Oil Markets and Prices

Oil Markets and Prices
The Brent Market and the Formation of World Oil Prices

PAUL HORSNELL
ROBERT MABRO

Published by the Oxford University Press
for the Oxford Institute for Energy Studies
1993

Oxford University Press, Walton Street, Oxford OX2 6DP

Oxford New York Toronto
Delhi Bombay Calcutta Madras Karachi
Kuala Lumpur Singapore Hong Kong Tokyo
Nairobi Dar es Salaam Cape Town
Melbourne Auckland Madrid

and associated companies in Berlin Ibadan

Oxford is a trade mark of Oxford University Press

© Oxford Institute for Energy Studies
1993

All rights reserved. No part of this publication may be reproduced, stored in a retrieval system, or transmitted, in any form or by any means, without the prior permission in writing of the Oxford Institute for Energy Studies,
57 Woodstock Road, Oxford OX2 6FA.

British Library Cataloguing in Publication Data
A catalogue record for this book is available from the British Library

ISBN 0-19-730013-8

Cover design by Moss, Davies, Dandy, Turner Ltd.

Typeset by Philip Armstrong, Oxford

Printed by Bookcraft Ltd. Bath

PREFACE

The purpose of this book is to enhance our understanding of the complex working of the world petroleum market and of the formation of oil prices in international trade. It devotes particular attention to the Brent market which involves spot, physical forward and futures trading of a blend of North Sea crudes known as Brent which has become one of the most important markers for world oil prices. And because the Brent market is central the research presented here examines its relationship to the constellation of other oil markets: those which deal on a spot basis with the main export crudes of Africa, the Gulf, the Far East and the North Sea, the market for Dubai, another marker crude, and that for West Texas Intermediate (WTI). Finally an analysis of pricing mechanisms used by OPEC and many non-OPEC exporting countries for their oil sales under term contracts and which use Brent prices as one of their references complete this study on oil markets and prices.

This book describes as fully as possible the ways in which oil is traded, the structure of the various markets, their institutional features and the behaviour of market participants and assesses the main implications for prices. The economic analysis is based on a solid foundation of facts and data, and the hope is that this approach will yield conclusions that are relevant to the industry and to policy-makers.

The authors' objective was to present, explain and assess the actual modes of behaviour of oil markets not, at this stage of their research, to build and test *a priori* models or construct a general theory. The tools and concepts of economics are used to analyse these modes of behaviour and the issues they raise providing insights which may be useful to readers familiar with the oil industry and to those who wish to understand the process through which the prices of a most important commodity are determined and change over time.

This book presents the results of work undertaken at the Oxford Institute for Energy Studies as part of a long-term programme of advanced economic research on oil markets, trading instruments and prices. This programme which began years ago has resulted in a number of publications, the most relevant to the issues addressed here being: R. Mabro et al, *The Market for North Sea Crude Oil*, Oxford University Press 1986, R. Mabro, *OPEC and the Price of Oil*, 1992, J. Gabillon, *The Term Structure of Oil Futures Prices*, 1991 and D. Long *European Gas Oil Markets: Price Relationships, Hedging and Efficiency*, 1991 (all published by the Oxford Institute for Energy Studies).

The main author of this book is Dr Paul Horsnell, Assistant Director for Research at the Institute and Fellow of Lincoln College. Robert Mabro wrote most or all of Chapters 1, 5, 6, 7, 15 and 16 and parts of Chapter 4. However, both take joint and full responsibility for the work. Other members of the Institute research staff, Juan Carlos Boué, Seana Lanigan and Maxence Trigano, contributed working papers on which parts of the book depend. The final draft was scrutinized with immense care by Mr Walter Greaves whose knowledge and understanding of oil trading is difficult to surpass, by Robert Bacon, Peter Beck and Paddy Spence. They all applied to the text the 'sharp compassion of the healer's art'.

We are grateful to Karen Exley who administered the research project with great competence and Vicki Harper who looked after the typescript deciphering the authors' handwriting with an amused smile.

This is the place for the Institute to thank the companies and organizations that sponsored the study.

> Amerada Hess
> British Petroleum (BP)
> British Gas
> Commission of the European Communities (EC)
> Conoco
> Cosmo Oil
> Elf Aquitaine
> Enterprise Oil
> International Energy Agency (IEA)
> Mitsubishi
> Mobil
> Neste Oy
> ÖMV
> Organization of the Petroleum Exporting Countries (OPEC)
> Petro-Canada
> Petróleos de Venezuela S.A. (PDVSA)
> Petróleos Mexicanos (Pemex)
> Petrosun
> Repsol
> Royal Ministry of Petroleum and Energy Norway
> Shell
> Statoil
> Texaco
> United Kingdom Department of Trade and Industry (DTI).

The sponsors are in no way responsible for the contents of this work, and in no way does their sponsorship represent any endorsement of any part. Their representatives attended three meetings in Oxford, read through drafts, provided comments and the opportunities for interviews, and represented a major resource of the study. It was above all a pleasure to work with them, and we thank them for their patience and generosity with their time. The panel of representatives was comprised of the following;

Kuniharu Akamatsu (Cosmo), Mohammad Amin (OPEC), Gro Anundskaas (Royal Ministry of Petroleum and Energy Norway), Bev Atkins (Neste Oy), Frederic Baule (Elf), Oynstein Berentsen (Statoil), Alberto Briceno (PDVSA), Raul Cardoso (Pemex), Alan Dalziel (British Gas), Malcolm Drew (BP), William Dougherty (Texaco), Tony Fountain (BP), Liz Gall (Enterprise), Amalio Grai:o Betrand (Repsol), Ivan Gutierrez (PDVSA), Marshall Hall (IEA), Tony Hepworth (Petrosun), Russell Hill (ÖMV), Marcel Kramer (then Petro-Canada), Gunter Lawson (Conoco), Vicente Llatas (PDVSA), Mike Loya (then Amerada Hess), Leonard Magrill (Texaco), Luis Mañas (Repsol), Y Masuda (Cosmo), Sidney Price (DTI), Koji Shimizu (Mitsubishi), Dan Sorochan (Petro-Canada), Seenu Srinivasan (Mobil), Peter Thompson (EC), Peter Ward (Shell), and David White (BP).

Over the course of the study many others helped, giving their time for interviews or other assistance. We would like to thank the following, for whom all the above disclaimers also apply.

Les Atkinson (BP), Doris Balzer (Rheinoel), Julia Barclay (Petroleum Argus), Adrian Binks (Petroleum Argus), Nick Black (Petroleum Argus), Alban Brindle (IPE), Paul Butcher (Cargill), Colin Bryce (Morgan Stanley), Peter Caddy (Petroleum Argus), Daniel Carr (NYMEX), Cristophe Chassard (International Time Services), Ron Davidson (BP), Cliff Evans (Czarnikow), Chris Evans (Shell), Marcus Green (Arcadia), Pedro Haas (Pemex), David Hufton (PVM), Brian Johnson (NYMEX), Timothy Knight (Paribas), Robert Levin (NYMEX), Alan Lovett (Shetland Islands Council), Tom Mackie (London Oil Reports), Onnic Marashian (Platt's), Aaron Markley (Cargill), Daniel Masters (Phibro), Bruce McCrodden (BP), Gustavo Mohar (Pemex), Jorge Montepeque (Platt's), Diane Munro (Energy Compass), Jan Nasmyth (Petroleum Argus), Mike Roffey (Paine Webber), Kemal Saiki (OPEC), Gordon Watson (Czarnikow), and Neil West (J Aron).

Other companies, individuals and organizations talked to us but did not wish to be acknowledged. Let them know, however, that we appreciated enormously being taken into their confidence.

Special gratitude is due to Adrian Binks for supplying us with the invaluable database of Petroleum Argus, and to the Shetland Islands Council which faxed us regularly the tanker loading schedules. Finally the Institute wishes to thank here the publishers of trade journals and data services who support our research endeavours with free or generously discounted subscriptions to their services, particularly MEES, PIW, Energy Compass, Wood Mackenzie and Platt's.

CONTENTS

Preface		v
Contents		ix
Tables		xi
Figures		xiv
Abbreviations		xvii
Chapter 1	Introduction	1

Part I : The Physical Base, Trading Instruments and the Fiscal/Institutional Framework of the Brent Markets

Chapter 2	The Physical Base of Brent Blend	11
Chapter 3	Physical Trading	31
Chapter 4	Description of Brent Markets and Trading Instruments	39
Chapter 5	The Fiscal Regime	56

Part II : The Forward and Dated Brent Markets

Chapter 6	The Historical Development of the Brent Market	73
Chapter 7	The Structure of 15-Day Brent Trading	83
Chapter 8	The Dated Brent Market	113
Chapter 9	Behaviour, Performance and Future	121

Part III : Oil Prices

Chapter 10	Oil Price Reporting	155
Chapter 11	Prices and Price Movements	167

Part IV : World Oil Markets

Chapter 12	The Brent Futures Contract and its Relationship to the Forward Market	193
Chapter 13	The Markets for Dubai, WTI and European Petroleum Products	207

Chapter 14	World Oil Spot Trade	243
Chapter 15	The Export of Crudes at Market-Related Formula Prices	291
Chapter 16	Conclusions	315

TABLES

2.1	Brent and Ninian System Fields. Dates of Discovery, Authorization and Production Start-up. Reserves in Million Barrels.	12
2.2	Oil Production by Field and System. 1986–91. Thousand Barrels per Day.	16
2.3	Oil Production and Reserves of Major UKCS Oilfields. 1986 and 1991. Million Tonnes.	18
2.4	Ownership in Brent and Ninian System Fields. January 1993. Percentage Shares.	23
2.5	Changes in Brent/Ninian Ownership. 1986–92.	24
2.6	Entitlements to Brent Blend by Company. 1986–92. Thousand Barrels per Day.	27
3.1	Destination of Brent/Ninian Loadings. 1987–92. Thousand Barrels per Day.	32
3.2	Destination of Brent/Ninian Loadings. 1987–92. Per Cent.	32
3.3	UK Consumption of Brent/Ninian. 1987–92. Thousand Barrels per Day.	33
3.4	US Imports of Brent/Ninian. 1987–91. Thousand Barrels per Day.	34
3.5	Average Cargo Size. 1987–91. Thousand Barrels.	35
3.6	Tax Receipts from UKCS Activity. 1984–5 to 1991–2. £ Million.	36
3.7	World Oil Production. 1992. Million Barrels per Day.	38
4.1	April/May Brent-Dubai Box Trade.	45
7.1	Composition of 15-day Brent Deals. Outright and Spreads. 1986–91. Number of Deals.	86
7.2	Time Pattern of Trading of the July 1990 15-Day Brent Deal. Number of Deals Made in the Periods Shown.	92
7.3	Continually Active Participants. 1988–91.	94
7.4	Number of Active Participants. 1986–91.	94
7.5	Top Participants in the 15-Day Brent Market. Rank and Market Shares. 1986–91. Per Cent.	96
7.6	Top Ten Participants by Categories. 1986–91	103
7.7	Shares of Top Ten Participants by Category in the 15-Day Brent Deals. 1986–91. Per Cent.	104
7.8	Patterns of Trading Between Various Categories of Participants. Aggregate Deals. 1987–91.	106

8.1	Frequency of Dated Brent Deals by Days to Loading.	114
8.2	Dated Brent. Ten Top Participants. Rank and Market Shares. 1986–91. Per Cent.	117
8.3	Pricing Basis of Dated Brent Deals. 1986–91. Percentage of Total Deals.	118
9.1	Prices of Outright 15-Day and Dated Brent Deals by Delivery Months. 1988–91. US Dollars per Barrel.	125
9.2	Extent and Duration of First Month Premia. 1988–92	133
9.3	Crude Oil Production. Brent and Forties Systems. 1993–2000. Thousand Barrels per Day.	147
9.4	Shares in Forties Production 1990 and 2000. Per Cent.	148
10.1	Crudes Assessed Daily by Argus, LOR and Platt's.	159
10.2	Timing of Brent Price Assessments. Hours of the Day. Greenwich Mean Time (GMT).	163
11.1	Average Price Change of First-Month IPE Brent. January 1989–May 1992. US Cents per Barrel.	178
11.2	Regression of IPE Price Volatility on its Lagged Values. Statistics.	179
11.3	Normality Tests on Brent Price Changes.	187
13.1	Equity Shares of Dubai Production by Company. 1993. Per Cent.	208
13.2	Composition of Dubai Deals. Outright and Spreads. 1986–91. Number of Deals.	212
13.3	Main Participants in the Dubai Market. Rank and Market Shares. 1986–91. Per Cent.	216
13.4	Determinants of Dubai Price Changes. Dependent Variable: Change in Dubai Price.	220
13.5	UAE Exports to Europe and Japan. 1988–91. Thousand Barrels per Day.	220
13.6	NYMEX Contracts, 1993.	225
13.7	NYMEX Deliverable Grades.	226
13.8	Total Volume and Deliveries, NYMEX Sweet Contract 1984–92. Million Barrels.	228
13.9	Platt's Price Quotations for Petroleum Products, ARA Area. 1993.	232
13.10	Representative Refinery Yields for Brent. Per Cent.	236
13.11	Causality Tests Between Brent and Product Prices.	238
13.12	Regression of Gasoil Price Changes. Statistics.	239
13.13	Regression of Dated Brent Price Changes. Statistics.	240
14.1	Major North Sea Spot Traded Crudes.	246
14.2	Pricing Basis of North Sea Crude Spot Deals. 1986–91. Percentage of Total Deals.	248
14.3	Main Buyers and Sellers in UK Crude Oil Spot Trade. Rank and Shares. 1986–91.	252

14.4	Main Buyers and Sellers in Norwegian Crude Oil Spot Trade. Rank and Shares. 1986–91.	253
14.5	West African Traded Crudes.	257
14.6	Main Buyers and Sellers in West African Crude Oil Spot Trade. Rank and Shares. 1986–91.	260
14.7	Pricing Basis of West African Spot Deals. 1986–91. Percentage of Total Deals.	261
14.8	Major Mediterranean Trade Crudes.	262
14.9	Pricing Basis of Mediterranean Spot Deals. 1986–91. Percentage of Total Deals.	264
14.10	Major Gulf Spot Traded Crudes.	265
14.11	Dubai Prices and Gulf Official Selling Prices. 1991.	267
14.12	Pricing Basis of Omani Crude Deals. 1986–91. Percentage of Total Deals.	268
14.13	Pricing Basis of Abu Dhabi Crude Deals. 1986–91. Percentage of Total Deals.	269
14.14	Pricing Basis of Qatari Crude Deals. 1986–91. Percentage of Total Deals.	269
14.15	Major Far Eastern Spot Traded Crudes.	271
14.16	Pricing Basis of Indonesian Spot Deals. 1986–91. Percentage of Total Deals.	276
14.17	Pricing Basis of Malaysian Spot Deals. 1986–91. Percentage of Total Deals.	276
A14.1	US Crude Oil Imports by Country of Origin and Users by Company. 1991. Thousand Barrels per Day.	284
A14.2	US Imports of North Sea and Mediterranean Crude Oil by Company. 1991. Thousand Barrels per Day.	285
A14.3	US Imports of West African Crude Oil by Company. 1991. Thousand Barrels per Day.	286
A14.4	US Imports of Middle Eastern Crude Oil by Company. 1991. Thousand Barrels per Day.	287
A14.5	US Imports of Canadian and Far Eastern Crude Oil by Company. 1991.	288
A14.6	US Imports of Latin American Crude Oil by Company. 1991.	289
15.1	Saudi Arabian Pricing Formulae. 1988–91.	300
15.2	Comparison of the Adjustment Factor in Saudi Arabia's Pricing Formula (Aramco/Europe) in Month M with GPW, Freight and Refining Costs Difference in Month M-2, Dollars per Barrel. 1988–91.	302
15.3	Comparison of Arabian Light and Iranian Light Prices as per Formulae. Far East. Dollars/Barrel. 1989–91.	305
A15.1	Mexico's Pricing Formulae 1987–92.	310

FIGURES

2.1	The Brent and Ninian Systems.	14
2.2	Brent Field and System Oil Production by Month. 1978–92. Thousand b/d.	17
2.3	Gravity of the Brent and Ninian Crude Oil Streams by Month. 1980–92. API°.	20
2.4	Combined Exxon and Shell Percentage Share of Brent Blend Production by Month. 1980–92.	28
7.1	Average Forwardness of Brent Deals by Month. 1986–91. Number of Days.	90
7.2	Number of Participants in the 15-day Brent Market by Month. 1986–91.	95
7.3	Concentration in the 15-day Brent Market by Month. 1986–91. Inverse Herfindahl Index.	100
7.4	Market Shares of Various Categories of Participants in the 15-day Brent Market by Month. 1986–91. Percentages.	102
8.1	Number of Dated Brent Cargoes Traded by Month. 1986–91.	115
9.1	Frequency of Loadings of Standard Cargoes at Sullom Voe by Tonnage. Aggregate 1991 and 1992.	123
9.2	Frequency of Loadings of Large Cargoes at Sullom Voe by Tonnage. Aggregate 1991 and 1992.	123
9.3	Daily Price Differentials between First-Month and Dated Brent and First and Second-Month Brent in Squeezes. January 1988, August 1989, November 1989 and March 1991.	136
11.1	Weekly Average Prices of First Forward Month Brent. 1984–92. Dollars per Barrel.	168
11.2	Crude Oil Price Changes, Year on Year. 1860–1990. Percentages.	171
11.3	Monthly Standard Deviations of Daily Forward Brent Price Changes. 1984–92. Percentages.	172
11.4	Weekly Volatility of Daily IPE Brent Prices. 1989–92. Percentages.	174
11.5	Average Intra-Day Price Range of IPE Brent by Number of Trading Days to Expiry of Contracts over January 1989 to May 1992 (excluding the Kuwait crisis). Dollars per Barrel.	177

11.6	Weekly Average Price Differentials between Brent Prices. 1988–92. Dollars per Barrel.	184
12.1	Daily Average Number of IPE Brent Contracts Traded. 1988–92.	194
12.2	Number of Contracts Traded per Delivery Month. 1989–1992.	194
12.3	Maximum Open Interest per Contract Month. 1989–92. Number of Contracts.	196
12.4	Average Open Interest by Trading Days to Expiry. 1991. Number of Contracts.	196
12.5	Average Number of Contracts Traded by Days to Expiry. 1991.	197
12.6	Average Forwardness of IPE Brent Contracts by Month. 1989–92. Number of Days.	197
13.1	Market Shares of Various Categories of Participants in the Dubai Market by Month. 1986–91.	214
13.2	Concentration in the Dubai Market by Month. 1986–91. Inverse Herfindahl Index.	217
13.3	Number of Participants in the Dubai Market by Month. 1986–91.	217
13.4	Weekly Average Price Differentials between Brent and Dubai (Comparable Delivery Months). 1987–92. Dollars per Barrel.	223
13.5	Weekly Freight Rates to NW Europe from Dubai and Sullom Voe (Brent). 1987–92. Dollars per Barrel.	223
13.6	Map of US Gulf Crude Oil Pipelines.	229
13.7	Weekly Average Price Differentials between WTI at Cushing and WTI at Midland. 1987–92. Dollars per Barrel.	230
13.8	Weekly Average Price Differentials between WTI at Cushing and Brent (Comparable Delivery Months). 1987–92. Dollars per Barrel.	230
13.9	Weekly Average Prices of Gasoline, Distillates and Heavy Fuel Oil in the Antwerp-Rotterdam-Amsterdam (ARA) area. 1989–92. Dollars per Barrel.	235
13.10	Weekly Average Refining Margins from Brent in the ARA area. 1989–92. Dollars per Barrel.	237
14.1	Quarterly Composition of North Sea Spot Trade by Crude. 1986–91. Number of Deals.	247
14.2	Pricing Basis of North Sea Spot Deals (other than Brent) by Month. 1986–91. Percentage of Total Deals.	249
14.3	Weekly Average Price Differentials between Forties and Brent. 1988–92. Dollars per Barrel.	254

14.4	Quarterly Composition of West African Spot Trade by Crude. 1986–91. Number of Deals.	258
14.5	Quarterly Composition of Mediterranean Spot Trade by Crude. 1986–91. Number of Deals.	263
14.6	Quarterly Composition of Gulf Spot Trade by Crude. 1986–91. Number of Deals.	266
14.7	Quarterly Composition of Far Eastern Spot Trade by Crude. 1986–91. Number of Deals.	272

ABBREVIATIONS

ADNOC	Abu Dhabi National Oil Company
ADP	Alternate Delivery Procedure
AIG	American International Group
ANS	Alaskan North Slope
API	American Petroleum Institute
APPI	Asian Petroleum Price Index
ARA	Antwerp, Rotterdam, Amsterdam Area
ARCO	Atlantic Richfield Company
b/d	barrels per day
BBQ	Brass River, Bonny Light, Qua Iboe
BNOC	British National Oil Corporation
BP	British Petroleum
CBOT	Chicago Board of Trade
CEPSA	Compañia Española de Petróleos SA
CFD	Contract for Differences
CFP	Compagnie Française des Pétroles, or Total
CFTC	Commodities and Futures Trading Commission (USA)
CRT	Chicago Research and Trading
DNO	Det Norske Oljeselskap
DTI	Department of Trade and Industry (UK)
c.i.f.	cost, insurance and freight
f.o.b.	free on board
EC	European Community
ECM	Error Correction Mechanism
EFP	Exchange of Futures for Physical
EFS	Exchange of Futures for Swap
FLAGS	Far North Liquids and Associated Gas System
GNP	Gross National Product
GPW	Gross Product Worth
GTCs	General Terms and Conditions
HLS	Heavy Louisiana Sweet
ICCH	International Commodities Clearing House
ICI	Imperial Chemical Industries
ICP	Indonesian Crude Price
IEA	International Energy Agency
IOC	Indian Oil Corporation
IPE	International Petroleum Exchange of London
IPL	Interprovincial Pipeline

LLS	Light Louisiana Sweet
LOR	London Oil Reports
mb	million barrels
mb/d	million barrels per day
LASMO	London and Scottish Marine Oil
LOOP	Louisiana Offshore Oil Port
MPM	Ministry of Petroleum and Mines (Oman)
NGLS	Natural Gas Liquids
NWE	North-West Europe
NYMEX	New York Mercantile Exchange
ODECO	Ocean Drilling and Exploration Company
OECD	Organization for Economic Co-operation and Development
ÖMV	Österreichische Mineralölverwaltung Aktietgesellschaft
OPEC	Organization of the Petroleum Exporting Countries
OPA	Oil Pipelines Agency
OSP	Official Selling Price
OTC	over the counter
OTO	Oil Taxation Office
PAD	Petroleum Administration for Defence District
PDO	Petroleum Development Oman
PDVSA	Petróleos de Venezuela SA
Pemex	Petróleos Mexicanos
PNOC	Philippine National Oil Company
P-Plus	Postings Plus
PRT	Petroleum Revenue Tax
PTT	Petroleum Authority of Thailand
PVM	Patrick Victor Mazzarolli Oil Associates
QGPC	Qatar General Petroleum Corporation
SITCO	Shell International Trading Company
TENI	Texas Eastern Norwegian Inc.
TENSI	Texas Eastern North Sea Inc.
TWO	Transworld Oil
UAE	United Arab Emirates
UKCS	United Kingdom Continental Shelf
UMC	Underwater Manifold Centre
URBK	Union Rheinische Braunkohlen Kraftstoff
USGC	United States Gulf Coast
VLCC	Very Large Crude Carrier
WTI	West Texas Intermediate
WTS	West Texas Sour

CHAPTER 1

INTRODUCTION

1. Themes

The fundamental question which continually presents itself to the minds of all those concerned with energy in general, and oil in particular, and more broadly with the role and impact of developments in the energy sector on the economy is: what determines the price of internationally traded oil?

In the 1970s the conventional answer to this question was simply 'OPEC'. Hence, the considerable interest manifested during that decade in the OPEC phenomenon, an interest which extended from a fascination with the behaviour, psychology and statements of oil ministers to research on the political economy of an organization perceived by many as an oil cartel. News about OPEC made the headlines during the 1970s and early 1980s; the pronouncements of the Shah of Iran, the King of Saudi Arabia and Sheikh Yamani were avidly listened to and widely quoted, and their portraits appeared on the cover page of popular magazines. Library shelves filled up with books about OPEC, often written in haste and most of them, sadly, poor in understanding and insight. The price of oil was construed as an OPEC affair, but the question of how and why OPEC set this or that price in any relevant instance was rarely, if ever, answered in a fully satisfactory manner. This failure may be partly due to the inability of over-specialized academic disciplines – be it economics, international relations, political science, sociology or psychology – to come to grips with an institutional phenomenon whose study involves them all.

Sometime in the 1980s, and increasingly nowadays, the answer to the question of what determines the oil price has become encapsulated in two deceptively simple words: 'the market'. But this answer, like the previous one, straightforward and almost self-evident as many may perceive it to be, does not have much explanatory content. As before, it only points like a forefinger to a major phenomenon. In the 1970s, it pointed at OPEC, said to be a cartel with the power to set the price of oil. Now it points to the market, the locus where the economic forces of supply and demand interact and generate a price that brings them into balance.

If we were none but passers-by asking from a fellow on the road the broad indication of a direction, we would still not be satisfied with these answers. They are insufficient even for the most basic understanding. OPEC did not operate in an economic vacuum in the 1970s; it did not, indeed could not, abolish the economic forces of supply and demand, and could not prevent its administered oil price from influencing the behaviour of these forces. There was then, as always, a market. And the market which gained both in extension and depth in the 1980s did not abolish OPEC. The organization still exists and its members remain major agents on the supply side of the world oil system.

At their most basic level, answers that appear initially to single out first OPEC and then the market, in fact raise the issue of their relationship; a relationship that has undergone significant transformation from one episode to the next of recent oil history. These very simple observations have already taken us well beyond the starting point. If the key lies in an understanding of the relationship between OPEC and the market, one needs to ask first: what is OPEC and what is the market? The relationship between them would remain unintelligible if their mode of operation, behaviour, and performance is not fully investigated.

The 'self-evident' truths that the determination of oil prices was in the past an OPEC affair and more recently the market's, like many assertions that are accepted without questioning as being well understood, are not evident at all. They are not definitive conclusions, thoroughly argued and solidly established truths, merely preliminary statements which on close examination open a research agenda.

On the issue of the crude oil price in international trade the scope of this agenda is daunting both in size and complexity. The research presented in this book does not cover the whole field but focuses mainly on a critical area: a particular market which has been playing a central and increasing, though not exclusive, role in crude oil price formation since the mid-1980s. The core of this study is an analysis of the nature, development and mode of operation of what is conventionally labelled as the Brent market, in effect a set of markets where a crude consisting of the blended output of the Brent and Ninian pipeline systems is traded under various kinds of contracts. These include spot, physical forward and futures deals, options on futures and swaps.

The market for a crude oil which through historical circumstance, or for compelling economic or structural reasons, or merely by default, provides a reference for world oil prices is, for this very reason, a prime candidate for research. All the important features of the Brent market that carry implications for the level and/or volatility of world oil prices matter to a much wider constituency than the relatively small number of participants that trade this crude spot, forward or futures. They matter to those who live from oil and to those, everywhere in the world, who need to purchase it; to governments and companies; to those responsible for the management of their country's economy; and to everyone who gains or loses, however little, however indirectly, through the economic effects of changes in the price of oil. The scholarly interest in the subject parallels the interests of different publics without identifying with any one of them.

The features of a market that may matter include first the commodity traded and the trading instruments used. The second set of relevant features refers to those that characterize participants, behaviour and motivations. How many or how few are they? If there were a few participants, each with a large market share, would that necessarily have an impact on the behaviour of oil prices? The motivations of participants cannot be ignored since it is open to question whether they matter or not. The third set of features relates to the mechanics and performance of the market in question. The future of a market depends to some extent on how well it functions and on how much its functions satisfy important needs.

We dwell at some length on these aspects because Brent is central to oil price formation, a hypothesis evidenced throughout the study. We shall see that its price is a marker for other crudes in the North Sea, the Mediterranean and West Africa and sometimes in regions outside the area where it physically moves; that it provides a benchmark for Dubai generally traded as a spread from Brent rather than on an outright basis; and that it is widely used in the pricing formulae of oil-producing countries for their exports to Europe and in some cases to the USA.

And precisely because Brent is central, our book does not confine itself to the boundaries of this market. After a detailed analysis of its structure and performance, the study moves to consider other oil markets and the pricing systems of petroleum-exporting countries, tracing and assessing their relationships with Brent. This book, therefore, has something to say on the trading of major world crudes; the Dubai, WTI and ANS markets; and pricing formulae. The relevant items of the research agenda on the oil price issue are not all treated with the same amount of detail, but the incursions made in the major areas related to Brent, and the focus put on their links, enable us to propose a tentative synthesis. Like all research on vast and complex subjects, the present endeavour adds something to knowledge but by the same token raises new issues and improves the formulation of old questions.

2. Method

There is no single methodology for the study of a market. The choice of a particular approach depends on the objective of the research, or more precisely on the nature of the knowledge sought. There are no perfect tools but often several good instruments, each one more suitable than the others for a particular task. If the purpose of the research is to predict prices, it would be necessary to build a forecasting model; if the objective is to establish or refute the validity of a hypothesis, for example the market economic efficiency theory, the appropriate methodology will be found in an econometric toolbox.

Our objectives are different. In a sense, they relate to research work which should be thoroughly undertaken *before* seeking to design forecasting models or to test an economic theory. Our objectives are to establish and develop a knowledge about oil markets, their actual mode of operation, their participants; about their performance and relationships with each other; and their role in the formation of oil prices. This calls for both the discovery of facts and phenomena and their analysis with the help, where appropriate, of economic concepts and econometric methods.

Like all other markets, those that trade oil have features of their own, both institutional and economic, which usually evolve historically in response to particular forces or needs, and reflect ways in which markets adapt to specific circumstances. Actual markets do not conform in fundamental respects to the theoretical paradigms, and precisely for this reason one always needs to consider them both. The methodological question at issue is not: 'fact or theory?' The question is 'in what order and relationship?' The correct answer is unambiguously that one must have them both. In our approach we look first at markets as they actually are, but continually assess and analyse the implications of their features in reference to the relevant concepts and propositions of economics. As Professor Adelman often taught, to understand how a market actually works, how much and what type of competition there is, and what is its influence on price, we need such theoretical concepts as, for example, those of economic efficiency or of a perfectly competitive market structure. These never describe what is. They do not exist except in the sense in which, as Adelman is fond of putting it, 'the absolute zero in physics exists'; and in this lies their usefulness.

Markets are historical phenomena. They emerge at a particular moment, develop over time, and their essential features often change. An applied economics study of a market and of the price movements which it generates is inherently a historical study. When the subject matter is essentially about processes which the analysis seeks to unravel, there is no escape from history, and our approach incorporates this important dimension whenever necessary.

Finally, our approach concerns itself with policy but not with general policy prescriptions. Policy is both an important influence in the development of oil markets and a major factor in the determination of oil prices; and the analysis of actual policies is therefore an integral part of the story. To provide advice is something else, and we have deliberately kept it out of the brief. The reason is that the interests relating to both the functioning of the markets and the price of oil are often divergent. A policy cannot be prescribed in a vacuum but in relation to the objectives, interests or welfare of a particular party. If the world were a homogeneous entity, it would have been possible perhaps to suggest remedies for the 'good of the world'. The main contribution of the book, in this respect, is to enable the various parties – companies and governments on opposite sides of the producer/consumer divide – to gauge the discrepancy between what they expect from the oil market and from the pricing mechanisms adopted by oil producers, and their actual performance. Real world markets do not always deliver what the market ideology prevailing in many industrialized countries wants us to believe they do. The prices they generate do not always correctly signal the degree of scarcity either because of concentration, or poor information or slow adjustment processes to name a few difficulties. In oil markets, the process of price formation largely results from the operations of economic agents mostly concerned with price relatives – with spreads between the prices of different crudes, the prices of a crude at different dates or between petroleum products and crude oil prices – rather than absolute levels. This is different from what it is generally thought that markets do; and the implication may be important. Also, the claims often made that the pricing formulae of exporting countries track the world market price of oil do not always appear to be very well founded. Some formulae track, in the case of ANS, the assessed price of a crude traded in markets which register very few transactions per month. This may be expedient but hardly justifies a meaningful market-orientation claim. The diagnostic of these discrepancies enables the various parties, if they so wish, to re-assess policy and evolve their own responses. 'Knowledge is neutral stuff, which men use according to their lights.'[1]

As researchers, the motivation of our endeavours is to gain greater understanding, a motivation which by itself does not preclude the possibility of errors. Many helped us tremendously in the task; a few retreated behind the shield of commercial and official confidentiality; some disclosed partial truths; and some dearly wished that we applied our efforts to other topics and were honest enough to say so. We are grateful to all because, in different ways, we learnt something from each – facts, interpretations, ideas, and from those who said nothing we caught a glimpse about attitudes. We would have liked, of course, to learn more.

For this reason, and more fundamentally because research in adding to knowledge increases the length of the boundary between the known and the unknown that lies outside, this book does not close the study of oil markets and the determination of oil prices. It signals, on the contrary, opportunities to go further in the enquiry. Our hope is that it will induce many others to join on a fascinating path of discovery.

3. Data

Empirical research is helped or hindered by the availability and quality of data. There are no official sources, indeed no published statistical sources, on the forward Brent market or on any of the spot markets for crude oil in the world. The only source on forward and dated Brent which records on a daily basis a proportion of the transactions effected is the database of Petroleum Argus. The records, which go back to 1973, include the names of the buyer and seller, the month for which the deal is made, and the price or the pricing formula at which the transaction was made. The coverage is not always complete since disclosure to press reporters is voluntary. In any analysis great care must be taken to avoid wrong references from a large, but not random, sample. We are extremely grateful to Adrian Binks, the editor of *Petroleum Argus* for providing us with access to this unique database.

Data on futures oil markets have been obtained from the relevant exchanges, IPE and NYMEX. Futures prices are also published in *Platt's Oilgram Price Report* and other trade journals. Data on futures oil deals cover the whole statistical population for prices, daily volume of transactions and open interest. But there is no public information on the participants' identity. In this respect we know something about participants in the Brent, Dubai and spot crude oil markets; very little, if anything, about who is who, and who is doing what, in the IPE and the NYMEX.

We have built up a comprehensive database on oil prices at the Oxford Institute for Energy Studies using Platt's and Petroleum Argus as sources. The statistical analysis of prices throughout this study has used this database. For oil production we have used the invaluable North Sea Service publications of Wood Mackenzie.

Other information was sought from interviews which we conducted extensively in London and in the USA. Invaluable knowledge was gained from discussions with oil company executives, traders, civil servants, oil journalists, the officials of oil futures exchanges and other authorities. Those who sponsored our study were generous with their time. Once more we wish to thank them all here.

Trade journals are a major source of facts and stories about oil markets.

This source cannot be ignored given the paucity of other information; but its use requires both caution and critical skills. In this area the historian's training is more relevant than the economist's. It must always be remembered that journalists are mainly concerned with *news*, not with the accuracy of archival records. They do not necessarily revise facts, figures or stories published yesterday if they find out today that these were wrong. Yesterday's story or statistic is no longer news today. This can pose problems for the researcher who has nowhere to go but through old issues of trade journals.

4. Plan of the Study

This book consists of an introduction (this chapter), four parts, and then a conclusion. Parts I and II are concerned with the Brent market which, as mentioned earlier, is a set of markets in which different types of transactions are carried out. These include the spot, or in the terminology of the industry, dated Brent market; forward physical commonly referred to as 15-day Brent market, because of a clause in the contract that stipulates a 15-day notice for lifting nominations, and the International Petroleum Exchange of London, a formal futures exchange where a futures contract for parcels of one thousand barrels of Brent blend is transacted. Parts III and IV extend the study to the wider issue of the market determinants of world oil prices. The outline by chapters is as follows.

Part I, which consists of Chapters 2 to 5, considers the physical base of Brent trading which is now a crude resulting from the co-mingling of the Brent system and the Ninian system blends. By physical base we mean the constituent crudes themselves and all the relevant characteristics of production (including ownership), the lifting infrastructure and physical trading. It then moves on to describe in detail the wide range of trading instruments used in the various Brent markets. Finally, the UK oil fiscal regime which is not neutral as regards the modality of disposal by producers of the crude oil gained from UK fields – as it makes a crucial distinction between arm's length and non-arm's length transactions – is carefully discussed.

Part II concentrates on the forward or 15-day Brent market and its relationship with the dated market. It starts in Chapter 6 with a history of the origins and early development of the forward market. This takes the story from the beginning in the very early 1980s to the critical year of 1986 when the oil price collapsed and the world petroleum market was in turmoil. The rest of the study covers in detail the period from January 1986 to December 1991, a complete span of six years. Chapter 7 provides an empirical analysis of the characteristics of transactions – liquidity, composition between spreads and outright deals, the degree of forwardness and so on – and of participants – identity, composition by categories, their shares in total recorded transactions and therefore the degree of concentration of the market. This is not based on a snapshot of the market at a given point in time but an analysis of changes throughout the period covered, 1986–91. As mentioned earlier, the empirical material was mainly obtained from the Petroleum Argus database.

Dated Brent and its relationship with the forward market is the subject of Chapter 8. Finally, Part II examines aspects of behaviour and performance of the Brent spot and forward markets (Chapter 9). We try to identify and analyse the economic motivations of participants and define the complex concepts of risk management hedging and speculation (in the economic, not the pejorative sense of the term) and their role. Chapter 9 then studies the performance of the market, more precisely the robust way in which it deals with the occasional squeeze or default. Finally it concludes by looking at its future. The question addressed is which crude is likely to succeed Brent should the physical base shrink too much in the future.

Part III is concerned with prices. The all important price reporting arrangements in place are examined in detail (Chapter 10). The study then analyses in Chapter 11 the behaviour of relevant oil price series and their volatility; in Chapter 12 the relationship between Brent forward and futures; and in Chapter 13 the relationships between the markets and prices of Brent and Dubai, WTI, and petroleum products at Rotterdam.

Part IV addresses the issue of Brent as marker for the pricing of other crudes both in world spot markets (Chapter 14) and in the pricing formulae applied by important oil-exporting countries, both OPEC and non-OPEC (Chapter 15).

The concluding chapter of the book provides a tentative synthesis on the fundamental issue of oil price determination in international trade today.

Notes
1. M.A. Adelman (1972), The World Petroleum Market, p. 4.

PART I

The Physical Base, Trading Instruments and the Fiscal/Institutional Framework of the Brent Markets

CHAPTER 2

THE PHYSICAL BASE OF BRENT BLEND

1. Introduction

The crude oil stream that currently makes up Brent blend is a mixture of the production from nineteen separate oilfields, collected through two distinct pipeline systems (the Brent and the Ninian systems) which carry the crude oil to the terminal at Sullom Voe in the Shetland Islands. The fields that supply crude for this commodity at Sullom Voe are:

(a) Brent, North Cormorant, South Cormorant, Deveron, Don, Dunlin, Eider, Hutton, North West Hutton, Murchison, Osprey, Tern and Thistle (the Brent System), and
(b) Alwyn North, Heather, Lyell, Magnus, Ninian and Staffa (the Ninian System).

Other fields or accumulations are currently in the planning or development stage. By the start of 1993 three (Strathspey, Dunbar and Hudson) had received permission from the UK government to move into production (i.e. Annex B permission), and will begin to produce in 1993, 1994 and 1995 respectively. A series of other developments are likely to receive Annex B permission and to come on stream in the mid 1990s.

The dates of discovery, Annex B permission and production start for the nineteen producing fields and the three with Annex B permission are shown in Table 2.1, together with estimates of their original recoverable reserves in millions of barrels. With the exception of Hudson and the small Staffa field, all were discovered in the five-year period after the discovery of the Brent field in July 1971. Brent began production in late 1976, and within the next eight years a further ten fields were brought on stream (seven in the Brent system and three in the Ninian system), all with reserves of 100 million barrels (mb) or more.

Since 1984, with the major exception of the Alwyn North field, developments have been much smaller and more marginal accumulations, whose development has been made viable by the rapid improvement in

12   Oil Markets and Prices

North Sea production technology. Only one-eighth of the total original recoverable reserve base of the two systems is held in the eleven fields whose Annex B permission has been granted since the start of 1981.

Table 2.1: Brent and Ninian System Fields. Dates of Discovery, Authorization and Production Start-up. Reserves in Million Barrels.

Field	Discovery Date	Annex B Authorization	Production Start-up	Oil and NGL Reserves (mb)
1. *Brent System*				
Brent	Jul 71	Aug 72	Nov 76	2180
Thistle	Jul 73	Jul 74	Feb 78	453
Dunlin	Jul 73	May 74	Aug 78	370
South Cormorant	Sep 72	May 74	Dec 79	200
Murchison	Sep 75	Sep 76	Sep 80	410
North Cormorant	Aug 74	Apr 79	Feb 82	410
NW Hutton	Apr 75	Jul 79	Apr 83	135
Hutton	Dec 73	Aug 80	Aug 84	215
Deveron	Sep 72	Sep 84	Sep 84	20
Eider	May 76	Oct 85	Nov 88	85
Tern	May 75	Jan 85	Jun 89	170
Don	Jul 76	Mar 88	Oct 89	25
Osprey	Feb 74	Nov 88	Jan 91	60
Hudson	Jun 87	Jan 93	– 95	85
2. *Ninian System*				
Heather	Dec 73	Aug 74	Oct 78	100
Ninian	Apr 74	Jun 74	Dec 78	1160
Magnus	Jul 74	Dec 78	Aug 83	790
Alwyn North	Oct 75	Oct 82	Nov 87	220
Staffa	Jul 85	Oct 90	Mar 92	8
Lyell	Jun 75	Jan 91	Mar 93	40
Strathspey	Feb 75	Oct 91	– 93	90
Dunbar	Nov 73	Nov 92	– 94	120

Source: UK Department of Trade and Industry, *Development of the Oil and Gas Resources of the UK*, several issues, Wood Mackenzie *North Sea Report*, various issues.

Twenty-one of the fields shown in Table 2.1 lie entirely in the UK sector of the North Sea, with one, Murchison, straddling the boundary between the UK and Norwegian sectors. While all Murchison production is landed at Sullom Voe, part counts as Norwegian output. Before August 1990 Brent blend was made up solely of oil landed at Sullom Voe through the Brent pipeline system. Output from the four fields of the Ninian system producing then was also loaded from Sullom Voe, but constituted a separate blend with its own storage facilities. On

1 August 1990 the Brent and Ninian streams were co-mingled and Ninian ceased to exist as a separate tradable crude oil blend. Hence, after August 1990 the term Brent blend refers to production from both the Brent and Ninian pipeline systems.

2. The Pipeline and other Lifting Systems

Schemata for the two pipeline systems that collect Brent blend and take it to Sullom Voe are shown in Figure 2.1. Possible future developments in the two systems are italicized, with their most likely connections to the pipeline systems shown. In the Brent system the crude oil streams meet at Cormorant Alpha and then flow to Sullom Voe through a 36 inch diameter pipeline. For the Ninian system the streams meet at Ninian Central before flowing along another 36 inch diameter pipeline to Sullom Voe. The two systems have four key pivotal points, Cormorant Alpha, Brent Charlie, Dunlin Alpha and Ninian Central, with flows being particularly sensitive to maintenance, pipeline problems and other disruptions at these points.

The nineteen separate producing fields shown in Figure 2.1 do not necessarily all have fixed platforms, nor does a single fixed platform necessarily exploit only one field. Many recent developments have involved the use of underwater manifolds over smaller accumulations of oil which are then tied back to an existing fixed platform. For example, the Osprey field is tied back to Dunlin, and Don is tied back to Thistle. The Deveron field is exploited by wells drilled directly from Thistle Alpha, and Cormorant Alpha is (for tax purposes) assumed to be exploiting both South and North Cormorant in the ratio of 40 to 60 (output from the North Cormorant platform and the Cormorant Underwater Manifold Centre are both attributed solely to North Cormorant). Likewise most future developments in the Brent and Ninian systems will involve the use of tiebacks to, or the deviation of wells from, existing fixed platforms, thus greatly improving the economics of exploiting smaller accumulations as well as extending the useful life of existing fixed structures.

Production began in the Brent field in November 1976, but the pipeline through Brent Charlie on to Cormorant Alpha and then on to Sullom Voe only became operational in November 1979. In the interim period production was loaded directly onto tankers (between 70 thousand and 110 thousand deadweight tonnes) through Brent Spar, a loading buoy. Brent Spar remained operational until 1991 for loading cargoes of oil from Brent Alpha and Brent Bravo. In combination with the large storage capacity of the Brent platforms (3.1 mb of storage in

14 *Oil Markets and Prices*

The Brent System

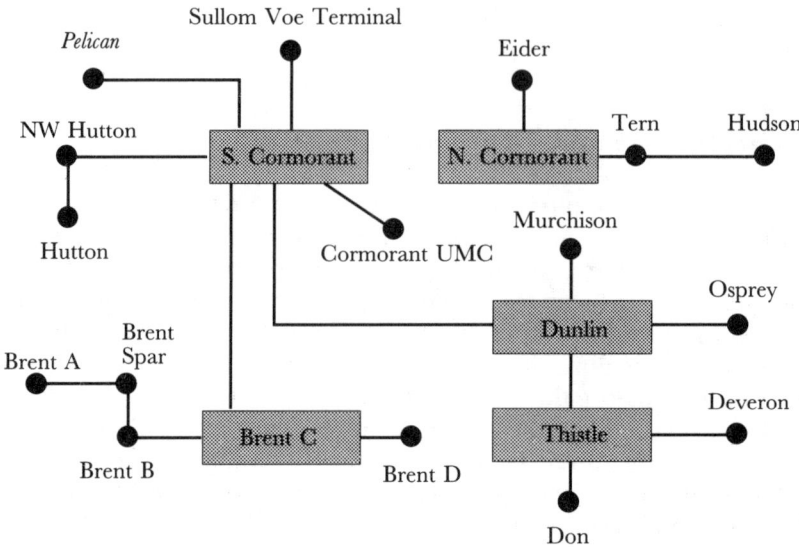

The Ninian System

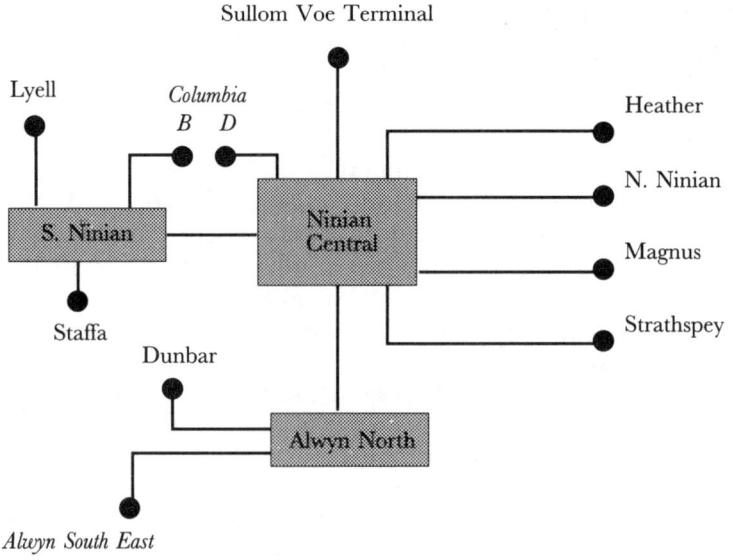

Figure 2.1: The Brent and Ninian Pipeline Systems.

total), this gave a considerable degree of flexibility in the face of any operational difficulties. Crude oil loaded through Brent Spar was pure Brent field crude oil and, as it did not flow to Sullom Voe, did not constitute part of Brent blend. While output from other fields in the North Sea can be loaded offshore, Brent was the last field in the Brent and Ninian systems with operational offshore loading facilities, and was thus the only field whose output could be obtained separately from the blend. While there are offshore loading facilities in the Thistle field these are also currently inoperative.

Theoretically Brent Spar could load at a rate of about 250 thousand barrels a day. However actual loadings in the last few years of its life were only a small proportion of the maximum that could be loaded. The level of loadings from Brent Spar was about 63 thousand b/d in 1988, 37 thousand b/d in 1989, 23 thousand b/d in 1990 and 27 thousand b/d during the period that Brent Spar was operational in 1991. In August 1991 Shell announced its intention to close Brent Spar, and the last loading occurred on 21 September 1991.

3. Production

Production profiles are shown by year, field and pipeline system in Table 2.2, with figures for 1990 also being split into the two periods before and after the co-mingling of the Brent and Ninian streams. Most of the fields have already passed their peak production – in the case of Dunlin as early as 1979. Only eight current fields (Alwyn North, Don, Eider, Lyell, Magnus, Osprey, Staffa and Tern) reach their peak production in the early 1990s. Indeed for some of the existing fields (in particular South Cormorant and Dunlin), the major reason for their continued exploitation is fast becoming their strategic infrastructural positions and the ability to access other accumulations from their existing fixed structures. The first Brent field to be abandoned will be NW Hutton, likely to come off stream over the course of 1993.

Figure 2.2 shows the production of the Brent field and the other fields of the Brent system by month from 1978 to 1992, and shows the decline in both since the mid-1980s. Brent field production shows a very marked seasonal pattern, with the low point in each year normally occurring in June. This is due to maintenance, which, given weather conditions, is best effected during the summer. As June is the last month of a six-month tax reporting period, it is preferable to carry out maintenance in June rather than July, i.e. defer production into the next reporting period.

Output from the Brent field remained below normal from the start

Table 2.2: Oil Production by Field and System. 1986–92. Thousand Barrels per Day.

	1986	1987	1988	1989	1990 (a)	1990 (b)	1990	1991	1992
1. *Brent System*									
Brent	421	386	342	203	118	17	76	183	233
Cormorant	47	40	43	11	25	24	24	22	22
North Cormorant	108	88	86	60	68	53	62	35	30
Deveron	6	6	5	3	5	3	4	1	2
Don	-	-	-	2	7	4	6	6	6
Dunlin	42	52	51	39	35	35	35	26	27
Eider	-	-	3	39	42	39	41	35	32
Hutton	75	62	63	41	30	27	29	18	22
NW Hutton	50	33	33	18	19	19	19	9	10
Murchison	75	70	58	37	37	36	37	30	35
Osprey	-	-	-	-	-	-	-	19	27
Staffa	-	-	-	-	-	-	-	-	6
Tern	-	-	-	18	32	37	34	53	74
Thistle	61	55	52	31	31	27	30	15	19
Total Brent	885	791	734	503	450	320	396	450	547
2. *Ninian System*									
Alwyn North	-	3	75	89	101	85	94	92	82
Heather	20	19	15	12	12	10	11	10	9
Magnus	127	126	141	145	128	142	134	135	151
Ninian	199	154	142	128	125	107	118	87	67
Total Ninian	346	302	373	374	366	345	357	324	309
Total Blend(c)	885	791	734	503	450	665	540	773	856

Notes: (a) January 1 to July 31 1990 before co-mingling
(b) August 1 to December 31 1990 after co-mingling
(c) Includes liftings from Brent Spar
Source: Wood Mackenzie *North Sea Report*, various issues

of 1989 through to 1992, owing to a series of large maintenance and refurbishment programmes on each of the four Brent platforms. In January 1989 a gas leak on Brent Delta forced a shutdown, and output remained restricted until October 1989. In May 1989 electrical work shut down Brent Charlie until October 1990. A series of refurbishments restricted output throughout 1990 and 1991. In April 1991 the entire Brent system was shut down for the installation of emergency safety valves.

The only other major shut-down of the entire system took place consequent to the Cormorant Alpha disaster of 18 April 1989. The gas

The Physical Base of Brent Blend 17

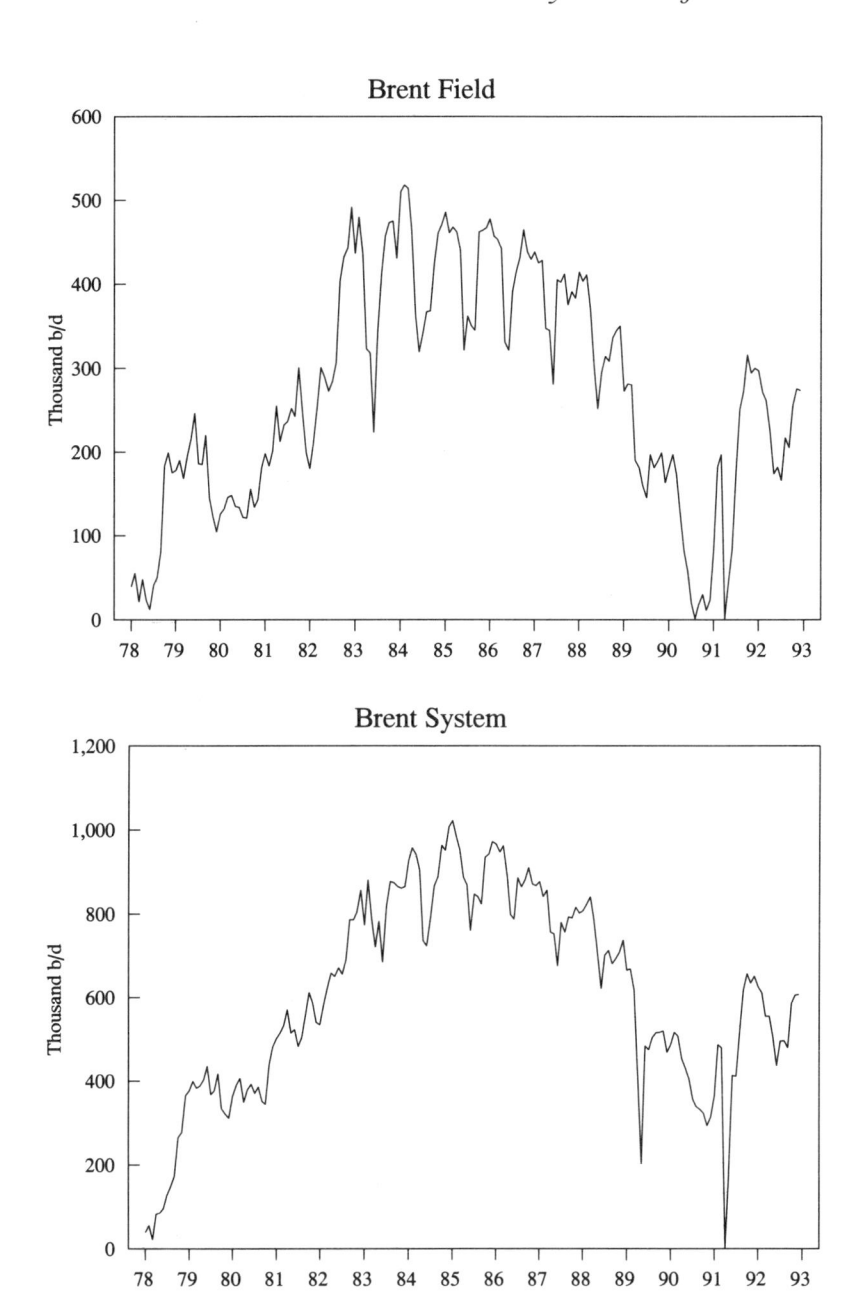

Figure 2.2: Brent Field and Brent System Oil Production by Month. 1978–92. Thousand Barrels per Day.

18 *Oil Markets and Prices*

explosion on Cormorant Alpha meant that no production from any field could reach Sullom Voe through the Brent pipeline, given the lynchpin position of the platform as shown in Figure 2.1. The system remained shut down until 29 May 1989, causing the dip in production shown in Figure 2.2. Throughout this period restricted Brent field production continued, with output from Brent Alpha and Brent Bravo being loaded onto tankers through Brent Spar. Cormorant Alpha did not become operational again as an oil-producing platform until February 1990.

The major fields within the Brent and Ninian system are large in terms of UKCS oil and oil condensate production. Table 2.3 shows the twenty largest UKCS oilfields ranked by production in 1986 and 1991, as well as in terms of their original recoverable reserves, with Brent and Ninian system fields shown in italics. Despite its reduced output, Brent was still the largest producer among UKCS fields in 1991, and the two

Table 2.3: Oil Production and Reserves of Major UKCS Oilfields. 1986 and 1991. Million Tonnes.

Field	1986 Production	Field	1991 Production	Original Recoverable Reserves	
Brent	19.5	*Brent*	8.5	Statfjord (Total)	446
Forties	16.5	Forties	8.2	Forties	333
Ninian	9.7	*Magnus*	6.4	*Brent*	263
Piper	8.4	Fulmar	5.0	*Ninian*	157
Fulmar	7.5	Statfjord UK	4.6	Piper	136
Magnus	6.0	Beryl	4.6	Beryl	127
Statfjord UK	5.4	*Ninian*	4.2	*Magnus*	102
Brae S	5.1	Alwyn North	4.0	Claymore	77
N Cormorant	5.0	Tern	2.6	Fulmar	72
Beryl	4.6	Brae N	2.6	Brae	70
Claymore	3.9	Claymore	2.5	Scott	60
Hutton	3.8	Maureen	1.7	*Thistle*	60
Maureen	3.6	Clyde	1.7	Nelson	57
Thistle	3.0	*N Cormorant*	1.7	*N Cormorant*	55
Murchison UK	2.8	Rob Roy	1.7	*Murchison*	51
NW Hutton	2.3	Eider	1.7	Alba	51
S Cormorant	2.2	Arbroath	1.6	Dunlin	49
Dunlin	2.0	Balmoral	1.3	Brae East	37
Beatrice	2.0	Scapa	1.3	Miller	32
Highlander	1.3	Kittiwake	1.3	Alwyn North	29

Note: Italics denote Brent or Ninian system fields.
Source: UK Department of Trade and Industry, *Development of the Oil and Gas Resources of the UK*, various issues.

systems have five fields among the largest ten producers.

The Brent and Ninian systems are relatively far less important in UKCS gas production, with only Alwyn North, Brent and Magnus having sizeable gas reserves. Gas from Alwyn North is transported via the Frigg pipeline system, while gas from other fields in the two systems (as well as from Statfjord), is transported to St Fergus by FLAGS (Far North Liquids and Associated Gas System).

By 1991 among the Brent and Ninian system fields only Brent and Magnus were producing significant volumes of gas through FLAGS, with minor amounts produced by the two Cormorant fields and Murchison. Among the new developments Pelican and Strathspey will probably produce gas to be transported by FLAGS. In 1991 FLAGS produced 4.5 billion cubic metres (bcm) of gas, with Alwyn North producing 3.1 bcm.

4. The Quality of Brent Blend

As the characteristics of the crude oil vary across the producing fields, Brent blend is not a completely homogenous commodity. The characteristics of the blend vary as relative production profiles differ across the fields, maintenance programmes are phased and because accidents and other supply disruptions tend to remove fields from production individually or in clusters determined by pipeline logistics. Further, as there tends to be some layering within storage tanks at the point of loading of the blend, the characteristics of the oil loaded by two tankers on the same day may vary significantly. Over time the development of new fields and the decline of older ones can lead to significant shifts in quality.

Brent blend can be characterized as a light, sweet (i.e. with a low sulphur content) crude oil. The gravity of its constituent parts varies from 30–31 degrees API (the Hutton and Osprey fields) to 39–40 degrees API (the Brent, Alwyn North, Don and Staffa fields). Sulphur content varies from 0.2 per cent by volume for the Brent and Alwyn North fields, up to 1 per cent for the Tern field.

It has been the Ninian system that has provided the bulwark against the rapid decline in physical supplies of Brent blend, with two large fields (Magnus and Alwyn North) both peaking in the early 1990s. These two fields produce crude oil that is significantly lighter and sweeter than that from Ninian and Heather, the first two fields developed in the Ninian system. By contrast, the incremental developments in the Brent system have tended to produce oil that is both heavier and with a higher sulphur content than the existing fields, and this has combined with a relative decline of the importance of the lightest and sweetest field in the system, the Brent field itself. Consequently, the relative characteristics of the Brent and Ninian streams have changed dramatically over the period from 1980 to 1992 as is shown in Figure 2.3. For the period after co-mingling in August 1990 the quality of the blend is also shown. There are two breaks in the Brent system series which correspond to the dislocations caused by the Cormorant Alpha explosion in April 1989 which restricted output through May, and the maintenance in April 1991 that reduced output to zero, and for these two months data has been interpolated.

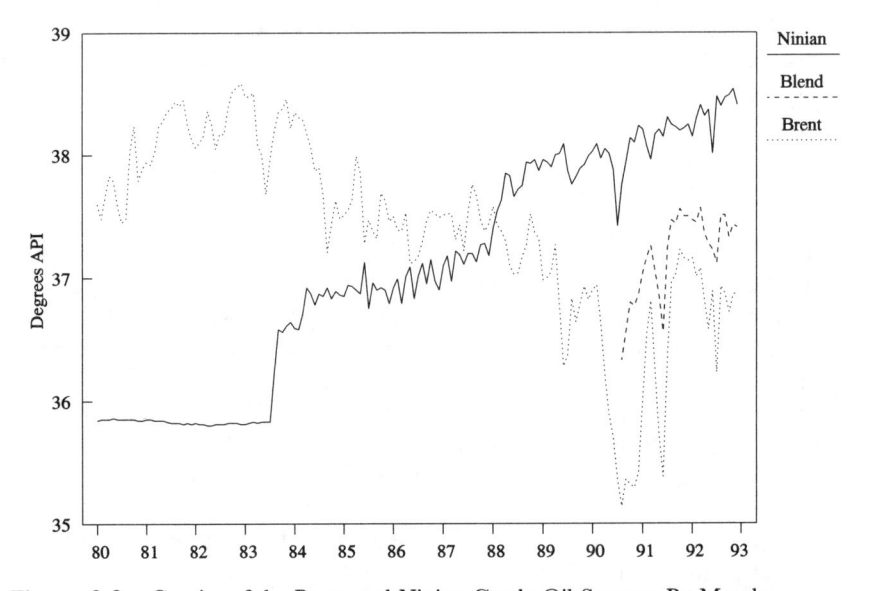

Figure 2.3: Gravity of the Brent and Ninian Crude Oil Streams By Month. 1980–92. API°.

The gravity for Brent blend given in reference texts is normally around 38 degrees API. While this was accurate before 1984, Figure 2.3 shows that the Brent stream has been getting progressively heavier and in quality terms considerably more erratic. Immediately prior to co-mingling the Brent stream, and therefore Brent blend, had fallen below 35.5 degrees API. By contrast, the quality of the Ninian stream has improved significantly, becoming lighter than the Brent stream in 1988, with the gap reaching a full 2 degrees API by the time of co-mingling, and 3 degrees in mid-1991. Since the end of 1991, with the four Brent field platforms getting back to normal production, the gap had settled to between 1 and 1.5 degrees API.

The addition of the Ninian stream has led to a dramatic improvement in the quality of Brent blend, and helped to smooth out some of the volatility of its gravity. Indeed with the Brent system down for maintenance in April 1991 the gravity of the production of the blend returned briefly to its reference book value above 38 degrees API. The average quality of oil actually loaded would have been somewhat lower than this as there was a heavy draw on the stocks held at Sullom Voe over this month, and hence cargoes loaded would have contained some of the heavier Brent system crude oil. Maximum storage capability at Sullom Voe amounts to some 10 mb, i.e. about two weeks' production.

5. Ownership

The majority of the producing oilfields of the Brent and Ninian systems tend to straddle at least two contiguous licensing blocks (in the extreme case the Dunbar field is spread out over five separate licensing blocks). Only five fields (Brent, Deveron, Heather, NW Hutton and Tern) are exploited in solely one block. In some cases the licensee structure for the adjoining blocks is the same and hence the ownership structure of the field is unproblematic (for example the North and South Cormorant fields, Eider and Magnus). In the other cases the ownership of the field is an amalgam of the licensees for each block, weighted by an assessment of each block's contribution to the production of the field as a whole.

This process of the unitization[1] of an oilfield can result in highly complex ownership structures. Company percentage interests in each field (either producing or with Annex B permission) in the Brent and Ninian systems are shown in Table 2.4, together with the names of field operators as they stood on 1 March 1993. The structure of ownership is simpler than in some fields in the North Sea (for example the Claymore field has thirteen licensees and the Forties field no less than eighteen), with at most eleven licensees and an average of between four and five licensees per field. Where an interest is declared in the name of an oil company wholly owned by another, Table 2.4 gives the name of the parent company. Defined in this way there were thirty-five companies with interests in the Brent and Ninian systems as of March 1993. The operatorships of the fields are split across ten companies, with Shell having seven operatorships, BP four, Conoco three, CFP two and Amoco, Amerada Hess, Chevron, LASMO, Texaco, and Unocal one each.

Because the percentages used in the unitization of a field are a function of geology, geological reappraisal and production experience can lead to reunitizations. In some cases a field may have to be reunitized more than once, for example the Dunlin, Ninian and Murchison fields have both been unitized on three occasions. Since 1987 there have only been two reunitizations carried out in the Brent and Ninian systems, in the Hutton field effective from 1 January 1987, and in the Dunlin field effective 1 April 1987. As a reunitization implies that some companies would have been in effect lifting oil beyond the levels to which they were later shown to be entitled, a period of payback is necessary.

During a payback period those companies whose shares have been reduced by the reunitization accept an entitlement to production less than their new share would imply to compensate for their previous overlifting. Thus the effective production entitlements will differ from the paper licensee shares. The figures given in Table 2.4 are all nominal shares. However the Dunlin field is still in a period of payback following the 1987 reunitization, (payback in the Hutton field was achieved by early 1988), and hence the effective shares of production from the field differ from those shown.

The Dunlin field straddles two blocks, 211/23a and 211/24a, the former held entirely by the Shell/Exxon partnership and the latter by a consortium originally headed by Conoco. The initial unitization gave 64 per cent of the field to block 211/23a, which was increased to 70.7 per cent in 1980, and then reduced to 56.85 per cent by the 1987 reunitization. As Dunlin's peak production was reached as long ago as 1979 and the latest reunitization was a major one, the payback period involves the reallocation of a large amount of oil. In total the payback arrangements mean that the effective share of Shell and Exxon combined is 36.7 per cent compared to their nominal share of 56.85 per cent. Likewise the effective share of the production from Dunlin of Aran Energy, OMV and Oryx is 21.1 per cent each rather than their nominal shares of 14.38 per cent each. No other fields in the Brent and Ninian systems are currently affected by the operation of any payback arrangements consequent on a reunitization.

Shares in a field can also change on the asset market. The market for assets in producing Brent and Ninian fields does exist, but is fairly limited. Table 2.5 lists the thirty-six transactions since 1986 that have resulted in a transfer of production entitlements in the Brent and Ninian systems. These transfers have resulted from twenty-two distinct deals, with the two major companies in the Brent system, Shell and Exxon, having been involved in none of them.

Of these deals three have involved corporate takeovers. Atlantic Richfield's takeover of Tricentrol in 1988 resulted in transfers in two fields, while the BP takeover of Britoil also in 1988 for £2.5 billion

Table 2.4: Ownership in Brent and Ninian System Fields. January 1993. Percentage Shares.

Field	Operator	Ownership Shares
Brent System		
1. Brent	Shell	Exxon (50.00), Shell (50.00)
2. North Cormorant	Shell	Exxon (50.00), Shell (50.00)
3. South Cormorant	Shell	Exxon (50.00), Shell (50.00)
4. Deveron	BP	Deminex (42.50), Santa Fe (22.50), BP (15.95), Arco (10.00), Premier (8.05), Monument (1.00)
5. Don	BP	BP (42.72), Deminex (30.96), Santa Fe (18.32), Arco (7.28), Monument (0.72)
6. Dunlin	Shell	Aran Energy (14.38), OMV (14.38), Oryx (14.38), Exxon (28.42), Shell (28.42)
7. Eider	Shell	Exxon (50.00), Shell (50.00)
8. Hudson	Amerada Hess	Amerada Hess (28.45), Itochu (25.77), Mobil (20.00), Exxon (12.89), Shell (12.89)
9. Hutton	Conoco	Oryx (22.17), Chevron (22.17), Conoco (22.17), Amerada Hess (9.53), LASMO (8.63), Itochu (8.63), Mobil (6.70)
10. NW Hutton	Amoco	Amerada Hess (28.46), Amoco (25.77), Itochu (25.77), Mobil (20.00)
11. Murchison	Conoco	Conoco (28.15), Chevron (25.93), Oryx (25.93), Statoil (11.10), Mobil (3.33), Exxon (2.22), Shell (2.22), Saga (0.42), Amoco (0.23), Amerada Hess (0.23), Enterprise (0.23)
12. Osprey	Shell	Exxon (46.70), Shell (46.70), Santa Fe (3.13), Deminex (2.81), Arco (0.66)
13. Tern	Shell	Exxon (50.00), Shell (50.00)
14. Thistle	BP	Deminex (42.50), BP (18.41), Santa Fe (16.88), Arco (10.00), Premier (8.40), Monument (2.41), LASMO (1.41)
Ninian System		
1. Alwyn North	CFP	Elf (66.67), CFP (33.33)
2. Dunbar	CFP	Elf (66.67), CFP (33.33)
3. Heather	Unocal	British Gas (31.25), Texaco (31.25), Unocal (31.25), DNO (6.25)
4. Lyell	Conoco	Chevron (33.33), Conoco (33.33), Oryx (33.33)
5. Magnus	BP	BP (85.00), Repsol (5.00), Sun (5.00), Goal (2.50), Petrobras (2.50)
6. Ninian	Chevron	Oryx (21.37), Enterprise (18.52), LASMO (17.26), Chevron (17.10), Ranger (11.50), Murphy (5.00), ODECO (5.00), Neste (4.24)
7. Staffa	LASMO	LASMO (60.00), Ranger (40.00)
8. Strathspey	Texaco	Texaco (67.00), Exxon (13.25), Shell (13.25), Shell (13.25), Oryx (6.50)

Source: Wood Mackenzie *North Sea Report*, various issues

Table 2.5: Changes in Brent/Ninian Ownership 1986–92.

Field	Purchaser	Vendor	Share	Effective from
Don	Sante Fe	Chevron	1.50	Nov 1991
Deveron	Premier	Burmah	8.05	Jul 1986
	Arco	Tricentrol	10.00	Feb 1988
	BP	Britoil	15.95	Feb 1988
	Monument	Petrofina	1.00	Dec 1988
Dunlin	BP	Britoil	14.38	Feb 1988
	OMV	Conoco	14.38	Jan 1990
	Oryx	BP	14.38	Jan 1990
	Aran Energy	Chevron	14.38	Jul 1992
Heather	British Gas	Tenneco	31.25	Dec 1988
Hutton	BP	Britoil	22.17	Feb 1988
	Oryx	BP	22.17	Jan 1990
	Amerada Hess	Texas Eastern (TENSI)	3.48	Nov 1990
	Ultramar	Amoco	8.63	Jan 1991
	LASMO	Ultramar	8.63	Dec 1991
	Itochu	Enterprise	8.63	Dec 1992
NW Hutton	Amerada Hess	Texas Eastern (TENSI)	10.38	Nov 1990
	Itochu	Enterprise	25.77	Dec 1992
Magnus	Repsol	BP	5.00	Jan 1989
	Sun	BP	5.00	Jan 1989
	Goal	BP	2.50	Jan 1989
	Petrobras	BP	2.50	Jan 1989
Murchison	BP	Britoil	25.93	Feb 1988
	Oryx	BP	25.93	Jan 1990
	Enterprise	Texas Eastern (TENI)	0.23	Jan 1989
Ninian	Enterprise	ICI	18.52	Dec 1986
	BP	Britoil	21.37	Feb 1988
	LASMO	BP	8.63	Jul 1988
	Ranger	BP	5.75	Jul 1988
	Oryx	BP	21.37	Jan 1990
	Neste	Murphy	2.12	Jul 1990
	Neste	ODECO	2.12	Jul 1990
Thistle	Arco	Tricentrol	10.00	Feb 1988
	BP	Britoil	18.41	Feb 1988
	Monument	Petrofina	2.41	Dec 1988
	LASMO	Ultramar	1.41	Dec 1991

Source: Wood Mackenzie *North Sea Report*, various issues.

resulted in the transfer of production entitlements in seven fields in the Brent and Ninian systems. LASMO's takeover of Ultramar in 1991 brought a transfer in two fields. BP's desire to rejuggle their North Sea portfolio after the acquisition of Britoil led to a further set of deals, the most notable being the sale of large interests in Dunlin, Hutton, Murchison to Oryx effective in 1990 – which immediately made Oryx the fifth largest producer in the two systems.

Another series of transactions was spawned by the battle for control over the North Sea assets of Texas Eastern held in their TENSI (UK North Sea) and TENI (Norwegian North Sea) subsidiaries. A bid by Enterprise for all the assets was blocked by court action in 1989, and Enterprise took just 30 per cent of the assets. In the Brent system Enterprise gained, from TENI, just a small share in the Norwegian part of Murchison. The remaining North Sea assets of Texas Eastern were bought in 1989 by a consortium of British Gas and Amerada Hess, with a two-thirds share for Amerada Hess. These assets were then split between the two companies in the consortium in November 1990. The split gave British Gas no extra involvement in the Brent and Ninian systems, but Amerada Hess added TENSI's shares in Hutton and NW Hutton to their existing interests in those fields.

Under the fiscal regime that operated in the UK North Sea before April 1993, partial sale of shares in a field was often motivated predominantly by tax reasons. A company with an involvement in a field that moved out of tax safeguard and became subject to the full rate of Petroleum Revenue Tax (PRT) could find it efficient to scale back that involvement. Companies with costs that could be set against PRT, but no PRT paying fields, had an interest in buying into such fields.[2] If the producing company could already more than offset its own costs, then sale of a partial share became attractive. An example of this was BP's attempt to sell 20 per cent of their 100 per cent stake in the Magnus field, for which bids were accepted for a total of 15 per cent from Repsol, Sun, Goal and Petrobras effective at the beginning of 1989.

6. Prime Suppliers

In all, other than the three companies subject to corporate takeover, only five companies (ICI, Burmah, Texas Eastern, Petrofina and Tenneco)[3] have sold all their interests in the Brent and Ninian systems since 1986. However, through purchases and the development of new fields, thirteen new firms have obtained interests, nine in the Ninian system, three in the Brent system and one in both. Considering only production entitlements in the fields that make up Brent blend, asset market activity and new field developments had resulted in there being in total just one more company with interests immediately prior to the co-mingling of the Brent and Ninian streams than at the start of 1986.

The effect of co-mingling was to increase the number of producing companies dramatically, from nineteen to thirty-four, with the addition of the then four Ninian system fields. The number of companies with interests in the Brent and Ninian systems and thus with entitlements to production of Brent blend stood at thirty-five in early 1993. The geographical spread of these companies is considerable with companies from no less than thirteen countries (Austria, Brazil, Canada, Finland, France, Germany, Ireland, Japan, Kuwait, Norway, Spain, UK and USA) having entitlements to Brent blend production.

Within this large spread of companies with primary access to Brent blend there are considerable variations in volumes of production entitlement, with the largest three companies accounting for over 60 per cent of the total in 1992, and the largest ten for about 90 per cent. Table 2.6 presents entitlements to Brent blend by company derived from production figures and ownership shares by field. Where a field has been subject to reunitization the effective shares (i.e. allowing for the payback of overlifted oil) have been used for the appropriate period.

Production is still dominated by the Shell/Exxon partnership, but the degree of concentration in production has been reduced significantly by co-mingling. One measure of concentration is the inverse Herfindahl index, i.e the inverse of the sum of the squared shares out of total production across companies. In 1986 this was 4.2, i.e. the level of concentration was similar to an industry with four equal sized producers. The high degree of concentration was maintained until 1990 – the index was 4.1 in 1987, 4.2 in 1988, and 4.0 in 1989. With the restricted output of the Brent field in 1990, the degree of concentration lessened in the seven months of 1990 before co-mingling, moving out to 4.6. The addition of the Ninian system fields greatly reduced the concentration of Brent production, with the value of the index being 6.9 in 1991 and 6.3 in 1992.[4]

In total, asset market activity, the development of new fields and most importantly the co-mingling of the Brent and Ninian streams have brought about a considerably more diversified and less concentrated pattern of ownership compared to that which obtained in 1986. Another manifestation of this is the decline in the percentage share of Brent blend produced by the Shell/Exxon partnership. Figure 2.4 shows this percentage by month from 1980 to June 1992, with the two breaks in the series represented by the Cormorant Alpha explosion and the shut-down of the Brent system for installation of emergency safety

Table 2.6: Entitlements to Brent Blend by Company. 1986–92. Thousand Barrels per Day.

	1986	1987	1988	1989	1990 (a)	1990 (b)	1990	1991	1992
Exxon	297.4	268.0	247.7	173.3	135.0	75.0	125.5	178.1	214.4
Shell	297.4	268.0	247.7	173.3	135.0	75.0	125.5	178.1	214.4
BP	-	-	42.5	34.1	10.7	128.8	59.5	120.1	135.3
Elf	-	-	-	-	-	56.9	23.9	61.2	55.0
Oryx	-	-	-	-	23.5	45.4	32.7	35.8	34.3
Chevron	44.9	42.8	39.8	27.1	23.9	41.0	31.0	32.2	29.5
CFP	-	-	-	-	-	28.5	11.9	30.6	27.5
Enterprise	19.5	13.7	13.9	8.4	7.6	27.2	15.8	19.7	17.0
LASMO	-	-	-	-	-	18.4	7.7	15.0	15.7
Conoco	46.6	44.3	41.1	27.9	17.2	16.0	16.7	12.4	14.9
Deminex	28.6	26.0	24.4	15.2	17.3	13.8	16.2	9.0	11.9
Ranger	-	-	-	-	-	12.3	5.1	10.0	10.2
Repsol	-	-	-	-	-	7.1	3.0	6.8	7.6
Sun	-	-	-	-	-	7.1	3.0	6.8	7.6
OMV	-	-	-	-	7.4	7.3	7.4	5.5	5.8
Santa Fe	11.7	10.7	10.0	6.3	7.4	5.8	7.0	4.3	5.8
Amerada Hess	13.9	9.8	9.8	5.9	5.4	5.9	5.6	4.0	5.0
Mobil	17.6	13.0	12.7	7.7	7.1	6.9	7.0	3.8	4.6
Amoco	19.7	13.9	14.0	8.4	7.6	7.4	7.5	2.5	4.5
Statoil	8.3	7.8	6.5	4.1	4.1	4.0	4.1	3.3	4.0
Goal	-	-	-	-	-	3.6	1.5	3.4	3.8
Petrobras	-	-	-	-	-	3.6	1.5	3.4	3.8
Murphy	-	-	-	-	-	5.3	2.2	4.3	3.4
ODECO	-	-	-	-	-	5.3	2.2	4.3	3.4
Neste	-	-	-	-	-	4.5	1.9	3.7	2.9
British Gas	-	-	-	-	-	3.1	1.3	3.1	2.8
Texaco	-	-	-	-	-	3.1	1.3	3.1	2.8
Unocal	-	-	-	-	-	3.1	0.4	3.1	2.8
Arco	-	-	5.2	3.6	4.1	3.2	3.8	2.1	2.8
Aran Energy	-	-	-	-	-	-	-	-	2.0
Premier	5.4	5.1	4.8	2.9	3.1	2.5	2.8	1.3	1.8
DNO	-	-	-	-	-	0.6	0.3	0.6	0.6
Monument	-	-	0.1	0.8	0.9	0.7	0.8	0.4	0.5
Saga	0.3	0.3	0.2	0.2	0.2	0.2	0.2	0.1	0.1
Ultramar	0.9	0.8	0.7	0.4	0.4	0.4	0.4	1.4	-
Britoil	57.2	53.9	7.8	-	-	-	-	-	-
Burmah	0.3	-	-	-	-	-	-	-	-
Petrofina	1.5	1.4	1.3	-	-	-	-	-	-
Texas Eastern	8.0	5.7	5.7	3.3	3.0	2.3	2.7	-	-
Tricentrol	6.7	6.1	0.6	-	-	-	-	-	-

Notes: (a) January 1 to July 31 1990 (before co-mingling)
(b) August 1 to December 31 1990 (after co-mingling)
Source: Own calculations from Wood Mackenzie *North Sea Report*, various issues.

28 *Oil Markets and Prices*

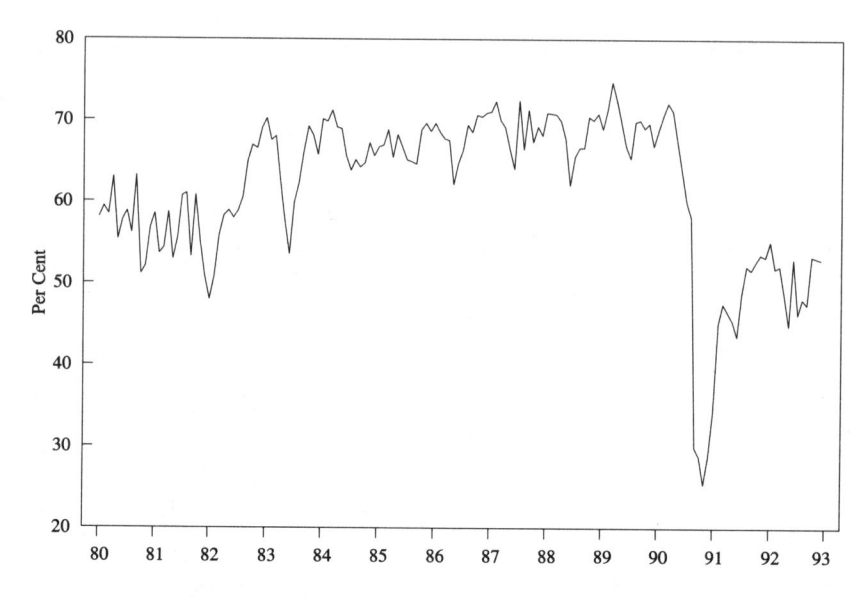

Figure 2.4: Combined Exxon and Shell Percentage Share of Brent Blend Production By Month. 1980–92.

valves having data points interpolated. From a steady state of between 60 and 70 per cent the Shell/Exxon combined share has fallen to about 50 per cent.

7. The Lifting of Brent Blend at Sullom Voe

At Sullom Voe Brent blend is available for loading at the terminal in standard parcels of 500 thousand barrels (or some 65 to 67 thousand tonnes). The size of the standard parcel has been varied twice in the past. It was 500 thousand barrels until the end of 1984, then 600 thousand barrels (about 80 thousand tonnes) from January 1985 to August 1988 at which time it was set once again at 500 thousand barrels.

Trade in the Brent physical forward cargoes is for a transaction volume equal to the standard lifting parcel, at present 500 thousand barrels. The relationship between transaction contracts and the physical lifting of the Brent blend, rigid as it may appear at first sight, involves some elements of flexibility. On the transaction side it has been possible to deal on the forward market with mini-contracts of 50 thousand barrels in recent years. The difficulty with these partial contracts arises from the obligation on their holders to 'resolve' their position before maturity either by reducing the number of contracts held to zero or by adjusting their numbers to multiples of ten, thus transforming them into standard 500 thousand barrel transactions. On the lifting side, the buyer of Brent blend enjoys a tolerance of plus or minus 5 per cent. This means that the contract is deemed fulfilled if the buyer lifted any volume between 475 thousand and 525 thousand barrels per cargo. The implications of this lifting tolerance is taken up in Chapter 9.

The specification of the parcel size is not the only, or indeed the most significant, feature of loading arrangements at Sullom Voe in terms of market and other economic implications. As in all oil-export terminals, loading operates according to pre-arranged schedules which are planned as follows:

(a) The companies producing (or holding entitlement to) crude in the Brent/Ninian system at Sullom Voe nominate their preferred loading dates for oil produced at the relevant month by the 5th of the preceding month.

(b) Shell UK which organizes the loading programme on behalf of the Brent blend participants (the terminal itself is operated by BP and the port by the Shetland Islands Council) finalizes it through negotiations with participants by the 15th of the previous month at the latest. The participants' preferences for loading slots, when first expressed, are to be distributed over the relevant month in a manner consistent with smooth operations at the terminal; and one suspects that much bargaining takes place on occasions between Shell UK and the participants. The loading programme allocates to sellers the requested number of slots on the dates agreed upon. The loading slot is specified as a three (consecutive) day window.

(c) The loading programme is finalized at the latest by the 15th of the preceding month.

(d) A producing company or any other entity selling Brent blend through the forward market is required to give the buyer 15 days notice of the first date of a three-day loading window. To illustrate, September Brent can be loaded between the 1 and 30 September. The first three-day loading window is 1–3 September, the last window is 28–30 September. The seller with a loading slot in the programme on, say 7–9 September, must give notice to the buyer before the end of business on 22 August. The notice must be given not later than by the end of business on the 16 August for the first loading window in September (1–3 September) and not later than by the end of business on 12 September for the last loading window (28–30 September).

(e) The buyer, once notified of the relevant loading window, must then nominate a vessel acceptable to the terminal no later than seven days before the first loading date.

Notes
1. Unitization is a procedure through which the production, development costs etc. of a field that straddles over several blocks (or countries) are distributed between the different companies with licences for these blocks.
2. The PRT regime is explained in Chapter 5.
3. In early 1993 LASMO announced an intention to sell its interests.
4. For the period after co-mingling in 1990, i.e. from August onwards, the index showed even less concentration at a value of 10.5, as the effects of co-mingling were mixed with the effects of low production in the Brent field.

CHAPTER 3

PHYSICAL TRADING

1. Introduction

In the last chapter we detailed the production of Brent blend. This chapter provides a picture of its consumption, and its importance in the context of the world market. In the next section we provide details of the trade pattern in Brent, compiled on the basis of data on shipping movements out of Sullom Voe. The final section very briefly documents the position of oil in the UK economy, and the position of UK North Sea oil in the oil market as a whole.

2. Trade in Brent Blend

A weekly shipping list is produced by the Ports and Harbours Department of the Shetland Islands Council, which documents the name of vessel, cargo size and stated destination of cargoes loaded at the Sullom Voe terminal during the previous week. While a few cargoes may be traded in transit and change their eventual destination, we believe that the shipping list provides an accurate picture of where loadings from Sullom Voe are eventually discharged.

On the basis of the shipping list alone, or with any publicly available information, it is impossible to distinguish between Brent and Ninian cargoes in the period before co-mingling in August 1990. Brent and Ninian are therefore aggregated for this period in the tables that follow. Our collation of the data includes all loadings of crude oil from Sullom Voe from the start of 1987 to the end of 1992, a total of 2,956 cargoes.

Table 3.1 shows the volume of loadings from Sullom Voe by country of destination and by year, with Table 3.2 presenting this information in percentage terms. In 1992 over 70 per cent of Brent blend went to refineries in the UK, the USA, Canada, and Germany.

With UK refineries taking more Brent in 1992 than Brent and Ninian in 1987, combined with lower availabilities, the amount of Brent exported has fallen sharply. In 1992, 73 per cent of Brent blend was exported, compared with 81 per cent of Brent and Ninian in 1987. In total, 200 thousand b/d less was exported from Sullom Voe in 1992

32   *Oil Markets and Prices*

Table 3.1: Destination of Brent/Ninian Loadings. 1987–92. Thousand Barrels Per Day.

	1987	1988	1989	1990	1991	1992
Canada	109.4	101.3	119.6	143.7	134.2	101.0
Caribbean	8.3	13.1	0.0	35.7	8.0	0.0
Eire	27.6	23.8	22.8	15.9	2.7	0.0
France	184.7	142.3	49.6	48.7	75.1	55.8
Germany	123.5	127.2	113.0	104.7	73.1	108.1
Holland	53.8	68.6	66.8	48.4	38.6	39.1
Italy	39.8	38.8	5.6	7.1	23.1	20.9
Poland	0.0	0.0	2.6	0.0	7.6	42.6
Scandinavia	47.1	23.0	10.2	7.0	29.5	49.3
Turkey	0.0	0.0	0.0	0.0	26.8	5.3
UK	187.3	250.3	248.6	178.6	206.0	225.7
USA	210.5	208.0	162.6	130.6	98.9	172.2
Other	13.4	23.0	15.3	6.2	6.8	19.4
Unknown	0.0	10.7	1.7	0.0	0.0	2.6
Total	1005.6	1030.1	818.6	726.5	730.3	841.9

Source: Own calculations from Shetlands Islands Council data.

Table 3.2: Destination of Brent/Ninian Loadings. 1987–92. Per Cent.

	1987	1988	1989	1990	1991	1992
Canada	10.9	9.8	14.6	19.8	18.4	12.0
Caribbean	0.8	1.3	0.0	4.9	1.1	0.0
Eire	2.7	2.3	2.8	2.2	0.4	0.0
France	18.4	13.8	6.1	6.7	10.3	6.6
Germany	12.3	12.4	13.8	14.4	10.0	12.8
Holland	5.3	6.7	8.2	6.7	5.3	4.6
Italy	4.0	3.8	0.7	1.0	3.2	2.5
Poland	0.0	0.0	0.3	0.0	1.0	5.1
Scandinavia	4.7	2.2	1.2	1.0	4.0	5.9
Turkey	0.0	0.0	0.0	0.0	3.7	0.6
UK	18.6	24.3	30.4	24.6	28.2	26.8
USA	20.9	20.2	19.9	18.0	13.5	20.5
Other	1.3	2.2	1.9	0.8	0.8	2.3
Unknown	0.0	1.0	0.2	0.0	0.0	0.2
Total	100.0	100.0	100.0	100.0	100.0	100.0

Source: Own calculations from Shetlands Islands Council data.

compared to 1987. Brent is primarily an Atlantic basin crude oil, of which in 1992 26.7 per cent were used in the UK, 31.7 per cent in the rest of Northern Europe, and 32.5 per cent going to North America. A total of 7.9 per cent went to ports in the Mediterranean. There are currently no restrictions on the export of UK crude oil except to countries subject to economic sanctions. In January 1979 restrictions had been placed that essentially required special permission for any cargoes going to a non-OECD country. These restrictions were lifted in March 1991.

The consumption of Brent by UK refineries is shown in Table 3.3. Refineries have been aggregated in cases where they use the same ports and therefore no decomposition is possible.

The major UK users of Brent are Shell's Stanlow and Shellhaven refineries and the Milford Haven refinery, accounting for three-quarters of consumption in 1992. One strong implication that can be drawn from Table 3.3 is that among the major equity producers of Brent only Shell uses a significant amount of their entitlement in their UK refineries. In Chapter 2 we found that the entitlements of Shell and Exxon were about 180 thousand b/d each in 1991, and that of BP was 120 thousand b/d. Their UK use of Brent in 1992, from Table 3.3, was respectively 131.6 and 10.9 thousand b/d, and zero in the case of BP. The BP refinery at Grangemouth is primarily geared to the use of Forties blend production, in which BP is the major equity producer.

Table 3.3: UK Consumption of Brent/Ninian. 1987–92. Thousand Barrels per Day.

Refinery	Owner	Capacity	1987	1988	1989	1990	1991	1992
Fawley	Exxon	300	10.0	18.7	47.7	17.9	13.0	10.8
Stanlow	Shell	260	28.5	50.2	44.4	62.0	64.1	87.3
Coryton	Mobil	200	1.6	0.0	5.7	7.3	16.2	5.7
Pembroke	Texaco	180	27.1	54.1	36.1	28.3	25.0	22.1
Grangemouth	BP	198	1.6	0.0	2.7	2.6	0.0	0.0
S.Killingholme	Total/Fina	190 }	7.6	15.3	2.7	1.4	5.6	6.9
Killingholme	Conoco	130 }						
Milford Haven	Elf/Murco	100 }	89.4	76.6	87.8	53.4	70.2	43.9
Milford Haven	Gulf	105 }						
North Tees	Phillips/ICI	100	0.0	0.0	0.0	2.7	0.0	0.0
Shellhaven	Shell	90	13.1	29.1	19.9	2.9	11.8	45.0
Other/Unknown			8.4	5.0	1.4	0.0	0.0	4.1
Total UK			187.3	250.3	248.6	178.6	206.0	225.7

Source: Own calculations from Shetlands Islands Council data.

34 *Oil Markets and Prices*

As seen in Table 3.1, US consumption of Brent/Ninian fell every year between 1987 and 1991 before rebounding in 1992. Within this fall there has also been a significant shift in the refineries that use it. Table 3.4 shows US-bound loadings since 1987 split by geographical area of destination. While the total has fallen sharply, consumption in the Gulf Coast refining area has risen. By contrast, the Atlantic Coast refineries, particularly the Chevron and Sun refineries in Philadelphia and the BP and Sun refineries in Marcus Hook Pennsylvania, have reduced their consumption.

Table 3.4: US Imports of Brent/Ninian. 1987–92. Thousand Barrels per Day.

	1987	*1988*	*1989*	*1990*	*1991*	*1992*
Atlantic Coast (PAD 1)	147.0	83.9	41.9	15.3	8.3	42.6
of which Philadelphia	*89.0*	*48.5*	*19.3*	*2.8*	*5.4*	*21.0*
Marcus Hook	*33.2*	*12.9*	*4.5*	*2.9*	*1.4*	*20.3*
Gulf Coast (PAD 3)	50.2	93.7	107.0	107.0	90.6	129.6
Unknown	13.3	30.4	13.7	8.3	0.0	0.0
Total USA	210.5	208.0	162.6	130.6	98.9	172.2

Source: Own calculations from Shetlands Islands Council data.

Whereas Brent used to compete with the stream of primarily light sweet imports, mainly from West Africa, in the Atlantic Coast market, in the Gulf Coast it is part of an import stream that is much heavier and sourer, and dominated by Saudi Arabian, Mexican and Venezuelan crude oils. Whereas in the Atlantic Coast Brent's closest substitutes and main competitors are imported grades, especially Nigerian, in the Gulf Coast the competition is mainly domestic US light sweet grades. On the Atlantic Coast the bulk of the competing grades are priced on Brent related terms, whereas on the Gulf Coast Brent is competing with US domestic grades. It is then possible that the shift in Brent use in the US market from the Atlantic to the Gulf Coast may have increased its sensitivity to changes in its price differential with domestic grades.

Table 3.5 shows the average size of cargo leaving Sullom Voe by selected destinations and in total. The size of the average cargo leaving Sullom Voe was higher in 1992 than in 1987. However, in 1987 the standard forward market cargo size was 600 thousand barrels, compared to the current 500 thousand. What has happened is that far more

Table 3.5: Average Cargo Size. 1987–92. Thousand Barrels.

	1987	1988	1989	1990	1991	1992
Canada	583.9	658.6	586.9	621.3	641.2	592.9
Caribbean	1513.0	1191.4	-	1295.0	966.5	-
France	664.1	709.5	948.7	842.4	736.6	781.7
Germany	605.9	538.6	506.5	506.9	520.1	587.3
Holland	557.7	580.8	551.6	532.3	518.8	569.8
Italy	723.3	831.1	1012.5	854.8	645.8	844.0
UK	618.2	566.0	527.8	540.2	510.4	526.8
USA	676.5	772.6	1157.5	1102.3	1056.4	964.8
Overall	629.5	636.7	623.0	643.3	631.3	638.6

Source: Own calculations from Shetlands Islands Council data.

cargoes of 1 mb or more are being loaded. In particular, the average cargo size for US liftings is now equivalent to a double standard cargo size.

3. The North Sea in World Oil Trade and the UK Economy

In 1991 oil and gas production contributed £7.6 billion to UK Gross National Product at factor cost, about 1.5 per cent of total UK GNP, and the offshore industry employed more than 33 thousand people.[1] While the sector is relatively unimportant compared to other UK industries in terms of employment and contribution to GNP, it has (at least in the past) been a major source of revenue for the UK government. The details of the fiscal regime affecting the sale of Brent blend are discussed in Chapter 5. Table 3.6 provides an idea of the magnitude of the tax receipts from the whole North Sea.

Tax receipts have fallen sharply since their high point in 1984–5, mainly due to lower oil prices and reduced production. The first element is royalty, payable on sales for fields that received Annex B development permission before 1 April 1982. Within the Brent and Ninian system this includes (as shown in Table 2.1) eleven of the fields including the Brent and Ninian fields themselves. The price collapse of 1986 reduced royalty payments drastically, and they have continued to fall as the production of the older fields has gone into natural decline.

The second element is Petroleum Revenue Tax (PRT), which was designed as the main rent-taking instrument, taking 75 per cent of each

36   *Oil Markets and Prices*

Table 3.6: Tax Receipts from UKCS Activity. 1984/5 to 1991/2. £ Million.

	1984/5	1985/6	1986/7	1987/8	1988/9	1989/90	1990/1	1991/2
Royalty	2575	2079	939	1051	607	608	637	550
Petroleum Revenue Tax	7177	6375	1188	2296	1371	1050	860	-200
Corporation Tax	2432	2916	2676	1298	1210	768	1032	650
Total	12184	11370	4803	4645	3188	2426	2529	1000

Source: UK Department of Trade and Industry, *Development of the Oil and Gas Resources of the UK*, various issues.

field's revenues minus costs and allowances, before being reduced to 50 per cent in the March 1993 Finance Bill. As Table 3.6 shows, PRT alone brought in over £7 billion in 1984–5. However PRT payments have since declined sharply, to the extent that in 1991–2 PRT was actually a negative element in the government fiscal balance, with a net payment of £200 million made to the oil companies. This arose from particularly high levels of investment in 1991, both in new field development and expenditure on existing fields. Before 1993 exploration and appraisal expenditure could be set against PRT payments on other fields. The third element is corporation profits tax, which in recent years has become the major source of the government take from North Sea activity. The government also receives money from the Gas Levy, which contributed £282 million to the Exchequer in 1992.

The decline in the importance of PRT is due to lower prices, lower production and because new developments are smaller higher cost fields. This is emphasized by calculations from the present value statistics by field generated by Wood Mackenzie. The present value in 1991 of the tax paid by the largest tax paying fields, i.e. the Brent, Ninian and Forties fields, over the course of their life is £103.2 billion. The present value of their PRT payments alone amounts to £49.1 billion. For these three fields as a whole, 53.6 per cent of the present value of revenue generated, gross of costs, was paid in tax (net of costs the take is over 80 per cent). The 1993 Finance Bill abolished PRT on future field development. In fact this is less generous that it might seem. The present value of the total tax that would have been paid by the next forty-eight oil and gas fields expected to receive Annex B development permission amounts to just £5 billion under the old tax regime, with PRT making up £1.1 billion. The tax take-out of the present value of total gross revenues is just 18.2 per cent. The total recoverable oil reserves of these forty-eight fields are almost exactly the same as the original reserves of the Brent field, and their gas reserves are five times as much. Yet the present value of the PRT that would have been paid by these fields is just 4 per cent of that paid by Brent. In addition, Brent pays royalty whereas the new fields will not. With Brent already having produced two-thirds of the present value of its PRT payments, and Forties and Ninian over 90 per cent, it appears that the PRT system has already collected the bulk of the rent it was designed to tap into. In particular, removing PRT on new fields does little to encourage development, and any such effect is swamped by the negative effects of the removal of the tax break represented by offsetting exploration and appraisal expenditures against the PRT paid by other fields.

While the North Sea is not the benefit to the Exchequer that it was in previous years, it should be noted that the taxes shown in Table 3.6 only represent a small proportion of the UK government's total take from the oil sector. Taxes are also collected downstream on the sale of petroleum products and from corporation taxes on refining and retailing activities. For example, the average prices in the UK of a litre of leaded gasoline, unleaded gasoline and transportation diesel in the last week of June 1992 were respectively 51.51 pence, 47.64 pence and 45.22 pence.[2] The total tax payable per litre for these products, including excise taxes and value added taxes, equates to 35.5 pence, 30.5 pence and 29.6 pence.[3] Based on average consumption in the first four months of 1992, these figures are the equivalent of annual tax receipts taken by the UK government from the sale of leaded gasoline of £6.2 billion, from unleaded gasoline of £4.3 billion, and from transportation diesel of £3.8 billion. Further to this £14.3 billion receipt from the sale of transport fuels, there is also the tax on profits in retailing, taxes on the income of employees in retailing as well as taxes on other petroleum products. In terms of absolute taxation, the take from the downstream sector (which falls mainly on consumers of oil products) in the UK now dwarfs that from the upstream.

In terms of the international oil industry the UK was only the eleventh largest producing country in the world in 1992 (even in a year when Kuwait and Iraq were not in full production). This is shown in Table 3.7 which shows all countries with a 1991 production of over 1 mb/d. In world terms the UK is not a major producer, providing less than 3 per cent of world supplies and holding 0.4 per cent of proven world reserves.[4]

However the UK is more important in terms of world trade. Total international trade in crude oil in 1991 amounted to about 30 mb/d, 21 mb/d produced by OPEC countries and 9 mb/d outside OPEC.[5] Net UK exports of crude oil amounted to only about 110 thousand b/d.

Table 3.7: World Oil Production. 1992. Million Barrels per Day.

	CIS Republics	8.95
	Saudi Arabia	8.31
	USA	7.15
	Iran	3.46
	China	2.84
	Mexico	2.67
	UAE	2.29
	Venezuela	2.34
	Norway	2.14
	Nigeria	1.90
	United Kingdom	1.85
	Libya	1.49
	Canada	1.61
	Indonesia	1.35

Source: *Oil and Gas Journal*, 8 March 1993.

However this represents the balance between exports of 1.05 mb/d and imports of 0.94 mb/d.[6] Brent blend constitutes almost exactly one-half of UK crude oil exports.

UK exports then make up about 3.3 per cent of total world trade, and over 10 per cent of non-OPEC exports. However, the UK's major importance is as a supplier of light low sulphur crude oil in the Atlantic basin. With the bulk of Middle East OPEC production being heavier and higher in sulphur than the bulk of UK exports, in this role only the exports of Norway, Nigeria and other West African countries, Algeria and Libya represent major competitors, and only Libya, Nigeria and Norway export more light sweet crude oil (US production of crude oil cannot be exported by US law). Hence UK production has more influence than might be suggested by being less than 3 per cent of world production, just over 3 per cent of world trade, and 0.4 per cent of world reserves.

Notes
1. From UK Department of Trade and Industry (1992), *Development of the Oil and Gas Resources of the United Kingdom*, often referred to as the Brown book.
2. Source: *Petroleum Times Energy Report*, 3 July 1992.
3. By way of comparison, crude oil at $20 per barrel equates to about 8 pence per litre.
4. Figures from *BP Statistical Review of World Energy*, 1992.
5. Shell (1992) *Energy in Profile*.
6. Calculations from UK Department of Trade and Industry (1992), *Digest of United Kingdom Energy Statistics*.

CHAPTER 4

DESCRIPTION OF BRENT MARKETS AND TRADING INSTRUMENTS

1. Introduction

Crude oil is traded on world markets with a variety of instruments, including spot, physical forward and futures contracts. Recently other instruments have been introduced, and their use has been expanding rapidly – the most important of which are options on futures contracts, swaps and warrants. While the oil market has lagged far behind other commodity markets in its range and use of trading instruments, the gap has closed considerably in the last ten years.

These sets of trading instruments apply to a small number of crudes, the most important being West Texas Intermediate (WTI), Dubai, Alaska North Slope (ANS), and Brent blend. These various crudes or blends define each particular oil market with locational and institutional characteristics of its own. All these markets are linked together through arbitrage but the linkages are not so complete or so perfect as to ensure total integration. There are continual tensions between the local forces and particular features which separate markets and the links which tie them together and seek to bring different price movements into a uniform pattern.

Our concern here is with the set of trading instruments or contracts which deal with Brent blend, thus constituting the Brent market. Until the mid-1980s, the term 'Brent Market' only referred to spot and physical forward transactions involving this particular blend. Now, the Brent market includes partial forward transactions, a futures contract traded in London on the floor of the International Petroleum Exchange (IPE), options on this contract, and swap deals. In this chapter we shall describe the main institutional features of these various instruments with a view to the economic, rather than technical or legal, implications of these characteristics.

2. Dated Brent and 15-day Brent

There are two types of transaction in the physical Brent blend market: one known as a 'dated Brent' cargo and the other as a '15-day Brent' or 'forward Brent' cargo. For all intents and purposes the former is a conventional spot transaction, and the latter is a forward deal. 'Dated Brent' refers to the sale of a specific cargo that is either available in a specific loading slot or that is already loaded and in transit to some destination. The 15-day cargo is a standard parcel that will be made available by the seller to the buyer on an unspecified day of the relevant month.

In both cases the oil is sold f.o.b. (insurance, freight and ocean losses are the buyer's responsibility, but demurrage at the terminal is the seller's) with payment made thirty days after the date of the bill of lading. For 15-day Brent, the contract is a standard telex, often, but not always, using as part of the contract the format defined by Shell UK in a document, known as Agreement for the Sale of Brent Blend Crude Oil on 15-Day Terms (July 1990). The format is straightforward, including as one might expect names of buyer and seller, the specified delivery month and price and so on. The price is calculated f.o.b. at the loading terminal at Sullom Voe and no gravity adjustment applies. The main legal clauses are that the contract shall be governed by English law; the parties submit to the exclusive jurisdiction of the English courts without any recourse to arbitration; the United Nations Convention for the International Sale of Goods (1980) shall not apply; each party warrants that in entering the contract it is not contravening the United Kingdom Financial Services Act, 1986.

Participants deal with each other on a purely bilateral basis, buying and selling cargoes at any time for forward delivery months. There are usually many more forward contracts for a given month than physical cargoes; the former can be as numerous as participants wish them to be while the latter are constrained, among other things, by the volume of production in that month.

In the 15-day Brent market, there is no exchange to match sellers and buyers and guarantee deals; no end-of-day closing when the open interest is established for all forward months; no unique date at which the deals for a month mature all at once and no 'marking to market'. There is no obligation on either party to a deal to reveal its existence or details to any other party. The clearing of the market involves all participants. It essentially consists of two different operations – book-outs and the seller's nominations which can take place on any day in the period starting fifteen days before the beginning of the relevant month and closing eighteen days before its end. The month is said to have become wet on the first day on which sellers can begin to serve 15-day notices.

A book-out is an agreement between a set of participants to cancel their contracts with a cash settlement for the difference between an agreed reference price and the contract price. A book-out may take place whenever a set of claims on forward cargoes held by different participants can be arranged in a chain starting and ending with the same participant (the 'circle'). For example, the set of trades – A having sold to B, B to C, C to D, and D to A – can give rise to a book-out. It may be proposed by any party in an identified circle. No participant is obliged to enter a book-out when invited if he does not wish to do so. The 1990 Shell UK terms, referred to above, specifically state also that no reason need be given by the participant who refuses to join a book-out. It is said that book-outs sometimes clear up to 50 or 70 per cent of the contracts for a relevant month.

In essence the book-out converts a contract for physical delivery into an agreement for financial settlement. In determining the terms of the proposed financial settlement, the parties assume that there will be a deemed delivery of 500 thousand barrels taking place on the 15th day of the relevant month or on the middle day of the loading window if the seller has already notified the buyers of the dates of the three-day loading range.

Contracts not cleared by a book-out cancellation are cleared through the nomination process. This works as follows. Sellers with entitlements to Brent blend at Sullom Voe who have sold it through the forward market, serve 15-day notices to participants who had bought cargoes for the relevant month. For example a buyer who receives a 15-day notice to take delivery may either accept it, or pass it on to somebody else who had entered into a buying contract with him. Each time the nomination is passed, it must be passed with the specific cargo number it relates to. This process can continue between participants until 5 p.m. London time on the last day on which the notice can be validly served given the nominated three-day loading window. A company left with a nomination having been unable to pass it on in time, is said to have been '5 o'clocked'.

For example, the last nomination day for a cargo loading in the first September loading slot, i.e. 1–3 September, is 16 August, leaving fifteen clear days before the first day of the slot. At 5 p.m. London time on 16 August that cargo becomes 'wet', and nominations for it can no longer be passed on in the 15-day market. The cargo has now become a dated Brent cargo. Likewise, the latest date a September cargo can become wet is 5 p.m. on 12 September, i.e. leaving fifteen clear days before the first day of the 28–30 September loading slot. September Brent is therefore the 'wet' month from 16 August to 12 September.

Sellers of equity Brent know when their cargoes will load, as soon as the loading schedule for Sullom Voe is finalized, as was explained in Chapter 2. Consider a producer who has three cargoes loading in September, all of which have been sold in the 15-day market. Assume the first of the three loading slots is the 10–12 September, and the producer has made a total of three buys and six sells in the 15-day market, none of which have been booked out. The last nomination day for the first loading slot the producer has is 25 August. On or before that date the producer will pass a nomination to the holder of any one of the sells they have made, the choice being at their discretion, and that agent can then accept the nomination or pass it on, in which case the procedure continues. This will be repeated for both of the other loading slots the producer has. Since in this example the producer has also bought three cargoes, they will also have nominations passed to them as part of any chain formed in the delivery month, and they can in turn pass these on using one of their remaining sells.

There is no earliest date on which the nomination procedure for a given slot can begin. However cargoes do not have specific loading numbers, nor are the loading slots for a producer's cargoes known before the loading schedule is confirmed, at the latest by the 15th of the month prior to delivery.

This 'pass-the-parcel' game creates a chain between a 'primary' seller (somebody with a physical entitlement) and the 'ultimate' buyer (the participant who has voluntarily accepted the notice or who has been unable to pass it on either because it has reached him at 5 p.m. on the last day or for some other reason).

The set of contracts between the primary seller and the ultimate buyer is called a chain. Before a month becomes wet, forward cargoes constitute participants' portfolios, with participants holding long, short or balanced positions. There are no actual chains at that stage, and the number of alternative chains that can be charted, with full information about deals made, is very large given the range of possible combinations and permutations.

The clearing process is complex. It involves the search for and negotiation of possible book-outs, and the peculiar pass-the-parcel procedure which can be clumsy or troublesome on occasions. One of its odd features is that a participant who holds a balanced portfolio (with an equal number of buys and sells) may still end up acquiring a wet cargo. This can easily happen if the 15-day notice for one of his purchase contracts reaches the office too close to the 5 o'clock deadline for the cargo to be passed on. This participant will now have one wet cargo, and one more outstanding sell than buy in the forward market for the relevant delivery month. If the participant has no use for the cargo it must be sold as a dated cargo. Regardless of what is done with the wet cargo, a forward market cargo must be bought to rebalance the portfolio of forward cargoes held by the participant.

The clearing process can run into difficulties when some participants without entitlement to Brent blend at Sullom Voe find themselves with short positions (more sells than buys) during the wet month and have to scramble for late purchases of 15-day contracts.

When the last nomination for a cargo in a delivery month has either been accepted, or the holder has been 5 o'clocked, all deals for that month have not necessarily been resolved. Companies may still be holding claims on cargoes after the last cargo has been accounted for. These deals have to be resolved and booked out *ex post*, and this resolution may go on for a few days after the last nomination has been passed.

In summary, the most interesting features of the 15-day market are as follows. First, the buyer's uncertainty regarding the exact date of delivery in the relevant month which may lead to 'secondary' hedging through transactions of dated cargoes or trading on other markets. Secondly, the imbalance between the discretion (however limited this may be) enjoyed by primary sellers and the uncertainty that affects buyers as regards delivery. Thirdly, the lack of perfect price/volume transparency of a market which, though rooted in physical trade, is significantly used for financial operations.[1] Finally, the oddity of certain procedures, particularly the notice/chain mechanism.

3. Spread Trading

There are two major forms of 15-day Brent market trading. Forward cargoes can either be traded as single cargoes with an absolute price agreed, or in spread trading that involves the simultaneous sale and purchase of two or sometimes more cargoes. Spread trading comes in a variety of forms which we now document, some of which involve trading first differences in two prices, others which involve trading second order differences in prices.

(a) Inter-Month Spreads

The most common form of spread trading in the Brent market, in recent years, is the trading of the difference in price between Brent for delivery in different months, and involves the trading of two Brent cargoes. For example, if trader X has bought an April/May spread from trader Y, then X has bought an April cargo from Y and simultaneously sold a May cargo to Y. If the price of April Brent was $19 a barrel and that of May Brent $18.50, then trader X has bought an April/May spread at 50 cents. Hence, the transaction involves the trade of two cargoes and two separate contracts will be written.

While in 95 per cent of all such trades reported to Petroleum Argus since the beginning of 1987, the spread has involved adjacent delivery months, spreads can be traded for delivery months further apart. Some 4.5 per cent of inter-month spreads in the Brent market involve trading the spread between delivery months two months apart, e.g. April/June spreads, with a further 0.5 per cent involving a three month difference in delivery dates. Less than one in a thousand spread trades involves a four month difference, e.g. April/August, and no longer spread than this has been recorded. Occasionally a trader may not find another willing to take up the offsetting position, in which case a legged spread can arise. In this the spread is achieved by making two outright trades with other parties, a buy for one month and a sell for the other.

The inter-month spread is a position on the absolute level of the backwardation or contango[2] between the delivery months. In the example above, trader X will gain if the price of April Brent strengthens relative to that of May Brent (i.e. if a backwardation increases or a contango decreases), regardless of whether the absolute price of April Brent has increased or decreased.

(b) Inter-Crude Spreads

A less common form of spread trading is to trade the differential against another crude oil, which in the Brent market normally means trading against either Dubai or WTI. For example, the purchase of an April Brent-Dubai spread by trader X involves the purchase of an April Brent cargo by X simultaneously with the sale of an April Dubai cargo. The spread almost always involves cargoes for the same delivery month in both markets. An inter-crude spread is a position taken on the path of the price differential between the crude oils, in our example trader X will gain if the price of Brent strengthens relative to that of Dubai. The only relevant number in the trade is the differential itself, with the trade carrying no information about the level of absolute prices, only the relative price of Brent compared to Dubai.

Other more elaborate forms of spread trading are also occasionally found in the 15-day market. Of these the most important is the box trade.[3]

c) The Box Trade

A box trade is essentially a position taken on the movement of the relative backwardation (or contango) between two crude oil markets. It involves the simultaneous sale and purchase of two inter-crude spreads, and as such involves the trading of four cargoes.

The most common box trade encountered in the Brent market involves Dubai spreads. For example, a typical Brent-Dubai box involves for one party the simultaneous purchase of a Brent cargo and the sale of a Dubai cargo for the same delivery month, together with the sale of a Brent cargo and the purchase of a Dubai cargo for another delivery month – and vice versa for the other party. Hence the schemata for an April/May Brent-Dubai box trade involving traders X and Y could be structured as shown in Table 4.1.

Table 4.1: April/May Brent-Dubai Box Trade.

Cargo	Trader X	Trader Y	Cargo	Trader X	Trader Y	Prices Brent	Dubai
April Brent	Buy	Sell	April Dubai	Sell	Buy	20.00	17.00
May Brent	Sell	Buy	May Dubai	Buy	Sell	19.00	15.50

In this example trader X has bought an April Brent-Dubai spread with a $3 per barrel differential, and sold a May spread with $3.50 differential. The only relevant number in this trade is the 50 cents difference between the two spread differentials (i.e. the difference between the Dubai and Brent April/May backwardations), and in reporting the trade it could be summarized simply as an April/May Brent-Dubai box at 50 cents a barrel.

The only factor determining the profit and loss for the trade is how the inter-month difference in the Brent-Dubai differential moves. For example, suppose that in the above example the April/May Brent backwardation increases from $1 to $1.50, while the April/May Dubai backwardation increases from $1.50 to $1.75. The value of the box has now fallen to 25 cents, i.e. the difference between the April/May Dubai and Brent backwardations, and so trader X has made a profit on the box trade of 25 cents per barrel.

4. The IPE Brent Futures Contract

The International Petroleum Exchange of London (IPE), launched the third version of its Brent futures contract on 23 June 1988. With some modifications this contract has provided the base of a successful and liquid market in contrast to the failure of previous versions. We quantify the scale of this success in Chapter 12, and this section concentrates on the structure of the contract and of IPE trading. The problems of establishing a successful contract rested on the potentially contradictory qualities it needed to have. The contract needed to be traded in small enough lots to generate the speculative interest from non-industry concerns that might otherwise be constrained, either by the size of their capital base or by the participants' attitudes to the risks involved in trading large lots. However, it also needed to be linked to the 15-day market in such a way that sufficient price convergence between the contract and the physical market would render it a viable hedging tool for industry participants.

To promote volume of trading, all versions of the IPE contract have traded one thousand barrel lots of Brent, the same size lot as the light sweet crude oil contract on the New York Mercantile Exchange (NYMEX).[4] However, while the physical base of the NYMEX contract is pipeline scheduling at Cushing Oklahoma of one thousand barrel batches, the IPE contract is based on a physical market that trades cargoes of 500 thousand barrels. The first IPE contract (launched in November 1983 and relaunched in October 1985), attempted to establish a contract based on physical delivery of Brent blend. Delivery could take place in the Antwerp-Rotterdam-Amsterdam area (ARA), through inter-tank (physical) or in-tank (book) transfer, or through an Exchange of Futures for Physical (EFP) mechanism whereby delivery can be made at any location in any crude oil by bilateral bargaining between participants.

The physical delivery provisions of the first IPE contract, while paralleling those in other oil and non-oil futures contracts (including the IPE's own gasoil contract), proved to be the source of the contract's failure. It received little industry support as it appeared to be an attempt to usurp the 15-day market and centralize it into a formal exchange. Further, the Brent that does reach ARA tends to be internal major company transfers, with no liquid physical trading base. Likewise, non-industry speculators saw the danger of being hit by delivery squeezes, which in particular meant that they could not participate in the IPE on an equal basis with those involved in the physical Brent market. The failure had therefore demonstrated that the characteristics of the Brent market were such that a standard contract based on physical delivery would be inappropriate, at least without the direct co-operation of the operator and users of the Sullom Voe terminal. The collapse in 1990 of a similar Brent futures contract in the now deceased Rotterdam oil futures market, has merely reiterated the lesson.

The solution to the problem was to be a contract based on cash settlement and not on physical delivery. This has two main advantages. First, it presented the IPE contract to the industry as being auxiliary to the physical market with no pretensions to dominate that market through the formal exchange. Secondly, cash settlement is more attractive to non-industry participants as it greatly reduces the possibility of any purely futures market based squeeze, and thus puts potential IPE participants on a somewhat more equal footing with the large industry participants. However the role of small speculators (the so-called 'doctors and dentists') is far less on the IPE than on NYMEX. The major fillip to the IPE contract from non-industry sources came from the finance houses (the Wall Street refiners), who used it to offset their risks on the partial Brent market (which is explained in the final section of this chapter).

The details of the IPE Brent contract are sometimes changed. However at the time of writing the major characteristics are as follows. The contract trades paper lots of one thousand barrels of current quality Sullom Voe pipeline Brent blend quoted in dollars and (complete) cents. There are no limits placed on daily price fluctuations. Up to nine months of contracts are traded with all open positions being marked to market daily. Those with any open positions are required to put up on a daily basis a margin (essentially a deposit) against those positions. The margin system reduces the risks of default, and in particular the risk that position takers could overreach themselves and face financial collapse to the detriment of confidence in the exchange. Nevertheless, there is an element of margin risk as margins can be changed according to the volatility of the market. To provide a measure of the usual scale, the margin as of August 1992 stood at $700 per contract, i.e. 70 cents per barrel.

Trade in the IPE's pits is carried out by a system of open outcry rather than by the automated trading systems used in some non-petroleum futures markets. However there has been a move to automate the trade reporting and matching systems, and the trade registration system developed by the London International Financial Futures Exchange, which allows the resolution of all trades within an hour, was implemented on 5 June 1991.

The final day of trading per Brent contract is the day prior to the month of the contract becoming wet in the 15-day market; for example, the January 1993 contract had its final trading day on 14 December

1992. Thus, the first futures month traded equates to the second forward delivery month in the 15-day market. This became the practice from the July 1990 contract onwards, before which the final trading day for a given month was the 10th (or closest trading day before) of the previous month. Not trading the wet month in the 15-day market prevents the IPE settlement price being set on the basis of any 15-day market squeeze. The drawback is of course that, unless a non-IPE instrument is used, physical barrels would have to be hedged on the previous month IPE contract thus incurring a time spread risk depending on the degree of backwardation or contango in the 15-day market. This particularly affects those wishing to hedge physical cargoes priced on dated Brent related terms. Hedging on the forward market leaves the risk of a Brent specific squeeze, while hedging on the IPE leaves the time spread risk.

Brent contract trading hours are 0931 to 2015 London time, with no lunchtime cessation of trading. This became the practice effective from 11 January 1990, before which trading ceased at 1730. The change enabled participants to cover the close of the New York market, and led to a considerable expansion of IPE trading.

If a contract is allowed to expire the settlement price is the Brent index. For example, if a contract was bought at $25 and the Brent index was calculated at $28 for the day of expiry, then the holder of the contract has made a gross profit of $3 per barrel, i.e. $3000 for the contract. The Brent index is calculated from six media sources (London Oil Reports, Petroleum Argus, Platt's, Reuters, Rim and Telerate). Each source reports all 15-day Brent deals (dated, all forward months, spreads and book-outs) believed to have been concluded during the period from Tokyo office opening to Houston office closing. The index is calculated as the average of three elements in the following manner.

The first element is the weighted average of confirmed outright deals for the appropriate delivery month, say July. The IPE take all deals for July forward Brent in which an absolute price was reported, i.e. not spread deals. If more than one source has reported a deal at a particular price, then in the averaging this is assumed to be one and the same deal. Likewise if, say, one source has reported three trades at a given price and another has reported two at the same price, then three deals at this price are used. The second element in creating the index for July derives the average price of outright deals for August Brent in the same manner as above, and the simple average of all spread deals between July and August. The average July/August spread is then added to the average of August outright deals to derive a second measure of the price of July Brent. The third element takes the average of the price assessments produced over the day by each of four reporting agencies.

The three Petroleum Argus quotes produced during the course of the trading day are averaged, as are the five London Oil Reports quotes, the nine Reuters quotes, and the fourteen Telerate quotes.[5] The simple average of these four numbers then produces the third element of the index. The index is then calculated as the simple average of the three elements and is produced and published every day for the previous day's trading; but it is only of importance in its role of a settlement price, on the day when a contract expires.

The current formulation of the Brent index as a calculation over one day's trading solved the problem of the lack of convergence in which the five-day average used in the second IPE Brent contract could often result. Convergence is not of course absolutely complete as the index is a measure of average prices over a day. It is not a measure of 15-day market prices at the exact minute of the expiration of a contract. However this correction certainly removed the reason for the failure of the second contract. There is a slight problem of circularity in that forward market traders tend to bear the IPE screen prices in mind when establishing their perception of the level of 15-day prices, particularly when 15-day market trade in single cargoes rather than spreads is thin. This perception is reflected in their conversations with the price reporting services, and therefore in the published assessments of 15-day prices. Hence IPE settlement prices can be in part derived from the feedback from IPE futures prices.

IPE Brent contracts actually represent two contracts, one between the buyer and the clearing house and one between the seller and the clearing house. The IPE's clearing house is the International Commodities Clearing House Ltd (ICCH) who levy a fee for each contract in addition to the IPE's own levies. The ICCH is completely independent and autonomous of the IPE (indeed its foundation predates the IPE by nearly a century). As well as its clearing house function the ICCH also guarantees the fulfilment of IPE contracts traded between clearing members of the exchange.

The IPE has seventy floor members' seats with voting rights. Each seat gives the right to have up to four traders in the trading pits at any given time. This arose from a splitting of the previous thirty-five seats, giving the existing members the right to either retain, sell or lease the additional seat they were given. Some have retained the second seat, and others have sold it, resulting in a total of forty-eight floor members as of January 1993. Most of the major 15-day market participants now have their own floor memberships.

The IPE has thus far managed to avoid the well publicized malpractices that have been found in some US (non-oil) futures markets. The rigours of the UK Financial Services Act and the need for the maintenance of confidence in equality of opportunity make the minimization of such malpractices a matter of keen concern. There are two major forms of explicit futures market based malpractice, both involving prior knowledge of information that is not available to participants on an equal basis.

The first form is classical insider trading, the forewarning rather than the extrapolation or guessing through analysis of significant market developments. The problem is particularly acute within integrated or state-owned oil companies which are large enough to affect the market through actions or announcements. This necessitates the maintenance of 'Chinese walls' between the trading and operational or management divisions of these organizations, in such a way that the walls are not perceived as being too thin by other participants.

The second is a variant of insider dealing, where the special knowledge is of deals in the market that have yet to be made. It is only a problem in markets with a relatively small volume, or markets in which there is the possibility of identification of trades made on behalf of an agent considered to be a market maker who can swing sentiment. This is best exemplified by the practice of 'front-running'. A front-runner is a broker who enters the trading pit with an order which they feel will move the market. The broker then trades on their own account before transacting that deal so as to profit from the market move. So far oil trading in futures exchanges has been spared the worst of these malpractices.

5. Exchange of Futures for Physical (EFPs)

An EFP represents a physical link between the IPE Brent futures contract and North Sea spot market or the 15-day market. It can be used to exchange an IPE position for a spot cargo. In the context of the 15-day market it represents the exchange of a futures market position of 500 IPE lots, (i.e. 500,000 barrels), for a 15-day cargo and as such it can be thought of as a spread trade between forward Brent and futures Brent. It is the exact opposite of a book-out in the 15-day market. A book-out turns claims on forward cargoes into a series of paper financial transactions. By contrast, an IPE EFP turns a paper contract into a claim on a forward cargo.

There are four possible outcomes from an EFP, considering transactions by traders X and Y.

Description of Brent Markets and Trading Instruments 51

(i)   X and Y Exchange Futures Positions

Trader X has initially bought 500 IPE contracts. In this case the EFP involves an exact swap of the futures position with X selling Y their futures position in exchange for a 15-day cargo. X will have then cleared their futures position, but be long of one 15-day cargo, while Y has a futures long position and has sold an extra cargo in the 15-day market. Hence 15-day volume has increased by one cargo, IPE volume by 500 lots and IPE open interest[6] is unchanged.

(ii)   X any Y Both Clear Futures Positions

X has initially bought 500 IPE contracts and Y has sold 500 IPE contracts. After they agree an EFP for one 15-day cargo both futures positions are cleared and thus IPE open interest falls by 500 lots. Meanwhile IPE volume increases by 500 lots and the volume in the 15-day market increases by one cargo, a sale from Y to X.

(iii)   X and Y Initiate Futures Positions

Neither X nor Y initially holds a futures position. After the EFP is transacted one party finishes short 500 lots on the IPE but long one 15-day cargo, and vice versa for the other party. Hence IPE open interest increases by 500 lots and, as before, IPE volume increases by 500 lots and volume on the 15-day market by one cargo.

(iv)   The 'False' EFP

The false EFP is one with a sting in the tail. X sells 500 lots to Y through an EFP in exchange for a 15-day position as before, but simultaneously sells a 15-day cargo back to Y. Hence the trade leaves both X and Y's net positions on the 15-day market unchanged, but has resulted in a change in their IPE positions. At first sight this might appear to be a rather peculiar manoeuvre, after all the end result could have been achieved by simply trading on the IPE without any use of the 15-day market. However there are four reasons why the false EFP is used.

IPE EFPs can be transacted at any time, whether or not the IPE is physically open for trading, and hence the false EFP is a way of trading futures when the IPE is closed. In other words, the false EFP is a way of enabling 24-hour futures trading through the back door. Secondly, in market conditions where the sale or purchase of a large number of lots might move the IPE price structure, a false EFP avoids this by keeping the trade out of the trading pits. Thirdly, the false EFP represents a neat way of closing positions with known prices, without leaving contracts to expire and be settled on the, unknown immediately at expiry, IPE index. The final reason for a false EFP arises from what is known as 'Platt's risk'. This is further explained in Chapter 10, but it arises because the quotations used most widely in valuing physical oil trade and term deals are evaluated over an hour after the IPE closes. In a fast moving market this can be a significant risk, and so the false EFP provides a way of closing IPE positions at prices closer to the structure of those evaluated by Platt's.

The EFP is not available to all IPE participants. In particular, it is only allowed to regular spot or forward market participants, and the IPE needs to see proof of the physical transaction involved.

As will be seen in section 7 of this chapter, IPE futures positions can also be exchanged for a swap trade.

6. IPE Brent Options

The IPE's Brent options contract was launched on 11 May 1989 trading lots of one thousand barrels of Brent blend and using the IPE Brent futures contract as its underlying contract.[7] The contract is for an American rather than a European option. That is to say, the option may be exercised (i.e. transferred to a Brent futures contract), at any time before its expiry date. By contrast, European options can only be exercised at expiry.

An IPE Brent contract can be exercised at any time up to one hour after cessation of trading on the expiry date of the contract – the hours of trading being 0925 to 2000 London time. Up to six months of contracts are quoted, with expiry being three trading days before the cessation of trading of the underlying futures contract. It is then a fourth layer of the Brent market, an options market based on a futures market which is in turn based on a forward market based on a spot market.

A call option gives its holder the right to buy the underlying futures contract, and a put option the right to sell. The price at which the exercise of the option occurs is known as the strike price, which for the IPE's contract is defined in multiples of 50 cents per barrel. The price of each option is then the premium paid by the buyer to the option writer in return for the right to exercise that option. The price of option for at least seven strike prices is quoted on any given trading day. Of these three are 'out-of-the-money', three 'in-the-money', and one 'at-the-money', the definitions being based on the previous day's futures settlement price.

An 'at-the-money' option is a call or a put for which the underlying futures price is equal to the option's strike price. If the underlying futures price is above a given options strike price, then the option is 'in-the-money' if it is a call, and 'out-of-the-money' if it is a put. Likewise if the underlying futures price is below the strike price then puts are in the money and calls out of the money. In the case of IPE contracts for any option that is not exercised by one hour after the close of business of the final trading day, such options that are more than 25 cents in-the-money are automatically exercised, i.e. settled against the futures settlement price of that day.

The theory of the correct price for an options premium is discussed in Chapter 11. In broad terms it is a function of the strike price, the current futures price, time to expiry and the volatility of the market. For example, the cost of a call option will be greater the greater is the difference between the strike price and the current futures price, the longer there is to expiry and the greater is the level of volatility. To give rough orders of magnitude, on 18 August 1992, during a period of fairly normal levels of volatility, October IPE Brent closed at $20 exactly. The price of a call option at $20 was 18 cents, at $19.50 it was 36 cents and at $20.50 it was 8 cents.

In reality behaviour in the options market is more than a simple exercise of in-the-money options when they are considered to be most in-the-money, and non-exercise of out-of-the-money options. Options give rise to a series of possible strategies normally involving the purchase of more than one option, each strategy conferring a different profile of upside and downside risks and rewards. To give but one example,[8] one of the many possible strategies is a long straddle, which represents the simultaneous purchase of a call and a put at the at-the-money strike price.

Whereas in a futures market the simultaneous sale and purchase of a contract is offsetting, in an options market the long straddle is not. This arises due to asymmetry between in- and out-of-the-money options. An out-of-the money option has cost a premium, but incurs no further losses regardless of the absolute difference between the futures price and the strike price, whereas the reward for an in-the-money option is valued by this difference. Hence if a long straddle is taken the worst possible case is that the futures price remains constant right up to the expiry of the option, in which case two premia have been lost. If the price moves at all then one of the options held will move into the money, and the strategy becomes profitable if the difference between the strike price and the underlying futures price exceeds in either direction the combined cost of the two initial premia.

It is this asymmetry in options that generates the appeal of options.

Attitudes towards risk tend to be highly asymmetric, with a given company normally being far more worried about price changes in one direction than the other. For instance, an upstream oil company is most concerned with the risk of a sharp fall in crude oil prices, while a refiner is more concerned with the risk of a sharp rise. Options provide a method of designing very flexible and company-specific risk management strategies that cannot be achieved by the use of futures or forward market transactions.

In 1992 IPE Brent options achieved the growth that has finally made the contract a success. From January to May 1992 over 226.6 thousand Brent options were traded, i.e. the equivalent of over 226 mb. For the same period in 1991 only 37.5 thousand were traded. Options have then become an important part of the Brent market. This growth has continued so that by January 1993 the equivalent of 125 mb was traded in that month alone.

To illustrate how a company uses Brent options, consider the strategy of Chevron.[9] Chevron normally runs a position of between one thousand and three thousand contracts, i.e. between 1 mb and 3 mb, split evenly between NYMEX and the IPE. It trades in clip sizes of fifty to one hundred lots at a time. While trading strategy is of course highly flexible, a brief description of the basic strategy runs as follows. Chevron's major preoccupation is to protect against falling oil prices, so they buy put options to place a floor on the price. To reduce the cost of the premiums incurred, they collect premiums by selling call options at higher prices. Hence they limit their downside risk, as well as reducing the upward potential should prices move above the strike price of the calls they have sold.

Options may also be traded on Brent delivery month spreads, and in 1992 the IPE introduced the category of 'volatility' or 'delta-neutral' trades, utilizing trades of both futures and options contracts.

Growth in the IPE options market was helped by two statutory and institutional changes. First, with effect from 3 January 1990, the market was opened up to US participants by the exemption of the IPE contract from the US Commodities and Futures Trading Commission's prohibition on the trading of foreign options. Secondly, options and futures trading income for pension funds and authorized unit trusts was exempted from UK tax in 1990.

However, the major factor that prevented IPE Brent options from gaining its current level of liquidity earlier is the existence of an informal market in options. There is still a substantial 'Over the Counter' (OTC) trade in options made by some of the larger financial institutions. Morgan Stanley, CRT, Merrill Lynch and Société Générale are particularly active in this market, which can provide tailor-made options on deals of any size while still using the IPE as the underlying futures contract. As it essentially represents a series of personalized bilateral deals, the OTC market can also arrange options for longer maturities than the six months of the IPE contract, without necessarily having to maintain and quote an options structure for every forward month. Hence while there may be default risk facing the buyer of options in the over-the-counter market, there can be more convenience in a tailor-made option.

The OTC market has absolutely no transparency at all in either prices or volumes, and it is impossible to quantify how much trade it does. Nevertheless, from interview evidence, we believe that it is very substantial. While it dominated the volumes on the IPE before 1992, the relative position now is less clear. However, again from anecdotal evidence, we believe that IPE options have now begun to overtake the OTC market.

7. Swaps

A swap represents another method, other than a futures, forward or options contract, of locking in a price or a margin for either the producer or consumer of crude oil or oil products. The main sellers are finance houses and the trading departments of large oil companies. The potential use of swaps is very wide. For instance a Brent producer could lock in the price of their expected level of output over a very extended period, but their use to date in the context of the Brent market has been in a narrower and more specialized form.

The principle underlying a swap is essentially very simple. For example, a producer can arrange a swap for a given volume over a given period at a price equating to an estimate of the weighted average market price over that period. At the end of each predetermined settlement period, the actual market prices for the agreed volume in that period are compared to the value of that volume under the fixed price specified in the swap. If market prices are higher the producer pays the swaps provider the difference, and vice versa if market prices are less than the fixed price multiplied by the agreed volume. Hence a swap requires no physical exchange of oil, just a series of netted transactions or 'contracts for differences'.

In a perfect swap, the swaps provider can find an oil consumer who wished to consume the same volume of oil in each period as that specified in the swap given to the producer. By fixing a price above that given to the producer, both producer and consumer receive fixed prices and the swaps provider receives a profit. If, say, the consumers pay more in the market than the price given in the swap, they receive payment from the swaps provider who will in turn receive a greater payment from the producer.

In reality such perfect swaps are almost impossible. The swaps provider will be left with at least some residual risk that they will have to 'warehouse', i.e. dissipate the risk by the use of other instruments such as options and futures. Hence the growth of swaps does not necessarily imply the loss of liquidity in futures markets. In fact the tendency has been for futures volumes to grow with the development of oil swaps, as futures markets have been relatively unattractive to those seeking the long-term price protection offered by swaps.

Swaps have the advantage over futures for long period risk management and in their relative administrative ease, since rolling a futures position over a period of years requires considerable management and is fraught with its own pitfalls. Hence much of swaps demand has not come from existing futures market users, and the need to warehouse risk has led to increases in futures market activity by swap providers unable to find perfectly offsetting swaps. It should be noted that swap providers tend to use futures more than options to warehouse risk, and thus in particular the growth in IPE options is not attributable to any explosive growth in the use of swaps.

The IPE futures contract allows futures positions to be exchanged for swap deals through an EFS. This works on exactly the same principles as an EFP except that the futures position is exchanged for a swap rather than a forward Brent cargo.

The major use of swaps in the Brent market to date has been the dated Brent swap, which is essentially a very short-term swap. In this instrument the spread between prompt physical cargoes and the forward market is swapped. This has two main applications. Buyers of Brent or other North Sea grades can use the dated Brent swap to increase the effectiveness of hedging on the forward market or the IPE. The swap locks in a spread and protects from any short-term physical squeezes. The swap may also be useful for buyers of crude oil that is linked to the Brent market through formulae pricing, so that the combination of the Brent forward market and a dated Brent swap provides price protection.

One particular form of this swap is the CFD (Contract for Differences) market, which trades the difference between Platt's assessments for dated Brent and first month forward Brent, and can be used to manage the risk arising from differential price moves between the dated and the forward market.

The market for dated Brent swaps would not exist if the relationship between prompt and forward prices displayed little volatility. As such, the variability of all the factors that influence this relationship will affect the potential size of this market.

8. Partial Brent

The partial Brent market arose out of the entry of the Wall Street refiners into the Brent market in the mid-1980s. Before the advent of a successful IPE futures contract, this provided a way of trading Brent in less than full cargo sizes. Partial Brent is cash settled, and trades paper lots of 50 thousand barrels of Brent.

The Wall Street firms act as market makers, with J Aron and Morgan Stanley being particularly active in this role. Contracts can be bought from or sold to a market maker, and essentially consist of a standard 15-day Brent contract with one added feature. This specifies that by expiry the holder of the contract must fulfil one of two conditions. They can balance it with an offsetting deal with the same market maker. Alternatively they can combine it with others, also from the same market maker, into the standard forward market cargo size, in which case the contract would be exchanged for a 15-day cargo. The market maker receives a premium for trading contracts on demand at some agreed measure of prices at the time of the deal.

The success of IPE Brent has taken most of the liquidity out of the partial market. The IPE provides a way of trading at lower cost and without the default risk that dealing with a Wall Street firm entails. However, partial trades are still made, particularly outside IPE Brent trading hours and in the Far East.[10] During periods of high volatility the market does gain significant liquidity. In particular, during the Kuwait crisis large volumes were traded outside IPE hours on the partial market.

Partial Brent is now a rather minor feature of the collection of markets and instruments that constitute the Brent market. It is perhaps best seen as the precursor of the success of IPE Brent. The partial market showed the potential of a cash settled market based upon the operations of the 15-day market.

Notes
1. A major contribution to the transparency of the market for those trading in it is made by the role of brokers. This is discussed further in Chapter 9.
2. A contango arises when prices are higher for more distant delivery months, e.g. prices for May delivery are higher than prices for April delivery, and a backwardation is the reverse. Backwardations and contangos are discussed further in Chapter 11.

58 *Oil Markets and Prices*

3. Other forms of trading second order differences have sometimes been reported to Petroleum Argus. For instance a butterfly trades the difference between two inter-month spreads, i.e. an April/May/June butterfly involves one party selling the April/May spread and buying the May/June spread, and so four separate cargoes are traded in a butterfly deal.
4. The NYMEX contract is detailed in Chapter 13.
5. Platt's is not used in this exercise since it only produces one quote per day, when the intention of the index is to provide a measure of the average over a day. Rim is not used since it does not assess Brent prices but just produces a trading range. Price assessment agencies are detailed in Chapter 10.
6. The summation of the long (or short) positions across participants in the market.
7. Crude oil options are also traded on NYMEX using the light sweet contract as the underlying futures contract. For an analysis of this market see G. M. Phillips and R. J. Weiner (1992), 'The Crude Oil Options Market: An Empirical Investigation', John F. Kennedy School of Government, Harvard University.
8. There are many textbooks on options strategies. For example see G. Chamberlain (1982), *Trading in Options*, Woodhead-Faulkner, or W. Labuszewski and J. C. Sinquefield (1985), *Inside the Commodity Option Markets*, Wiley.
9. As reported by J. Parry in 'Chevron Chooses its Options', *Pipeline*, Autumn 1991, IPE London.
10. See *Weekly Petroleum Argus*, 15 April 1992.

CHAPTER 5

THE FISCAL REGIME

1. Introduction

The oil fiscal regime, in the UK as elsewhere, is not neutral because its provisions elicit responses and changes in the behaviour of economic agents. It has a significant influence on patterns of incentives for production, trading, investments in exploration and development, sales and purchases of oil assets. In the UK certain features and principles of petroleum taxation have also created an incentive for vertically integrated oil companies with producing interests in the North Sea to sell, in certain well-defined circumstances, their equity crude in arm's length transactions instead of transferring it directly to their downstream subsidiaries for use as a refinery input. They have also provided a more general incentive for trading in the forward market. In fact, the birth of the Brent market and its early development are partly due to attempts by oil companies at tax optimization.

Trading arm's length has fiscal relevance for two reasons. First, it enables companies that produce North Sea crudes to establish a price for fiscal purposes. In the absence of a developed market and a visible process of price formation (a situation that would obtain if most crude oil transactions between upstream and downstream remained internal to the firm), tax liabilities would inevitably be based on oil price assessments made by the fiscal authorities. It is not difficult to understand why oil companies prefer prices to be set by markets rather than by cautious tax inspectors who will always be tempted to err on the high side and often involve them in time-wasting negotiations, and on occasions in costly litigation. Secondly, trading provides oil companies with opportunities to arrange the pattern of their crude oil sales from North Sea fields (and oil purchases for their refineries) in a tax efficient manner.

There are therefore important relationships between North Sea oil taxation and the Brent market. On the one side, the market may offer opportunities for tax optimization; on the other side, attempts at tax optimization may have an impact on the economic efficiency of the market and the process of price formation. The first aspect is of some interest but tends to attract more attention than the second aspect, which is usually ignored because of the analytical difficulties involved in determining the exact effects of non-neutral fiscal regimes on the economic performance of markets.

2. The Oil Taxation Regime

The oil fiscal regime in the UK comprises three elements: (a) royalties, (b) petroleum revenue tax (PRT), (c) corporation tax.[1] In a sense, this is a layered tax system. Royalties, where applicable, are levied in kind or cash and then expensed, that is treated as costs when computing liability for other taxes. PRT comes next, construed as a 'profit' tax levied field by field on the difference between the value of output and allowable costs including royalties. Finally, corporation tax applies to the profits of the company as they arise in the whole of its UK operations upstream, allowing for costs, royalties and PRT.[2]

There are four features of the UK oil fiscal regime that are relevant to an analysis of taxation and the oil market. The first is the concept of a fiscal ring-fence; the second, the differential rates of PRT and corporation tax; the third, the principles for valuing oil production for PRT purposes; and the fourth, the rules and procedures which govern the nomination of sales contracts for PRT purposes by producing companies.

(i) Ring-fence

There is a fiscal ring-fence around an activity (or set of activities) undertaken by a corporation when the profits and losses of this activity cannot be aggregated or set against profits or losses made by the corporation in other parts of its business in the computation of tax liabilities. The UK oil fiscal regime involves a ring-fence around every oilfield for PRT purposes (the field-by-field principle) and a ring-fence around upstream activities in the UK for the purposes of corporation tax. Until early 1983 the ring-fence provisions were extremely tight. They were subsequently relaxed in some respects in order to encourage exploration and development in a low oil-price period. For example, the ring-fence round the oilfield was partially lifted by the 1983 Finance Act to allow exploration and discovery appraisal expenditures incurred elsewhere in the UK to be set against PRT taxable profits. This tax break was removed by the 1993 Finance Bill.

These ring-fence provisions are not neutral in their effects. The following example of such an effect is of some interest. The field-by-field principle was a disincentive to exploration for all companies when exploration costs other than abortive exploration expenditure in one area were not allowed for PRT against the profits of another field. Allowing for these costs in 1983 removed the disincentive for companies with actual PRT liabilities but kept it unchanged for companies without fields paying PRT. It thus provided an incentive for the latter to buy into fields with actual PRT liabilities from companies with (PRT) profits larger than their exploration expenditures. In this example, neither the imposition of a ring-fence, nor its *partial* relaxation were neutral in their effects. Both involve certain disincentives; and the latter also leads to a redistribution of income as well as assets.

(ii)   Differential Rates of Taxation

Oil profits generated in the UK upstream are subject to both PRT (in oilfields which received development authorization before March 1993) and corporation tax, while profits from downstream activities and from trading are only liable to corporation tax. The total tax rate on an oil company is therefore higher upstream than elsewhere whatever the relative PRT and corporation tax rates are. Since the tax rates are in fact higher for PRT than corporation tax the differential taxation rate on profits generated upstream as compared with other activities is in fact very large. As one of the purposes of the ring-fence is to separate areas subject to different tax rates from each other, the two features of the UK oil tax regime are indeed related.[3] Taken together, they obviously provide an incentive for transferring profits across the ring-fence from the high to the low tax rate activities, that is from the upstream to the downstream or trading, whenever this can be done by lawful means. By definition this particular issue of tax optimization only arises for oil companies with both crude oil producing interests *and* downstream or trading activities in the UK. Paradoxically, the opportunity to reduce overall tax liabilities by transferring the source of some profits from the upstream to trading and the downstream is provided by a third important feature of the UK oil fiscal regime – the output valuation principle – to which we now turn.

(iii)   The Valuation Principle

The UK oil fiscal system bases the valuation of crude oil production for the purposes of determining taxable profits for PRT on market prices, that is (a) on price realized in the sale of the oil liable to tax in a genuine arm's length deal, or (b) on an assessment by the Oil Taxation Office of the market price of similar transactions when the oil liable to tax is appropriated by the producer, transferred or sold in a non-arm's length transaction.

The valuation of an arm's length transaction does not pose any problem as regards prices as these are stated in contracts. However, the deal must qualify as 'arm's length' by fulfilling all the following conditions: (a) the contract price is the sole consideration for the sale; (b) the sale is between unconnected parties; (c) neither the seller (nor any person connected) has any interest in the subsequent resale of the oil or any produce derived from it. Thus, deals between subsidiaries of the same corporation or companies related through part ownership do not qualify. Similarly deals involving other consideration than price, be it a benefit in kind or cash, or a clause bestowing on one party some indirect benefit, or back-to-back deals (for instance A sells to B and almost simultaneously B sells to A the same volume at a similar price) all violate the criteria listed above and do not qualify as arm's length deals.

The valuation by the OTO (Oil Taxation Office) of non-arm's length deals had an unsettled history in the period before March 1987. The principle guiding this valuation is that it should be based on the prices of 'contemporary and comparable' arm's length deals. Despite its apparent simplicity this principle involves many ambiguities. The meaning of 'contemporary' unless precisely defined could refer to a period as short as a day or as long as several months, even a fiscal year. The term 'comparable' is also vague. It could refer to all market transactions for the crude in question effected in a given period of time, or to spot transactions only, or to the arm's length deals in which the company itself was engaged at a given time.

The OTO always remained firm on the 'contemporary and comparable' principle but has often varied its precise interpretation. Until 1984 the OTO considered the BNOC[4] term price as that of 'comparable' arm's length transactions. The term price was that posted by BNOC for the purchase of participation crude; it was 'supposed to reflect the exchange value of a barrel of oil for willing buyers and sellers striking a bargain in a free market'.[5] So, the 'contemporary' BNOC term price was used for the valuation for PRT purposes of non-arm's length deals. Sometime early in 1984 the OTO recognized that the BNOC term price was no longer representative, and the valuation of non-arm's length deals became more complex. To remove uncertainties about the precise method of calculations the OTO defined a valuation method in early 1987. The 'market value' of non-arm's length deals of a participator (i.e. producing company), is now determined by taking the average of the prices of contracts for sale of oil of the kind in question. The relevant sales contracts (spot and forward) are those entered upon within the period beginning at the start of the previous month and ending on the middle day of the month in question. Thus the valuation for PRT purpose of non-arm's length deals made in September is the average of the prices of sales contracts for September delivery made between 1 August and 15 September. All participators are obliged to report all their transactions to the OTO. It is interesting to note that the OTO does not possess comprehensive information on North Sea trading. The data immediately available to it are the returns of participators only, that is of companies with producing interests in the UKCS. The 1993 Finance Bill, however, vests the OTO with new powers that enable it to obtain data from non-participators.

A vertically-integrated oil company normally has the option of either selling crude oil from its production to third parties, or retaining the oil for its own use. If the tax regime were neutral the decision as to whether the crude oil is sold or retained would be determined by the relative costs of the alternative courses of action. In the UK, taxation strongly influences this decision since it will pay the vertically-integrated oil company to sell its oil arm's length whenever it expects the realized market price to be lower than the OTO's valuation of a non-arm's length deal; and to appropriate the oil whenever it expects the realized market price to be higher than the OTO price. In both cases the vertically-integrated oil company chooses to make less pre-tax profits upstream but this is exactly compensated for by higher pre-tax profits downstream. There is an overall gain in after-tax profits since the tax rate is lower downstream than upstream.

There are therefore circumstances in which vertically-integrated oil companies are better off selling their crude oil output arm's length than retaining their production for their own use. It is important also to note that unless the company is long on crude (i.e. if it produces more crude than required for its own needs, a rare occurrence after the nationalizations of their upstream interests in most OPEC countries in the 1970s) it will also be buying crude for its refineries, some of which will effectively compensate for the amounts sold arm's length.

The recourse for fiscal reasons to sales and purchases of crude oil by oil companies to third parties when it would have been cheaper and more convenient otherwise to internalize the transactions within vertically-integrated structures, is referred to in the literature as 'tax spinning'. And it is tax spinning which was partly responsible for the birth and many features of the Brent market. Not only does the fiscal regime favour the recourse to arm's length sales in situations where normally they would not be needed, but it makes it necessary for companies to multiply and diversify these arm's length transactions. This is necessary to ensure that the sale of oil to a third party and the compensatory purchase (which the vertically integrated company may have to make to supply its refineries) does not take the form of a back-to-back deal. Such a deal does not qualify as an arm's length transaction and sales to third parties which end up in back-to-back deals would defeat their tax-optimization objective.

There is thus a need to separate a fiscally-motivated oil sale from the compensating purchase with several other transactions, to drown, as it were, certain sales and purchases in a sea of other deals. The Brent market, where the number of contracts exchanged for a particular month is a high multiple of the number of physical cargoes available, fulfils this need very well. It is said that necessity is the mother of invention; a fiscal necessity has indeed played a part in the invention of a forward market for North Sea crudes.

(iv) Nomination Procedures

In the period until March 1987 an oil company was able to select freely from its portfolio of contracts those which it wished to exercise for the physical sales of its own production. Thus, when the forward month had become wet it would choose the deals in its portfolio that provided the greatest fiscal advantage. PRT liability was calculated on the realized prices of these contracts.

As of March 1987 the OTO introduced a nomination scheme which rigidly constrained companies in the selection of contracts for sales of crude oil liable to PRT. The procedure stipulates that each participator should, for each producing field in which it has an interest, nominate sufficient actual transactions to match its share of equity production from the field in any chargeable period. The nomination must be made not later than five o'clock in the afternoon of the second business day following the date of the transaction. For instance, a deal made on Monday must be nominated by five o'clock on Wednesday at the latest; a deal made on Thursday or Friday by five o'clock on the following Monday or Tuesday respectively. The length of the nomination window effectively extends to four days when there is an intervening weekend. If a participator's nominations for a month exceed its production, then the most recent nominations are cancelled until the level of production is matched. If production is higher than nominations then the difference is taxed on the basis of the 'market valuation' procedure for non-arm's length transactions explained earlier on.

In the period before March 1987 a producing company, whether vertically integrated or not, could easily take advantage of trading in the 15-day Brent market to transfer profits from the highly taxed upstream (PRT plus corporation tax) to lightly taxed trading activities (corporation tax only). The rules of the optimization game were exceedingly simple.

The company every month would choose to 'wet' the sale contracts with the lowest prices in its portfolio. Since it was able to make the nomination to the OTO towards the end of the dealing period for the relevant month, it faced little uncertainty as to whether the prices of the nominated contracts were lower than the prices that may obtain in the rest of the period. The closer was the nomination to the end of the period, the lower the uncertainty. In other words, under the old scheme the company would nominate looking only at the cards it held in its hands as there were not many left in the deck; at the time and for the purpose of nominations it did not have to take a view about future price movements for the month in question.[6]

Given the portfolio of sells and buys held by the producing company, it is clear that it always pays to choose the lowest priced contract for a crude oil sale subject to PRT. This is shown by the following example. Assume that the taxable oil output of a producing company for a given month is one cargo. This company also trades on the Brent market and has constituted a portfolio of five sells and four buys for that month. (There is one more sell than buys to dispose of the physical cargo). The sells were made at prices p_1 to p_5, and p_5 happens to be lower than any of p_1 to p_4. The buys were at prices p_6 to p_9. By nominating the contract made at p_5 for a physical disposal the company has lower upstream profits than by nominating any of p_1 to p_4 but its trading profits, in consequence, would be higher by an equivalent amount. Given differential taxation rates on upstream and trading profits, it always paid to select under the old nomination scheme the lowest price contract of a given portfolio.

Trading thus extended the scope for tax spinning to non-integrated producing companies willing to participate in the Brent market. It is important to stress however that tax spinning of a cargo through trading by a non-integrated company is not always more profitable than a direct disposal of the cargo through a single sale. We have identified above the rule which maximizes profits when the company engages in trading, but this rule does not imply that trading is necessarily the best alternative. Another condition must apply for the tax spinning of a cargo through trading to be more profitable than a single sale. The formal condition is that the net of tax trading profits for the relevant month must exceed the difference in after-tax profits between the single sale (the no tax spinning case) and the lowest priced sales contract in the trading portfolio (the tax spinning case).

The OTO judged that it was losing revenues on a large scale by allowing so much flexibility in nominations; hence the change in procedure which applied from March 1987. Under the new nomination procedure the oil company can no longer wait until the end of the trading period for a given month for selecting contracts in their portfolio for nomination. Instead of choosing *ex post* from a completely constituted portfolio the companies have only two days (or four days when a deal is made on Thursday or Friday) to decide whether they wish to nominate a deal after it has been entered upon. For perfect tax optimization they must take a view about future price movements in relation to the price of that deal when they consider whether they should nominate it or not. They may pick deal X for nomination hoping that its price p_x will turn out to be the lowest in their portfolio only to find in the end that it did not.

Despite its reduced flexibility the procedure introduced in 1987 still enables a company to make its nomination at the point where the oil price reaches a local minimum on its path. The trading strategy that yields this result is fairly simple. The company sells a cargo at a time when it contemplates the possibility of a nomination. If the oil price rises in the following two (or four) days it submits this sale for nomination. If, on the contrary, the price falls the company then enters into two new deals, a buy and a sell and continues to do so for as long as the price continues to fall. It would only nominate when the price rises again. By doing so the company would have picked for nomination for PRT purposes the lowest point in that particular segment of the price path. In this strategy the company holds a sub-portfolio of n sells and n-1 buys from which it picks, when prices move upward, the lowest priced sell and then matches the n-1 remaining sells with the n-1 buys. The reduced profit attributable to the upstream is exactly compensated for by an equivalent increased profit on trading operations, and the overall tax bill is thus reduced.

We have mentioned earlier that the 1987 procedures do not enable a company to identify for nomination purposes the lowest price that obtains in the whole trading period (the global minimum) but they involve an opportunity to pick local minima. The implication for the Inland Revenue is that the prices at which deals are nominated for tax purposes are often lower than the relevant average market price.

In November 1992 the OTO informed participators of its concern about, among other things, the effects of the nomination procedure on tax revenues, and it seems almost certain that the rules will be tightened again sometime in 1993.

3. Tax Spinning

Is it still possible to engage profitably in tax spinning after the redefinition of 'market valuation' procedures for non-arm's length deals and the tightening of nomination rules of March 1987? We have shown that there are two different tax spinning mechanisms. The first is only available to vertically-integrated companies and involves a choice between selling equity oil to third parties or appropriating it for own use. The second is available to all producing companies, whether integrated or not, if they choose to trade in forward markets.

In the early 1980s, when the vertically-integrated companies knew that their non-arm's length sales would be taxed on the basis of posted BNOC term prices, the decision to sell or appropriate was straightforward. It paid to sell to third parties when the BNOC price was higher than the market price (and to appropriate the oil when the BNOC price was lower than the market price). Since both prices were known on any day the correct decision could be made automatically.

Under the new method for valuing non-arm's length deals, the oil company has no simultaneous knowledge of the actual market and the 'market valuation' price except on the last day of the trading period (the middle day of the relevant month). Its decision at any earlier date on whether to sell its oil arm's length or appropriate it directly has to be based on a knowledge of the actual market price and a guess of the likely 'market valuation' price. Since the quality of this guess tends to improve as one progresses through the six-week period over which the average price that constitutes the 'market valuation' is computed, it is more efficient to postpone the decision (to sell or appropriate) towards the end of this period. At that time the vertically-integrated company has a good idea of what the average price of its own transactions over the six relevant 'computation' weeks is likely to be.[7] Since it also knows the current market price, the decision as to whether to sell or to appropriate becomes straightforward.

The constraints imposed by the early planning of lifting schedules, the allocation of loading slots before the middle of the previous month and more importantly by the need to spread loadings more or less evenly throughout the month, simply means that the integrated companies cannot postpone all decisions on whether to sell arm's length or to retain a cargo to the last minute. They will be able to obtain a few loading slots at the end of the relevant month; for other cargoes they have to nominate early on, and therefore guess in advance every day whether the current price will turn out to be higher or lower than the average price computed *ex post* for the 'market valuation' of non-arm's length deals. Thus, if the company expects oil prices to rise during the six-week computing period it would be tax efficient to sell (and to buy the compensating cargo) arm's length at the beginning of the period. If the expectations of a rising price turn out to be correct, the market price at the beginning of the period would be definitely lower than the 'market valuation' price. If the company managed to postpone the decision to the end of the period and the oil prices had indeed been rising over the six computation weeks, then it should retain the cargo in question since the market price then would be higher than the average computed over six weeks. Similar reasoning applies when prices are expected to fall or have been falling during the six-week period.

One market implication of these strategies is that the number of physical cargoes (given the level of production) that will be made available to third parties is likely to vary depending on the expectations of integrated companies as regards the direction of price changes during each six-week computation period. Variations of physical supply on the open market are often perceived more clearly by market participants than the concomitant variation in demand.[8] The perceived change in physical supplies can influence the course of prices.

The second method of tax spinning which reallocates upstream to trading profits, and which in principle can be attempted by any producing company, whether vertically integrated or not, involves a variety of strategies using the large number of trading instruments available in the petroleum market. Although spinning has become a more difficult exercise since March 1987, it has not been abolished by the tightening of procedures introduced at that time.

The fiscal optimization exercises through spinning which, in the past, involved *ex post* decisions based on actual price data and the final composition of the trading portfolio, now largely consists of *ex ante* guesses and decisions based on expected prices and incomplete information. Since March 1987, because of the changes in OTO regulation, fiscal optimization is not entirely a deterministic exercise. One major exception is the use of the nomination window which can automatically track the lowest price in any particular sequence of price movements which involves a fall followed by a rise. It cannot identify with certainty, however, the lowest price that obtains in the whole trading period for any production month.

Opportunities for tax optimization, however reduced by successive tightening of fiscal procedures, will exist so long as some oil production attracts PRT liability. They are the inevitable consequence of two features of the UK oil regime. The first is the differential rate of taxation on production and other activities (refining, trading and so on) and the virtual impossibility to erect impassable fences between the heavily and the more lightly taxed sectors. The second is the fundamental principle of taxation on the basis of market prices. This principle, sensible and valuable as it may be, invites participators to seek, whenever possible, the help of the vast array of trading instruments and hedging techniques on all the relevant oil markets, to reallocate profits from the highly taxed production sector to refining or trading where the fiscal border is lower. The continual development of new and more sophisticated trading instruments opens new opportunities which the fiscal authorities then try to close with tighter procedures and regulations. Since the UK government is unlikely to abandon the market price principle (and there are many good reasons for retaining it) the best that the OTO can hope to achieve is rules that turn all tax optimization exercises into trading gambles with uncertain outcomes. This is not easy as the experience of the past ten years abundantly proves. The difficulty is that a draconian tightening of the rules may adversely affect the very markets on which the fiscal regime depends to assess profits for tax purposes. The oil companies and the OTO both know that some tax spinning is unavoidable so long as PRT and the market price principle are retained. How little can be allowed without jeopardizing this principle is the question which naturally exercises the fiscal authorities. The oil companies' silence in response to the OTO request for views and comments on connected issues it raised in November 1992 suggests that they would rather let it guess the answer.[9]

Notes
1. The UK oil fiscal regime and its developments until 1984 is described in greater detail in R. Mabro et al. (1986), *The Market for North Sea Crude Oil*, Oxford University Press, pp. 109–18. The reader interested in a description of all the features of UK oil taxation will also find much useful information in Price Waterhouse (1990), *UK Taxation on the Profits from North Sea Oil*, Graham and Trotman. For a broader economic analysis of the subject, see C. Rowland and D. Mann (1987), *The Economics of North Sea Oil Taxation*, Macmillan.
2. The scale of tax receipts from these elements was quantified in Chapter 3.
3. Another purpose of the ring-fence is to enable the Inland Revenue to collect taxes on the profits of an oilfield as soon as they arise.
4. The (then) UK state oil company, the British National Oil Corporation. BNOC was abolished in 1985. Its importance as a factor in the birth of the Brent market is discussed in Chapter 6.
5. See R. Mabro et al., op. cit., p. 105.
6. Of course, views about future prices movements have to be taken all the time for trading purposes and actions taken in response to these views lead to the constitution of a portfolio of contracts. But while trading involves *ex ante* judgements, nominations to the OTO under the old scheme were essentially an *ex post* exercise.
7. Averages of a large number of readings are not normally very sensitive to the inclusion of a few additional readings.
8. There is of course an offsetting change in demand because when an integrated company sells a cargo it usually ends up buying one, and when

it retains a cargo its call on the open market is often reduced by one.
9. The Finance Bill of March 1993 introduced important changes to the PRT regime. First, the PRT rate is being reduced from 75 per cent to 50 per cent on all fields which received development authorization (Annex B) before 16 March 1993. This measure, however, does not remove the incentive for fiscal optimization through tax spinning. It merely reduces the benefits of any given optimization exercise (other things being equal) for a participator liable to PRT. Secondly, PRT is abolished on new oilfields (those which receive development authorization after 16 March 1993). The owners of these new fields will have no reason to engage in tax spinning when production comes on stream. In many instances, however, these new fields which are often small and expensive to develop, would not have attracted PRT liability under the pre-1993 regime. Thirdly, exploration expenditures are no longer allowable under PRT. This may lower the rate of future exploration activities in the UKCS.

Part II

The Forward and Dated Brent Markets

CHAPTER 6

THE HISTORICAL DEVELOPMENT OF THE BRENT MARKET

1. The Context

The emergence and growth of the 15-day Brent market in its various forms in the 1980s is part of broader and very fundamental developments in the structure of the world petroleum industry. The institutions, the technical modalities and the economic features of international trade in oil changed radically because of the de-integration of the industry in the 1970s. As a result of nationalization in the OPEC region and in other producing countries of the third world, the major companies lost many of the concessions which had provided them with equity oil. Large flows of oil in international trade ceased to move directly from source to refineries within the internal channels of the companies. The integrated structure divided into two distinct parts: the producing countries, or their national oil companies, which became sellers and marketers of crude rather than passive tax recipients, and the international companies which became purchasers of crude rather than tax payers on equity production. Nationalizations replaced the vertical integration links by an interface between sellers and buyers. In effect a market for arm's length transactions was born.

Initially there was almost everywhere a short transition period during which the producing country mainly supplied their former concessionaires. But the new structure was inherently open to multilateral trade relationships. The young marketing departments of national oil companies sought to increase the number of their customers and diversify the set. Oil companies deprived of privileged access to equity oil in this or that country, naturally began to buy from several other sources. The 1979 crisis which severed another privileged link, the long-term contracts under which the majors supplied Japanese and some European national oil companies, increased the number of firms seeking to purchase oil directly from the producing countries. De-integration created the conditions for a market to emerge and, soon after producing countries and oil companies found themselves engaged in a multiplicity of arm's length transactions, in the buying and selling of physical oil.

In the same period, another significant development, the growth of non-OPEC oil production, further enlarged the size of this physical petroleum market. The number of producers with crude oil to sell on the market place increased. De-integration was coincidentally associated with diversification on the supply side. As mentioned earlier there was also an increase in numbers and diversity on the purchasing side.

The third major development in the late 1970s and early 1980s, was the emergence of two distinct, though inter-related, systems of oil price determination. There was OPEC which at that time was setting an administered price for a marker crude (Arabian Light) and an increasingly active market for non-OPEC crudes in which oil prices were subjected to the pressures of economic forces while continuing to be strongly influenced by the OPEC system of price administration. This situation involved risks for oil buyers. Oil purchased from OPEC countries at OPEC f.o.b. prices often proved to be too expensive when it reached its destination compared with the price of non-OPEC crudes then available at the final location. Furthermore, on several occasions between 1982 and 1985 market pressures forced OPEC to lower the price of the marker crude. Long-haul crude bought at one price would reach refineries in Europe, the USA or the Far East after a few weeks during which a significant price cut may have been enacted. The need to hedge purchases (as well as sales) became paramount in a set-up where two centres of price determination were often pulling prices in opposite directions causing continual fluctuations in the market and occasional changes in the administered level of the marker crude.

All these developments spurred significant growth and diversification in market activity leading to the introduction of new trading instruments. The transactions set initially involved term contracts for the purchase of physical crude from producing countries and some spot deals. Very soon spot deals began to expand largely because of trading between holders of term contracts. Some of them did not have refinery outlets; some were obtaining more crude than their final requirements and others less. Also, most had to cope with continually changing circumstances between the date of nomination and the later dates of lifting and arrival at destination which always created discrepancies not only between the quantity, but also between the type and location of the crude purchased from the primary source, and the pattern of actual requirements that emerged when the crude was finally appropriated. Spot sales and purchases provided the obvious mechanism for balancing and adjustments. Finally, the need for hedging and for managing price risks created opportunities for markets to acquire a time dimension through the development of forward physical transactions, forward paper deals and futures exchanges.

2. The Logic Leading to the Emergence of Brent

The structural changes undergone by the world petroleum industry in the late 1970s and early 1980s, as mentioned in the previous section, provide the fundamental explanation for the birth of forward and futures markets, and the dynamic development over a fairly short period of seven or eight years of a wide variety of trading instruments. The context in which the 15-day Brent contract (and for that matter the light sweet crude oil futures contract on the NYMEX) emerged in the first half of the 1980s is therefore easy to understand. De-integration expanded the size of the external market which previously consisted of a small number of spot transactions undertaken either under distressed conditions, or for price discovery (finding out how much buyers are prepared to pay for the marginal barrels), or for disposing of small amounts of surplus crude. Initially, the growth of the external market simply meant an increase in spot trading. Markets, however, are organic entities which tend to diversify qualitatively when the volume of activity expands in a significant manner. The diversification occurs in response to the varied needs of the growing number of economic agents who enter the expanding market. The emergence of forward and physical then futures contracts are the first phase of this diversification which meets a demand for a time dimension in transaction.

These general propositions, straightforward as they may be, do not, however, answer by themselves specific questions of interest. Why did the demand for transactions with a time dimension find its point of application in the North Sea with Brent through a *sui generis* forward physical type of deal and in New York with a fairly conventional futures contract traded on the floor of a regulated exchange?

As often in history, the response to a significant need elicits a process of trial and error, an evolutionary process, in search of appropriate means to satisfy the demand. Sometimes a particular solution, rarely the ideal or perfect one since this is unobtainable, imposes itself through this process as the most appropriate or expedient, and the most robust. With hindsight, and through an analysis which moves by elimination from the general to the particular, one can explain why Brent (and WTI) became the object of forward (futures) trading.

In the early 1980s the set of crudes that satisfied eligibility criteria for a robust forward/futures contract was very small indeed. The eligibility criteria relate to ownership, volume of production, infrastructure for physical delivery and tradability. For a crude to be eligible it is highly desirable that its ownership be diversified. Concentration on the supply side tilts the balance of power in favour of primary sellers (producers) and naturally makes potential buyers reluctant to enter the market.

76 *Oil Markets and Prices*

This criterion excludes OPEC and some non-OPEC crudes (Mexican, Russian, and some North Sea varieties) from eligibility.

The second requirement is for the output stream to be sufficiently large to ensure physical liquidity. Considering the conditions prevailing in the early 1980s, these first two criteria virtually eliminated all crudes from areas other than the North Sea and the USA. The third criterion is the existence of an infrastructure capable of the delivery in both a reliable and flexible manner of the parcels specified in the trading contract.

The fourth is unrestricted, or more realistically almost unrestricted, tradability. Among North Sea crudes or blends, Brent and Ninian enjoyed some infrastructural advantages over other crudes or blends because of the excellent facilities extant at Sullom Voe. In the USA, the pipeline delivery system satisfies the criterion to some extent. The drawback is that bottlenecks occasionally impair the performance of the system. The North Sea, which is well-positioned strategically in the Atlantic Basin passes the tradability criterion; US crudes, though similarly located, fail it because of legal restrictions on exports.

This analysis strongly suggests that any search for a robust forward/futures trading framework, in the circumstances of the early 1980s, would have naturally focused first on the North Sea region. But here again a question arises: why a UKCS and not a Norwegian crude for this trading purpose? The most important factors that privileged the UK in this context are:

(a) The volume of the output stream. In the early 1980s the production levels of both Brent and Forties blend (830 thousand b/d and 520 thousand b/d in 1984 respectively) were higher than the largest Norwegian crude stream, namely Statfjord (475 thousand b/d).
(b) The institutional framework which was more market oriented in the UK than in the Norwegian North Sea oil industry.
(c) The availability of large volumes of crude oil to the British National Oil Corporation (BNOC) in the early 1980s. BNOC received, on behalf of the UK government, royalties paid in kind and was entitled to purchase from UKCS oil producers participation crude. In 1984 for example, the BNOC had claims on a volume of oil estimated at about 800,000 b/d.[1] BNOC being a non-integrated company was therefore a big potential supplier of crude to the open market.
(d) The fiscal regime. The valuation of transactions for tax purposes applies different principles in the UK and Norway. In the UK, as mentioned in Chapter 5, arm's length transactions are valued at the realized price of the deal and internal transactions at some estimate

of the ruling market price. Arm's length and internal transaction are not treated in the same way by the oil fiscal regime. In Norway valuation for tax purposes does not distinguish between types of transactions. Valuation in all cases is made on the basis of norm prices which are determined administratively in arrears for each quarter by the Petroleum Price Board, a commission consisting of five independent members appointed by the King. Since the UK fiscal regime is not neutral as regards arm's and non-arm's length transactions it provided an additional impetus to the trading of UKCS crudes on the open market.

Among the UKCS crudes or blends, Brent had clear advantages over all others because of its larger production volume, more diversified ownership, and excellent infrastructure. One can thus argue at the same time and without contradiction, first, that the emergence of the Brent market was not pre-planned, and, secondly that Brent blend was best suited to satisfy the powerful demand for a market framework for forward transactions in crude oil.

3. Historical Origins and Early Developments

Historically the 15-day Brent market emerged through the development of spot trading in North Sea crudes which began, as far as one can now establish, in the late 1970s. In 1977, UKCS oil production became significant at some 770 thousand b/d. By 1979 it had more than doubled, reaching 1,578 thousand b/d. A significant physical basis for spot trading was available at the time of the Iranian revolution and of the oil market disturbances of 1979–80.

In *The Market for North Sea Crude Oil*[2] it was suggested that:

The market itself appears to have evolved in a number of stages, moving from one stage to the next as surges in activity and changing market circumstances prompted new styles of trading.

There was spot trading because producers were keen to establish a market price for North Sea oil for both fiscal and commercial reasons; some vertically-integrated producers saw opportunities for fiscal optimization in spot transactions; many non-integrated companies involved on the UK side of the North Sea found it expedient sometimes to dispose of their limited volume of oil in a *hic et nunc* manner; BNOC, a very large seller, sought to diversify its transaction set rather than rely exclusively on buy-back arrangements and term contracts.

In 1981 the press began to report short selling by traders on a forward basis as 'traders were often trying to balance rather limited North Sea f.o.b. availability against c.i.f. arrivals of long haul crudes from the Middle East.'[3] Integrated companies, such as Conoco and BP, began to sell spot when spot prices were below the BNOC price. The first reports on what came to be known as tax spinning appeared in 1981.[4] During this period the most active market was one where delivery could take place in either Brent, or Ninian, or Forties. A forward dimension was already observed with transactions usually made one month and occasionally two months ahead.[5]

In 1982 the time horizon moved further forward as suggested by a report that a number of May barrels were done in early March. Spot cargoes and forward contracts are both eminently tradable. A cargo bought by B from A can easily be sold by B to C, then by C to somebody else and so on; similarly any economic agent can sell and buy forward contracts balancing over the relevant period of time its portfolio. Balance for a buyer means that the number of forward buys for a given month could be any number n that exceeds its forward sells m by the number $z = n - m$ of physical cargoes it wishes to acquire. Balance of a seller implies an excess of sells over buys equal to the number of physical cargoes it plans to supply. Problems can arise, however, if some traders find themselves in an unbalanced position at the end of the relevant period and one such situation seems to have obtained in January 1983. As forward trading becomes more significant and complex, informal procedures to ensure smooth operation and clearing of the market becomes necessary.

These procedures slowly emerged in 1983. Initially BP seems to have been the most active in pressing for standardization of trading procedures, and the BP terms and conditions were used by most participants. At that time, the Brent/Ninian/Forties trades were gradually phased out over the year and activity focused increasingly on Brent which was a more suitable candidate for becoming a standard trading commodity. During 1984 most of the procedures which now characterize 15-day Brent trading were introduced, including nomination at Sullom Voe, the 15-day notice itself and the famous 5 p.m. London time formal end of business clause for the passing of nominations. A form of contract through which Shell trades Brent specifying these and other terms was later adopted by most participants.

By 1984 the 15-day forward Brent market was well established and thriving. It had emerged in an evolutionary manner settling into a particular framework which was to prove robust. It is informal in the sense of being unregulated by official authorities but formal in the sense of involving voluntarily accepted standard procedures. There is no enforcement mechanism other than the law of contracts. In our imperfect world, however, an informal but complex system does not always operate in a perfect and smooth manner simply through the existence of a strong implicit consensus. That such a consensus exists because the main participants are motivated by powerful economic interests – hedging, risk-management, profitability of trading, fiscal optimization, need for price discovery and so on – to maintain it in existence and ensure efficient performance is not in doubt. But this consensus does not prevent occasional disturbances caused by rogue behaviour or clearing problems due to accidental causes. An informal system only works well when some of the main participants discreetly intervene on the occasions where a reminder needs to be uttered privately or a clearing logjam sorted out.

Logic and the widespread and credible belief of most participants suggest that the major oil companies involved in Brent are the ultimate guarantor of informal discipline, the necessary condition of stability and success of an informal system.

4. The 1986 Crisis

The 15-day Brent market expanded rapidly throughout 1984 and 1985. By the end of that latter year, however, the world market entered a new crisis which had diverse implications for Brent. In September 1985, and after many hesitations, Saudi Arabia decided that it could no longer accept the relentless decline in the volume of its production and exports caused by a fall in world oil demand, increases in non-OPEC production and lack of cartel discipline within OPEC. Saudi Arabia decided to abandon the OPEC-administered price system and introduced netback pricing for its export sales. The initial Saudi aim was to re-impose discipline within OPEC and to elicit co-operation in production rationing from non-OPEC producers in order to stabilize prices at, or close to, the levels prevailing in 1985. Although the aims and the presentation of the policy changed while it was being implemented, largely because of political constraints and pressures, there was no escape from its major consequences: a radical transformation of oil pricing methods and an oil price collapse.

The Brent market went through a period of turmoil at the beginning of 1986. Although it had coped with apparent ease with the price crises of March 1983 and May 1984 – which may have fostered confidence, if not some complacency, in the robust features of its mechanism – the sheer size of the price fall between November and December 1985 and February 1986 was too big for smooth responses. Some of the performance problems which arose at the time are described later in this study in Chapter 9. Although these problems were solved, they gave rise to legitimate fears that the recurrence of clearing difficulties or performance crises (even if ways of settling them were to be found in the end), would reduce confidence, and therefore liquidity, in the Brent market, or bring about some form of government regulation.

In February and March 1986 many proposals for reforming the Brent market were mooted in various quarters; some schemes involving a clearing house, and other more modest suggestions for the tightening of certain rules and closer supervision of their implementation.[6] Interesting questions were also posed: (a) whether netbacks would reduce refiners' need for hedging, considering that they guaranteed a positive refining margin on most OPEC crudes? and (b) whether the netback pricing system could be extended to the North Sea which would only be feasible if the UK Oil Taxation Office were to accept this method for the valuation of crudes for PRT purposes? Had netbacks become the prevailing and continuing pricing method for crude oil the Brent market would probably have suffered because this development would have had implications for both hedging and fiscal optimization.

But the OPEC netback arrangements did not continue for long enough to induce their adoption in the North Sea. Radical ideas about reforms were not pursued for very long because they all involved, on closer examination, problems or flaws. In fact, the Brent market quickly recovered from the January–February 1986 difficulties, and April saw a renewal of activity. The number of active participants recorded by Petroleum Argus which had fallen from more than seventy in January 1986 to about fifty, two months later, in March, began to rise again in April and subsequent months until September when it almost reached the January level (see Figure 7.2). The number of transactions seems also to have grown modestly in the second quarter of 1986 compared with the preceding quarter, and much more significantly in the third quarter of 1986, as shown in the Petroleum Argus data presented and discussed in Table 7.1. A most interesting development, however, was the rising profile of big finance houses from Wall Street on the Brent market. The first to enter the market was probably Morgan Stanley in 1984, and within eighteen months they were followed by a series of other Wall Street firms. In January 1986 their share of total transactions recorded by Petroleum Argus was 10 per cent; by mid-year it had risen to 20 per cent; and it reached a peak of about 33 per cent in November of that year.

The big finance houses brought to the 15-day Brent market liquidity, wide experience in financial and commodity markets which helped the introduction of new trading instruments (such as spreads, mini Brent deals and so on), and a welcome addition to the group of intermediaries, then mostly commodity traders, between Brent producing oil companies and refiners. The significant participation of Wall Street houses in the 15-day Brent market continued to increase after 1986 irrespective of the important changes in the world oil and the North Sea environment.

The large oil price fluctuations of 1986 had important effects on fiscal optimization. As explained in Chapter 5, under the then prevailing procedures, producing companies could select *ex post* from their portfolio of contracts for a given month the lowest priced ones for nomination to the OTO for PRT purposes. In 1986 the price gap between contracts was sometimes very large and the OTO felt that the system allowed significant reallocation of profits from the heavily taxed upstream to the more lightly taxed trading sector. As already mentioned this led to a change in nomination procedures for PRT in early 1987 which restricted the scope and altered the nature of fiscal optimization strategies.

5. Introducing the 1987–91 Period

The 'price war', as many observers labelled the events of 1986, ended in the autumn of that year. The political and economic costs of continuing for much longer were too high for all producing countries. In mid-1986 Saudi Arabia ceased to believe in the possibility of a victory, that is a rally of all major producers (both OPEC and non-OPEC) around a common and efficient stabilization policy.

As always in such circumstances the crises ended up with compromises that changed important features of the petroleum world. The system of administered oil price was abandoned by OPEC which then contented itself with defining a price target. The pricing of crude oil by producing countries for physical sales to their customers was increasingly made through formulae which related the price of the country's crude to that of Brent, ANS or Dubai (see Chapter 15). As a result, Brent blend acquired the role of a marker crude, and price determination in the Brent market gained worldwide significance. Finally, oil prices found new levels at around $17 or $18 per barrel, well below those ruling in 1985.

The Brent market during the episode beginning in 1987 after the oil price crisis, the episode which is the subject of this study, continued to operate and thrive. The detailed features of its development during this period are presented and discussed in subsequent chapters.

Although the Brent market framework remained almost the same, there were changes in its functions and in the motivations to trade.

Although tax spinning, which had played a role in its birth, continued to provide an incentive to trade it has lost some of its previous importance. For many oil companies trading became a commercial activity in its own right, a semi-autonomous profit centre strongly related, but not exclusively, to the physical supply side of the company's operations. Above all, Brent had become a world marker. Oil companies with worldwide interests in producing and acquiring crude oil could no longer remain indifferent to the determination of the Brent price. To be in Brent is to be where the action is. The history of Brent is that of a market continually facing new circumstances and continually finding new functions to perform, new reasons to trade and prosper.

Notes
1. R. Mabro et al (1986), *The Market for North Sea Crude Oil*, Table 3.3, p. 37.
2. Ibid. p. 161.
3. Ibid., p. 163.
4. *Petroleum Intelligence Weekly*, 20 April 1981 and *Petroleum Argus*, 8 May and 5 June 1981.
5. See *Petroleum Argus*, 5 June, 10 July and 25 September 1981.
6. See *Petroleum Argus*, various issues March 1986.

CHAPTER 7

THE STRUCTURE OF 15-DAY BRENT TRADING

1. Introduction

In this chapter, the features of the 15-day Brent market, and their changes during the period 1986-91, are described and analysed empirically. The data used were kindly supplied by Petroleum Argus. The main aspects of the market covered in this chapter relate to transactions and participants.

The characteristics of transactions studied here are (a) their volume which is a measure of liquidity, (b) their composition as between outright and spread deals, and (c) the forwardness of transactions. The very significant increase in the volume of spread deals over the period considered and changes in the degree of forwardness, particularly during crises (e.g. the Iraq-Kuwait crisis of 1990) are interesting phenomena which will be discussed at some length.

The analysis then focuses on market participants. It identifies the various entities involved in 15-day Brent trading, assesses their share of transactions and derives measures of market concentration. Finally, an attempt is made to study the trading behaviour of main groups of participants and their motivation.

2. Transactions

(a) Data and their Limitations

The best publicly available source of data on deals in the 15-day Brent market is Petroleum Argus. As there is no legal obligation on participants to report details of deals in informal forward markets (with the exception of producers who need to provide extensive information to the OTO), the coverage of Petroleum Argus depends very much on the goodwill or the self-interest of participants and brokers and is therefore incomplete. This proviso needs to be constantly kept in mind when interpreting the numbers presented and analysed in this section. The main implications of incomplete coverage in this case are that:

(i) the volume of activity is always a multiple of the numbers recorded by Petroleum Argus;
(ii) apparent changes in the statistics over time may be partly due to changes in the rate of coverage;
(iii) information on certain characteristics of the deals (e.g. the identity of the buyer or seller or both) is lacking for a proportion of the recorded deals.

Less obviously, the rate of coverage of certain types of transactions, such as outright deals, may become adversely affected when their volume declines to low levels. The smaller the volume of a particular type of deal, the greater may become the reluctance of participants to reveal prices, and the greater is the likelihood that an increasing proportion of the shrinking volume of transactions will not be reported.

Our judgement is that the Petroleum Argus coverage of 15-day Brent market deals in 1990–91 was of the order of 40 per cent. This view was reached by comparing the results of two exercises. From interviews, we derived the assumption that the average length of a chain would be about thirty if there were no book-outs and all deals were cleared through the nomination process. The typical number of cargoes (500 thousand barrels each) was about forty-eight per month in 1990–1. This implies some 4,300 cargoes traded per quarter.

The second exercise assumed, also following soundings in interviews, that the average number of trades per trading day, though extremely variable, may be approximated at around forty. As the number of trading days in a quarter is about sixty-four, the number of trades per quarter would be 2,460. According to the Petroleum Argus data, 80 per cent of these are spreads, and 20 per cent outright deals. Applying these percentages to the 2,460 trades and counting spreads as two deals, we come up with an estimate of 4,430 deals per quarter. This is very close to the estimate of 4,300 arrived at in the first exercise. We must stress here that the two exercises were conducted independently; in other words the critical assumptions were derived from separate questions and interviews. We proceeded from assumptions to results and *not* from a guess of the results back to the assumption.

We also compared these estimates with information provided by a large trading entity on the average number of deals made in a month. Applying to this number the share of this trading entity in total transactions recorded by Petroleum Argus suggested that the number of transactions in a quarter was of the order of 3,600. This is lower than the estimates arrived at in the two exercises. Allowing for some understatement by the trading entity of its own activity would raise this estimate. (A big player in our experience is always inclined to understate its true profile.) If the understatement was a mere 10 per cent, the figure would rise to almost 4,000 deals; if 20 per cent we would reach the 4,320 level, the same order of magnitude as our previous guess estimates.

We infer from these exercises, given that the average number of deals recorded per quarter in the eight quarters – 1Q1990 to 4Q1991 – was about 1,800 per quarter, that the Petroleum Argus coverage was slightly less than 40 per cent.

(b) Liquidity of the Market

Always keeping these qualifications and assumptions in mind we may form some idea of the developments in the volume and pattern of transactions in the 15-day market. Table 7.1 suggests that the market does *not* suffer from a liquidity problem. During the years 1987–91, the volume of recorded transactions varied within a range bound by a low of 1,333 (3Q1989) and a high of 2,419 (1Q1988). If the coverage, as estimated above, was of the order of 40 per cent, the actual total volume would have varied between 3,325 at the lower end and 6,050 at the high end. We remind the reader that every outright deal counts as one and every spread deal as two since it involves two cargoes.

In the period 1984–5 which was covered in *The Market for North Sea Crude Oil*,[1] the volume of *recorded* transactions grew from 450 to 1,300. These volumes have been consistently, and often considerably lower than those recorded during 1987–91. Data for 1986 reveal that a significant rise in transaction volumes began in 3Q1986 and continued in the following six quarters to reach the peak of 1Q1988. Thereafter there is no discernible trend, rather marked fluctuations. Recorded volumes declined first in 2Q1988 down to 1,800–1,900, a level which remained fairly stable until 1Q1989 and then declined again down to the trough of 3Q1989. After that quarter there were fluctuations and we recognize in the variable pattern a burst of activity in 3Q1990, the quarter during which Iraq invaded Kuwait.

(c) Outright and Spread Deals

The more interesting feature of the 15-day Brent market as depicted from the Petroleum Argus data, is the dramatic change in the composition of deals as between outright and spread transactions. There was a most remarkable growth in spread trading, and an equally striking decline in the volume of outright deals in the period 1986–91 considered as a whole.

There are two types of spreads: the first is intra-Brent (between two

Table 7.1: Composition of 15-day Brent Deals. Outright and Spreads. 1986–91. Number of Deals.

	Total Deals	Outright Deals	Spread Deals	Brent Spreads 1 Month	Brent Spreads 2 Months	Brent Spreads 3+ Months	Total Brent Spreads	Inter-Crude Spreads Dubai	Inter-Crude Spreads WTI
1986									
Q1	1216	992	224	202	20	0	222	0	2
Q2	1381	860	521	396	80	30	506	15	0
Q3	1624	1258	366	288	48	4	340	14	12
Q4	1568	1051	517	402	78	0	480	17	20
1987									
Q1	1820	1220	600	492	34	0	526	55	19
Q2	1826	1206	620	518	48	14	580	24	16
Q3	2174	1628	546	448	44	10	502	33	11
Q4	2275	1650	625	566	38	2	606	7	12
1988									
Q1	2419	1560	859	674	86	12	772	38	49
Q2	1819	1173	646	458	48	6	512	76	58
Q3	1996	1178	818	558	26	2	586	125	107
Q4	1852	881	971	658	32	4	694	156	121
1989									
Q1	1908	542	1366	1112	20	2	1134	138	94
Q2	1524	413	1111	894	14	2	910	72	129
Q3	1333	429	904	694	6	4	704	80	120
Q4	1552	499	1053	820	34	2	856	97	100
1990									
Q1	1706	566	1140	924	26	10	960	100	80
Q2	1595	660	935	750	56	2	808	81	46
Q3	2282	785	1497	1286	66	8	1360	83	54
Q4	1789	529	1260	1102	46	4	1152	61	47
1991									
Q1	1834	331	1503	1310	58	6	1374	77	52
Q2	1666	370	1296	1086	28	4	1118	98	80
Q3	1681	386	1295	1118	46	0	1164	86	45
Q4	1769	383	1386	1196	52	8	1256	86	44

Source: Own calculations from Petroleum Argus database

forward Brent months), and the second, inter-crude spreads (between Brent and Dubai, and Brent and WTI). In the Petroleum Argus data, spreads represented 18 per cent of total deals in 1Q1986, and this share reached 79 per cent on average in 1991 with the volume of spread deals having increased by a factor of five. Meanwhile the volume of reported outright trades had by 1991 fallen by a factor of five from their peak levels at the end of 1987. There has then been a fundamental shift in the liquidity of the market with spreads increasing and outright trades decreasing over time. What then have been the determinants of these trends?

The fall in the volume of outright trades in the 15-day market is due to the conjunction of several factors. The first is the development of the IPE futures Brent contract, launched in its present form in June 1988, and which has gained increasing liquidity over time. Prior to the development of this contract the forward market was the only vehicle available for hedging UK and Norwegian North Sea oil without incurring very large basis risk. The IPE now provides another hedging vehicle. While large producers may remain wary of hedging large amounts on futures for fear of causing adverse market movements, the IPE tends to be preferred by smaller producers due to its flexibility.

Since 1987 there has been both an increase in the amount of crude oil directly priced off Brent (as is documented in Chapters 14 and 15), and also an increased sensitivity to risk and the value of hedging in the oil industry. *Ceteris paribus* these factors would be expected to increase the volume of outright Brent trades, and the decline observed in the forward market must then be seen in the light of both existing and incremental trading volumes tending to shift towards the IPE.

Other factors have also reduced the volume of outright trades. The period 1986–91 coincides with the withdrawal from the Brent market of several large traders of outright Brent as is detailed later in this chapter, in particular the Japanese trading houses, the sogo shosha. Indeed, of the ten largest traders of outright Brent in 1986 only four are still active traders. The exit of these players has further reduced the market for outright Brent as a purely speculative instrument. Only one of the ten major outright Brent traders in 1986 was an oil company; by 1991 five were, all with large volumes of Brent or Brent related crude oil to hedge, either as sales or purchases.

While the development of the IPE and the exit of some players have probably been the major factors behind the decline of outright trading in the forward market, a series of other factors may have been in play. The changes in the UK tax regime have reduced some of the incentives to trade outright. There is also less UKCS production to be hedged. While Norwegian production has more than compensated for this fall, the Norwegian tax regime has not provided the same incentives to trade as the UK regime.

While the volume of outright trades has been falling there has been a large increase in the volume of spread trading. It is worth noting the difference in risks between spread and outright trading. The risk in an outright trade is the variance of the level of prices, in a spread it is the variance of a differential. The risk in a spread is then not necessarily less than that of an outright, depending on the covariance between the two prices whose differential is being traded. However, since 1986 the variance of changes in spreads has usually, but not always, been less than that of the level of prices. On the other hand, while the variance of spreads may have been lower, the risk/return trade-off has generally been less favourable than for outright trades.

The increase in spread trading cannot necessarily be attributed to any increase in speculation relative to hedging in the Brent market. Spreads are not exclusively used for speculation purposes. They can serve as instruments for the hedging of an outright transaction. A Brent-WTI spread, for example, is a hedging instrument for a North Sea crude oil cargo bought at a Brent-related price which may have to be sold on the US East Coast at a WTI related price. An intra-Brent spread (say, between first and second month) can be used as a secondary, though imperfect hedge for an outright transaction in the Brent forward or futures market made for hedging purposes. Finally, a spread can be bought or sold to reduce basis risk. It follows that an increase in the volume of spread deals relative to outrights should not be interpreted as indicating an increase in speculation relative to hedging in the 15-day Brent market in 1988–91, the period during which the dramatic rise of spread trading was observed.

What then has determined the increase in the volume of spread trading? The first factor is a general learning effect. Spreads were introduced into the Brent market through the entry of Wall Street finance houses in the mid 1980s. Having used spreads as a trading instrument in other commodity and financial markets, Brent spreads were a natural evolution for them. The introduction of spreads has led to their adoption by other market participants as they learnt how to use and understand spread movements. In this early introduction and adoption stage there was probably some substitution from outright to spread trading. Any risk-averse market participant will find the overall risk of their portfolio of deals reduced by trading spreads compared to a portfolio of just outrights, given that movements in the absolute price of crude oil and in differentials are not perfectly correlated.

The initial learning effect and increasing sophistication among traders in the understanding of differentials has been reinforced by other factors. In particular the increase in the volume of oil priced from dated Brent since 1987 has increased the need to hedge differentials as noted above. However, now that the adoption and learning phase in spread trading is over and that the market is mature, the major determinant of the volume of spread trading is the volatility of absolute price levels. The economic function of spread trading is to restore price differentials as absolute price levels change. In both forward and futures Brent markets trading of outright positions tends to be very heavily concentrated in a single delivery month's trading. As the price of that month changes, arbitrage possibilities open in the differentials, and trading of spreads brings the structure of prices back into line. Hence the volume of spread trading will increase during periods of high volatility in absolute price levels as the number and scale of the arbitrage possibilities increases.

Before there was liquidity in trading spreads, there were traders who wished to profit from arbitrage possibilities in inter-month price differentials. However, the only way they could accomplish this was through a legged spread, i.e. two outright trades made in different months on opposite sides of the market with two different trading partners. These traders were effectively trading spreads, although the deals would have been recorded as two outrights. Thus, to an extent part of the decline in outrights is that traders who used to arbitrage between the prices of different delivery months can now trade spreads explicitly rather than having to achieve a spread position through the trade of outrights.

The developments of increased spread trading but reduced outright trade have had a fairly neutral effect on the liquidity of the market as a whole. However, this does mean that the 15-day market has become a market that is primarily concerned with price relatives. The general stability in total volumes shown in Table 7.1 masks the sharp decline in trades of the absolute price level. From the point of view of price assessment agencies, the implication is that their information set on absolute prices has been reduced, while that on relative prices has been greatly enhanced.

(d) Forwardness of Transactions

We have computed the forwardness of each recorded transaction for the whole 1986–91 period applying the following method.[2] Forwardness is measured as the number of days between the date at which the deal was entered upon and the middle of the period potentially available for loading in the relevant delivery month. Thus, the forwardness of a deal for an April cargo made on 10 February is the sum of the remaining eighteen February days, thirty-one March days and half of April, the delivery month, that is sixty-four days. A deal for an April cargo made on 27 March can only be loaded between 12 and 30 April, the mid point of which is 21 April. The forwardness of this deal is therefore the sum of the remaining four March days and twenty-one days in April, that is twenty-five days.

In Figure 7.1 we present the average degree of forwardness of deals made *in* every month (1986–91). The two highest peaks occurred in May and June 1986, at the time of the oil price crisis and in August and September 1990 when Iraq invaded Kuwait. In crises many hedgers try to lock prices as far ahead as they can and presumably find speculators willing to take the risk at a cost. The average degree of forwardness at these two peaks was seventy-one and sixty-nine days respectively, that is the average term of a deal made at the beginning of a month (say, May) was for the third month forward (July).

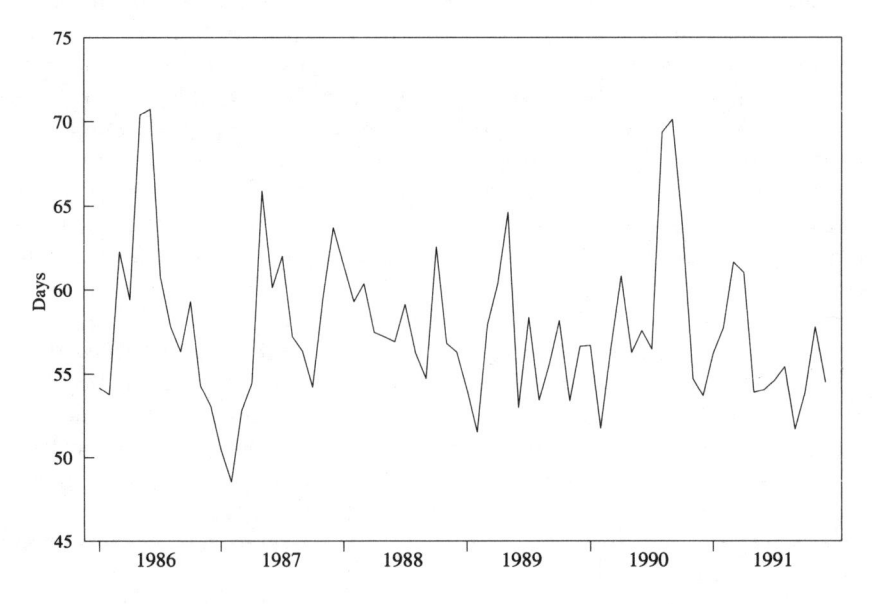

Figure 7.1: Average Forwardness of Brent Deals By Month. 1986–91. Number of Days.

During the troughs, the value of the index has fallen as far down as forty-eight days. In this case the average deal made at the beginning of January was for the second month forward (February). An interesting feature of the graph is the steep fall of the index, down to very low values, soon after high peaks were attained during crises. One interpretation is that crises at their beginning, as mentioned earlier, cause participants to seek more forward deals as a means to ride what is then perceived as a temporary bump. It is precisely because of this perception that hedgers find partners for their proposed deals. Soon after, uncertainty about the outcome of the crisis, uncertainty about such questions as 'how far the price fall or rise will go and for how long the collapse or the explosion will go', becomes so significant that hedgers who sought to lock the price far ahead find the operation too expensive for lack of speculators willing to accept the risks. In this situation market participants cease to look far ahead and like car drivers in thick fog, they fix their sight on what is nearest to them.

We also observe, amidst many fluctuations, a decline in average forwardness between 1987 and mid-1990. This period can be construed as fairly normal for it separates the two major crises of 1986 and 1990. Although the decline is very clearly visible, we should not exaggerate its importance as it is not statistically significant. The fluctuations in the degree of forwardness are however large, and are the result of several factors. The time pattern of prices is important, for as is explained in Chapter 11 contangos tend to be more stable than backwardations. As a result heavy backwardations create a disinclination to trade spreads far forward. Increased volatility in absolute price levels on the other hand creates an incentive to hedge further forward, note for instance the large increase in forwardness at the start of the Gulf crisis in 1990. Very large shocks can also dislocate price differentials several months out, and so lead to an increase in far forward spread deals to arbitrage those differentials.

We have so far discussed the forwardness of deals made *in* the month, and now turn to the analysis of deals made *for* a particular month. In Table 7.2 we chart the evolution of the trading of cargoes for a single representative Brent delivery month, in this case July 1990. All the reported trades made for this month were either outright deals, or inter-month or inter-crude spreads, and the number of reported deals of each type are shown by time period. Trading for July 1990 cargoes began some five months forward of the last possible nomination day for cargoes, with the trading of a single May/July spread in February. By the end of March trading was still very thin – a total of thirteen deals of which twelve were inter-month spread trades. Indeed July 1990 cargoes were only actively traded between three months and one month of the last nomination day, with trade in May alone accounting for over 50 per cent of all trades.

The time structure of outright and spread deals was very different, with the distribution of outright deals being concentrated over a much shorter time-span. July 1990 became the wet month on 16 June, when the first nominations for July delivery became possible, and could have

Table 7.2: Time Pattern of Trading of the July 1990 15-Day Brent Deal. Number of Deals Made in the Periods Shown.

Date of Deals	Outright Deals	Brent Spreads May	June	Aug	Sep	Other Spreads Dubai	WTI	Total Spreads	Total Deals
Feb	0	1	0	0	0	0	0	1	1
Mar	1	2	7	0	2	0	0	11	12
Apr 1–15	8	1	12	9	0	8	0	30	38
Apr 16–30	13	2	29	7	0	10	3	49	62
May 1–15	48	0	56	16	1	9	8	90	138
May 16–31	83	-	22	20	0	5	12	59	142
Jun 1–15	59	-	1	44	3	1	2	51	110
Jun 16–30	1	-	-	19	0	0	0	19	20
Jul 1–15	0	-	-	3	2	0	0	5	5
Total	213	6	126	118	8	33	25	315	528

Source: Own calculations from Petroleum Argus database.

been traded right up to 13 July when the last possible nomination could have been made and the last chain formed. However, over this month only one outright deal was reported. Nearly 90 per cent of all outright deals were made when it was the second delivery month forward, or in the latter half of the time when it was the third delivery month forward. By contrast, spread deals were traded in significant numbers from late March right up to the beginning of July, and some trade continued into July. Indeed while July was the wet month, all but one of the twenty-five deals transacted were spread deals.

Spread trading involving cargoes for a given delivery month tends to reach its peak before outright trading. In the example shown, the peak period for spread trading involving July cargoes was in the first half of May when both June/July and July/August spreads were being actively traded, while outright deals reached a peak in the second half of May. For July 1990 forward cargoes the volume of outright trades only exceeded the volume of spread trading while July was the second month forward delivery month. At all other points during the trading of July 1990 cargoes the spread trades dominated, and overall represented over 60 per cent of all trades. A strong pattern then emerges of outright trading determining prices in second month Brent, while other forward prices are primarily determined by interpolation from the second month through the trading of spread deals.

(e) Summary

The 15-day Brent market is liquid. We estimate the average number of transactions per quarter in 1990–91 as being somewhere between 4,000 and 4,500 deals (counting spreads as the trade of two cargoes). Of course this volume continually varies. There was growth between late-1986 and mid-1988 but no marked trend thereafter.

During our period the composition of the liquidity of the market has drastically changed. Spreads have gradually gained in importance (relatively to outright deals) until they became overwhelmingly dominant in the first half of 1991. We believe that the decline of outright trades is primarily due to the development of IPE futures Brent and the exit of key participants. Meanwhile over this period the market for Brent spreads has grown in volume and become mature after their introduction by Wall Street finance houses led to an adoption and learning process by other participants.

There is no doubt that, though a low risk/low reward instrument, spreads are an efficient tool of risk management when the exposure is to movements in price relatives. But the dominance of spreads in the transaction set raises important questions about the exact role of the Brent market in determining the price of oil. In spread deals the relationship between specified 'flat prices' and market prices may not be very tight. And since the focus is to a large extent on relatives, the search for price levels that correspond to the relevant market conditions becomes less broadly based and less active. The liquidity in that part of the market which concerns itself with the oil price level, has become a small proportion of the total liquidity of the forward market.

3. Participants

(a) Size and Concentration

The Petroleum Argus data for the period 1986–91 identifies 174 names of participants. This set includes all entities reported to have engaged in at least one deal during the period covered. Since reporting always picks up a much larger proportion of active participants than of deals, it is extremely unlikely that a major participant is missed out. Defining as 'continually active' participants with at least one trading record every year throughout a given period, we find that forty-three participants were involved in a continuing manner in 1986–91, and fifty in the most recent consecutive years, 1988–91. These are listed in Table 7.3.

The number of active participants by year is shown in Table 7.4.

94 *Oil Markets and Prices*

Table 7.3: Continually Active Participants. 1988–91.

J Aron, Phibro, Cargill, Shell International, CFP (Total), BP, Statoil, Morgan Stanley, Amerada Hess, Marc Rich, Elf, Shell UK, Neste, Dreyfus, Chevron, Nova, Arcadia, Bear Stearns, TWO, Mobil, Kanematsu, Texaco, Vitol, Sinochem, Exxon, Repsol, Norsk Hydro, Shell Germany, Conoco, Sun, URBK, Shell Netherlands, Nissho Iwai, Koch, Agip, Ultramar, Mitsui, Hill Petroleum, Sohio (BP America), Shearson Lehman, Marubeni, Coastal, C. Itoh, Clarendon, OK Petroleum, Enterprise, Mitsubishi, Phillips, Wintershall, CEPSA.

Notes: 1. These participants are ranked by descending order of number of recorded transactions in 1991.
2. The number of recorded transactions in 1991 is less than twenty for Sohio and all subsequent names in this list.

Source: Own calculations from Petroleum Argus Database

Table 7.4: Number of Active Participants. 1986–91.

Year	Number
1986	108
1987	109
1988	110
1989	83
1990	87
1991	67

Source: Own calculations from Petroleum Argus Database.

The comparison of these numbers with the total of identified names (174) suggests that those participants who have traded episodically in the period 1988–91, entered later than 1986 or exited before 1991 is fairly large. The number of continually active participants, as defined above, gives some idea of the size of the core group that has been trading in recent years. The definition adopted here may be criticized however for being too generous since it includes in the core participants which have traded as little as only once every year. A tighter criterion, a minimum of ten deals every year, reduces the number of continually active participants to thirty-seven in the period 1988–91.

Figure 7.2 shows a monthly breakdown for all these years. In the most crowded month of the period, there were more than seventy active participants, in the least active probably less than forty. Ignoring the hectic months of 1986, Figure 7.2 also reveals more clearly than the annual numbers mentioned above a regular decline in the number of active participants per month after 1987. The only exception to this pattern is the period that corresponds to the Kuwait crisis.

We have also computed the shares in total recorded transactions of the forty largest participants every year (Table 7.5). This provides an apparent ranking of participants and identifies the most active ones. Imperfect coverage affects adversely the accuracy of this table which can only be used to suggest orders of magnitude and approximate ranking. Despite these qualifications, it is difficult to dismiss some results derived from Table 7.5 relating to the size of a participants' core, and more importantly, the increase over time in market concentration.

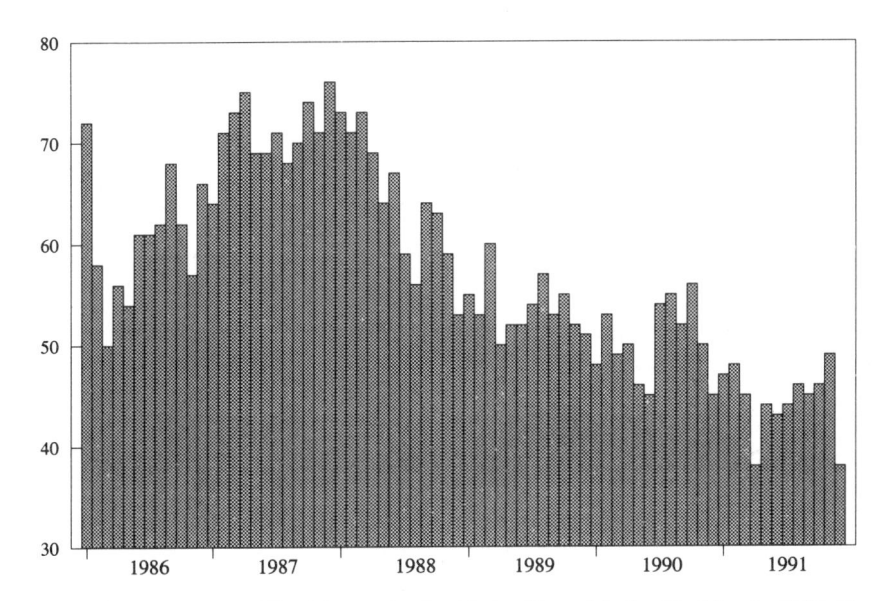

Figure 7.2: Number of Participants in the 15-day Brent Market By Month. 1986–91.

We have seen that the number of active participants by year has been declining in 1987–91. Table 7.5 suggests further that the number of participants with a market share of 1 per cent or more has also been declining from thirty-two in 1988 down to twenty-five in both 1990 and 1991. If market shares were to be used, instead of the notion of continual activity over time, to identify a core group it would appear that the number of reasonably active participants (those with 1 per cent or more of total transactions which we estimate at fifteen deals or more per month), was approximately twenty-five in 1990–91; and that the

96 Oil Markets and Prices

Table 7.5: Top Participants in the 15-Day Brent Market. Rank and Market Shares. 1986–91. Per Cent.

(a) Total Deals

Rank	1986		1987		1988		1989		1990		1991	
1	Phibro	8.7	Phibro	10.0	J Aron	14.7	J Aron	15.6	J Aron	15.6	J Aron	15.8
2	J Aron	7.4	J Aron	9.6	Phibro	12.5	Phibro	11.7	Phibro	12.6	Phibro	10.6
3	Nissho Iwai	6.1	Shell International	5.2	Drexel	4.7	Drexel	5.8	Shell International	5.6	Cargill	5.9
4	Shell UK	5.5	Nissho Iwai	4.7	Shell International	4.7	Bear Stearns	4.0	CFP	4.6	Shell International	5.8
5	Drexel	4.3	BP	3.6	BP	4.0	Cargill	3.9	Morgan Stanley	4.4	CFP	5.4
6	Marubeni	4.2	Marubeni	3.6	Nissho Iwai	3.8	Shell International	3.9	Cargill	4.3	BP	5.0
7	BP	3.6	Shell UK	3.5	Kanematsu	3.4	Nissho Iwai	3.5	Statoil	4.0	Statoil	4.7
8	Intermorth	3.5	Drexel	3.5	Shell UK	3.2	TWO	2.9	Neste	3.7	Morgan Stanley	4.3
9	Shell International	3.3	Exxon	3.3	Morgan Stanley	2.8	BP	2.9	Shell UK	3.2	Amerada Hess	3.4
10	Kanematsu	2.9	Kanematsu	3.2	Exxon	2.4	Morgan Stanley	2.9	Nissho Iwai	3.1	Marc Rich	3.4
11	TWO	2.7	Marc Rich	2.8	Mitsui	2.2	Shell UK	2.6	Marc Rich	2.8	Elf	3.2
12	Conoco	2.1	TWO	2.7	Mobil	2.2	CFP	2.5	BP	2.6	Shell UK	3.1
13	Nichimen	2.1	Avant	2.5	Cargill	1.9	Hill Petroleum	2.3	Sinochem	2.6	AIG	2.8
14	Enron	2.0	Mobil	2.1	Avant	1.8	Sinochem	2.0	Nova	2.3	Neste	2.7
15	URBK	2.0	Morgan Stanley	1.9	Dreyfus	1.8	Marc Rich	1.9	Amerada Hess	2.0	Dreyfus	1.9
16	Sun	1.9	Mitsui	1.9	Bear Stearns	1.7	Elf	1.9	TWO	1.7	Chevron	1.9
17	Gotco	1.9	Enron	1.9	TWO	1.5	Mitsui	1.8	Arcadia	1.3	Nova	1.7
18	Exxon	1.9	Kaines	1.8	Nova	1.4	Avant	1.7	Mobil	1.3	Arcadia	1.6
19	Mobil	1.7	C Itoh	1.6	Marc Rich	1.4	Statoil	1.6	Kanematsu	1.3	Bear Stearns	1.5
20	Nova	1.6	Elf	1.6	Scan	1.4	Scan	1.5	Sun	1.3	TWO	1.4

Source: Own calculations from Petroleum Argus database

Table 7.5: Top Participants in the 15-Day Brent Market. Rank and Market Shares. 1986-91. Per Cent. (continued)

(a) Total Deals

Rank	1986		1987		1988		1989		1990		1991	
21	Kaines	1.6	Dreyfus	1.6	Elf	1.6	Kanematsu	1.3	Bear Stearns	1.5	Mobil	1.3
22	Tradax	1.5	Nova	1.5	Kloeckner	1.3	Mobil	1.2	Dreyfus	1.4	Kanematsu	1.2
23	Sigmoil	1.4	Kloeckner	1.4	Conoco	1.3	Marubeni	1.2	Vitol	1.4	Texaco	1.2
24	Avant	1.3	Tradax	1.3	Statoil	1.2	Arcadia	1.2	Elf	1.3	Vitol	1.2
25	Mitsui	1.3	Conoco	1.3	CEPSA	1.1	Dreyfus	1.2	Chevron	1.3	Sinochem	1.1
26	Neste	1.3	Mitsubishi	1.3	Neste	1.1	Nova	1.2	Conoco	1.3	Exxon	0.9
27	Vanol	1.2	Marimpex	1.2	Mitsubishi	1.1	Conoco	1.2	AIG	1.2	Repsol	0.8
28	Dreyfus	1.2	Neste	1.2	CFP	1.0	Mitsubishi	1.1	Sucden	1.1	Norsk Hydro	0.8
29	Chevron	1.2	Vanol	1.2	Chevron	0.9	Exxon	1.1	Mitsubishi	1.1	Aerochem	0.7
30	Metallgesell	1.2	Chevron	1.2	Marimpex	0.9	Sun	1.0	Agip	0.9	Shell Germany	0.7
31	C Itoh	1.2	CEPSA	1.2	Shell Netherlands	0.8	Vitol	1.0	Marubeni	0.9	Conoco	0.5
32	Marc Rich	1.0	Scan	1.0	Coastal	0.8	Coastal	1.0	Texaco	0.8	Sun	0.5
33	Morgan Stanley	1.0	Statoil	1.0	Vitol	0.8	Chevron	0.9	Hill Petroleum	0.7	URBK	0.6
34	Scan	0.9	Britoil	0.9	Toro	0.8	Neste	0.9	Repsol	0.7	Shell Netherlands	0.4
35	Britoil	0.8	Vitol	0.8	Hill Petroleum	0.8	Sucden	0.8	Drexel	0.6	Nissho Iwai	0.3
36	Bomar	0.8	URBK	0.8	Texaco	0.8	Texaco	0.8	Mitsui	0.6	Crescent	0.3
37	Coastal	0.8	Metallgesell	0.8	Kaines	0.8	URBK	0.8	URBK	0.6	Koch	0.3
38	Mitsubishi	0.7	Coastal	0.7	Sun	0.7	Shell Netherlands	0.5	Shell Germany	0.5	Agip	0.2
39	Cedar	0.6	Bear Stearns	0.6	Marubeni	0.7	CEPSA	0.5	Exxon	0.4	Ultramar	0.2
40	Sohio	0.6	Shell Netherlands	0.6	URBK	0.7	Sohio	0.5	Shell Netherlands	0.4	Mitsui	0.2

Source: Own calculations from Petroleum Argus database

Table 7.5: Top Participants in the 15-Day Brent Market. Rank and Market Shares. 1986–91. Per Cent. (continued)

(b) Spread Deals

Rank	1986		1987		1988		1989		1990		1991	
1	J Aron	10.2	J Aron	9.4	J Aron	15.1	J Aron	15.5	J Aron	16.5	J Aron	15.8
2	Nissho Iwai	8.2	Phibro	9.3	Phibro	12.4	Phibro	11.9	Phibro	13.5	Phibro	10.7
3	Phibro	7.9	Nissho Iwai	6.8	Nissho Iwai	6.4	Drexel	5.6	Shell International	5.5	Shell International	6.0
4	Drexel	6.3	Shell International	5.4	Drexel	4.8	Bear Stearns	5.3	CFP	4.7	CFP	5.8
5	Shell UK	5.9	Avant	5.1	Avant	3.8	Nissho Iwai	4.5	Morgan Stanley	4.7	Cargill	5.6
6	Kanematsu	5.5	Kanematsu	4.6	Bear Stearns	3.7	Cargill	4.2	Nissho Iwai	4.3	BP	5.1
7	Internorth	3.8	Drexel	3.8	Dreyfus	3.5	Morgan Stanley	3.2	Cargill	4.3	Morgan Stanley	4.6
8	Nichimen	2.9	BP	3.6	Mitsui	3.5	Shell International	3.2	Marc Rich	3.6	Marc Rich	3.8
9	Dreyfus	2.9	Marubeni	3.5	Kanematsu	3.5	TWO	3.0	Neste	3.5	Statoil	3.8
10	Avant	2.7	Dreyfus	3.4	Shell International	3.4	CFP	2.8	BP	2.6	Elf	3.2
11	Marubeni	2.7	Marc Rich	3.0	Morgan Stanley	3.4	Hill Petroleum	2.8	Shell UK	2.5	Amerada Hess	3.2
12	Gotco	2.3	Shell UK	3.0	Scan	2.6	BP	2.8	Statoil	2.5	AIG	2.9
13	BP	2.3	Tradax	2.5	BP	2.4	Mitsui	2.4	TWO	2.4	Shell UK	2.7
14	Shell International	2.2	Kaines	2.4	Cargill	1.9	Avant	2.3	Amerada Hess	2.0	Neste	2.6
15	URBK	2.1	Morgan Stanley	2.2	TWO	1.8	Marc Rich	2.2	Arcadia	1.9	Dreyfus	2.4
16	Tradax	2.0	Enron	2.0	Shell UK	1.8	Scan	2.1	Bear Stearns	1.7	Chevron	2.1
17	Mitsui	1.8	Mitsubishi	1.6	Mobil	1.5	Shell UK	1.8	Dreyfus	1.7	Arcadia	1.9
18	TWO	1.8	Chevron	1.5	Marc Rich	1.5	Arcadia	1.8	Mobil	1.6	Bear Stearns	1.8
19	Sun	1.6	TWO	1.5	Mitsubishi	1.5	Marubeni	1.7	Nova	1.5	TWO	1.6
20	Enron	1.6	Bear Stearns	1.4	Hill Petroleum	1.3	Dreyfus	1.7	Kanematsu	1.4	Mobil	1.5

Source: Own calculations from Petroleum Argus database

Table 7.5: Top Participants in the 15-Day Brent Market. Rank and Market Shares. 1986-91. Per Cent. (continued)

(c) Outright Trades

Rank	1986		1987		1988		1989		1990		1991	
1	Phibro	9.1	Phibro	10.2	J Aron	14.5	J Aron	15.9	J Aron	16.5	J Aron	16.0
2	J Aron	6.3	J Aron	9.7	Phibro	12.6	Phibro	11.2	Phibro	11.2	Phibro	10.2
3	Shell UK	5.4	Shell International	5.2	Shell International	5.5	Drexel	6.2	Statoil	6.9	Statoil	8.1
4	Nissho Iwai	5.3	Exxon	4.5	BP	5.0	Shell International	5.6	Shell International	5.9	Cargill	7.1
5	Marubeni	4.9	Nissho Iwai	3.8	Drexel	4.7	Sinochem	5.4	Sinochem	5.4	BP	5.2
6	BP	4.1	Shell UK	3.8	Shell UK	4.1	Shell UK	4.4	CFP	4.4	Shell International	5.0
7	Shell International	3.8	BP	3.6	Exxon	3.7	Statoil	3.7	Cargill	4.4	Shell UK	4.6
8	Drexel	3.5	Marubeni	3.6	Kanematsu	3.4	Cargill	3.3	Shell UK	4.4	Amerada Hess	4.4
9	Internorth	3.4	Drexel	3.4	Mobil	2.7	Elf	3.1	Neste	4.0	Exxon	3.6
10	TWO	3.1	TWO	3.2	Morgan Stanley	2.4	BP	3.1	Morgan Stanley	4.0	CFP	3.5
11	Conoco	2.6	Marc Rich	2.7	Nissho Iwai	2.0	Exxon	2.9	Nova	3.8	Neste	3.3
12	Exxon	2.2	Kanematsu	2.6	Statoil	1.9	TWO	2.7	BP	2.5	Elf	3.2
13	Mobil	2.2	Mobil	2.4	Cargill	1.8	Nova	2.4	Amerada Hess	1.8	Morgan Stanley	3.2
14	Enron	2.1	Mitsui	2.1	Conoco	1.8	Morgan Stanley	2.1	Sun	1.4	Nova	2.9
15	Sun	2.0	C Itoh	2.0	Nova	1.7	Conoco	1.8	Elf	1.3	Sinochem	2.8
16	Kanematsu	1.9	Elf	1.9	CEPSA	1.7	CFP	1.7	Agip	1.2	AIG	2.6
17	URBK	1.9	Morgan Stanley	1.8	Neste	1.7	Mitsubishi	1.5	Marc Rich	1.2	Aerochem	2.2
18	Nichimen	1.8	Enron	1.8	Elf	1.6	Neste	1.4	Vitol	1.2	Marc Rich	1.6
19	Nova	1.8	Kaines	1.6	Mitsui	1.4	Shell Netherlands	1.4	Sucden	1.2	Shell Germany	1.4
20	Gotco	1.7	Kloeckner	1.5	Marc Rich	1.4	Marc Rich	1.3	Kanematsu	1.1	Kanematsu	1.0

Source: Own calculations from Petroleum Argus database

100 *Oil Markets and Prices*

number of participants with 2 per cent or more of total transactions, that is one deal or more on average per day, was about fifteen in 1990–91.

Although very different, the various criteria used here yield similar results. They suggest that the 15-day Brent market involved a significant group of about twenty-five to thirty-five participants and that the number of those who really mattered was about fifteen at the beginning of the 1990s.

The second important feature of recent developments is an increase in the degree of market concentration. Adding up the apparent market shares of the ten top participants in Table 7.5 shows a steady increase in their aggregate share from 49.5 per cent in 1986 to 64.3 per cent in 1991 (see Table 7.7). Another measure of concentration, the inverse Herfindahl index, was also computed and the results are presented in Figure 7.3. This measure expresses market concentration in terms of an equivalent number of equal-sized firms. When this number is close to one, there is monopoly; higher numbers up to five or six point to an oligopolistic structure; and the higher the value of the index beyond these small numbers, the more competitive is the market.

Figure 7.3 shows that the equivalent number of equal-sized firms was thirty-two at the beginning of 1987, and therefore large. But this

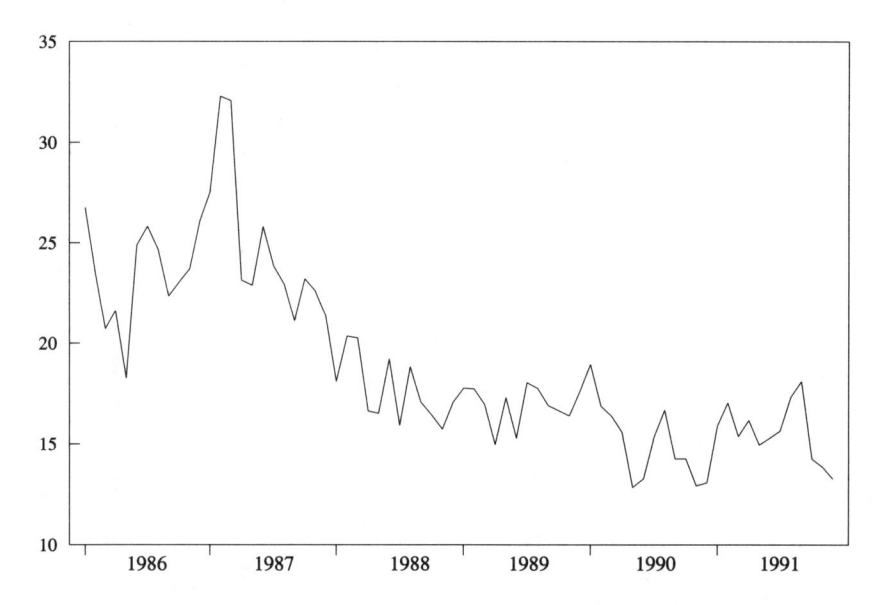

Figure 7.3: Concentration in the 15-day Brent Market by Month. 1986–91. Inverse Herfindahl Index.

number has been declining ever since down to thirteen at end-1991. This index confirms therefore the increase in concentration indicated earlier on by the fall in the total number of active participants (from some 110 in 1986–8 down to sixty-seven in 1991), and the increase in the market share of the top ten (which has reached 64.3 per cent in 1991). It shows, however, that despite this decline the market structure appears to remain reasonably competitive since an index value of thirteen is higher than the small numbers (one to five or six) that are typical of monopolistic or oligopolistic structures. Worries about concentration would become justified if the downward trend were to continue in future years.

(b) Type of Participants

An analysis of participants' behaviour calls for their classification into meaningful groups. The breakdown into categories is not a very neat exercise however because (a) the participants identified are not always independent entities as some of them are partly or wholly owned subsidiaries of companies similarly engaged in Brent trading or part of the same corporate group as other participants; and (b) many participants have characteristics which relate them to more than one category in any conceivable classification.

The grouping attempted here divides participants into six categories: Wall Street, traders, sogo shosha and other Japanese entities, Brent producers, non-Brent North Sea producers, and other oil companies.

Wall Street refiners are the Wall Street investment banks and their offshoots. We have classified Phibro as a Wall Street refiner, although any categorization of Phibro is problematic. On the one hand Phibro is close to being an integrated company. It owns four US refineries through its subsidiary Hill Petroleum[3] (which also trades on the Brent market on its own account). It is also in the process of acquiring upstream interests in Latin America and, through the 'White Nights' project, in Russia, has exported Soviet crude oil (the first foreign company to do so) and holds stakes in the exploration company Anglo-Suisse, its collaborator in the White Nights project. However Phibro's major activity remains oil trading, trading in virtually all futures markets, most crude oil and oil product spot markets, as well as the Brent and Dubai forward markets which would suggest that its classification should be as a trader. However we have classified Phibro as a Wall Street refiner as it is a wholly owned subsidiary of the Wall Street investment bank Salomon Brothers.[4]

Traders are companies that are either solely trading firms, downstream firms engaged in trading and downstream distribution, or oil companies

102 *Oil Markets and Prices*

Figure 7.4: Market Shares of Various Categories of Participants in the 15-day Brent Market by Month. 1986–91. Percentages.

from outside the area where physical supplies of Brent blend generally flow. For example, while Attock does run a refinery in Rawalpindi (Pakistan) its operations in the Brent market are essentially those of a pure trader. Likewise while the Papua New Guinea registered company Petrogulf has extensive exploration interests elsewhere, it has no interests in any sector of the North Sea and owns no refineries and is thus also classified as a trader.

The Japanese trading houses, the sogo shosha, are broken out as a separate category together with the Japanese refining companies Idemitsu, Cosmo Oil and Shell Japan. Brent and non-Brent North Sea producers have self-explanatory labels. Shell International has been included in the category of other oil companies which it dominates. The behaviourial assumption is that Shell UK is the Brent producer while SITCO trades partly to supply downstream operations.

Figure 7.4 shows the shares of total recorded transactions – buys and sells, of these six groups of participants for every month in the period 1986–91. Table 7.6 shows the composition by category of the ten major participants (those with the highest shares in a given year), and Table 7.7 the combined shares of the categories represented among the top ten in the years 1986–91.

According to these data, the Brent market has been dominated since 1987 by Wall Street participants. Their share peaked in late 1988 and 1989 at slightly more than 40 per cent; it decreased however in 1990 and early 1991 but rose again towards the end of that year reaching 38 per cent in December (see Figure 7.4). Furthermore, the share of Wall Street participants in the top ten group was the largest in all the years 1986–91. It almost doubled between 1986 and 1989 from 20.4 per cent to 40 per cent when five participants out of the top ten were Wall Street refiners. There is no doubt that the two most active participants in the

Table 7.6: Top Ten Participants by Categories 1986–91.

	1986	1987	1988	1989	1990	1991
Wall Street	3	3	4	5	3	3
Oil Companies	3	4	4	2	5	5
Sogo Shosha	3	3	2	1	1	-
Traders	1	-	-	2	1	2
	10	10	10	10	10	10

Note: Oil companies, here cover three relevant categories distinguished above: Brent producers, non-Brent North Sea and other oil companies.

Source: Own calculations from Petroleum Argus database.

104 *Oil Markets and Prices*

Table 7.7: Shares of Top Ten Participants by Category in the 15-Day Brent Deals. 1986–91. Per Cent.

	1986	*1987*	*1988*	*1989*	*1990*	*1991*
Wall Street	20.4	23.1	34.7	40.0	33.5	30.7
Oil Companies	12.4	15.8	14.3	6.8	21.1	24.3
Sogo Shosha	13.2	11.5	7.2	3.5	3.1	-
Traders	3.5	-	-	6.8	4.3	9.3
Total	49.5	50.4	56.2	57.1	62.0	64.3

Source: Own calculations from Petroleum Argus database.

15-day Brent market throughout the years 1986–91 were J Aron and Phibro. Their combined shares of the sum of total recorded buys and sells significantly increased from less than 20 per cent in 1986–7 to between 26.4 and 29.1 per cent in 1988–91. The peak of these two leaders in terms of market shares was in 1990, the year when the Wall Street share fell partly as a result of the demise of Drexel and a large drop in the activity of Bear Stearns.

Among traders, the most important is Cargill, generally perceived as the third largest participant in the 15-day Brent market. Most respondents in our interviews believe that Cargill's share is understated by the Petroleum Argus data.

Figure 7.4 and Tables 7.5 to 7.7 reveal two interesting developments. The first is the dramatic rise in the share of Brent producers over a stretch of time beginning in April 1989 when their share was at an untypical low level of 10 per cent and continuing through to February 1991 with a peak of 35 per cent. This development cannot be entirely explained by the co-mingling of Brent and Ninian in August 1990 (this involved a change in the composition of the two categories, Brent and non-Brent producers) since the rise began well before and continued for a while after August 1990. It cannot be explained either by a rise in the share of the three participants – Shell UK, BP and Exxon – who are major Brent producers. Their combined share declined in fact from 6.6 per cent in 1989 to 6.2 per cent in 1990, the period when the rise noted above took place. It is only in 1991 that their combined share increased significantly to 9 per cent but by then the share in transactions of the Brent producers category had peaked. What seems to have happened in 1989–90 is a significant increase in trading activity on the part of a group of European companies (that is continental in this context), particularly CFP (Total), Statoil and Neste whose combined share rose from 4.8 per cent in 1989 to 12.3 per cent in 1990.

Aggregating the three categories – Brent producers, non-Brent producers and other oil companies – into a single category of oil companies, also shows an increase in market share from 30.8 per cent in 1989 to 38.7 per cent and 44.3 per cent in 1990 and 1991 respectively. In these latter two years the number of oil companies in the top ten rose to five, and the market share of oil companies in this top group, although still lower than the Wall Street share, rose very significantly from a low of 6.8 per cent in 1989 to 21.1 per cent in 1990 and 24.3 per cent in 1991.

The second development is the gradual movement of the Japanese out of the Brent market. Their share was high in 1986–7 at about 18 per cent but it steadily fell thereafter to an insignificant 2–3 per cent in 1991. The past importance of the Japanese in the Brent market and their subsequent exit also clearly appears in Tables 7.6 and 7.7. There were three sogo shosha among the top ten participants in 1986 with a 13.2 per cent share of transactions. In 1991 there was none. In 1991 the share of the largest remaining Japanese participant, Kanematsu, was only 1.2 per cent of all recorded buys and sells.

We have also analysed the pattern of trade between the six groups of participants. The analysis compares observed trades between participants in 1987–91 with the numbers that would have been expected if deals between participants were entered into without there being any pattern in trading partners, i.e. if the choice of counterparty was random. The triangular matrix in Table 7.8 shows the percentage deviations of observed from expected trades. The interesting results are:

(a) Wall Street participants trade above expected levels with all oil company groups and traders.
(b) The Brent producers trade less than expected with all groups except Wall Street (+12 per cent). Similarly, the non-Brent North Sea producers trade less than expected with other groups than Wall Street (+14 per cent).
(c) The sogo shosha trade more with participants of their group than expected (+39 per cent), perhaps because of the constraints imposed by time zone differences and of the strength of national bonds.
(d) The pattern for traders shows negative deviations with all oil company groups. They trade within their own group less than under the random norm, and more than expected with Wall Street and the sogo shosha.

106 *Oil Markets and Prices*

Table 7.8: Patterns of Trading Between Various Categories of Participants. Aggregate Deals. 1987–91.

1. *Observed Trades*

		\multicolumn{7}{c}{SELLS}	
		N	P	O	S	T	W	U	Total
	N	122	380	173	233	398	799	177	2282
	P	253	1057	406	391	970	1843	459	5380
	O	144	441	115	331	460	1172	269	2932
BUYS	S	176	382	264	468	679	975	145	3089
	T	346	1097	472	762	1003	2131	481	6292
	W	700	2244	1165	1260	2151	1969	695	10184
	U	157	534	274	176	462	763	648	3014
	Total	1898	6135	2869	3621	6123	9652	2874	33172

2. *Percentage Differences Between Observed and Expected Total Trades*

		\multicolumn{6}{c}{SELLS}
		N	P	O	S	T	W
	N	-7	-13	-13	-4	-5	14
	P		-16	-16	-33	-4	12
BUYS	O			-55	1	-14	30
	S				39	15	-6
	T					-14	9
	W						-13

Note: N = North Sea (but non-Brent) Producers, P = Brent Producers, O = Other Oil Companies, S = Sogo Shosha, T = Traders, W = Wall Street Refiners, U = Unknown

Source: Own calculations from Petroleum Argus database.

These results are in some cases – Wall Street and oil companies – consistent with the perceived role of various groups. Oil companies, to some degree, are hedgers and Wall Street appears to provide the liquidity necessary for their hedging. They are, however, surprising in the case of sogo shosha and traders. As mentioned before, the sogo shosha traded between themselves and with traders much more than expected by the random pattern. They seem to have constituted a small club of their own within the larger market rather than providing on a scale commensurate to their participation the liquidity that speculators supply to hedgers. One would have also thought that the pattern of deviations in dealings between traders and other groups would have been similar to that of Wall Street. It was not. The deviations are negative for transactions between oil companies and traders in marked contrast with the large positive deviations noted in the case of oil companies and Wall Street. There seems to be, therefore, an interesting difference in the economic role played by Wall Street and traders. The former performed a function that enabled hedging to take place; the latter seem to have contributed much less in this respect.

4. Motivations of Traders

In a typically erudite and insightful review of *The Market for North Sea Oil*, Walter Greaves noted the lack of a discussion of the motives of non-tax spinners,[5] and wondered why the traders had not been asked, quoting in support the poet Dannie Abse:

> *While Freud was tracing the river to its source he met Itzig unsteadily riding.*
> *'Where are you going?' he asked that wild eyed rider.*
> *'Don't ask me', said Itzig. 'Ask the bloody horse'.*

As a part of our research we have interviewed most of the leading runners (and riders) from the Brent market stable, and hence seek to fill the omission made in the earlier study. We have then inclined to Itzig's advice rather than that of Virgil:

> *"Equo ne credite" (Don't trust the horse) Aeneid ii 48*

Drawn from these interviews, and from other sources, we now provide a pastiche that represents a typical company in several categories. We also profile the activities of 15-day market brokering companies. In each case the characterization does not apply to any particular company, nor should it necessarily be taken to be representative of all. Before presenting these, we first contrast between hedging and speculative motives for trading.

The common view of hedging tends to concentrate on hedging to reduce exposure to price risks. This view states that the motive of futures or forward trading is to reduce overall price risk by taking up offsetting positions in spot (actuals) and forward or futures. However, there is a far richer taxonomy of hedging operations, mainly due to the path-breaking work of Holbrook Working.[6] We follow Working's approach and taxonomy in the following. The first type of hedging is 'routine hedging'. This requires no views about market developments, and hence has no speculative component. The purpose of such routine hedging is to smooth the time-path of returns, i.e. reduce its variability. As long as the volatility of the basis, i.e. the difference between the price of the commodity being hedged and the futures price being used as a hedge, is less than that of the price of the commodity being hedged, then risk has been reduced.

Another form is 'selective hedging', which does involve a speculative element. Depending on price expectations, the trader will hedge all or only part of their commitments in the actuals market. Working's third type of hedging works through trading the basis itself, hedges are placed to try to profit from changes in the basis. This is known as 'carrying-charge hedging', or 'arbitrage hedging'. The hedger seeks to predict changes in the basis (and not in the absolute levels of prices). This can often be combined with selective hedging. For instance, imagine a producer who expects prices to fall, but also expects the basis to narrow. Optimally they should now have a larger short position in futures or forward markets than the volume of production they are trying to hedge.

Both selective and arbitrage hedging involve taking a view on price developments. Another of Working's classifications involves an even greater speculative element. This is 'anticipatory hedging', where operations in the futures or forward market are not matched by any commitments in the spot market. In the sense that hedging involves opposite positions in both markets, this is not strictly hedging as the positions are not opened simultaneously.

Most hedging operations in the oil market do involve a market view, with the minority of hedging being routine in Working's definition. It is already clear that it is inappropriate to consider the Brent market as being comprised of well-defined hedgers and speculators. Companies can do both simultaneously, and there is also an element of hedging in the operations of the firms that might be expected to constitute the speculators. Speculators take up the opposing positions to the hedgers. It might be thought that the Wall Street companies and other finance houses would make up the speculators. We now provide a characterization of a typical, but fictional, finance house.

The Wall Street refiners are the oil trading offshoot of large Wall Street finance houses. When they first entered oil markets in force in about 1984, their general strategy was to use all global contacts to source crude oil at competitive prices in order to resell it at a profit. Now the strategy is better encapsulated as the use of all global contacts and any or all markets, using any mechanism to make profitable deals. Typically they run their operations as a series of decentralized books, concentrating on particular profit centres. Typical books are physical trading, the Brent-Dubai spread, the Brent-WTI spread, options, outright positions and crack spreads (i.e. the spread between crude oil and oil product prices) and so on. Each book, while having a focus, can however trade in any market.

It is sometimes reported that some Wall Street firms seem to be losing interest in particular oil markets, a conclusion inferred from reduced levels of activity. However, normally reducing activity in one market can often simply mean that the company has put particular focus on the fields they consider to offer the best opportunities at any given time, switching the weight given to each activity as circumstances change. In particular, it is virtually impossible to define what is the usual division between their activities.

The forward Brent market is seen as by far the easiest and quickest way of taking either a long or a short position. The decentralized nature of the books means that the company does not, at least centrally, always know precisely their position at any given time. For example, if a piece of bullish news hits the market and each book starts buying forward Brent cargoes, the company can very quickly acquire a large open position without the decision necessarily having been taken centrally. This also means that a significant proportion of the trade the company does in forward Brent consists of internal offsetting and rejigging of positions between each book.

Drawing from mechanisms devised in other commodity or financial markets, the Wall Street refiners have been increasingly focused towards the market for oil derivatives, such as swaps (for producers, consumers and for refinery margins) and other long-term arrangements. Many see the future in oil of the Wall Street firms far more in these derivatives than in trading *per se*.

The move into derivatives signals a further motive for the activities of Wall Street firms in the Brent market. On their entry into the market their activity was purely speculative, and their role was to take and try to manage the risk the other companies transferred to them through the market. Now an increasing proportion of that risk is being transferred to them, not through open markets such as the Brent forward and futures market, but through the market for oil derivatives, or other integrated risk management packages that they offer to companies, or sometimes countries, without the Wall Street firms' comparative advantage in risk management. Hence, a part of their activity in the forward and futures markets is designed to manage the risk they have acquired elsewhere. Their activity in the Brent market has thus become less speculative, and has a greater element of hedging their overall risk. In offering oil derivatives they are, in the economic sense, speculators in the context of the oil market as a whole. However, in the narrower context of their operations in especially IPE Brent, there is a strong element of hedging. This means that, since forward Brent is seen as the best way of taking positions on movements in prices or in spreads, there is an increasing tendency for Wall Street firms to hedge predominantly on Brent futures, but speculate on forward Brent. Whereas in the past the reason they traded Brent was to earn profits through trading, now a part is in order for them to offset their own risks.

There is also another group of finance houses particularly, but not exclusively, European, many of whom have had a long association with the oil industry. These companies have had a major role in the financial operations of the industry, arranging letters of credit, countertrade deals, pre-financing of ventures, and general capital operations. Many of these companies also offer swaps and other oil derivatives, and as a result have begun to trade purely to hedge their own and their clients' risk, primarily using futures rather than forward Brent. Some have now acquired seats on the IPE and now also act as brokers for IPE trade. The major difference between the evolution of the trading patterns of these companies compared to the Wall Street refiners, is that the reason for their entry into trade was primarily hedging rather than speculation. In particular, they had in general gone straight to futures trading, without trading spot markets or 15-day Brent first.

Among major oil companies an important motive for trading Brent is for cross-hedging purposes. Their operations concern far more than their own production of Brent. It involves other UK and Norwegian production, plus their output from areas where prices tend to be Brent linked, in particular equity production from West Africa. The Brent market provides less basis risk than any other operative crude oil market for these operations. These companies tend to be overall net buyers of crude oil, and so the Brent market (forward and futures) is also used for risk management of oil purchased spot or through term contracts linked to Brent prices. The summation of the above volumes is a large multiple of the companies' Brent production. It follows that there need be no strong relationship, if any, between the level of their activity in the Brent market and the volume of their Brent production.

Some major oil companies also offer risk management packages to other companies, together with swaps, over-the-counter options, and long-term warrants. Like the Wall Street refiners, part of their motivation to trade is to offset that risk. They are then using hedging operations to reduce the risk incurred in other markets. Indeed, it is only the balance of activities that varies from Wall Street firms. They have the same motives in trading, with the addition of a physical production, procurement and supply function, together with the extra tax considerations that the first of these implies. They are certainly not routine hedgers, with their activities combining selective hedging with speculation.

Smaller producers of North Sea crude oil with no interests in the Brent and Ninian systems, use the Brent market for cross-hedging purposes. It was noted in Chapter 7 that these companies are not very active in the Brent forward market; rather, their production is now hedged on the IPE, or through arrangements with finance houses. Refiners also tend to risk manage either with finance houses or on the IPE. In particular, companies receiving oil through term sales find the IPE provides a better and more flexible hedge, mainly because most term prices are based on averages of prices over several trading days, rather than any one trading day.

Both finance houses and oil companies combine degrees of hedging and speculation in their activities. The closest approximation to a pure speculator is the trading company, but even then there can be an element of hedging in their Brent market operations. The typical trading firm is a much smaller operation than a Wall Street refiner, tends to have fewer financial resources and to concentrate on oil trading. However, there are larger trading firms, successful in other areas, that have entered oil trading as an additional activity. The original role of trading companies was to lift oil in one location and sell it on in others, with several producing countries (in particular, Iran and Iraq) having built up strong links with particular trading companies. Hence, Brent trading provided a method of hedging their activities in physical oil, as well as a means of outright speculation. While a company could be a very small operation, there is a minimum critical mass and financial resource necessary for any success, for instance the ability to load large vessels by combining Brent cargoes, and the ability to use operational tolerances.

Hedging and speculation play no role in explaining the motives of brokering firms. Brokers play an important role in the functioning in the forward market, taking a commission to transact trades on behalf of other companies. There are about six companies engaged in forward Brent brokerage, of which the main ones are PVM, Spectron, First National and United Crude. The books of these companies mainly comprise 15-day market trade, with some spot trade in addition. Most companies active in the forward market use a broker to arrange deals, with the exception of Wall Street firms and the major oil companies. The brokers can act as important opinion formers, since their wide contact with their clients puts them possibly in the best position to gauge the market, and to identify the sellers and buyers at any time. In this role the brokers are highly important contacts for the price assessment agencies.

The forward market is probably most transparent in both prices and volumes to the brokers, and they thus play an important role in information dispersion through their clients in the market, and beyond the boundaries of those active in the market through the brokers' conversations with the price assessment agencies. The forward Brent market is a small world, where the participants are very well known to each other. Brokers can then serve a very useful role in providing an anonymous method for information and opinions to be carried around the market. Put simply, potential friction can often be avoided by the use of a broker. This lubricating role is not just confined to dealings between different companies; in companies running more than one trading desk it is not uncommon for an external brokering firm to be called in to act as arbitrators between trading desks in the event of a dispute.

The role of brokers should not be underestimated, indeed they have become an essential part of the functioning of the market. While the market is certainly not transparent to any agent or company not directly involved in trades, the role of the brokers is a major factor in generating a level of internal transparency that is perfectly satisfactory to those that do trade.

Notes
1. R. Mabro et al (1986), op.cit.
2. The first study of forwardness of transactions on the Brent market is R. Bacon (1986) *The Brent Market: An Analysis of Recent Developments*, Working Paper WPM8, Oxford Institute for Energy Studies. The method applied here to measure forwardness, however, is different in some aspects.
3. Now known as Phibro Energy.
4. For an excellent history of this association (and the story of how the Marc Rich trading firm was spawned), see H. Waszkis (1992), *Philipp Brothers: The Rise and Fall of a Trading Giant*, (2nd edition), Metal Bulletin Books.
5. W. Greaves (1986), 'Ask the Horse!', *Petroleum Review*, October 1986.
6. See, in particular, H. Working (1953) 'Futures Trading and Hedging', *American Economic Review*, vol. 43. H. Working (1953), 'Hedging Reconsidered', *Journal of Farm Economics*, vol. 35. and H. Working (1960), 'Speculation on Hedging Markets', *Food Research Institute Studies*, vol. 1.

CHAPTER 8

THE DATED BRENT MARKET

The market for dated Brent is the spot market underlying the forward market, and, as is documented in Chapters 14 and 15, generates the most important price in international oil trade. A dated cargo can arise in two ways. First, an equity producer can, instead of selling their production in the forward market, sell it as a dated cargo, or simply transfer it to one of its own refineries (if it is an integrated company) without any recourse to the market. In both of these cases the cargo is not at any time part of a forward market chain. Alternatively, a dated cargo arises as the last stage of the forward market clearing process. As soon as a nomination has been accepted, or the holder of that nomination has been 5 o'clocked, the cargo becomes dated and cannot be sold again in the forward market. The owner of that cargo, i.e. the last company in a forward market chain, must either use it themselves or sell it on as a dated cargo.

Trade in dated Brent primarily represents trade in cargoes in the period between the close of nominations and the loading of the cargo. There are however other forms of dated Brent transactions. The cargo may, as noted above, not have been traded through the forward market. In such a case the cargo can be sold as soon as its loading dates are known, i.e. as soon as the loading schedule is finalized, which is normally on the 15th of the month preceding the delivery month.

Cargoes that are not put into the forward market can sometimes be sold on a dated basis even further forward. Consider the case of a producer who wishes to load six Brent cargoes at Sullom Voe during a given month, and of these only five have so far been sold in the forward market. Even before the loading schedule is finalized the producer can still feel fairly certain that they will get a loading slot during, say, the first ten days of the loading month, and so sell the cargo on a dated basis with a loading range of the first ten days of the month.

There is also some trade in cargoes after they loaded, or trade in cargoes sold on a delivered basis, particularly into the US Gulf Coast. Dated Brent cargoes may also be traded as part of date swap, which involves companies swapping the loading dates they have entitlement to. Brent may also be swapped for another crude oil at another location. Finally, there is a special category of spot Brent transaction that involves the trading, not of a complete cargo, but of a top-up parcel out of Sullom Voe storage. These parcels can then be loaded onto a tanker that is also taking oil from a forward market chain. The use of such small parcel trades is detailed in Chapter 9, and these trades have not been included in the following analysis, which refers solely to the trade in complete dated cargoes of Brent.

In 1991 over 80 per cent of dated Brent trades were for cargoes yet to load but with a known three-day range, rather than being sales in transit, on a delivered basis, or having longer loading ranges being sold before publication of the loading schedules. Among this 80 per cent, trade takes place on average about thirteen days before the first day of the loading range. Table 8.1 shows the frequency distribution of trades in 1991 by days to the first day in the range.

Table 8.1: Frequency of Dated Brent Deals By Days to Loading.

Days to Loading	Per Cent
21 or more	2.7
17 to 20	10.0
14 to 16	37.4
10 to 13	30.4
5 to 9	14.3
less than 5	5.2

Source: Own calculations from Petroleum Argus database.

The logistics of chartering tankers and getting them to Sullom Voe, together with the need for refiners to have their crude slate planned somewhat in advance, means that, as shown in Table 8.1, very few trades take place in the five days immediately before loading. Those that do have a strong element of being distressed sales.

The nomination procedure detailed in Chapter 4 gives fifteen clear days before the first day of a loading range. Nominations close at 5 p.m. sixteen days before that first loading date. The dated deals in Table 8.1 shown to have taken place more than sixteen days in advance are then either nominations that have been accepted well before the deadline, or sales made on a dated basis outside the forward market. Theoretically the latter could take place as much as forty-five days in advance, for example if a loading schedule is finalized on 15 July, a producer given a loading slot for 29–31 August could sell it on a dated basis immediately. However, in 1991 no recorded dated trade was carried out more than thirty days in advance of loading.

Chains of transactions for the same dated cargo can arise. From the deals reported in 1991 in the Petroleum Argus database, the longest such 'wet' chains we can construct for the same cargo contain three transactions. We believe that it is rare for longer wet chains to form. A comparison of reported deals with cargo departures from Sullom Voe, which is reported below, suggests that about one in eight cargoes traded on a dated basis has a wet chain of transactions attached.

The total number of dated Brent trades (except for trade in small parcels) reported to Petroleum Argus is shown by month from 1986 to 1991 in Figure 8.1. By the end of 1991 the level of reported trade had risen above two per trading day, and reported trade was significantly higher in 1992 than in previous years. Two months are shown in Figure 8.1 to have had abnormally low levels of trade, i.e. January 1988 and May 1989. In the former case one trader took possession of all but one of the cargoes in the month, and this is detailed in Chapter 9. The low level of trade in May 1989 was a result of the Cormorant Alpha explosion the previous month, as described in Chapter 2, which led to the shut-down of the system and meant that very few cargoes were loaded.

The major sellers and buyers of dated Brent are shown in Table 8.2, by year since 1986. The sellers of dated Brent are dominated by companies that are not equity producers. Either Phibro or J Aron has been the largest seller in each year since 1986. In 1991 none of the first

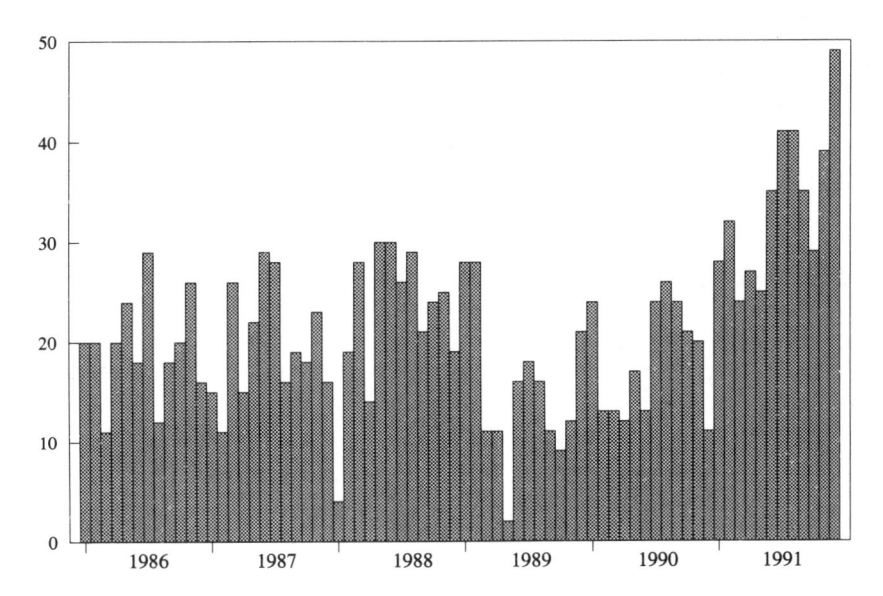

Figure 8.1: Number of Dated Brent Cargoes Traded By Month. 1986–91.

three in the list of the largest sellers were Brent producers, in 1988 none of the first four, and in 1987 none of the first six. In all years, companies without primary availabilities of Brent have made more than 50 per cent of all dated Brent sales; indeed in 1989 Phibro and J Aron alone accounted for 51.7 per cent.

All of these companies have sold on cargoes that they have acquired in the forward market. For example, in 1991 J Aron, Cargill and Phibro made 37.1 per cent of all sales of dated Brent, and only 12.7 per cent of buys. Thus, nearly one in four of all Brent chains in 1991 resulted in one of these companies being at the end of the chain. J Aron and Cargill own no refineries. Phibro owns four US refineries, but US import statistics report no purchases of UK crude oil in 1991 by these refineries. Hence the purchases of dated Brent by these companies must have been sold on to other companies, i.e. there has been a 'wet' chain of dated Brent cargoes. We return to a major reason for this intermediary trade below in the discussion of how dated Brent is priced. We have identified forty-six companies who made reported sales of dated Brent during 1991. Of these, eighteen were Brent producers, and all forty-six had made trades in the forward market during 1991.

Other than purchases of dated Brent for intermediary purposes, the main consistent buyers of dated Brent shown in Table 8.2 are major oil companies, in particular Shell, Exxon and Texaco. The German, Canadian and UK components of Shell have made most of Shell's purchases, but since 1986 trades have also been made by Shell France, Japan, Netherlands, Sweden, and Switzerland, as well as by Shell International.

In all, sixty-two companies were identified that had made reported purchases of dated Brent over the course of 1991. Of these, thirty-nine were also active in the forward Brent market. Among the twenty-three companies that made dated purchases but no forward trades, eleven are US refiners and three Canadian refiners. Among the others are refineries in Poland, Czechoslovakia, Austria and Ireland. Out of these twenty-three companies, sixteen had made recorded trades in the forward market before 1991, and hence, while exiting forward trading and its supply functions, still used the dated Brent market as a source of supply.

There has been a significant shift in the way prices are formed for dated Brent since 1986. This is shown in Table 8.3 which shows the proportion of deals priced by various methods.

Before 1988 most trades were made on an outright basis, i.e. the parties agreed a price for the cargo in dollars and cents per barrel. However, since 1988 outright trade has declined to virtually nothing in 1991. By 1991, 99.8 per cent of dated Brent deals were done as a

Table 8.2: Dated Brent. Ten Top Participants. Rank and Market Shares. 1986–91. Per Cent.

Main Sellers of Dated Brent

Rank	1986		1987		1988		1989		1990		1991	
1	Phibro	11.4	J Aron	11.4	Phibro	13.4	Phibro	26.4	Phibro	32.6	J Aron	14.6
2	Shell UK	10.0	Phibro	10.0	J Aron	12.9	J Aron	17.8	Cargill	19.1	Cargill	10.8
3	J Aron	6.4	Kanematsu	6.4	Kanematsu	9.5	Shell Internat.	7.8	Shell UK	6.2	Phibro	10.4
4	Drexel	5.5	Dreyfus	5.5	Dreyfus	6.9	Shell UK	4.5	J Aron	5.1	Elf	9.0
5	Exxon	4.6	TWO	4.6	Shell UK	5.2	Bear Stearns	4.5	Chevron	4.5	Shell Internat.	6.1
6	Kanematsu	4.6	Kaines	4.6	Chevron	4.3	Amerada Hess	3.7	Shell Internat.	3.9	Chevron	6.1
7	Mitsubishi	4.1	Shell UK	4.1	Marimpex	4.3	BP	3.7	Kanematsu	2.8	BP	5.2
8	OPA	4.1	Drexel	4.1	TWO	3.9	Cargill	3.7	Exxon	2.8	Shell UK	4.7
9	Statoil	3.7	Chevron	3.7	Shell Internat.	3.0	Mitsubishi	3.3	Amerada Hess	2.8	Marc Rich	2.8
10	Shell Internat.	3.2	Exxon	3.2	BP	3.0	Morgan Stanley	2.2	Morgan Stanley	2.8	Neste	2.8

Main Buyers of Dated Brent

Rank	1986		1987		1988		1989		1990		1991	
1	Exxon	7.7	CFP	7.7	J Aron	14.7	Phibro	9.1	Phibro	9.7	Shell Germany	10.3
2	Texaco	6.7	Texaco	6.7	CFP	7.3	Shell Germany	8.6	J Aron	9.1	Shell UK	7.1
3	Phibro	6.2	Exxon	6.2	Phibro	6.9	Shell Canada	8.2	Shell Canada	7.3	Shell Canada	7.1
4	Shell Germany	6.2	Mobil	6.2	Shell Germany	6.0	J Aron	8.2	Shell Germany	6.1	Texaco	7.1
5	CFP	5.3	J Aron	5.3	Texaco	5.5	Texaco	7.0	Exxon	5.5	J Aron	5.4
6	Drexel	4.3	Phibro	4.3	Exxon	5.0	Exxon	6.6	Texaco	5.5	Exxon	5.4
7	Sun	4.3	Sun	4.3	Cumberland F'm	5.0	Diamond S'rock	4.8	Shell UK	4.8	Cargill	4.3
8	BP	3.8	Shell Canada	3.8	Shell UK	3.7	Shell UK	4.1	Morgan Stanley	3.6	Shell Internat.	3.8
9	Sohio	3.8	Shell Internat.	3.8	Ultramar	3.7	Bear Stearns	4.1	Shell Internat.	3.0	Phibro	3.8
10	Shell UK	3.3	Conoco	3.3	BP	3.2	CFP	3.7	Cargill	3.0	Chevron	3.2

Source: Own calculations from Petroleum Argus database.

Table 8.3: Pricing Basis of Dated Brent Deals. 1986–91. Percentage of Total Deals.

	1986	1987	1988	1989	1990	1991
Outright Price	75.6	62.2	13.4	2.7	4.6	0.2
Differential Price to :						
Forward Brent	19.7	33.6	77.3	78.6	78.8	78.2
Dated Quotations	2.1	1.2	1.1	3.9	5.5	7.5
Other North Sea	1.7	1.7	1.5	2.1	0.9	1.3
WTI	0.4	1.3	6.7	12.6	10.1	12.5
Other	0.4	-	-	-	-	0.2

Source: Own calculations from Petroleum Argus database.

differential to another crude oil price. As is documented in Chapter 14, this trend has occurred throughout the world, not just in the market for dated Brent, as crude oil trade has moved to primarily a trade of differentials in prices, rather than trades in absolute prices.

While dated Brent is referred to as the spot market for Brent, transactions are not really in the strict sense spot. Dated Brent deals do have an element of forwardness in them, about thirteen days on average as noted above. There is then still some price risk in the period from the time when a deal is made, and when transfer of the physical oil occurs.

Most differentially priced deals for spot crude oil (other than trigger deals which are explained below) are done on the basis of assessed prices on or soon after the loading date, or an average of prices on days around the loading date. If refiners wish to guarantee that they will not pay above market prices at time of loading then the formula price removes their risk. In effect they are insuring against movements in the Brent price without having to incur the minor risk of default and the major risk of being five o'clocked that entering the Brent market explicitly would entail; or the transactions costs involved in IPE trade, together with the basis risk of differential movements between dated Brent and forward or futures Brent. A formula price deal made on the basis of prices a few days after the bill of lading also insures NW European refiners against market movements between loading and the arrival of the cargo at the refinery gate. An even later pricing date would give the refiner protection against crude oil price changes right up to the point of sale of the refined products derived from the cargo.

A very common variant of formula pricing is trigger pricing. A trigger mechanism in the contract allows the buyer or seller to activate the pricing formula at a time of their choosing. In most North Sea deals, but by no means all, it tends to be the buyer that is given the trigger.

A trigger price is then a formula related deal with a speculative element. Triggers have been sold by, in particular, Phibro, J Aron, Shell and BP. Trigger deals tend to be tailor made according to the individual requirements of the buyer or seller. There are then a multiplicity of possible forms for the deal; for example, for a cargo loading in, say, two weeks the trigger may give the buyer the right to choose a two or three-day window over those two weeks, or perhaps a longer period, over which dated Brent prices are to be averaged and used in the formula. Alternatively the deal may be that the seller will deliver a cargo at a fixed time after the trigger is activated. The trigger looks a little like a call option, but the difference is that the buyer is committed to buying a cargo and only has discretion over the timing for the determination of the price of the deal.

As Table 8.3 showed, the dominant marker used in formula prices for dated Brent is forward Brent. Most dated Brent deals are done as differentials to the price of Brent for a forward delivery month as assessed by a price reporting agency agreed upon by the parties to a deal. Thus the forward Brent market sets the level of prices, while the dated Brent market sets the relative position of dated Brent prices compared to forward prices. A significant number of deals are also done as a differential to the assessed price of dated Brent, or to the assessed prices of other North Sea grades.

One strong feature of Table 8.3 is the increase in the number of deals done as a differential to WTI, the key US marker crude oil. These deals represent sales to US refiners, with the bulk involving intermediary companies. Of dated Brent cargoes priced against WTI in 1991, 80 per cent were sold by Phibro, Cargill, J Aron and Morgan Stanley. A further 14 per cent were deals between independent US refiners with a US transfer point for the oil.

Comparing data on reported dated Brent deals with departures of cargoes from Sullom Voe can provide an estimate of what proportion of Brent cargoes are traded on a dated basis. Over the course of 1991 421 cargoes of crude oil left Sullom Voe. Some of these contained more than one standard sized (plus or minus loading tolerance) Brent parcel, and allowing for this the equivalent of 516 standard cargoes were loaded. Other than date swaps, a total of 324 deals were reported for three-day loading ranges for dated Brent due to load in 1991. Piecing together possible wet chains gives thirty-one chains of two transactions and four of three transactions. Hence the data implies that trades were made for 285 distinct cargoes, or 55 per cent of the total. An additional sixty-two deals were made for loading ranges greater than three days, or on a delivered basis, some, if not most, may have been cargoes that are also included among the 285 traded as a three-day range. Assuming that these sixty-two were separate cargoes generates an estimate that 67 per cent of all cargoes leaving Sullom Voe either had been or would be traded on a dated basis. The estimated range of 55 to 67 per cent of course only reflects reported deals, and would tend to be an underestimate for this reason. However, it is clear from this exercise that the supply function of the dated Brent market is greater than the forward Brent market, as in the majority of cases the company at the end of a forward market chain is not the eventual user of the crude oil.

CHAPTER 9

BEHAVIOUR, PERFORMANCE AND FUTURE

1. Introduction

This chapter draws together several strands that impact on the functioning, behaviour and performance of the Brent market, and the future of that market. The next section considers the implications of the loading tolerance procedures. Squeezes of the market, of various types, are considered in Section 3; and in Section 4 we detail litigations and default that have arisen from trading in the market. The final section is forward looking, and attempts to provide possible scenarios of the future of the Brent market in the light of declines in its physical base in future years. We suggest that while there will be a sufficient physical base for the continuation of a dominant North Sea forward market, that market may not be Brent.

2. The Use of the Lifting Tolerance

Section 1 (h) of the Shell General Conditions for the sale of Brent blend defines a cargo of Brent blend as '500 thousand barrels (the "nominal volume") plus or minus five per cent in buyers' operational tolerance of Brent blend crude oil'. Thus the lifter of a Brent cargo out of the forward market chains has the choice of loading any volume between 475 thousand and 525 thousand barrels, the flexibility being defined as operational tolerance.

Operational tolerance is widespread throughout the oil industry. There is for example a 5 per cent tolerance for loadings of equity production of Dubai Fateh, and the tolerance for Alaska North Slope loadings is 15 per cent (in the ANS case this tolerance is at the seller's rather than the buyer's discretion). However in the Brent market operational reasons for the tolerance compete with strong trading motives for utilizing the tolerance provisions. The 5 per cent loading tolerance gives rise to what is known as the tolerance game.[1]

Before explaining how the tolerance game works we consider how prevalent is the use of tolerance. Between the start of 1991 and the end of 1992, 886 separate liftings of Brent blend took place at Sullom Voe.

Very few of these liftings were for amounts that were close multiples of 500 thousand barrels, the vast majority of cargoes passing through the chains loaded at one end or the other of the tolerance range.

Figure 9.1 shows the distribution of cargo sizes lifted in 1991 and 1992 for cargoes of less than 90 thousand tonnes, represented in thousand tonne intervals. The information on individual cargo departures from Sullom Voe comes from the data produced by the Ports and Harbours Authority of the Shetland Islands Council, which was discussed in Chapter 3. We present the data in tonnes as tabulated by the Shetland Island Council. The standard cargo size or nominal volume roughly equates to about 66,300 tonnes, utilization of the minimum loading size equates to just under 63 thousand tonnes, and the maximum cargo size is just below 70 thousand tonnes.

Cargo sizes greater than 70 thousand tonnes shown in Figure 9.1 either represent internally transferred cargoes which, as they have not been through the chains are not subject to any volume restrictions, or are cargoes which have been lifted through the chains and then have had 'top-up' parcels for smaller amounts of oil added to them. While the amount lifted through any one chain must lie between 475 thousand and 525 thousand barrels, there is no requirement that only oil lifted through the chains be loaded on any given tanker.

It is clear from Figure 9.1 that few cargoes are lifted at or within 2 per cent either side of the nominal volume of a cargo, i.e. between about 65 thousand and 67,500 tonnes. The vast majority of cargoes are lifted at or close to the minimum or maximum values. Therefore, for whatever motivation, the tolerance provisions can be said to be almost always utilized. The apparent predominance of cargoes loaded at the maximum as opposed to the minimum may be a little misleading. For reasons explained below, many of the cargoes lifted at, or close to, the maximum are likely to contain the minimum amount lifted out of the chains together with a separate top-up parcel obtained in another deal outside of the 15-day market.

It is common (especially for tankers heading for US Gulf coast locations) to load oil from more than one Brent chain onto the same tanker.[2] As the cargoes are distinct as far as the chains are concerned, each loading carries full tolerance. Thus, for example, if two cargoes are to be loaded onto the same tanker the buyer has the discretion to load any amount between 950 thousand and 1,050 thousand barrels. Figure 9.2 shows the distribution of the larger cargo sizes of over 90 thousand tonnes (shown in 5 thousand tonne intervals) loaded at Sullom Voe in 1991 and 1992.

Lifting two cargoes at the nominal volume, or alternatively maximizing one and minimizing the other, equates to lifting about 132 thousand

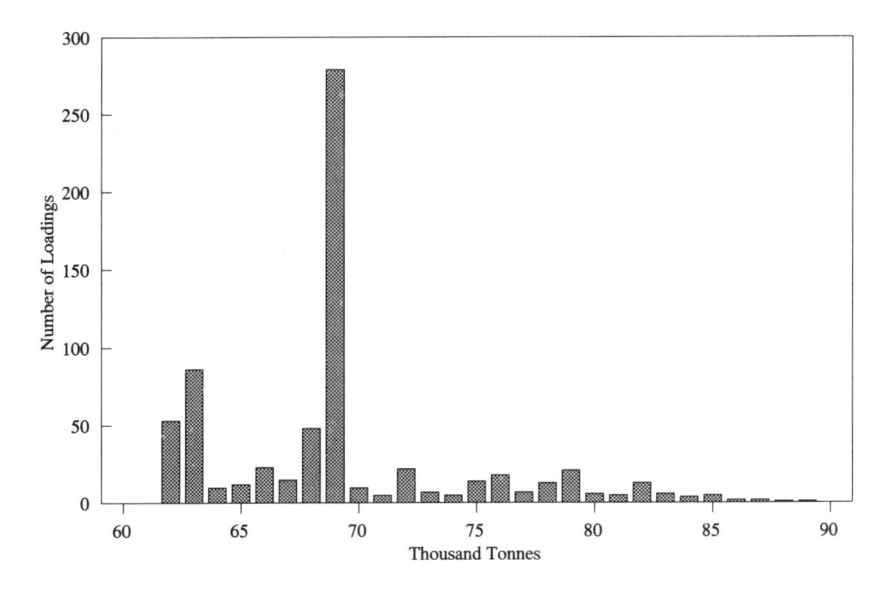

Figure 9.1: Frequency of Loadings of Standard Cargoes at Sullom Voe by Tonnage. Aggregate 1991 and 1992.

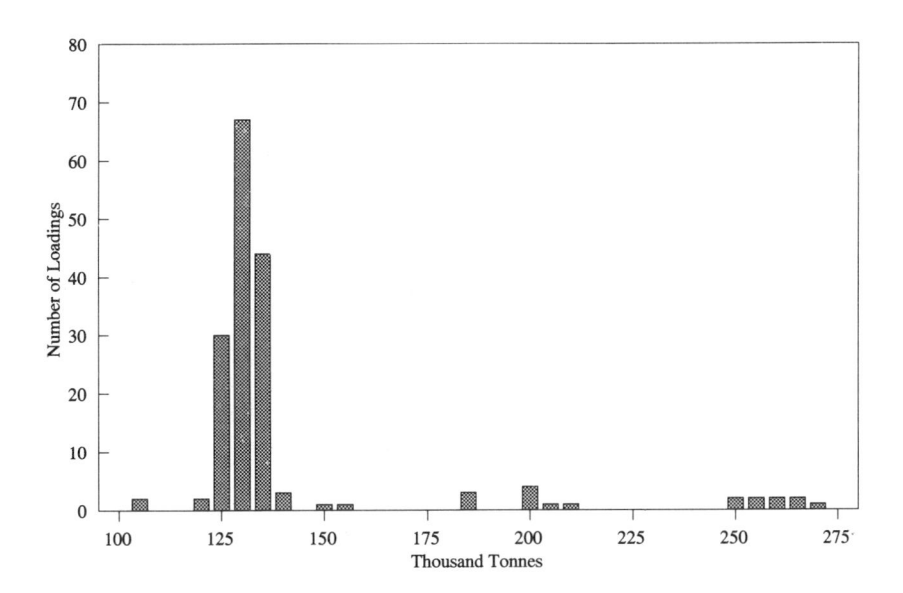

Figure 9.2: Frequency of Loadings of Large Cargoes at Sullom Voe by Tonnage. Aggregate 1991 and 1992.

tonnes. Figure 9.2 shows a distribution of double cargo sizes along the full scale between both being minimized and both being maximized. Further up the scale we also see the full utilization of the tolerance provisions for the relatively small number of triple and quadruple size cargoes (seven and eight respectively). In summary, there is no doubt that the use of the tolerance provisions is the norm rather than the exception, and it is relatively rare for cargoes to be lifted close to the nominal volumes. This then raises the question as to why lifters are usually motivated to invoke the tolerance clause.

The term 'operational tolerance' in the Shell General Terms and Conditions does not refer to operational flexibility due to the mechanics of actually loading the oil onto a tanker. Just as a motorist at a petrol pump can always get very close to the volume of petrol they desire, so can the storage and loading controllers at Sullom Voe in putting oil onto a tanker. The genuine operational tolerance from this source is closer to one-tenth of 1 per cent, not 5 full per cent. Instead, the original concept of operational tolerance has more to do with freight economics, the desire to minimize empty space on a tanker and so to minimize the per barrel cost of transport for a given tanker charter. However, the major motivation for use of tolerance is now more financial than practical, and arises from the structure of the chains themselves.

The tolerance game was first played on a large scale by the Wall Street refiners, in particular J Aron, in 1986 and has gradually become more and more widely played. The financial gains and losses involved are not negligible. To take one example, imagine a trader who has carried out six buys at prices at 50 cent increments starting from the lowest buy at $20 per barrel. The trader also has six sells at exactly the same prices. Based on standard parcel sizes the trader has therefore broken even with six buys at an average of $21.25 and six sells at an average of $21.25, and would indeed break even if they managed to book out all of their deals. The best possible case for the trader arises when, having failed to achieve any book-outs, their three highest priced buys and lowest priced sells are matched in chains that are minimized with respect to volume, and their three highest priced sells and lowest priced buys are matched in chains that are maximized. Thus the minimized chains contain an average buy price of $22 per barrel and an average sell price of $20.50, and vice versa for the maximized chains.

In this case the difference between the value of the trader's buys and sells is given by 3 x $1.50 x 50,000 = $225,000. If the minimized chains had been maximized and vice versa the trader would have made a loss of $225,000. The range between the best and worst outcomes is therefore equivalent to a margin of no less than 15 cents on each of

Table 9.1: Prices of Outright 15-Day and Dated Brent Deals by Delivery Months. 1988–91. US Dollars per Barrel.

		Mean Price	Min Price	Max Price	Range	Standard Deviation	Price of Dated Brent
Jan	88	18.00	15.52	19.38	3.86	0.38	16.84
Feb		16.60	14.43	18.45	4.02	1.03	15.67
Mar		16.42	13.95	18.09	4.14	0.53	14.75
Apr		15.74	14.11	17.00	2.89	0.74	16.57
May		15.18	14.27	17.50	3.23	0.65	16.33
Jun		16.68	14.46	17.59	3.13	0.67	15.53
Jul		16.51	13.90	17.57	3.67	0.51	14.91
Aug		15.58	13.81	17.50	3.69	0.75	14.88
Sep		14.91	13.77	16.62	2.85	0.55	13.16
Oct		14.58	11.47	15.91	4.44	0.74	12.42
Nov		13.37	11.34	15.26	3.92	0.77	12.95
Dec		12.61	11.35	13.98	2.63	0.67	15.33
Jan	89	13.36	11.73	15.31	3.58	0.91	17.11
Feb		14.48	12.05	17.73	5.68	0.91	16.91
Mar		16.12	12.56	17.18	4.62	0.68	18.74
Apr		16.43	15.25	19.33	4.08	0.75	20.21
May		17.95	15.90	21.00	5.10	1.13	18.68
Jun		18.65	15.74	20.32	4.58	1.07	17.60
Jul		17.31	16.35	19.15	2.80	0.46	17.54
Aug		17.11	16.03	18.16	2.13	0.66	16.75
Sep		17.00	15.95	17.65	1.70	0.40	17.80
Oct		17.03	16.10	18.30	2.20	0.39	18.91
Nov		17.89	16.90	19.59	2.69	0.49	18.70
Dec		18.53	17.13	19.12	1.99	0.45	19.92
Jan	90	18.71	17.90	20.40	2.50	0.52	21.30
Feb		19.69	15.34	22.20	6.86	0.98	19.78
Mar		19.75	18.70	21.35	2.45	0.48	18.33
Apr		19.17	17.87	19.79	1.92	0.40	16.42
May		18.48	15.70	19.50	3.80	0.53	16.33
Jun		17.30	16.22	18.80	2.58	0.63	15.08
Jul		16.86	15.25	18.74	3.49	0.82	17.22
Aug		16.37	13.60	18.75	5.15	0.72	27.44
Sep		18.98	16.02	27.10	11.08	2.38	35.18
Oct		25.71	16.47	40.00	23.53	3.44	35.95
Nov		30.96	19.52	40.30	20.78	4.55	33.03
Dec		33.65	20.65	38.60	17.95	2.75	28.13

Source: Own calculations from Petroleum Argus database and *Platt's Oilgram Price Report*, various issues.

126   Oil Markets and Prices

Table 9.1: Prices of Outright 15-Day and Dated Brent Deals by Delivery Months. 1988–91. US Dollars per Barrel. (continued)

		Mean Price	Min Price	Max Price	Range	Standard Deviation	Price of Dated Brent
Jan	91	30.04	25.60	36.70	11.10	2.62	23.47
Feb		26.89	18.97	34.30	15.33	2.37	19.45
Mar		23.27	17.10	33.00	15.90	4.15	19.04
Apr		18.72	16.15	28.50	12.35	1.79	19.14
May		18.42	15.95	27.50	11.55	1.24	19.16
Jun		19.14	16.95	20.30	3.35	0.68	18.13
Jul		18.99	17.80	20.22	2.42	0.61	19.46
Aug		18.99	18.12	20.26	2.14	0.55	19.77
Sep		19.56	18.33	20.46	2.13	0.33	20.55
Oct		20.11	19.24	21.00	1.76	0.35	22.24
Nov		21.13	19.60	22.93	3.33	0.83	21.03
Dec		21.82	19.70	23.61	6.91	0.72	18.30

Source: Own calculations from Petroleum Argus database and *Platt's Oilgram Price Report*, various issues.

their six buy/sell pairings.

Thus in a market where trade in a given delivery month has moved over a $2.50 price range, the tolerance game can be thought of as being worth at maximum 15 cents a barrel even to market players with a balanced portfolio whose average buy price equalled their average sell price. However, as Table 9.1 shows, the market often trades specific delivery months over a greater price range than this over the course of trading of cargoes for that month. In Table 9.1 we show the lowest and highest recorded price for outright deals reported to Petroleum Argus made for each delivery month from January 1988 to December 1991 over the course of its trading, the mean price for recorded deals done, and the range and standard deviation of the prices of recorded deals done. For cargoes in the delivery months of September 1990 through to May 1991 it was not unusual for market players to have deals with a range of greater than $10 in their portfolio. Table 9.1 also shows the average assessed price of dated Brent over the course of the delivery month.

To play the tolerance game a participant needs to end up at the end of the chain. The logic of the procedure is as implied above – if the average buy price is less than the average sell price (including the imputed price of dated Brent as one deal), then the chain should be maximized to collect up the profit on a greater volume of oil. Likewise, if the average sell price is less than the average buy price then the agent at the end of the chain has the incentive to minimize the cargo.

The player of the tolerance game does not always have to physically lift the oil, it is not uncommon for dated cargoes to be sold on the condition that the chain is maximized or minimized. For instance a player with a strong incentive to see a particular chain maximized, (i.e. they have a series of deals in the chain for which the average buy price is less than the average sell price), can accept a nomination for the cargo and then sell the cargo on with the condition that the final lifter will load as close to 525 thousand barrels as possible.

The tolerance game also gives a strong incentive to try to affect the build-up of a chain. For instance imagine that company A, among other deals, has sold a forward cargo to B and holds a buy from company C in their portfolio, and that A also knows that B has a sale to C. If A receives a nomination from another player and would like their sale to B and buy from C to be in the same chain, they will certainly ask B who they would pass the nomination on to if A were to pass it on to them. If B says anyone other than C, then A will seek other routes to getting the deals stacked in the way they wish. Companies will not, of course, always succeed in stacking deals in the way they want. However, the playing of the tolerance game does mean that companies are not indifferent to the way that chains build up, as they would be if all trades were settled on the basis of the nominal cargo volume of 500 thousand barrels.

The tolerance game has important implications for the functioning of the chains. Nobody intending to play the game in a given chain has any motivation to book out any deals that might find their way into that chain. Book-outs are settled assuming a standard cargo size, while the tolerance game works by keeping deals in the chain. The use of tolerance for trading rather than freight motivations has been growing and has led to a reduction in the proportion of deals booked out. There can be no exact figures for this, but our best estimate is that a participant with a balanced portfolio of deals in 1990 *seeking* to book out their deals would be successful in arranging a book-out in about 90 per cent of cases. In 1991 this figure may have fallen to about 70 per cent.

The failure of tolerance game players to book out has two main effects on the smaller participants. By leaving their cargoes in the pool of deals to which nominations can be passed, because of the lack of book-outs, it leaves open the possibility of them being '5 o'clocked' and having to lift the cargo. While the refusal of other players to book out may signal their intention to play the tolerance game and accept a nomination, some residual risk still remains for the other players. Secondly, it means that the actual size of the gains and losses made in

128   *Oil Markets and Prices*

the chain are unknown until the time of loading, i.e. when the size of cargo that passes through the chain becomes known. This can reduce the effectiveness of the forward market for hedging purposes since hedging strategies have little choice but to assume a standard cargo size, as it is impossible to guess whether a particular deal will find itself in a chain where the cargo will be maximized or minimized.

Freight economics will normally lead to an incentive to maximize cargoes. In cases where the trading motivation implies that the lifter of the oil should minimize but freight economics implies the reverse, there is a compromise solution. The tolerance game opens up a trade in small parcels of Brent for loading onto tankers that also collect oil out of the chains. The lifter can minimize the cargo as far as the chain is concerned so that the trades in the chain are settled on the basis of 475 thousand barrels, but still benefit from freight economics by loading 50 thousand barrels or more onto the same tanker, having made a deal with an equity producer for the partial cargo. Hence some of the cargoes which appeared to have been maximized in Figure 9.1 may in fact have been minimized and then had a top-up parcel added.

There are cases in which a player with a strong incentive to see a chain maximized or minimized can achieve this without physically lifting the oil. We have already noted that they could accept a nomination and then sell the cargo on a dated basis as either a maximized or a minimized cargo. However there are other cases.

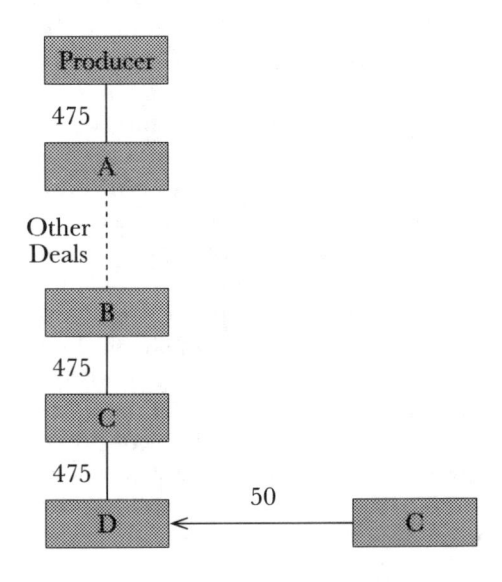

Consider the chain shown in the diagram below. Company D (the end of the chain) intends to lift 525 thousand barrels, perhaps on freight economics grounds. However, imagine that the stacking of company C's deals in this chain imply that C has a strong incentive to see the chain minimized (perhaps C expected the nomination to come back to them so that they could minimize the chain, but D was 5 o'clocked).

To ensure that only 475 thousand barrels are used to settle trades in the chain, C manages to sell D a top-up parcel of 50 thousand barrels, with the condition that D minimizes the chain. This top-up must either be equity crude that C was going to load in the appropriate loading window (if C is an equity producer), or be the resale of a top-up parcel that C had already bought and was scheduled to load in the same window as D's cargo. A further source of trade in 50 thousand barrel parcels has been created, and C has managed to get the chain minimized.

The second case, as shown in the following diagram, is more difficult, but it has been achieved. Imagine that in the case above, C has been unable to sell D a top-up and D intends to maximize the cargo. D informs C that their deal is for 500 thousand plus the tolerance. To meet this C, in addition to the chain, utilizes an existing deal with another agent, X, for a 50 thousand barrel parcel scheduled to load in the same window as D's cargo, allowing C to pass a nomination of 500 thousand minus the tolerance back up the chain. D loads 525 thousand barrels but only 475 thousand barrels has ultimately come from the chain, regardless of D's intention to maximize the whole chain.

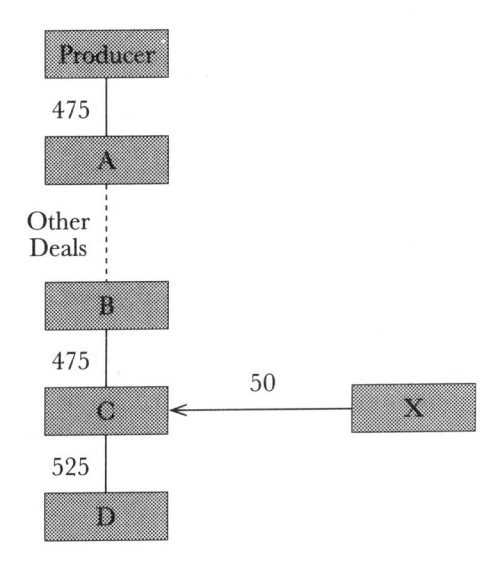

Pressure from the smaller Brent market participants led to Exxon, concerned with growing illiquidity due to a fall in the number of Brent market participants, coming out in opposition to the tolerance game in mid-1989 (Morgan Stanley, ICI and Neste have also been associated with attempts to change the procedures). Exxon proposed that deviations from the standard cargo size should be priced at an assessment of Dated Brent prices at time of loading, and that intermediate deals in a chain should be priced as if the standard cargo size had been lifted. The proposals failed to find support among the larger Brent participants and the use of the tolerance provisions for trading motives has grown considerably since 1989. Most of the companies opposed to the current use of tolerance seem to regard it as an unavoidable evil.

3. Squeezes of the Brent Market

Squeezes have been observed in virtually all commodity markets at some time, and have a long history. To mention only the more famous instances, there was the Secretan affair of the 1880s, the Cargill squeeze of wheat markets in 1963, the Hunt brothers' of silver in 1979 and 1980, and Sumitomo's of copper in 1991. There have also been squeezes in the Brent market at various times over the last few years. Indeed, as is detailed below, in the period we consider (from July 1987 to June 1992) several delivery months have been squeezed, including four in which the degree was particularly severe.

In this section we consider how squeezes arise, and in particular what motivates those undertaken deliberately. We note there is a taxonomy depending on the motivations of market players and on market conditions. We also find that despite the observed regularity of squeezes, it is not rational behaviour for any trader other than a fly-by-night company (playing the market as a one shot game rather than a repeated game) to squeeze the Brent market in a concerted fashion, and it will never be in the interests of any equity producer to do so (indeed it would be absolutely disastrous for the broader interests of the company as a whole). Yet even after the disappearance of some of the fringe players in the market since 1986, some of the most important companies (but never the equity producers) have attempted squeezes, often repeatedly. The squeeze is then an interesting phenomenon: it will rarely work, can easily be squashed by other players, and can cause serious longer-term damage to a firm's reputation and credibility as well as to the reputation of the Brent market itself. There is a parallel to killing the goose that lays the golden egg; yet squeezes can and do occur.

There is a problem in defining exactly what constitutes a squeeze in either legal or economic terms.[3] It is particularly difficult to provide a definition that does not in some way carry the imputation of some (unobservable) intention on the part of at least one party involved. To get around this problem we define a squeeze specifically in the context of the Brent market in terms of its effect on prices, thus removing the need to distinguish between 'deliberate' and 'accidental' squeezing. The definition we use, and whose rationale is explained below, is that a squeeze can be observed in the Brent market when the price of cargoes for the first forward delivery month traded rises above both the price of dated Brent and the price of second month forward cargoes. However, as is explained below, there are other circumstances apart from a squeeze that can produce this particular alignment of prices.

It is in practical terms almost impossible to squeeze the wet market for any specific North Sea grade, including dated Brent, since they have close and available substitutes. Any attempt to corner the market in dated Brent and force its price up above other grades will meet with very limited success, as refiners will simply switch to other North Sea grades or to imports. The wet cargo North Sea oil market as a whole will not be susceptible to squeezes simply because oil is too bulky and expensive a commodity to corner the entire market, and because there is too much oil available for the squeeze to work.

However squeezes can work in the oil market in one of two ways. The first is to utilize a bottleneck or to create one. For example the market for domestic US grades and the light sweet crude oil contract on the New York Mercantile Exchange can be (and have been) squeezed simply by booking up pipeline space or storage space in advance at key points such as Cushing Oklahoma. Alternatively if there is dislocation due to supply problems, for instance adverse weather leading to regionalizations of the market, it can become very easy to operate a squeeze. These methods have no direct parallel in the Brent market; for example it would be far too clumsy and expensive to book up all available tanker fixtures. The second method is to squeeze either a paper contract, or a market for forward cargoes. In the context of the Brent market while there are many close substitutes for dated cargoes, there is no substitute for, say, a forward March cargo. Agents in a long or short position for March Brent who wish to balance their portfolio can only do this by trading March Brent cargoes.

Consider how a successful deliberate squeeze of, say, March Brent would work. Traders wishing to attempt a squeeze would build up a large net buy position, i.e. they would go long in the market. For each net buy there must be other agents with a (in summation) matching net sell position. If these agents are not equity producers with enough scheduled cargoes to match all their sales, then they will need to balance their positions before the last possible nomination closes.

Ideally for the squeezer, these unbalanced agents will enter the market in such force looking to buy cargoes to balance their own positions, that the squeezer could sell cargoes at a profit. Thus, in the ideal case there is absolutely no need for the squeezer to take physical delivery of any oil. The attempt to squeeze essentially becomes a game of 'chicken' between the squeezer and those with a net sell position and no other cover.

In reality the squeezer must be prepared to take physical delivery of some oil. However the potential profit does not come from selling the physical oil on as dated cargoes; it comes from being able to sell at least some cargoes at an increased price as those with unbalanced positions try to buy cargoes. The squeeze will also impact most on the first traded month forward, i.e. the greatest effect of the squeeze should be felt in the period immediately before the close of nominations; before this point the unbalanced sellers of contracts can simply bide their time and wait.

A squeeze would therefore be expected to have two effects. First, the value of first month forward Brent would be expected to rise above the value of dated Brent for the reason stated above, i.e. dated Brent has many substitutes but a forward cargo for a specific delivery month has none. Secondly the value of the squeezed delivery month should rise above other months, i.e. the price of first month forward Brent should rise above that of second month Brent.

However, while during a squeeze first month forward Brent should trade at a premium to both dated Brent and second month forward Brent, this is not the only circumstance in which this can occur. In a market where there is an overhang of prompt cargoes but where there is some perception of medium-term supply tightness, it is not unusual for this configuration of dated Brent and the first two forward month Brent prices to occur. However, there are two major features that distinguish the prompt overhang case from the squeeze.

The first is the matter of timing. In a squeeze the premium of first month over other Brent prices will rise at some point towards the expiry of nominations for the delivery month. The second factor is the degree of the premium. In the case of prompt overhang the premium of first month is almost never more than 10 cents over both dated and second month simultaneously. In the case of a squeeze the premium over both is theoretically unbounded.

To illustrate this we define the first month premium for any given day on which first month prices exceed both second month and dated prices in the following manner. The first month premium is the minimum of the differential between first and second month Brent and the differential between first month and dated Brent. We then define the extent of the premium as being the maximum value the premium reaches over the course of the time that cargoes for the delivery month are being traded. Table 9.2 shows the extent of the first month premium for all delivery months from January 1988 to June 1992 in which a first month premium has occurred, and the number of trading days in which there was a premium.

In Table 9.2, by tracking the course of the two relevant price differentials for each delivery month, and referring to contemporary trade press reports as to whether there existed any perception among Brent traders of a prompt crude supply overhang, we only categorize the presence of a premium as being due to an overhang in fourteen of the delivery months. These months are listed in lower case in Table 9.2. The remaining twenty-four delivery months shown in capitals in Table 9.2, by our definition, display squeezes of various forms.

Table 9.2: Extent and Duration of First Month Premia, 1988–92.

Month	Max Extent	Days	Month	Max Extent	Days
1988			*1991*		
JANUARY	0.80	20	JANUARY	0.22	9
February	0.03	2	FEBRUARY	0.63	10
April	0.03	2	MARCH	1.35	6
August	0.03	4	APRIL	0.36	10
December	0.03	2	MAY	0.38	15
1989			August	0.05	4
JANUARY	0.32	5	October	0.04	1
FEBRUARY	0.30	4	November	0.05	9
MARCH	0.55	7	December	0.08	7
APRIL	0.13	6	*1992*		
June	0.13	2	JANUARY	0.17	5
July	0.05	5	February	0.09	7
AUGUST	0.75	17	March	0.03	2
SEPTEMBER	0.18	19	April	0.05	8
OCTOBER	0.13	10	May	0.07	7
NOVEMBER	1.53	19	JUNE	0.19	21
DECEMBER	0.13	17			
1990					
FEBRUARY	0.25	6			
JULY	0.38	7			
AUGUST	0.13	4			
SEPTEMBER	0.40	7			
OCTOBER	0.64	11			
NOVEMBER	0.37	10			
DECEMBER	0.27	7			

Note: Months in capitals are those which display squeezes.
Source: Own calculations.

We attempt a finer taxonomy of squeezes by distinguishing between three types. The first variety is a technical squeeze, what we call a paper 'scramble' i.e. a paper squeeze induced by a strong desire to lift physical oil, the second is the deliberate attempt at a squeeze (for example January 1988; August and November 1989), and the third is the 'accidental' squeeze (for example March 1991).

A scramble arises when cargoes are pulled out of chains (that is, nominations are accepted) by traders who had not originally intended to lift the oil. This can occur in both falling and rising markets. For example, as was shown in Table 9.1, the February 1991 delivery month traded over a price range of at least $15.33, and many traders had deals in their portfolio involving substantial losses. There was therefore a strong incentive for cargoes to be pulled out of the chains early so that the tolerance provisions could be utilized, and so by lifting only 475 thousand barrels losses could be reduced. Likewise, traders with large gains had a very strong incentive to maximize cargoes.

Another case arises if market sentiment changes after the peak trading time for a delivery month in such a way that the market is perceived as being tighter when the delivery month becomes wet than it was thought of when the bulk of deals were made. In this case refiner and inventory demand will encourage the early lifting of a cargo as the nominations begin.

In both of the above cases chains are short, and companies are given an incentive to lift more cargoes than their original portfolio of deals warranted, i.e. in lifting physical oil they will unbalance themselves in the paper Brent market. Hence the scramble results in traders needing to buy forward cargoes close to the end of nominations. The first month price is bid upwards and a first month premium can occur.

In a scramble the first month forward Brent price begins to move independently of all other prices, and the resultant first month to second month backwardation is essentially technically driven (during the February 1991 Brent scramble other markets remained in a state of contango even as Brent moved into very strong backwardation). Some element of this divorce from other prices of the first month Brent is likely to occur in any month, as traders' concerns late in the wet month begin to move away to the spread between dated Brent and the next delivery month rather than the expiring wet month. However, during a scramble this increasing lack of definition of first month prices can result in large first month premia.

We consider that the ten consecutive delivery months starting from August 1991 and covering the Gulf crisis and delivery months for which trades were made during the Gulf crisis, all have elements of either tolerance motivated or end-user demand motivated forward Brent scrambles. (In addition there were other elements that resulted in even greater first month premia in March, April and May 1991).

The deliberate squeeze can result in the most dramatic incidences of a first month premium. The three most severe deliberate squeezes were January 1988 (the squeezer being Transworld Oil), August 1989 and November 1989 (in the latter two cases the market was squeezed by Wall Street finance houses). The large-scale and deliberate squeeze is also the hardest case to comprehend in terms of the motivation of the squeezer, given the strong Quixotian element involved. Consider the case of the January 1988 squeeze.

A relatively successful squeeze of the April 1987 delivery month was made by Transworld Oil (TWO). Later in the year TWO decided to mount the operation again but on a much larger scale. In late November 1987 TWO started large-scale buying of January Brent cargoes, and by mid-December had a virtual stranglehold over the delivery month.

What distinguished the January 1988 squeeze from others was its duration. Figure 9.3 shows the path of the first month to dated Brent differential, shown as a dotted line, and the first to second month Brent differential, shown as an unbroken line, for the four major squeezes during the last calendar month of trading days for the delivery month. Prices are not assessed for the last few days of a contract, and so we can never observe these differentials at the point of expiry of trade in the delivery month (i.e. the point at which no more nominations can be made for loading in that month). Both of these differentials remained at very high levels throughout the last month of trading of January 1988 cargoes.

TWO did not sell cargoes during the nomination period, and refiners switched to availabilities of other North Sea grades. Thus the company had to take delivery of the cargoes. There were forty-two cargoes in the January loading programme, and TWO after a hectic spate of tanker chartering lifted no less than forty-one of them, which represented (given the then prevailing standard cargo size of 600 thousand barrels) a volume of about 25 mb of oil which hung over the market. Most of the oil was moved to the USA (note the very large level of liftings to the USA in January 1988 shown in Figure 3.1).

While the squeeze was not profitable, it had demonstrated that one trader could mount a corner of both forward and physical Brent. Further, in general such incidents often attract unwelcome publicity and rumours. The January 1988 squeeze had highlighted the dangers to the survival of the market. It had also given a severe dent to the confidence in the market of some of the smaller participants. The squeezes mounted in August 1989 and November 1989 were less severe

136   *Oil Markets and Prices*

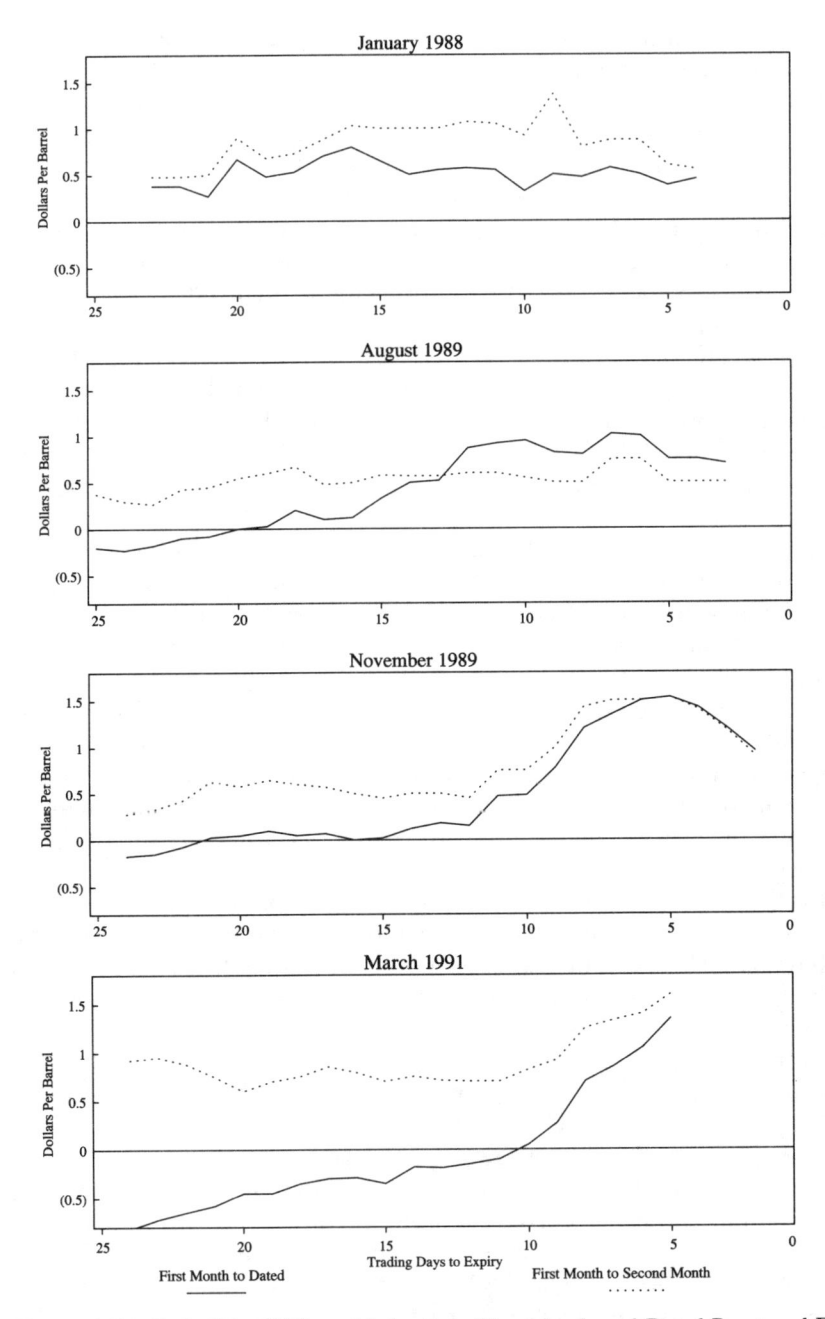

Figure 9.3: Daily Price Differentials between First-Month and Dated Brent and First and Second-Month Brent in Squeezes. January 1988, August 1989, November 1989 and March 1991. Dollars per Barrel.

than the January 1988 squeeze in terms of their duration, but, as is shown in Figure 9.3, far more severe in terms of their effect on prices.

Much of the economic literature on squeezes is concerned with deliberate manipulation by producing companies with market power. There is no doubt that the major equity producers of Brent have a considerable degree of power to mount either a long or a short position squeeze. They control the amount of oil available to the chains through their decision on whether to transfer cargoes internally or to sell at arm's length. They can also affect the flow of oil through changes in inventory levels at Sullom Voe. If Brent trading was simply (in terms of economic game theory), a one-shot game, then they could easily mount a highly effective squeeze. However, it is not a one-shot game, it is repeated. This means that the major equity producers have little incentive to squeeze the Brent market, and a focus on their potential to do so through use of their market power, is misplaced.

Put simply, trading gains on the Brent market are very low indeed in the list of priorities of these companies. Their major objective is to preserve the market, maintain the conditions necessary for it to keep liquidity, and seek to keep the market unregulated. The purpose of the market is to establish prices, both for tax reference purposes in the North Sea, and to serve as input into the pricing formulae adopted by producer countries, a status quo that companies are happier with compared to the uncertainties of any alternative mechanisms. Any squeeze inspired by a major equity producer would simply lead to a mass exit of smaller market participants, and a loss of liquidity and confidence in the market. Other participants will only enter a market with companies with such market power if they are confident that power will not be used against their interests.

Further, it should not be forgotten that all the major producers in the Brent and Ninian systems are overall net buyers of crude oil, much of which is directly linked to Brent prices. While they might gain in trading profits through a Brent squeeze, the overall financial position of the companies is likely to suffer.

What then of firms other than producers, whose main aim is trading rather than the preservation of the market itself? There are several factors that would tend to limit any inclination to squeeze the market by all but the most short-term or naïve companies. This is not to say that they will not squeeze the market, rather that any such operation they mount is likely to be part of a learning experience. Certainly the largest trading firms have learnt that large-scale squeezes are not a good strategy, but unfortunately they needed to try the exercise before they became convinced that it was not a profitable occupation in the longer term.

The potential market power of the equity producers to mount a counter-operation combined with their intention to avoid squeezes acts as a very large deterrent. Further, the threat of litigation from a squeezed company will act as far more of a deterrent than it might have done in the past. Finally, the credibility of a company within the market can be seriously affected if it tries to squeeze. There are certainly companies who still feel very strongly opposed to the participants who squeezed the market in 1989. In the final analysis the unwritten code of conduct in the Brent market is similar to that of a private club, and in the longer term no serious trader wishes to be blackballed.

As well as technical scrambles and deliberate squeezes, a squeeze can arise accidentally, for instance a trader who builds up a large long position intending to either close out later or to take delivery. If the trader then has difficulty in closing out in sufficient time before the month becomes wet, or alternatively if they find that they are not being passed nominations, either because cargoes are being lifted early (i.e. the scramble) or because other traders also have large long positions, all the symptoms of a squeeze can occur. This 'accidental squeeze' scenario arose in the March 1991 delivery month.

In summary, we have no doubt that the Brent market can be squeezed. However there appears to be very little incentive for any company to do so on a large scale, unless they are prepared to undertake what would be a very high risk, one-shot game. This means that the bulk of apparent squeezes in the Brent market are likely to be either technical scrambles or in some sense accidental. However, much of this is predicated on the continuation of a solid physical base for the market; it is much easier and more tempting to squeeze a twenty cargo loading programme in a month than a sixty cargo programme. As we document in the last section of this chapter, the next decade will see a considerable shrinkage in the size of the average Brent loading programme, which may ultimately motivate the creation of another forward market to take on the current role of Brent.

4. Litigation and Default in the Brent Market

The Brent market is informal and unregulated, and as such it has gone through a period of maturation. While the Brent market of today is very clean in comparison with some other commodity markets, this advanced stage has been reached only after going through some particularly difficult episodes. Today most of the fringe players that were at the heart of the major problems of the past have left the market. The market has settled down to a stage where the amount of self-policing needed is fairly minimal compared to previous periods.

However, there have been occasions in the past when the market has risked falling into disrepute. It says much for the success of the damage limitation exercises mounted by key participants in the past, that the market has reached its mature form with the minimum of external regulation impinging upon it. The worst time was 1986, and we concentrate on the roles of two firms whose problematic involvement dates from this time, namely Gatoil and Transnor. We then consider whether such incidences can still occur in the modern Brent market, and conclude that the scope has been very dramatically limited.

Saudi Arabia's change in policy at the end of 1985, whereby it decided not to attempt to defend the oil price any longer, indirectly led to the near collapse of the Brent market. The precipitous price falls of late 1985 and early 1986 meant that cargoes for the January to April loading programmes traded over a considerable price range during the trading life of the cargoes. For example, February 1986 cargoes traded at prices as high as $29 in November 1985, and as low as $18 in January 1986. Given the predominance of outright position taking in the Brent market at this time, as opposed to the current dominant *modus operandi* of taking spread positions, the magnitude of some of the potential losses created by the price collapse was enormous.

The collapse in prices and the size of the losses incurred by some firms put considerable strains on the functioning and the mechanics of the market. Those faced with the prospect of large losses were tempted to dispute the small print of contracts and to seek legal recourse, believing that delays in the law were preferable to meeting the immediate losses (indeed the major case that arose during this period took over four years to settle, and even then it was settled out of court). The result was a series of open defaults, haggling over technical contractual details, the threat of substantial litigation claims and the creation of a regulatory time-bomb that looked set to explode in 1990. It was certainly the greatest threat to the survival of the market, yet it was one through which 15-day trading eventually emerged relatively unscathed.

The problems with the Brent market chains in 1986 began with a series of events during the nominations for and the loading of the January programme. In one case a chain extended to over 150 deals, with the wrong loading dates being passed down at several points in the chain. The chaos grew in the February programme with the dates being changed in at least five chains, and hence the phenomenon of 'phantom cargoes' or 'dry chains' arose, i.e. market participants receiving nominations for cargoes that did not actually exist in the loading dates specified in the nominations.

On 11 February 1986 the Swiss based company Gatoil sent a telex to Exxon, Shell, Texaco, Sun, Nichimen and Rheinoel advising them that Gatoil was in receipt of no less than seven nominations for the loading window 26–28 February, and was the final user for five cargoes in this range.[4] In fact only two cargoes were scheduled to load in this window. Gatoil had received nominations from Shell UK, Sun, Exxon, Texaco, Rheinoel and Nichimen, and had passed nominations to Shell UK and Conoco. Gatoil was also the buyer of a dated cargo from Mitsubishi who had originally purchased it from the UK Oil and Pipeline Agency. Gatoil therefore stated its intention to lift only one of the cargoes from the chains in the disputed loading range, as it had no intention of accepting any loading date changes, and Gatoil was therefore defaulting on the others.

The failure of the number of nominations for the loading range to match the number of cargoes was due to false nominations being made, i.e. the loading dates were being changed as the nominations were passed on and hence phantom cargoes were being created. For example, in a telex to market participants Shell detailed their understanding of how one of the disputed chains had arisen. The chain was as follows:

Exxon-BP-Shell UK-Nichimen-Gotco-Marubeni-Occidental-Internorth-Kanematsu-Internorth-Conoco-Exxon-Phibro-Citizen-Shell International-Gatoil-Mitsubishi-OPA-Shell UK-Phillips-Gotco-Clarendon-Marc Rich-Vanol-Clarendon-Marc Rich-Conoco-Clarendon-Marc Rich-Neste-Conoco-Shell International-Kanematsu-Nichimen-Gatoil

Gatoil appear twice in this chain, with nominations being passed to it from Shell International and Nichimen. The key in resolving the progress of this chain is that only the Nichimen nomination was listed by Gatoil in its telex as one of the seven nominations it had received for the 26–28 February range. The nomination from Shell International had in fact been for the 25–27 February range, but by the time the cargo nomination reached Gatoil for the second time the dates had been changed elsewhere in the chain.

The other key feature of this chain is the three appearances of Marc Rich, in all three cases the nomination having been passed from Clarendon (a company that began life as Marc Rich's US operation). According to Shell,[5] nominations for the cargo should have finished at 5 p.m. on 10 February at which time it was in the hands of Marc Rich. However Marc Rich was unable to pass it on in time and thus was five o'clocked. The nomination was however still passed on by Marc Rich who changed the loading dates to 26–28 February without informing other parties. Hence Gatoil ended up with the final nomination for loading dates that did not match the dates of Exxon's original cargo. Similar events occurred in other chains leading to the excess of nominations for the 26–28 February loading range.

Informal talks were held in London in the week after the Gatoil telex between BP, Shell, Sun, Conoco and Gatoil to attempt to resolve the situation.[6] Remarkably the situation was resolved without the threatened avalanche of litigation. The chains were by and large sorted out. In the words of one trader at the time, 'I think that Shell and Conoco and Exxon made sure everything gets taken care of, and we'll worry about the money later'.[7] While some facets of the incident did end up in court, the scale of the litigation had been very much minimized. One other case of default in the February programme for a trade between Gatoil and Avant for a cargo loading in another range did end in litigation. In mid-January 1986 Avant sold Gatoil a February cargo, on 4 February they passed a nomination for a cargo in the 19–21 February loading range to Gatoil, and on 6 February called upon Gatoil to open their letter of credit. Gatoil failed to do so and also failed to nominate a vessel by 5 p.m. on 17 February. Avant therefore telexed Gatoil to accept that Gatoil's breach of contract had brought the contract to an end. Avant then sold the cargo on to its parent company Mitsui, and claimed the difference between the price of the original cargo and that of the deal with Mitsui, a claim worth about $3.9 million plus interest.

The chains for March 1986 delivery also had problems,[8] but again the problems were resolved. The problems in early 1986 brought about a spate of proposals for changes to the operation of the market. In February 1986 it became clear that BP thought performance bonds could be considered, and an 'operations room' to monitor deals.[9] At this time most deals were conducted on the basis of the existing BP contract. Significantly, BP produced a new set of conditions for sale.[10] These included compulsory book-outs and the introduction of a margin, i.e. deposit, system for trades. Shell also introduced a new contract without margin calls and with compulsory book-outs,[11] which then became the basis for most trade.

Gatoil made their last Brent market trade on their own account in 1987, although they continued to trade actively in the Brent market after this point working through Kloeckner, who, perhaps among others, were known to trade for companies with whom other participants were either unwilling or unable to trade. In October 1990, charges of embezzlement were filed in Dusseldorf against the head of Kloeckner, Wolfgang Zeschmar. Zeschmar was jailed in May 1991 for trading in Kloeckner's name on behalf of Gatoil from 1986 to 1988. These Brent trades accounted for no less than $316 million of the $352 million losses that led to Kloeckner's withdrawal from oil trading. One major casualty in 1986 was the state-owned Austrian firm Voest Alpine, primarily an engineering firm. It had sustained losses reported to be over $300 million in oil trading.[12]

Kloeckner's withdrawal from the market went smoothly. In October 1988 both Kloeckner and Marimpex had built up large net buy positions in a falling market. There were plenty of signs to the other traders that both companies were in extreme difficulties. Yet no repeat of the 1986 experience occurred. One device that minimizes the chances of any default and was used particularly in the case of Marimpex was the 'total-out', where the seller of a forward cargo to a troubled firm simply bypasses it altogether and passes the nomination straight to a buyer from this troubled firm. The potential chaos was resolved relatively smoothly, just as the collapse of Drexel in 1990 spawned no defaults or litigation. The market had learnt from the lessons of early 1986.

The other major incident caused by the price collapse of 1986 proved to be longer running and further reaching, and managed to cast a large shadow over the market for more than four years. Indeed some of the ambiguities created by the case are still in force. In December 1985 a small Bermudan based trading company called Transnor bought two March Brent cargoes, from Shell International and from Nissho Iwai, at an average price of $24.50 per barrel. After the price collapse Transnor defaulted on the contracts by refusing to take delivery, leaving a debt owed to Shell International and Nissho Iwai of about $5.4 million each. On 21 February 1986 Transnor lodged a writ at a New York district court against Conoco, Exxon, Shell and BP, the allegation being that in January 1986 the four companies had for tax spinning purposes rigged the price of Brent downwards.

Before the case could be heard it had to be established whether a New York district court had power to rule on events in the Brent market. Under the US Commodity Exchange Act US courts have a power to rule over futures markets in which US commercial interests participate. In particular section 4(a) of the act states that it is illegal for US companies to trade in futures contracts that are neither subject to the rules of a non-US exchange or market, nor subject to a CFTC approved exchange. However, the act does have a forward contract exclusion which, if it could be invoked, would put the Brent market outside US law. The relevant questions were then whether the Brent market could be deemed to be a US market, and whether it constitutes a forward or a futures market. Thus, a necessary stage in the proceedings was to get a court opinion on those issues.

The problem is that the Commodity Exchange Act does not define the difference between a forward and a futures contract, other than stating that in forward contracts delivery is deferred for reasons of 'convenience or necessity'. The difference between futures and forward contracts and thus the implied categorization of the Brent market was therefore left to a New York district judge, Judge D. Conner who was hearing the case.

Judge Conner's first opinion on the appropriate categorization of the Brent market came on 5 August 1987. The opinion was that not only was Brent a US market, it was also a futures market. Such an opinion should have given market participants plenty of warning about the judge's later stance, and it was certainly a contributory factor in the change in the willingness of two of the defendants to continue to fight the case. Shell and BP settled out of court with Transnor in 1988. It was later revealed in a court ruling in May 1990 that part of Shell's settlement was that Transnor would not have to pay the $5.38 million it owed to Shell until or unless it had recovered the sum of at least $20 million in the other pending lawsuits.[13] Exxon and Conoco continued to fight on. It is a point of speculation as to what motivated the difference in behaviour of Shell and BP on the one hand and Exxon and Conoco on the other.

The Conner opinion of 18 April 1990 came as a bombshell to the market (even though in large part it was merely a restatement of the August 1987 opinion) and led to a period of very thin Brent trading in the UK, and virtually no Brent trading in the USA while companies awaited a clarification of the situation from the US CFTC. Exxon withdrew from the market temporarily on the advice of its lawyers, and Koch also completely stopped trading Brent. Many other US firms moved all their Brent trading activity to London in the immediate aftermath of the Conner opinion.

From the point of view of the UK government, the Conner opinion represented an outrageous and unjustified breach of UK sovereignty with important implications for other UK based commodity and financial markets. In the words of a communication from the UK Department of Trade and Industry to the CFTC, 'there are elements of the opinion that on one interpretation would assert US jurisdiction to an extent objectionable to the UK . . . Under this interpretation of the opinion, the jurisdictional reach asserted is, in the British government's view, contrary to international law and damaging to the British national interest.'[14]

In a bid to calm the market fears, and to respond to calls from US based Brent market participants, on 25 April 1990 the CFTC announced that it was considering the steps that would be necessary to maintain access to the Brent market by US firms and in the meantime was taking a no action policy. The next day the CFTC entered into talks with the UK DTI. Fears by market participants of a regulatory minefield being opened up were heightened by a speech by Senator D'Amato on 2 May calling for Brent to be taken 'within the control of long overdue effective regulation',[15] criticizing the CFTC for its lack of action, and claiming that price manipulation had occurred.

The Transnor case itself then moved swiftly to a close. On 10 May Judge Conner made a ruling which cut the damages that Transnor could seek dramatically, to a total of $43.2 million compared to the $265 million Transnor had been looking for. Transnor could only seek damages for three transactions, the potential profit of $8 million from sale of the two disputed cargoes, the $5.38 million from its transaction with Shell International and the money it had already paid Nissho Iwai, i.e. $1 million out of a total debt of $5 million.[16] Under US law since the claims involved a charge of conspiracy they could be trebled. However, while good financial news for the remaining two defendants in the case, the major importance of the case was unaffected, i.e. that the Brent market was deemed to be a futures market subject to US commodity laws, and therefore the ruling did nothing to relieve the disruption and dislocation caused to the market.

Without a formal ruling by the CFTC the situation could not be cleared, and the market was endangered. However relief for the market came on 16 May. The discussions between the CFTC and the UK DTI resulted in a joint statement that the Brent market was 'an international market' which 'cannot be regarded as or regulated as if it were exclusively a US market'. This statement does appear to have fallen well short of the UK government's original and more general concerns, with no reference to the Conner opinion as being any violation of UK jurisdictional sovereignty and the principle involved. On the same day the CFTC released another statement suggesting that Brent trading was likely to be formally exempted from US regulation.

These developments, together with a recent favourable Supreme Court ruling in another case with some similar features, were enough to lead to a request being put before Judge Conner by Exxon and Conoco that the original ruling be reconsidered. The request was refused on 18 May, just three days before the trial was due to begin. One hour before the trial should have started discussions over whether an out-of-court settlement was possible began and became prolonged. A tentative settlement was reached the next day and finalized soon afterwards.[17]

The CFTC was expected to give a quick exemption from the provisions of the Commodity Exchange Act to the Brent market. However dissent within the CFTC commissioners slowed the process down, and an exemption was not given until September 1990, some three months later than expected, and even then only by a majority three to one verdict.[18] Some of the regulatory risk was therefore cleared, but theoretically the original Conner opinion still held. While US participants have become more relaxed in their attitude to the Brent market it should be noted that the issue is still not formally settled once and for all. First, a US court can choose to ignore the CFTC ruling, should it so wish, and relate its conduct closer to the April 1990 Conner opinion if another writ concerning the Brent market is lodged in the USA. Secondly, the CFTC statement itself is a little ambiguous. Formally it only gives Brent trading exemption from section 4(a) of the Commodity Exchange Act, i.e. it is perfectly legal as far as the CFTC is concerned for US companies to trade in Brent. However this still leaves unclear the issue of whether any of the other sections of the act apply to that trading, and some of those other sections are fairly draconian.

The Brent market still produces occasional litigation. In July 1992 the High Court in London found against Cargill in an action brought by Nissho Iwai.[19] The charge against Cargill was that in March 1992 it had all but refused to pick up its telephones until after 5 p.m. when Nissho Iwai were trying to pass a nomination. The cause for disputes has then become one of procedures, particularly in the nomination process, rather than the open defaults of 1986. Tangles can easily arise that bring about disputes. For instance, it was reported that on 17 July 1992, several incorrect dates were accidently passed down chains, with the situation being worsened by one company not answering its telephones promptly.[20]

The question is then begged as to whether the market has really changed and matured enough to lessen the chances of any further Gatoil or Transnor type problems. The answer is positive for a variety of reasons. The first is the changes since 1986 in the terms and conditions for trading in the market. In particular, a nomination now has to be passed down a chain with a specific parcel number which equates to a specific loading range. This greatly cuts down the possibility of any further reoccurrence of the phantom cargoes of 1986.

The second reason is that most of the fringe players have gone, mainly because other companies in the market are now more likely to refuse to trade with participants they suspect. They are far more worried about the credit-worthiness of trading partners than they were in the past. Companies running into financial difficulties tend to find that the number of those prepared to deal with them dries up very quickly, as for example the troubled refiner Aerochem found in 1991.

The third reason is the development of the IPE Brent futures contract. Fringe players find it much easier to trade on the IPE than on the 15-day market. Likewise a company attempting to use another as a front (for example the Gatoil/Kloeckner link) will find IPE trading more conducive as they trade on equal terms rather than having to pay the premium the front company would normally demand.

Fourthly, the overall financial standing of the average 15-day Brent trader is considerably more robust than in previous years due to the departure of many of the smaller trading companies and because many of the smaller companies left are direct subsidiaries of other larger companies. This is why the price collapse of January 1991 did not spawn the defaults and near defaults caused by the gyrations in prices in 1986 and October 1988. So few companies were trading the absolute price level that the losses involved were relatively minor compared to the previous cases, and companies who had losses were financially robust.

The fifth reason is that the internal policing of the market has improved. The costs of further litigation to the future of the market have been much increased by the Transnor case, and hence so have the incentives to detect the build-up of any dangerous situation well in advance. Finally there has been a significant shift in the composition of 15-day Brent participants. In particular the share of companies with production interests giving them Brent equity entitlements has been much increased, from below 10 per cent in early 1989 to over 30 per cent in 1991 (as shown in Chapter 7). More trade is therefore concentrated in the hands of the companies with the greatest vested interest in preserving the market, and who therefore will be more likely to behave in a responsible fashion.

All the above points to a considerable improvement compared with previous years. However that is not to say that the market is completely mature and that absolutely all the fringe or potentially disreputable players have gone. Just as in any other market there are still some such players. Indeed participants in the market itself do perceive that there are some potentially problem companies still trading.

Nevertheless, the major dangers to the Brent market are now external rather than internal. In particular, from 1990 the Wall Street firms behind the subsidiaries that trade in the Brent market have all become distinctly accident prone in other markets. A repeat of Drexel's sudden departure from the Brent market due to factors outside the market cannot be ruled out, but the danger is that it could involve a company even more active in trading than Drexel was. There is a financial risk involved in dealing with Wall Street firms that is not present with producer countries or major oil companies, and it would be foolish to believe that there could never be another Drexel type collapse. Although the market could survive another such crash, the transition period could be rather difficult.

There are of course firms currently in the market who commit certain undesirable peccadillos, for example those who sit on nominations for an inordinate length of time, trying to sell the cargo on as a dated cargo before having accepted the nomination, and then pass them on close to 5 o'clock. As the Cargill/Nissho Iwai case shows, disruptions in the nomination procedure are now the major source of any possible litigations.

5. A Conclusion to Part II: The Future of Brent

Chapter 2 detailed the path of production in the Brent system, and revealed a gradual fall of output that had necessitated the co-mingling with the Ninian system to preserve the physical base of Brent blend. We also noted that less than 8 per cent of the original recoverable reserve base of the fields in the two systems was held in the fields that had received Annex B development permission since 1981. Further, the potential new developments were all of a relatively small magnitude. This then raises the question of how the physical base of Brent blend will evolve, and whether an alternative North Sea blend could provide a larger base. By its very nature, this exercise is a speculative one. However, some firm conclusions do emerge.

Using Wood Mackenzie projections on a field basis for current and potential developments, we have constructed a possible path for Brent blend output. This is shown in Table 9.3 for the period from 1993 to

Table 9.3: Crude Oil Production. Brent and Forties Systems. 1993–2000. Thousand Barrels per Day.

Year	Brent	Forties
1993	857	559
1994	802	844
1995	798	1043
1996	722	1030
1997	621	1022
1998	536	980
1999	460	920
2000	384	820

Source: Own calculations from Wood Mackenzie, *North Sea Report*, various issues.

2000, together with the possible production path of the Forties system, both series expressed in thousand b/d.

Two main provisos need to be made about these series. First, the current capacity of the Forties pipeline is 950 thousand b/d, and hence production greater than this could not all be transported by the pipeline unless it were upgraded. Secondly, there have recently been a number of potentially very large discoveries in the Forties area, for example Mungo, Erskine, Monan and Medine. Data on these fields are not currently available, but if they joined the Forties system they could significantly reduce any fall off in Forties system output towards the year 2000.

Table 9.3 shows that potential Forties system output surpasses that of Brent blend in 1994, and then remains significantly higher. By the year 2000 Brent blend output is below 400 thousand b/d, and equates to a loading programme of just twenty-three cargoes in the average month. While Brent has only minor fields to come on stream, Forties has a series of major producing fields.[21] No other UK system comes close to the levels of production expected from Forties; after Brent the next highest projections for the year 2000 are Gannet/Fulmar (122 thousand b/d) and Flotta (117 thousand b/d).

This then is one of the reasons why a forward market formed for Brent rather than Forties is about to disappear. The second major reason was concentration of ownership, with Forties being dominated by just one company, i.e. BP. However, this reason is also fast disappearing. In Table 9.4 we show the percentage division of Forties output by major producers in 1990, and a projection for 2000, based on current shares in producing fields and potential developments.

Asset market activity could of course change the projection

Table 9.4: Shares in Forties Production. 1990 and 2000. Per Cent.

Forties 1990		Forties 2000	
BP	45.5	BP	23.1
Marathon	12.1	Enterprise	7.7
Sun	6.2	Amerada Hess	6.1
Bow Valley	4.3	British Gas	5.3
Clyde	3.1	Agip	4.9
Enterprise	2.7	Marathon	4.3
British Gas	2.5	Fina	4.3
Kerr McGee	2.5	Amoco	3.8
Amerada Hess	2.0	Exxon	3.5
Amoco	1.9	Shell	3.5

considerably. However, unless BP buys a large number of Forties area assets, which we consider unlikely, Table 9.4 does carry the strong implication that a high concentration of ownership will become less of a feature of Forties system output.

With the advantage of higher production being lost, together with the diversification of ownership in Forties, Brent retains just one major advantage. Sullom Voe is by far the best harbour in the North Sea, combining ease of access with the ability to accommodate the largest tankers, together with large storage facilities.[22] This raises two possibilities beyond the emergence of a Forties market to take the place of the Brent market. One is the emergence of a Brent/Forties market along the lines of the Brent/Ninian/Forties market that existed in the early 1980s. The other is that Sullom Voe is an ideal entrepôt centre, and could receive other crude oil than Brent through incoming tanker movements. We return to this possibility below.

So far we have only considered the UK North Sea. However, as is discussed further in Chapter 14, Norwegian output has climbed steeply over the course of the late 1980s. Nevertheless, a parallel projection exercise on fields and potential developments for existing Norwegian lifting systems (both pipeline and offshore), reveals none with an output greater than that of Brent blend in the year 2000. However, Norway does have a set of future developments in the Haltenbanken area that, we believe, could produce over 750 thousand b/d by 2000, with further discoveries in the area possible. Early feasibility studies seem to have ruled out blending through a pipeline system on grounds of cost, and favoured offshore tanker loading. No single field could produce enough to support a market, and offshore loading is less flexible than terminal loading, as well as reducing the number of tankers that can technically load. In particular, offshore loading makes transatlantic trade very difficult.

On grounds of physical base, there does not then appear to be a Norwegian system that could take the place of Brent. However, this does not rule out Norwegian crude contributing to the liquidity of the Brent market through the use of Sullom Voe as an entrepôt, particularly the output from the fields of the Haltenbanken area. If a Norwegian onshore terminal for this oil is ruled out, it is not inconceivable that it may prove efficient to take it to and market it out of Sullom Voe, thus producing a fresh lease of life for the Brent market.

In interview evidence several traders suggested that a market based on Russian crude oil pipeline deliveries into Western Europe could eventually take over from Brent. Others, however, strongly disagree. It was also suggested that any non-North Sea European successor to Brent may no longer trade in dollars per barrel, but instead shift to trade in

European Currency Units (ECUs) or D-Marks.

In summary we can provide one firm conclusion. There will be a physical base for a viable North Sea market until well into the next century. However, this still leaves the issue of precisely which market that will be, with the most likely eventuality being a switch to a Forties market. Our view is that if maximum achievable Brent blend production does fall below 400 thousand b/d as is projected, particularly if Forties maintains a significantly higher output, then the Brent market will not survive in its current form. The role of trader confidence is of prime significance, in that it could survive on a small physical base as long as faith in the efficiency of the mechanisms of the market survives. As we document in Chapter 13, the Dubai market survives on a physical base of twenty cargoes a month, but our analysis of that market suggests that it survives mainly due to the existence of Brent.

On current projections, Brent system output will cease about the year 2010, and Ninian system output about five years later, and so the eventual death of the Brent market as it stands today cannot be postponed indefinitely. We offer three possibilities if enhanced recovery technology fails to preserve the physical base of Brent blend. First, and most likely, a forward Forties market will take over from forward Brent, building on the base of the small forward market in Forties that already exists. Secondly, either as a transition to a Forties market or as a permanent replacement to Brent, a Brent/Forties market could grow. Thirdly, Sullom Voe could become an entrepôt centre receiving other North Sea oil to take advantage of its superior facilities.

Notes
1. Also known as the 'op-tol' game, 'min-max' game, or chain trading.
2. Average cargo sizes by destination were derived in Chapter 3.
3. For legal definitions see E.T. McDermott (1979), 'Defining Manipulation in Commodity Futures Trading: the Futures Squeeze' *Northwestern University Law Review* vol. 74, no. 2, pp. 202–25. For economic interpretations see L.N. Edwards and F.R. Edwards (1984), 'A Legal and Economic Analysis of Manipulation in Futures Markets', *Journal of Futures Markets*, vol. 4, pp. 333–66; G. Chichilnisky, 'Manipulation and Repeated Games in Futures' in R. Anderson (ed.), *The Industrial Organisation of Futures Markets* (1984) Lexington; and A. Kyle, 'A Theory of Futures Market Manipulations' in R. Anderson, ibid.
4. The full text of the telex, and Shell's reply, is contained in a *Petroleum Intelligence Weekly* supplement, 'An Inside Look at the Brent Market Crisis', 24 February 1986.
5. Ibid.
6. *Platt's Oilgram News*, 19 February 1986, 'Companies Said Huddling in London to Salvage Brent Forward Market'.

7. Quoted in *Platt's Oilgram Price Report*, 20 February 1986.
8. See *Platt's Oilgram Price Report*, 18 March 1986.
9. See *Platt's Oilgram News*, 21 February 1986.
10. Detailed in *Weekly Petroleum Argus*, 21 May 1986.
11. Ibid., 9 June 1986.
12. *Platt's Oilgram News*, 17 March 1986.
13. Ibid., 14 May 1990.
14. Ibid., 2 May 1990.
15. *Platt's Oilgram News*, 3 May 1990.
16. Ibid., 14 May 1990.
17. Ibid., 23 May 1990.
18. Ibid., 21 September 1990.
19. See *Platt's Oilgram News*, 27 July 1992, 'Brent Trade Finds its Unique Policies Still Controversial'.
20. Ibid.
21. For instance in 1993 and 1994 alone, the Forties system is increased (among others) by the addition of Scott, Nelson, East Brae, and T-Block all with peak production of over 100 thousand barrels per day.
22. Although considerable improvements in Forties facilities and procedures are in progress.

Part III

Oil Prices

CHAPTER 10

OIL PRICE REPORTING

Price reporting has become an important part of the oil industry, and the assessed prices produced by journalists have become increasingly significant. Oil price reporters are now far more than mere observers of crude oil and oil product markets. If they were, then their only role would be to add to the price transparency of the market. However, deals worth hundreds of millions of dollars per day ride on published assessments, and the nature and structure of oil reporting create trading opportunities and new markets, and affect the behaviour of oil traders. Price reporting does more than provide a mirror for oil markets; the reflection in the mirror can affect the image itself.

While price reporting for oil products began in the 1920s, daily assessments of crude oil prices are more recent, only becoming important with the growth of the spot markets for crude oil in the 1970s. Indeed, before the mid-1960s the major oil companies were their own price assessors, calling out prices unilaterally, a role taken up by OPEC through to the end of the 1970s. The growth of spot markets for crude oil created a need for price assessment, at first simply as a contribution to price transparency and as a service for those within the market. However, the assessed prices gradually went through the same evolution as product price reports had been through, and they began to be used in trade rather than merely as an aid to trade.

Three main factors have led to the growth in the importance of crude oil price reporting over the course of the 1980s and into the 1990s. The first is the movement by producer nations towards market related pricing. The move to netback pricing in 1986 led to a considerable growth in the value of trade priced from product assessments at the US Gulf Coast, the Antwerp-Rotterdam-Amsterdam area and Singapore. However, starting in 1986 and accelerating through 1987 and 1988, most of the major exporting countries moved to marker crude oil related formula pricing, rather than the product market related pricing embodied by netbacks. The published assessments of a handful of crude oils, in particular Brent, Dubai and Alaska North Slope, suddenly acquired a whole new role. Millions of barrels of crude oil per day were to be priced directly from the numbers produced by the price assessment agencies. Countries using retrospective pricing also tend to use averages of price assessments to form the retrospective price. As a result nearly all the direct sales made by national oil companies are in some way valued on the basis of price assessments.

The second factor was the shift to differential pricing for spot trade in the non-marker crude oils. For example, deals done for UK and Norwegian grades other than Brent, as well as spot sales of West African and Mediterranean crude oil, are normally done as a differential to the price of dated Brent. Differential pricing in spot markets has changed the definition of 'marker crude'. Brent is a marker now not just because it is a representative crude used to gauge the general price level, but because it sets the general price level in many markets with only differentials from Brent being traded.[1]

The third factor has been the growth in financial oil derivatives provided by, in particular, the Wall Street finance houses. The swaps market is not very transparent, the volume of crude oil which is swapped by each company is a jealously guarded commercial secret. However this volume is very substantial indeed, and there are oil-importing countries which have swapped their entire expected volumes of oil imports. In a return to the world before spot markets much oil trade, and in particular purchases on a national level, is being based on fixed prices. The Wall Street refiners have in a sense taken over from the oil companies and OPEC in being the price fixers of the oil business. A cynic might argue that we have been through a forty-year cycle that has returned us to fixed prices, but the new price fixers are considerably less financially solvent or involved in the grass roots of the business than the old ones were.

An oil swap is a fixed price agreement with an arrangement for financial transfers in the relevant direction when the market price is either above or below the fixed price in the swap. The market price used is a price assessment. A company or nation who has made a swap is totally indifferent to the price they trade at, unless the transfers within the swap are based on price assessments, rather than the actual trades made by the party involved. Hence the growth in the swap market has led to a further boost in the importance of price assessments.

There are two types of agencies that assess Brent prices. The first and most important, since to the greater extent these prices are the ones used in deals, are hard copy services producing reports at least daily, and sometimes more frequently. This group consists of Platt's, Petroleum Argus (Argus), and London Oil Reports (LOR). We will concentrate on this group given its importance in the pricing of physical trade, but there are also screen services attempting to provide frequently updated prices and news. These are primarily an aid to trade rather than a means of pricing, and the most important are Reuters, Telerate, Bloomberg, Knight Ridder and a screen service provided by Platt's.

In addition to the seven main companies mentioned there are also a series of agencies which are essentially regional or seek to serve niche oil product markets. We first provide a brief sketch of the three major reporting agencies.

i) Platt's

Platt's prices are the most widely used in contracts in the oil industry, a pre-eminence mainly achieved through the virtue of being the first agency to be established. In 1924 Platt's became the first oil price reporting agency, reporting US prices for oil products. Gradually the oil industry began to use Platt's prices in the settlement of deals. The first recorded use of Platt's prices was by the Iraq Petroleum Company, using Platt's US Gulf Coast assessments for gasoline to price some of its gasoline production. Platt's (now a part of McGraw-Hill) had nearly a fifty-year start on other companies in its reporting of product prices, but lagged behind Petroleum Argus in crude oil price reporting, producing its first daily crude oil prices in 1983. It now runs offices for price reporting in New York, California, Houston, London, Singapore and Tokyo. Platt's produces a daily price report, *Platt's Oilgram* covering world crude oil and product prices and US domestic product prices, as well as a daily and a weekly newsletter.

ii) Petroleum Argus

Petroleum Argus grew out of Europ-Oil Prices, founded in 1970 by Jan Nasmyth. It initially focused on European product prices, before branching into worldwide crude oil and product price reporting. Argus was the first service to make daily assessments of crude oil markets, beginning its coverage in 1979. Before this it assessed crude oil prices first weekly and then bi-weekly, and has a database containing all the confirmed deals reported to it since 1973, which has been drawn on in the current study. Petroleum Argus now has offices in London, Houston, Singapore and Tokyo, producing a daily crude oil market report as well as four regional product price reports. It also produces a weekly newsletter and weekly market reports together with a monthly data collation report.

iii) London Oil Reports

London Oil Reports was founded in 1978, initially as a weekly newsletter with some price assessments, before moving into oil market and price reporting. In 1985 it was merged with Independent Chemical

Information Services, an agency which since 1980 has assessed petrochemical prices, to form the ICIS-LOR group. Oil reporting is now based in London, Houston and Tokyo, with additional offices, mainly for chemicals, in Paris and Hong Kong. LOR's main product is its World Crude Report, produced on a daily basis with two updates. It also produces a daily oil products report, daily jet report and a weekly feedstocks (including LPG) report. The ICIS-LOR group also publishes on a weekly or bi-weekly basis, reports on petrochemicals, chemical tanker shipping, gasoline additives and lube oils.

All three of these companies combine, to differing degrees, the role of price reporters with the role of journalists. Before considering their coverage and mode of operation in crude oil markets, we briefly mention the on-screen services. The market leaders among screen services are Telerate and Reuters, both of which combine price information screens and deal reporting with a news service (Telerate uses AP Dow Jones while Reuters relies on its own network). A screen service is also provided by Platt's which is known as Platt's Global Alert. The screen services are essentially trading aids, especially in their role of conveying the news reports which move the markets.

The use of the prices produced by screen services for contractual pricing purposes is not very widespread, for the oil trade prefers to work from the faxes and telexes produced by hard copy services. However that is not to say that Reuters and Telerate prices are not used at all. Reuters has been used in German contracts and Telerate does have a toehold for some contracts made in California. Sales made by the US government from the Strategic Petroleum Reserve over the course of the 1990-91 Kuwait crisis were linked to the average of Reuters and Telerate assessments (which also form part of the input in the compilation of the IPE Brent index as was detailed in Chapter 4). However, the vast bulk of trade is priced off the hard copies produced by Platt's, Argus and LOR, either alone or sometimes in combination. For example, the average of assessments is widely used, particularly by the sogo shosha, by some major traders in key markets (for example Phibro), and for some sales by exporting countries, in particular for oil products (for example Russia, Saudi Arabia, Abu Dhabi, Algeria and Venezuela).

Table 10.1 shows the crude oils which are assessed by Argus, LOR and Platt's on a daily basis as of August 1992, split by geographical markets. Generally prices are assessed on a f.o.b. (free on board) basis at their normal point of loading rather than on a delivered c.i.f. (cargo, insurance, freight) basis. The exceptions to this among waterborne crude oils are Russian Urals (assessed c.i.f. in NW Europe and in the Mediterranean), Bonny Light (which Argus assesses at both the US Gulf

Table 10.1: Crudes Assessed Daily By Argus, LOR and Platt's

	Argus	LOR	Platt's		Argus	LOR	Platt's
North West Europe				*Far East*			
Dated Brent	X	X	X	Ardjuna			X
Forward Brent	X	X	X	Arun Condensate		X	X
Ekofisk	X	X	X	Attaka		X	X
Flotta	X	X	X	Bima			X
Forties	X	X	X	Cinta	X		X
Oseberg	X	X	X	Daqing		X	X
Statfjord		X	X	Duri	X	X	X
Urals c.i.f. NWE		X		Gippsland	X		X
Mediterranean				Handil			X
Brega		X		Jabiru	X		X
Es Sider	X	X	X	Labuan			X
Iranian Light		X	X	Minas	X	X	X
Iranian Heavy	X	X	X	Miri			X
Saharan Blend		X		Shengli			X
Suez Blend		X	X	Tapis	X	X	X
Urals c.i.f. Med	X	X	X	Widuri	X		
Zarzaitine		X		*US Market*			
West Africa				ANS Gulf Coast	X	X	X
BBQ *			X	ANS California	X		X
Bonny Light	X	X		Bonny Light	X		
Bonny Medium	X	X		Cano Limon			X
Brass River		X		Eugene Island			X
Cabinda	X	X	X	HLS Empire	X		X
Forcados	X	X	X	Kern River			X
Gulf				Line 63	X		X
Dubai	X	X	X	LLS	X	X	X
Murban	X	X		THUMS			X
Oman	X	X	X	WTI Cushing	X	X	X
Oman MPM	X		X	WTI Midland	X	X	X
Qatar Land		X		WTI Postings Plus			X
Qatar Marine		X		West Texas Sour	X	X	X
				Canada			
				Bow River/Hardisty			X
				Mixed Lt Sr			X
				Par Crude			X

* A basket of three Nigerian crudes

Coast as well as f.o.b. Nigeria), Alaska North Slope which is assessed c.i.f. Long Beach California and at the US Gulf Coast, and Cano Limon at the US Gulf Coast. Iranian grades are assessed f.o.b. at the Egyptian port of Sidi Kerir. Crudes with an underlying forward market (Brent, ANS, WTI, Tapis), are often quoted for two or more delivery months. Two of the prices shown in Table 10.1 are differentials rather than absolute prices (namely the Oman MPM market and the WTI Postings Plus market). The interpretation of these two differentials is explained in Chapter 14.

The methodology used in assessing prices is of crucial importance. In the days when spot oil trading involved very little intra-day volatility and primarily consisted of outright trading in absolute prices, the method could be very straightforward. The assessed price could simply be a range given by the lowest and highest prices at which trades were concluded over the relevant day. That methodology was undesirable because prices could be reported for unusual cargo sizes or for oil with other non-standard characteristics, whether in terms of location or quality. Further, as intra-day volatility increased the range implied by this methodology became increasingly large, and thus the quotes had increasingly little worth or meaning.[2]

The high-low methodology is not currently in use; instead price assessment agencies use a bid-offer range evaluated at a specific point in time. This involves expressing the oil price as a range denoted by the lowest selling price and the highest buying price indicated in the market at the specified time of assessment. This time is known as the 'time-stamp' and all price assessments produced are time-stamped. Further the price quoted is that of a standardized commodity for each crude oil type, with the agencies producing lists of specifications. For example dated Brent reflects the price of a 500 thousand barrel cargo of Brent due to load at Sullom Voe, in the case of Platt's specifications within five to fifteen days of the assessment, for other agencies between ten and twenty days of the assessment. Cargoes close to their loading dates are excluded to prevent the sale of distressed cargoes from influencing price levels.

The time-stamped bid-offer range of a standardized cargo methodology does rely on the skill of the reporter. Price assessment is more of an art than a science, the reporter having to judge on the basis of the talk within the market and the deals done during the day, precisely where prices are at the time-stamp. The use of market talk in thin trading conditions, i.e. asking market participants and brokers at which price levels they would be negotiating, prevents the assessment being too heavily skewed by a handful of deals. On the other hand, it comes close to meaning that price assessments have an element of panel pricing in them (considered below).

In some markets there is no alternative but to use market talk because the market concerned is highly illiquid. The most obvious case of this is the quote for Alaska North Slope c.i.f. the US Gulf Coast. Long periods can elapse between physical cargoes of spot traded ANS arriving at the Gulf Coast. Most ANS goes to California, and most of what does arrive in the US Gulf is internally transferred by the equity producers of ANS. There is little trade in the forward market for ANS and the quote is therefore highly reliant on market talk. This is a highly unsatisfactory state of affairs. ANS is the third most important crude oil in the world (after Brent and Dubai) in terms of the volume of oil directly priced off its quotation.[3]

Market talk in an active market such as Brent is usually fairly accurate. While the positions that people have will influence their opinions, the balance between the long and the shorts in the market should cancel this out. Further, reporters are constantly observing actual trades taking place, normally confirmed with both parties to the transaction, and as a final check there is a futures market in operation during most of the trading day. However, ANS currently has no liquid underlying futures market, and few deals actually take place for US Gulf Coast delivery. There is therefore an element of necromancy in producing ANS price assessments.

Price reporters often have to use subjective judgements in interpolating information from trades that may not exactly match the specifications they are trying to assess. For example we have noted that dated Brent is the single most important price in the world oil trade, given the volumes either spot traded differentially to it or directly priced off it through formula pricing. However, not all trades match up to the specifications for which the dated Brent price is meant to match. First, as we saw in Chapter 9, very few cargoes of close to 500 thousand barrels actually leave Sullom Voe, with cargoes often being traded on a dated basis as the standard size corrected for a specified tolerance. These cargoes may be priced below that of a standard sized cargo. The buyer of such a cargo knows that it is being sold on this basis so that the seller can realize gains from the tolerance game, and therefore might be able to achieve a discount to cargoes where the buyer is left with the choice of how to exercise the tolerance.

Secondly, dated Brent cargoes are sometimes traded further than fifteen days in advance. An equity producer can sell loading dates as soon as they know them. Alternatively, dated Brent can be traded more than fifteen days ahead specifying a wider loading window than the conventional three days. In this case the seller is either trying to retain flexibility over which cargo is sold, or does not yet know its loading dates other than being certain that they will have at least one in, say, the second half of the month. Thirdly, price assessment agencies may also have some of the trade in physical top-up parcels of Brent reported to them, which are sometimes carried out at differentials to assessed dated Brent prices.

All the above examples are cases where the agencies may have prices reported to them which, while the deals do contain some useful information, would have to be subjectively standardized. This requires skill on the part of the reporter demonstrating that price reporting is more of an art than an exact science.

Given the necessity of time-stamping, the assessments produced by different agencies are not always strictly comparable as the time-stamp used varies. Further, the times used have implications of their own. Table 10.2 shows the timing of Brent price assessments made by Argus, Platt's and LOR, based on Greenwich Mean Time (with the appropriate local times shown) for a representative trading day when summer time is not in operation. The table also shows the hours of trading of the IPE and NYMEX in comparison with the assessment times.

Platt's only produces one published assessment of Brent prices per trading day, the time-stamp being between 4 p.m. and 4.30 p.m. New York time. By contrast Argus produces three assessments per day and LOR produces five (see Table 10.2). Both Argus and LOR produce reports for London mid-day, as well as the end of the day in Houston. In addition LOR produces a report after NYMEX closing.

The timing of the most widely used assessment (i.e. Platt's) is critical. It does not conform to any logical break in the trading day, coming about an hour after the close of trading on the IPE and NYMEX, and well before trading in the US spot markets for crude oil begins to wind down. This has several implications.

First, Platt's prices can be well off the actual values when Houston traders leave their offices and the (world) market takes a break before Tokyo opens. In particular, the influential US inventory and production figures issued by the American Petroleum Institute (API), normally on a Tuesday, appear after the Platt's assessments for that day are made. The API figures can move oil markets very significantly. LOR, being the last to make assessments, gauges the impact of the figures and reflects this in its reported prices at Houston close.

Secondly, Platt's assessments are made at a time when both NYMEX and the IPE are closed, leaving an hour's price exposure to hedgers. This can be a significant price risk. For example, consider a European refiner who is about to receive a million barrels of Nigerian crude oil. This oil is being priced off Nigerian formula terms, i.e. a five-day average of Platt's dated Brent assessments, with adjustment factors, five days from the loading of the cargo. The refiner is hedging this purchase by having sold 1,000 IPE Brent contracts (i.e. one million barrels), with the intention of buying back 200 lots on each of the five days when prices are used in the average. (The refiner is also using a combination of spread deals to hedge the difference between the IPE Brent price and

Table 10.2: Timing of Brent Price Assessments. Hours of the Day. Greenwich Mean Time (GMT)

GMT	Argus	LOR	Platt's	Notes
0800				
0830		0845 (1745 Tokyo)		
0900				
0930				0930 IPE opens
1000				
1030				
1100				
1130				
1200	1200 London			
1230		1230 London		
1300				
1330				
1400				
1430				1445 NYMEX opens
1500				
1530				
1600				
1630				
1700				
1730				
1800				
1830	1830 London	1830 London		
1900				
1930				
2000				2010 NYMEX closes
2030				2015 IPE closes
2100		2115 (1515 Houston)		
2130			2130 (1630 New York)	
2200				
2230				
2300	2300 (1700 Houston)			
2330				
0000		0000 (1800 Houston)		

the price of dated Brent.)

If the refiner buys 200 IPE contracts close to the IPE closing time, there is still about an hour to go before the Platt's assessment is made from which his purchase will be priced, and the market can (and often does) move sharply in that hour. The efficiency of the refiner's hedge is therefore weakened, and the refiner can lose (or gain) large sums from this residual risk. This risk can be called 'Platt's risk', i.e. that which arises from movements in the general price level between the closure of the exchanges and the Platt's assessment. This risk goes beyond Brent and Brent related crude oils, and confronts anyone who has entered into a crude oil or oil product transaction based on Platt's prices which they have attempted to hedge by taking positions on the formal exchanges (together perhaps with a variety of spread deals).

Platt's risk does affect the way oil is traded. One facet of this is the 'false' IPE Exchange for Physical outlined in Chapter 3, which is one way around Platt's risk. Another is the creation of a market in Platt's risk. There are trading companies that, for a premium, are prepared to collect up the Platt's risk of other companies, i.e. they accept to pay (or be paid) the difference between hedged prices and the Platt's assessment. Such companies can and do make money on what is termed the 'dated to paper' market, especially as many of the risks they are incurring may be offsetting. Hence the timing of Platt's price report creates a new market in Platt's prices themselves.

Table 10.1 presented a large selection of crude oils for which the agencies attempt to produce absolute prices. However, most spot traded crude oils are not traded as absolute prices but as differentials. The crude oils shown in Table 10.1 for NW Europe, the Mediterranean and West Africa (except for Brent itself) all tend to be traded as a differential to published assessments to dated Brent. Dated Brent itself tends to be traded as a differential to published assessments of the price of forward Brent. Likewise the spot trade in Middle Eastern grades is carried out in terms of differentials to the level of expected official prices, trade in US cash markets is quoted against WTI, and in the Far East crude oils are often quoted against the expected level of official selling prices such as the Indonesian Crude Prices (ICP). The spot oil trade has increasingly become the trade of a differential against either a published assessment or an expectation of an official selling price.[4]

Producing absolute prices for crude oils is then in effect a matter of filling in a matrix. One schemata of filling in the prices for those crude oils traded off Brent would be as follows. The first step is to assess the price of Brent for the forward month in which there has been the most trade in outright prices (generally the second month forward, sometimes the third). The reporters obtain bid/offer ranges from the market (both from traders and brokers), and to a lesser extent have the knowledge of deals done reported to them over the day, and will infer from this the value of Brent at the time-stamp they are using. If that time is during trading or immediately after the close on the IPE, they also have a check arising from knowledge of what price EFPs are being talked at, i.e. the difference between the IPE price and the forward Brent price for a comparable month. Having achieved one absolute Brent forward month price other prices can then be derived.

The next step is to get the other Brent forward prices, which is achieved from the current market bid/offer ranges. Then dated Brent prices can be derived from market talk and from deals done (if any) which allows the assessment of the differentials between dated Brent and the forward prices. Having achieved a price for dated Brent the prices of all the crudes traded as differentials to dated Brent can then be derived.

The process of filling in the matrix does not stop there. Since there is virtually no reported trade in outright prices in the Dubai market, the only way to gauge the level of Dubai prices is to derive them from forward Brent assessments and knowledge of the talk of the bid/offer in the Brent-Dubai differential. Having derived one Dubai price the prices for the other Dubai forward months can be derived from the intra-Dubai spreads. Hence for the purposes of price assessment, the price of second forward month Brent is the single most important absolute price to tie down. Implicit in this process of subsequent matrix filling is that the differentials between crude oils are considerably less volatile on an intra-day basis than the absolute levels of prices.

While producing countries continue to price oil as a differential to a marker crude oil, rather than adopting alternative mechanisms, using price reporting agencies to gauge the level of the marker crudes is better than the possible alternatives. For example, instead of using an assessed marker crude oil price against which to quote differentials, one alternative is to use a panel. In panel pricing the assessments of prices are made by those who participate in that market and are then averaged. This method has been tried in the Far East where the panel price derived is known as the APPI (Asia Petroleum Price Index) and some crude oils, in particular Tapis, have been traded against it. However, in general panels are seen as being sluggish in the face of prices movements (the APPI is produced weekly), potentially biased depending on the balance between and motivations of the buyers and sellers on the panel.[5]

A second alternative to price assessments would be to use the prices generated by futures markets. However, there are very strong reasons why IPE Brent prices would not serve as an adequate substitute for price assessments. First, there is no IPE dated Brent contract and indeed the IPE currently does not trade the wet forward month. Trading prompt oil as differentials from IPE Brent would then have to take into account the time spread of the market and thus lose its simplicity. Secondly, the cash settled IPE market can become divorced from the physical oil trade, as in late 1990 when the IPE Brent price was sometimes as much as 50 cents below the comparable forward market delivery month's price – a premium demonstrating that the IPE contract is a purely paper one and not a contract for physical crude oil. Thirdly, futures market prices tend to show great volatility in the closing minutes of trading. Increasing the volumes of oil priced off exchange closing prices leads to even greater incentives for agents to attempt to move the market significantly in the last few minutes, leading to a series of distorted final prices, which many may be highly wary of using as a basis for spot trades. For all practical purposes neither panels nor futures prices can improve on the output of the price reporting agencies in assessing the levels of the key marker crude oils.

Notes
1. This is quantified in Chapter 14.
2. See P. Caddy (1991), 'The Problems of Defining the Price of the "Marker" Crude Oils and Products', *Petroleum Review*, February 1991.
3. Details of ANS trade are given in Chapter 14.
4. The method of price formation in each market is detailed in Chapter 14.
5. A full critique of APPI prices and their use in the construction of the official Indonesian Crude Price is given in Chapter 14.

CHAPTER 11

PRICES AND PRICE MOVEMENTS

1. Introduction

In the last chapter we explained how price series for the Brent forward market are assessed. In this chapter we consider some of the features of these prices, as well as the prices generated by trading of the IPE contract in Brent futures. After a brief overview of the path of prices since 1984, we consider the volatility of prices, and then the role and determinants of price spreads between crude oil for different delivery months. In the final section we consider questions of price dynamics within the functioning of the market, and the properties of the distribution of price changes.

2. Price Developments Since 1984

The path of the price of first forward month Brent for the period from 1984 to the end of 1992 is shown, as a weekly average, in Figure 11.1. The daily price has averaged $20.61 over this period, ranging from a low of $8.82 per barrel in 1986 to a high of $41.65 per barrel during the Kuwait crisis. In this section we give a brief overview of the period, which splits into four separate subperiods with the movement between them representing distinct, if sometimes only temporary, regime shifts in either policy or the supply balance.

The first identifiable period is the end of the era of administered OPEC prices and the 1986 reverse oil shock. This has been discussed extensively elsewhere,[1] but it is worth noting how sharply oil prices can fall without OPEC production discipline. In just nine months, in 1986, the price fell from over $30 per barrel to less than $10. The collapse was halted by the production cuts agreed at the 75th Meeting of the OPEC Conference which finished on 5 August 1986, with the cuts being implemented with effect from 1 September 1986. Following this we have the period up to the start of the Kuwait crisis, with a shift to market related OPEC pricing. The price over this period moves in two large cycles without showing any significant trend. Prices showed occasional upward spikes due to market squeezes or specific political or

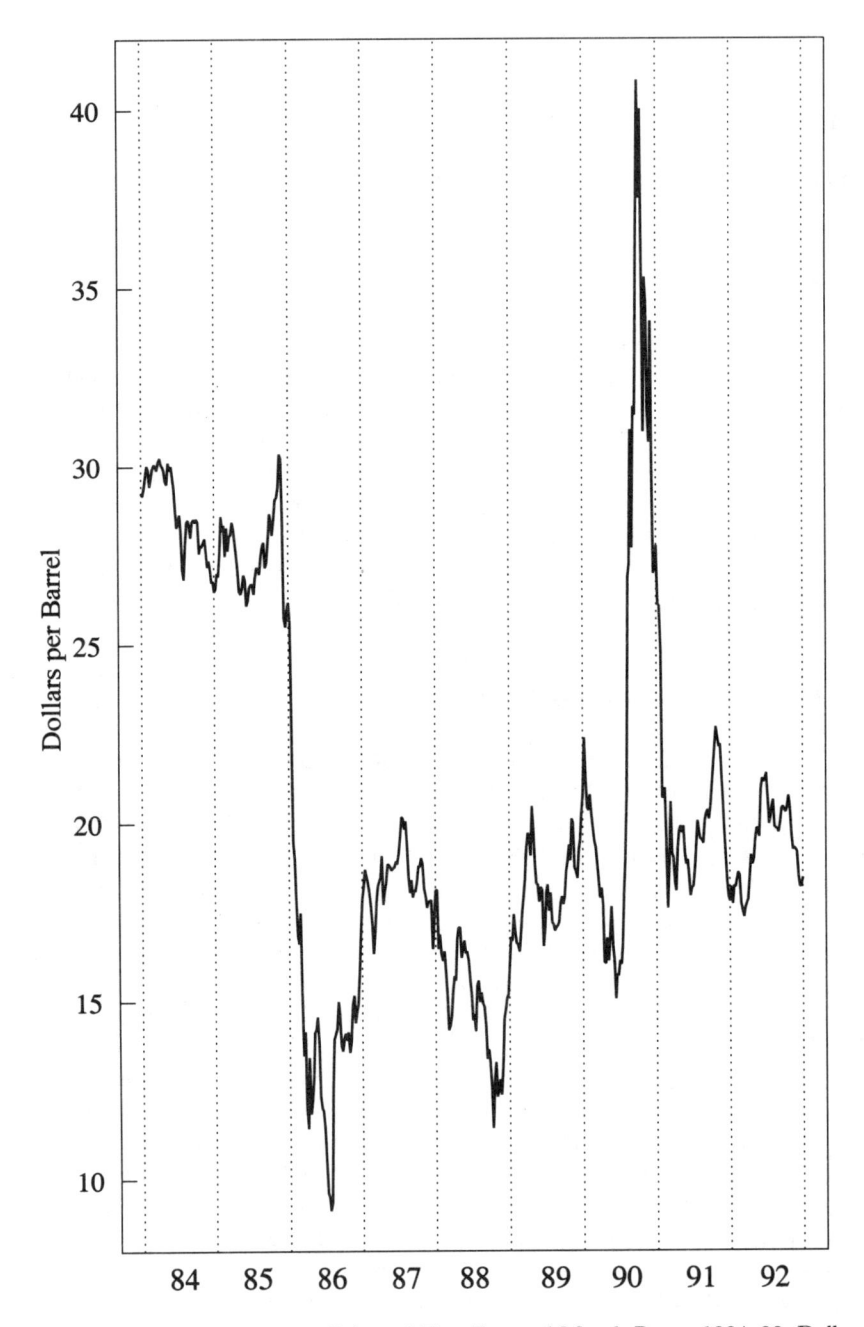

Figure 11.1: Weekly Average Prices of First Forward Month Brent. 1984–92. Dollars per Barrel.

supply related incidents, such as the explosion on the Cormorant Alpha platform in May 1989 which greatly disrupted the supply of Brent. There were also two longer periods of high prices caused by supply tightness in conjunction with the knock-on effects from other markets, in particular the gasoline squeeze in the USA in the early summer of 1989, and the US heating oil squeeze in the extremely cold conditions of the 1989 to 1990 winter.

However these effects were dwarfed by the impact of the Iraqi invasion of Kuwait on 2 August 1990. Prices had already strengthened before the crisis in response to Iraqi belligerency and the run-up to, and bullish outcome of the 87th Meeting of the OPEC Conference of 26 and 27 July 1990; and in particular its introduction of a $21 desired reference price for the OPEC basket.[2] Prices had risen from $15 in early July to $18 immediately prior to the invasion. The immediate embargo of Iraqi supplies and loss of Kuwaiti production combined with growing military tension, had forced the price of Brent to over $40 per barrel by mid-October. From that point prices weakened until the end of the year as other OPEC countries, and in particular Saudi Arabia, made up the supply shortfall of some 4.3 mb/d in international trade. By the start of 1991 it was the threat to Saudi facilities rather than the loss of Iraqi and Kuwaiti production that was keeping prices high.

Prices increased again in the run-up to and expiry of the UN deadline to Iraq on 15 January 1991, once more passing $30 per barrel. When US forces began their attack on Baghdad on the night of 16 January the immediate effect was to send prices spiralling upwards. While both NYMEX and the IPE were shut, the cash WTI and forward Brent markets could operate. Deals for Brent were reported as high as $37 per barrel, and for West Texas Intermediate over $40. However, deals were soon being done below $30 as the perception grew that Saudi oil facilities were not in danger, and by the time the IPE opened in the morning Brent was trading at $23, $7.20 below the previous night's close, and then fell a further $3.30 over the course of the day to finish at $19.70 per barrel. It is important to note that this sharp adjustment was achieved almost entirely by overnight trading in the forward markets. It remains a matter of speculation as to what might have happened had news of the attack on Iraq emerged when NYMEX and the IPE were trading.

Prices firmed before the start of the ground war in Kuwait on 24 February but fell back again on news of the allied military success. The volatility associated with the crisis was not fully curbed until after the outcome of the meeting of the OPEC Ministerial Monitoring Committee on 12 and 13 March became known, after which the immediate post-war policy regime became clearer.

The post-war period until mid-1992 was marked by four main factors. First, world production minus Kuwait and Iraq was close to capacity, with very little additional supply possible were it to be needed. Secondly, the OECD economies were entering a period of deep economic recession and declining oil demand, with perceptions of when that recession might end and therefore when oil demand might pick up becoming a major factor. Thirdly, Iraq continued to be a source of uncertainty, with the market affected by perceptions as to when the UN embargo might be lifted and exports resumed. It should be noted that the price first reacted to (incorrect) rumours that a resumption was likely soon, that is as early as in April 1991. Finally a series of other potential (and actual) political crises that might affect the supply balance emerged (Russia, Algeria and Libya).

The result of these factors was that the price resumed a cyclical pattern caught between two bounds. On the one hand, if Iraq stayed out of the market and demand recovered then prices might move very sharply upwards, particularly in the peak demand period in the fourth quarter of a year, given the lack of spare capacity. On the other hand, with weak demand and a return of Iraqi exports, prices could weaken significantly. Given these extremes the market showed two large cycles. From mid-1991 a perception of possible tightness in the fourth quarter of that year led to a concerted run-up of prices. When demand fell well below expectations, due to the combined effects of recession and warm weather, prices fell back, helped by the overhang of precautionary stocks that had been built up in the autumn.

Over the course of 1992 the cycle repeated itself. A very weak current market was combined with expectations of tightness later in the year leading to another sustained run-up in prices beyond $20 per barrel, only to be brought down again as the realities of recession led to another spate of downwards revisions of demand. These cycles are a normal aspect of oil market behaviour. The extreme disutility attached to having low stocks in a tight market combined with any degree of risk aversion leads to behaviour which, while rational, tends to create overshooting.

3. Volatility

The one common factor throughout the period 1984 to 1992 has been volatility in prices. Without volatility forward and futures markets would not exist. Volatility creates the risk which leads to the desire to hedge, it also provides the incentive for speculators to enter the market. There is a widely held view that volatility in oil prices has been created by the greater reliance by the oil industry on forward and futures markets for price discovery over recent years. In fact oil prices have a long history of volatility. Figure 11.2 shows annual percentage price changes for crude oil since 1860,[3] the year after Drake's well created the oil industry. The period of control of prices by the seven sisters during the 1950s and 1960s was the only period of stability in prices in an industry that has been prone to sharp fluctuations since its birth. In fact the debate as to whether the presence of speculators in forward and futures markets leads to increased volatility is an old one, and there is no empirical evidence that it is the case.[4]

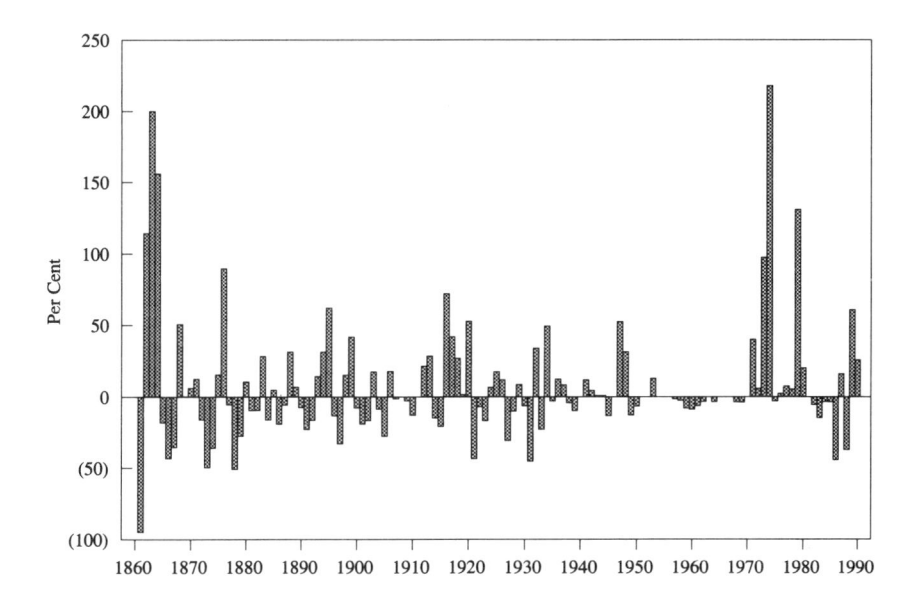

Figure 11.2: Crude Oil Price Changes, Year on Year. 1860–1990. Percentages.

While year-on-year volatility has been common for crude oil, the feature that is new is large-scale day-to-day and intra-day volatility in prices. Even outside times of political crisis, risk management has become an activity that requires constant attention.

There are several ways of quantifying volatility. The first is to evaluate the variance of percentage changes in daily prices over the whole period 1984–92. The results of this method in standard deviation form are shown, on a monthly basis, in Figure 11.3 for the first month forward Brent price. The observation for each month is evaluated as the standard deviation of daily percentage price changes over the month. For days when the delivery month represented by the first

172 *Oil Markets and Prices*

forward month has switched, changes were taken from the previous day's second forward contract.

Figure 11.3 also shows several strong features beyond the demonstration of quite how volatile prices were during 1986 and during the period of the Kuwait crisis. First, since the 1986 crisis, volatility has never returned to the low levels of 1984 and 1985. There has been a statistically significant increase in the average level of volatility since 1985, even when extreme periods are excluded. This could be the result of two factors; either the market is now hit by more information, or the speed of adjustment to new information has increased.

The truth is probably a combination of the two. In particular, even if the amount of new information hitting the market on a day-by-day basis has remained the same, the relevance of any given piece of information in the determination of price levels is greater today than under a policy regime of administered prices with Saudi Arabia acting as swing producer. Saudi Arabia's swing role in the years before 1986, while not ultimately a sustainable policy in itself, was certainly a major factor in dampening volatility. For example, the impact of a piece of news suggesting that supply is running ahead of demand will be greater now than under the regime where traders' perceptions were that any such gap would be eventually removed by changes in Saudi production.

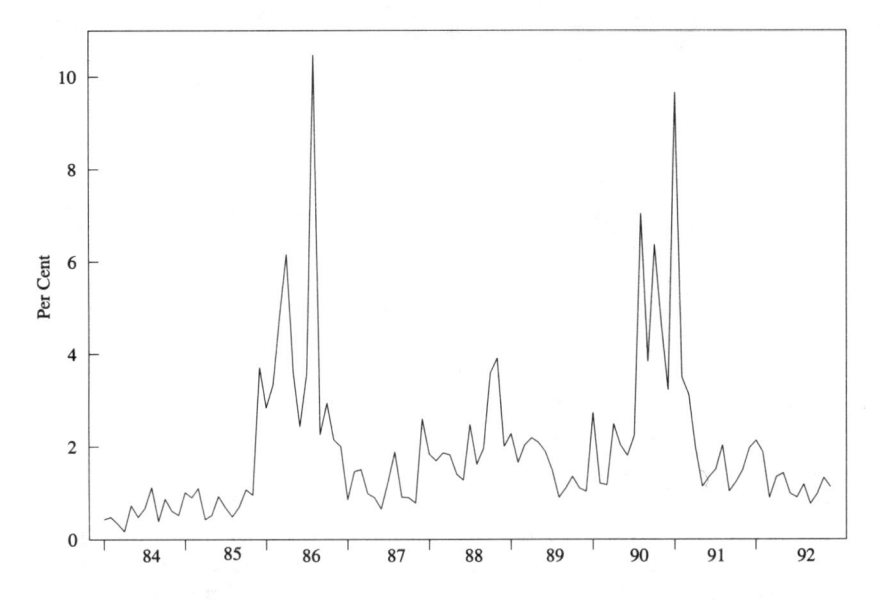

Figure 11.3: Monthly Standard Deviations of Daily Forward Brent Price Changes. 1984–92. Percentages.

A pattern of seasonal volatility is also shown in Figure 11.3. Since 1986, excluding the special circumstances of the Kuwait crisis, there has been a predominance of peaks of volatility in December and January. This effect proves to be statistically significant.

A second approach to volatility, beyond that which was employed in the construction of Figure 11.3, derives from observed behaviour in options markets. The Black-Scholes formula[5] provides an expression for the value of a call premium on a European option. A European option is one that can only be exercised at expiry, as opposed to an American option that can be exercised at any point up to expiry. While most options markets, including all those for crude oil and oil products, trade American options, the formula is used as an approximation to the value of the call premium for an American option.[6] The Black-Scholes formula is as follows;

$$Premium = PN(x_1) - WN(x_2)$$

$$x_1 = \frac{\log_e(P/W) + 0.5V^2T}{V\sqrt{T}}$$

$$x_2 = x_1 - V\sqrt{T}$$

Where: P = Current price of the underlying futures contract
T = Time to expiry of option
W = Present value of the strike price of the option, calculated using a riskless discount rate
V = Volatility
N = Cumulative normal function

All of the necessary inputs into the Black-Scholes formula are directly and exactly observable, except for the level of volatility. Thus by using the actual value of the call premium being traded, and assuming that it is correctly priced according to Black-Scholes, the formula can be solved in terms of V, and an estimate of volatility, known as implied volatility, can be derived. However, for the purposes of the current analysis, we have chosen to use another method, as IPE options do not, as yet, generate a long enough meaningful series.

The third method utilizes data on daily trading ranges where available. The full daily trading range in the Brent forward market is not directly observable given that no price assessment agency achieves anywhere near full coverage. However the range is observable for IPE Brent contracts. A proxy for the variance of prices on any given day t, is given by the following equation;[7]

$$Variance_t = \frac{[\log_e(high_t) - \log_e(low_t)]^2}{4\log_e 2}$$

Using this method for the nearest month Brent contract traded on the IPE for the period from January 1989 to end of May 1992, and converting into annualized standard deviation form, results in the series shown, as a weekly average, in Figure 11.4.

The effects of the Kuwait crisis are again highly visible. Note that, apart from the very end of December 1990, volatility remained above average levels throughout the crisis. Remembering that our measure of volatility only includes data from the day concerned and no historic element, it is clear that price behaviour was marked by above average intra-day movements throughout the crisis. By contrast, the 1986 crisis was characterized by a series of discrete events causing price movements but with relative stability in prices between those events. It is also worth noting that the abortive military coup in Russia in August 1991 shows up in Figure 11.4 as a period of short lived but dramatic volatility. We use the daily data used in the construction of the figure in testing for non-randomness in, and the determinants of the level of volatility.

One possible determinant of volatility is the maturity effect first advanced by Samuelson.[8] This argues that the volatility of a futures or

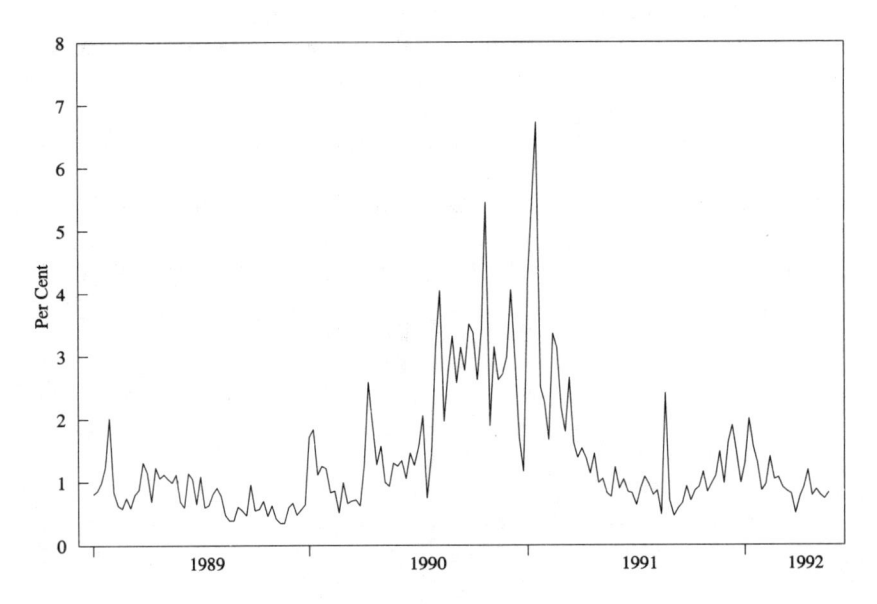

Figure 11.4: Weekly Volatility of Daily IPE Brent Prices. 1989–92. Percentages.

forward contract increases the closer that contract is to maturity. Samuelson's formulation rested on some very strong assumptions, in particular that spot market prices follow an exogenous first order autoregressive process. However other theories have also produced arguments for maturity effects.

Andersen and Danthine[9] start from the natural idea that volatility is affected by the flow of information into the market. If the major source of uncertainty is demand, then volatility is likely to increase as maturity approaches, as demand uncertainty tends only to be resolved close to expiry. If the major source of uncertainty is supply, then volatility may even decrease with contract age, since supply uncertainty in most markets tends to be resolved earlier.

An alternative to the Andersen and Danthine argument rests on the idea that new information will have greater impact the nearer a contract is to maturity, since its effects are normally more easily quantifiable in the near future. For instance, we can have more certainty concerning the effect of an immediate political event on the supply balance in the next month rather than the month beyond that. This argument provides support for the 'cantilever theory' of prices,[10] i.e. that the long-run price of oil is relatively stable and so the impact of news is akin to striking a cantilever, with more vibration produced at the free rather than the tethered end. Observationally, the long-run price of oil has been highly stable, with the Kuwait crisis for instance having had very little impact on prices for oil traded beyond eighteen months out on NYMEX.[11]

Empirically Brent prices are more volatile for contracts closer to termination in both the forward and futures markets. For example, for the period from the start of 1989 to mid-1992 the daily trading range for the first month traded IPE contract was less than that of the second month traded on only 16 per cent of all trading days; it was equal on 6 per cent and greater on 78 per cent of trading days. Regression analysis confirms for IPE Brent delivery months the result of Serletis,[12] who analysed light sweet crude oil and oil products contracts on NYMEX, i.e. that while not true for every delivery month traded there is generally an increase in volatility as maturity nears.

The above approach detects a general increase in volatility over the life of a contract, but provides no clues as to the behaviour of prices very close to expiry. As opposed to the maturity effect caused by the impact of information flows on the cantilever, there are several reasons why there might be a distinct expiry effect. Volatility could change close to expiry as positions in one delivery month are closed and rolled over into the next, or due to changes in the volume of trading as attention shifts away from the expiring contract.

Alternatively, volatility could increase due to squeezes. However, as we have already noted in Chapter 4, the IPE Brent contract is not prone to squeezes. It should be noted that the first delivery month traded in the IPE is actually the second in the forward market. The IPE contract at expiry converges to a forward market contract as it becomes wet. The IPE contract is cash settled, and squeezes and scrambles are very unlikely as much as a month away from the expiry of the forward market contract. However, there is a possible expiry effect arising from activity in the options market. We explained in Chapter 4 that IPE Brent options expire three trading days before the expiry of the underlying futures contract. It is theoretically possible that a trader with a large enough marginally 'out-of-the-money' options position may find it profitable to move these options 'in-the-money' through trading of the underlying futures contract.

Figure 11.5 shows the average trading range over the last thirty trading days to the expiry of the contract for IPE Brent delivery months between January 1989 and May 1992, excluding trading made during the course of the Kuwait crisis. It therefore shows the average pattern of intra-day volatility in approximately the last one and a half calendar months of a contract's life. Compared to the trading period shown as a whole, there is significantly lower volatility on the last day of trading, and significantly higher on the second and third to last days of trading. There does then appear to be a distinct expiry effect in addition to the maturity effect already detected.

We found no patterns in the volatility of the first month traded IPE contract in relation to expiry of light sweet crude oil contracts on NYMEX.[13] However, in interview evidence several IPE participants said that they did expect higher volatility on days close to or at NYMEX contract expiry. Even though this effect is not statistically significant it certainly exists in perceptions. There were also no significant day of the week effects detected in the absolute price change from the previous day's closing price to current day's opening price. In particular there was no Wednesday effect. The weekly data on refinery production and crude oil and oil product stock levels published by the American Petroleum Institute is influential as a measure of the short-term supply balance. It is normally released on Tuesday evenings after the close of NYMEX and the IPE. However, the effect of these figures does not create statistically significant greater changes between Tuesday closing and Wednesday opening prices for IPE Brent than on other days.

A forward trade for Brent can be made at any time and hence forward market prices, while not constantly observable, can change at any time. However the IPE works within fixed exchange hours, and

Prices and Price Movements 177

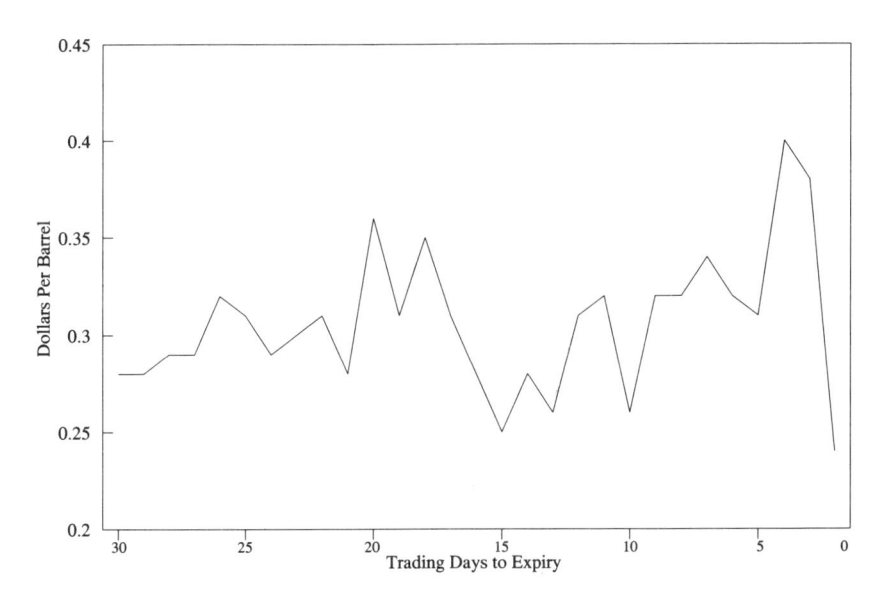

Figure 11.5: Average Intra-Day Price Range of IPE Brent by Number of Trading Days to Expiry of Contracts over January 1989 to May 1992 (excluding the Kuwait crisis). Dollars per Barrel.

hence the impact of any overnight information has to be reflected in a difference between the opening price and the previous night's closing price. The question then arises as to how the decomposition of price changes varies between times the IPE is open and when it is shut, i.e. how the difference between the opening price and the previous day's closing price relates to the movement in price from IPE trading start to finish.

In Table 11.1 we show the average absolute changes in the price of the first delivery month traded on the IPE over the period from January 1989 to the end of May 1992 as a whole, and by subperiods. The first of these equates to the time before 11 January 1990 when the IPE changed its Brent contract trading closing time from 5.30 p.m. to 8.15 p.m. London time. The second relates to the period with the extended hours before the Kuwait crisis, and the third and fourth to the periods during and after the Kuwait crisis respectively. It is clear that most price variation now occurs in the ten and three-quarter hours that the IPE is open for Brent trading. By contrast, before the hours were extended there was movement in prices outside rather than inside IPE trading hours. Table 11.1 also shows the comparative advantage the IPE enjoyed over NYMEX throughout the Kuwait crisis due to its longer

178 *Oil Markets and Prices*

Table 11.1: Average Price Change of First-Month IPE Brent. January 1989–May 1992. US Cents per Barrel.

Period	IPE Shut	IPE Open
1 Jan, 1989 to 31 May, 1992	21	29
Sub-Periods		
1 Jan, 1989 to 10 Jan, 1990	15	13
11 Jan, 1990 to 1 Aug, 1990	11	20
2 Aug, 1990 to 13 Mar, 1991	61	83
14 Mar, 1991 to 31 May, 1992	9	19

Note: IPE Shut is defined as the average difference between opening price and the previous day closing price; IPE open is the average difference between closing price and the opening price of a trading day.

hours and better time zone position in relation to the Middle East. Over this period the greater proportion of price changes occurred while the IPE was open.

Oil market volatility is in part predictable in terms of its own history. This is shown in Table 11.2 which presents the results of the regression of the IPE trading range on its own past values. Again, we have excluded the period of the Kuwait crisis. The hypothesis that the trading range is a stationary variable (i.e. has constant mean and variance) cannot be rejected by a Dickey-Fuller test and hence the regression does not have to be run in first difference form. We find statistically positive significant effects arising from the first, second, third and fifth lagged trading days volatilities. Thus high volatility today implies that volatility will also be higher over the course of the next calendar week.

In Table 11.2 volatility levels in previous days are shown to have a strong explanatory power. Again it should be remembered that our measure of volatility uses daily trading ranges and has no inbuilt historical element. The idea that there is serial correlation in price volatility is perhaps not too surprising, for example the run-up to OPEC meetings and the meetings themselves take longer than one day and most political news takes more than a day to be fully resolved. However the regression does show clearly that oil market volatility does not take a random walk, each trading day is not a fresh day with a priori completely unknown and random volatility.[14]

In sum, we have discovered that there are predictable elements in price volatility, arising from seasonal, maturity and expiry effects as well as from the recent past history of volatility. We cannot maintain the

Table 11.2: Regression of IPE Price Volatility on its own Lagged Values. Statistics.

Variable	Coefficient	T-Statistic
Constant Term	1.3586	5.029*
Lagged Volatility:		
1st Lag	0.2697	7.236*
2nd Lag	0.0801	2.106*
3rd Lag	0.1412	3.685*
4th Lag	0.0059	0.154
5th Lag	0.0812	2.118*
6th Lag	0.0425	1.111
7th Lag	0.0495	1.289
8th Lag	0.0017	0.044
9th Lag	0.0260	0.671
10th Lag	0.0440	1.168

Other Statistics: R-Squared 0.269, Log Likelihood -896.5, F-Statistic 24,587

Note: * Significant at 5 per cent level

hypothesis that volatility is an exogenous and completely unpredictable variable. We return to the implications of this finding in section 5 of this chapter.

4. The Time Structure of Prices

The time structure of prices refers to the relative prices for the same commodity for delivery at different points in time, for example the price of Brent for April delivery compared to that for May delivery. The differences between these two prices is a spread, and as was quantified in Chapter 7, the trading of spreads has become the dominant form of trade in the Brent forward market.

Two important pieces of terminology are backwardation and contango. A backwardation occurs when the prices are higher for delivery dates closer to the present. Thus a situation where Brent for April delivery has a higher price than Brent for May delivery represents a backwardation. A contango arises when prices are higher for more distant delivery dates, e.g. May Brent being priced above April Brent. The time structure of prices refers to the whole pattern of backwardations and contangos across the possible delivery dates. Thus it is perfectly conceivable that some time spreads may be in contango while simultaneously others are in backwardation. Indeed, such cases are not uncommon in the Brent market.

Considering how the time structure of prices might be arbitraged by traders generates two important propositions concerning the relative behaviour of backwardations and contangos. Consider first a market in contango between the prompt cash price and prices in the future, e.g. where dated Brent is at a discount to, say, second month forward Brent. If the degree of contango exceeds the carrying or storage costs of the crude oil, then profit can be made by buying spot Brent, selling it forward and putting the physical oil into storage. This is sometimes referred to as cash and carry arbitrage. This generates the proposition that the degree of contango is limited by the value of transaction and storage costs, unless there is no storage available. Storage in this sense includes both onshore tankage and holding oil offshore in crude carriers. Even if all onshore tankage was used up, the degree of contango should not exceed the per barrel costs of tanker chartering for the relevant time period. This implies that the degree of any contango between any forward traded months is also limited. For example the contango between, say, January and February delivery is limited by the difference in storage costs today between storing a physical cargo until January and storing it until February.

The one major exception to the rule that, as long as storage is available contangos are limited, may occur close to the expiry of a contract, and affects the spread between the physical commodity and the expiring contract. In the case of Brent this means the spread between dated Brent and first month forward Brent close to its expiry.[15] As was explained in Chapter 9, when a market squeeze or scramble is in operation the price of first month forward Brent can be forced far above dated Brent. As trade in forward Brent tends to be very thin indeed in the last two weeks before expiry, there need be no upper limit to this particular form of contango. This case is discussed further below.

If the costs of cash and carry arbitrage set a limit to the degree of contangos, it would seem plausible that the costs of reverse cash and carry arbitrage, i.e. selling prompt and buying further forward, should limit the degree of backwardations. However the symmetry tends not to hold, at least not in the case of oil. Consider the case where the degree of backwardation does exceed the cost of reverse cash and carry arbitrage, noting that this cost is essentially made up only of transactions costs and does not involve the storage costs of cash and carry arbitrage. In theory, selling prompt and buying forward should depress prompt prices and bid forward prices up. Indeed, in a world of zero transaction costs this would imply that backwardations could never persist. However, for this arbitrage to work the trader must have stocks of crude oil to sell. This is not true for most market participants. Further, backwardations tend to be associated with periods of real or perceived shortage where unavailability of physical cargoes prevents reverse cash and carry arbitrage from removing the backwardation. This generates the proposition that there is no upper limit on the degree of backwardation. While contangos are limited (except in the face of a shortage of storage), backwardations can be theoretically unlimited in their degree.

An agent holding enough inventory above minimum operating levels[16] during a period of backwardation enjoys a 'convenience yield' from these stocks. For the stocks to be willingly held this must be at least equal to the extent of the backwardation plus carrying and capital costs. Considered in these terms it becomes clear why backwardations can be unlimited. As short-term markets can move into large-scale excess demand and the calls on stocks increase, there need be no limit to the implicit valuation agents put on holding existing stocks. There need then be no limit to the backwardation necessary to induce agents to part with those stocks. It also follows that as this is a product of short-term market tightness, which tends to correct itself, very large backwardations will not be maintained for long. Therefore the larger the degree of backwardation, the more unstable it would be expected to be.

This asymmetry between contangos and backwardations was generated in the example above with reference to a cash price and a forward price. The lack of any ceiling on a backwardation was caused by the impossibility of selling a physical cargo if you have no access to a cargo, i.e. you cannot take a short position on a physical commodity. However, you can of course take a short position on a forward cargo. At first sight this might be taken to imply that while there can be no limit on the degree of backwardation between prompt cargoes and forward cargoes, reverse cash and carry arbitrage might limit the degree of backwardation between forward delivery months. For example, in a heavily backwardated market why not sell the first forward month and buy the second forward month? The problem is of course that in the prompt versus forward argument there was no price risk involved; the price of both prompt and forward trades are known at the point the arbitrage is arranged. By selling the first to second month spread, the trader still has to acquire a physical cargo to deliver in the first month. They also do not know what the level of spread will be when they close their positions. In other words, selling the spread between two forward months is not a reverse cash and carry arbitrage operation and cannot put any limit on the degree of backwardation. Hence not only is there no limit on the degree of backwardation between prompt cargoes and forward cargoes, there is also no limit to the backwardation between

182 *Oil Markets and Prices*

forward months.

The theory of 'Normal Backwardation' was propounded by Keynes[17] and Hicks[18]. This argues that there is more flexibility in consumption than in production, and so it is the producers who look further ahead in trading forward contracts. Overall the net effect is that the hedgers (i.e. producers and consumers) have a short position in the forward market. To encourage speculators to take up the opposing long positions, a premium must be created for prompter delivery months. Hence the market will always tend to be in backwardation, with this backwardation representing a risk premium paid by the hedgers to the speculators. Further, this would imply that prices for forward months are biased downwards.

There are several problems with the theory of normal backwardation. First, it does rest crucially on the idea that hedgers are net short in the market, i.e. that there is less volume hedged by consumers than by producers at any point of time. Secondly, speculators do not necessarily need to be paid a risk premium to enter a market. As was pointed out by Dusak,[19] logically a speculator would enter as many markets as possible (commodity and financial), to diversify risk. As long as there is no systematic relationship between risk across markets there need be no risk premium and thus no downward bias in forward prices. There is no systematic relationship between risk in crude oil markets and in markets for other commodities or for financial assets. Thirdly, the theory of normal backwardation, when applied to crude oil, would imply that the large major oil companies would prefer to pay Wall Street refiners to carry their risk, rather than to cope with that risk in house.[20] Both observationally and from interview evidence, we believe that there is no truth in this implication. Finally, there has been little empirical evidence in any market to suggest that forward prices are biased downwards – indeed there have been as many cases of upward as of downward bias reported,[21] so contradicting the theory.

Empirically there is also no evidence of any downward bias in Brent forward prices. Comparing average prices for dated Brent over the course of delivery months since 1988 with the average price of the matching forward contract, when it is the second month forward contract, provides an estimate of the gain to the speculator of matching the hedger's short position. Over the whole period this averages at 32 cents per barrel, with a standard deviation of $3.59 per barrel, and hence is not significantly different from zero. Taking out of the analysis the months affected by the Kuwaiti crisis gives an average of an 11 cents per barrel gain with a standard deviation of $1.74 per barrel, again not significantly different from zero.

Backwardation and contango in the Brent market is normally taken to apply to the spreads between prices of cargoes in different delivery months. However, we first consider the very special spread represented by the difference between the price of dated Brent and first month forward Brent. This spread essentially represents the gain or loss that is realized by accepting delivery from the forward market and selling it on as a dated cargo. It has two important implications.

First, it represents a risk to those attempting to hedge through Brent market operations the purchase or sale of a cargo priced on dated Brent related terms. It will be seen in Chapters 14 and 15 that this includes virtually all oil produced in or imported into Europe, together with a substantial proportion of trade into North America. This risk has given rise to the contract for differences market, essentially a swap based on published assessments of the spread. Secondly, the spread determines the willingness of Brent market participants to lift cargoes out of the chains rather than to pass on nominations. When the spread is positive, chains tend to be very short, since there is a gain in lifting the cargo. When it is negative chains tend to be very long, and are very often only terminated by a party being five o'clocked and unable to pass on the nomination. Hence the spread is an important determinant of behaviour in the Brent market.

Figure 11.6 shows weekly average time spreads in the forward Brent market. The difference between the dated to first month spread and the first month to second month spread is striking. The latter rarely moves between backwardation and contango. Most of 1988 was spent in contango, while 1989 was a year of backwardation. In 1990 after a period of relatively deep contango, the Kuwait crisis occasioned a movement into deep backwardation. This spread has mainly been a backwardation, only having been negative on 34.3 per cent of trading days during the period. It also shows the theoretical asymmetry explained above. The average backwardation over the whole period has been 55 cents, the average contango only 19 cents.

By contrast the dated to first month spread has not only been highly volatile with frequent switches between regimes, it has also been mainly in contango. Over the whole period the spread has been zero on 12.8 per cent of trading days, in backwardation on 28.7 per cent, and in contango on 58.5 per cent. It should be noted that observation of the dated to first month spread gives little information about the first to second month spread. In fact it has been in contango or zero on more than half the occasions the first to second month spread has shown a backwardation. It also does not show the theoretical asymmetry, indeed the deepest contangos are greater than the deepest backwardations. The average contango has been 17 cents, compared to 22 cents of average backwardation.

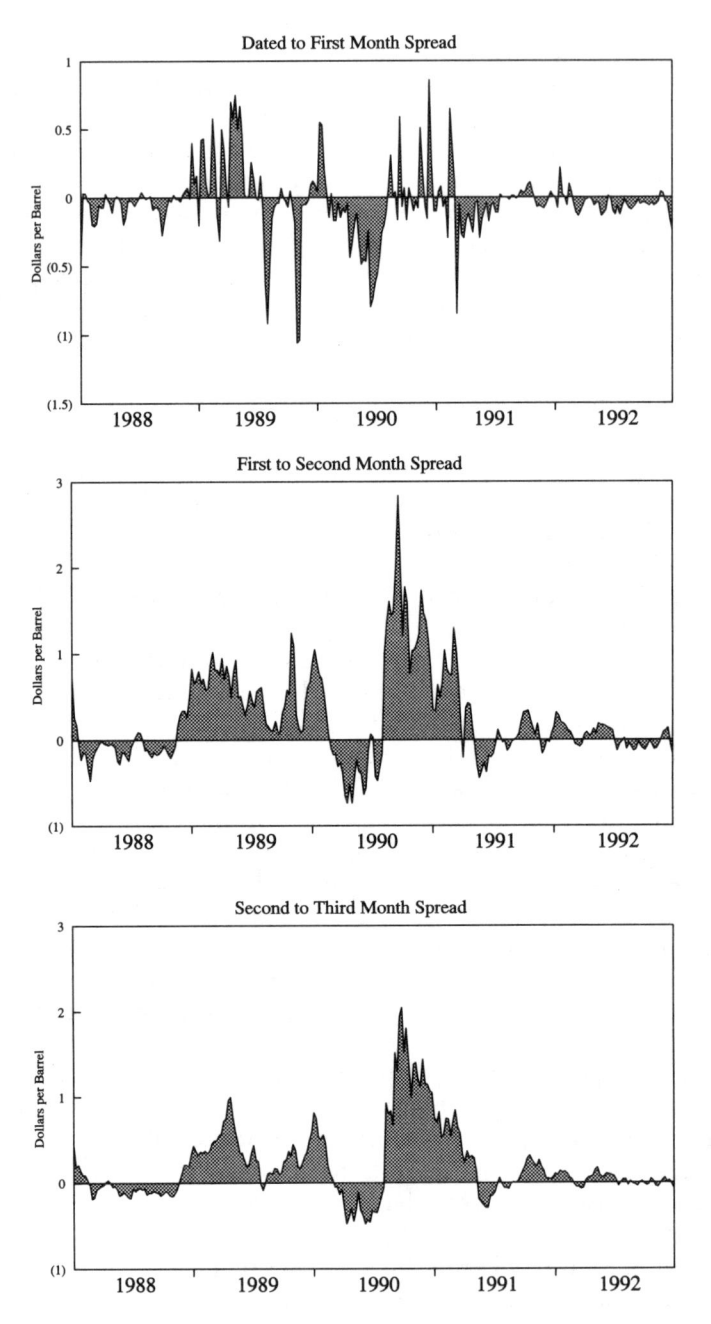

Figure 11.6: Weekly Average Price Differentials between Brent Prices. 1988–92. Dollars per Barrel.

The deep spiked contangos in the dated to first month spread are all associated with days very close to the expiry of the first month forward contract, at times when a squeeze or scramble is in operation. While cash and carry arbitrage will be effective if second month forward Brent rises too far above dated Brent, if the same pattern occurs for first month Brent close to its expiry it may well prove impossible to make the trade necessary for the arbitrage in the remaining time, in a thin market with very few cargoes left to pass down the chains. As noted in Chapter 9, in such circumstances a forward contract and physical Brent do not represent identical commodities, since while an agent wishing to buy a physical cargo can buy Brent or any other North Sea grade, there is no substitute for a forward Brent contract for an agent caught in a squeeze or a scramble.

The second to third month spread is also shown in Figure 11.6. It is considerably less volatile than the first to second month spread and it is not affected by the spiked backwardations associated with a squeeze or scramble in an expiring contract.

5. Market Efficiency

In economic terminology a market is considered efficient if all currently available information is contained in the current price at all times,[22] and hence it is impossible at any time to forecast future changes in prices on the basis of past changes in prices. If the market efficiency hypothesis holds then the only unexploited predictable price movements are those for which the gains are less than the trading costs (including the cost of capital) involved in realizing those gains.

There are traders in all commodity and futures markets who rely on what is known as 'technical' trading or chartism. Chartists look for patterns in past price movements (e.g. 'head and shoulder' patterns), from which they infer future price movements.[23] It is fairly common in oil futures market reports to see terms such as 'resistance level' indicative of a technician's view of the market. Technical trading does not conform to an economist's view of the market. If future trends are predictable on the basis of past performance then in theory all agents in the market will eventually learn the signs, and prices will simply adjust immediately. Otherwise traders would be making systematic repeated errors which does not fit with any concept of economic rationality. Maintenance of the efficient markets hypothesis also rules out the occurrence of speculative bubbles or fads.[24]

The efficient markets hypothesis is usually taken to come in three levels. The weak form says that all the information contained in past prices is reflected in current prices. The semi-strong form says that current prices reflect all publicly available information, i.e. that analysis of the fundamentals will not guarantee profits. Finally the strong version says that all information, be it public or inside, is reflected in prices, i.e. the holders of inside information will through their actions reveal it to the rest of the market. Most attention has been given to the weak form, as that is the easiest to test. If the weak form holds, there should be no correlation between successive price changes. As the only factor that can change prices is new information, which is not forecastable, then no patterns in price changes should emerge.

The implication of the weak form of the efficient markets hypothesis is that price changes follow a random walk.[25] In section 2 we showed that volatility in oil prices is in part predictable from its own past history, as well as terms of seasonality, maturity and expiry effects. These results imply that oil prices cannot take a random walk. While not meaning that the weak form of the efficient markets hypothesis is necessarily violated (since price changes could follow a more complicated process than the random walk that is still consistent with the hypothesis), it makes testing of the hypothesis difficult. This is compounded by another feature of oil prices, that they are neither normally nor log-normally distributed. We expand on this below.

Another implication of there being a forecastable element in future levels of volatility is that there should be interdependence between prices and volatilities as long as there is at least one agent in the market who is not risk neutral. For instance, imagine that volatility on the next trading day is expected to be higher than on the current day. If all other parameters in the oil market remain unchanged, a risk averse market participant will be less willing to trade tomorrow at current prices. In other words, prices may be lower on days that a priori are expected to be volatile. The risk averse participants may also reduce their volume of trade. In interview evidence some Brent market participants stated that they tended to stay on the sidelines keeping a watching brief on days that they expected in advance to manifest above normal levels of volatility. This implies that prices, volatility and volume of trade are simultaneously determined with a complex series of causalities, both forwards and backwards, running between them.

In Table 11.3 we show the result of tests for the normality of price changes in the first forward Brent market contract, and in changes in the log of prices (i.e. percentage changes in prices), for a series of time intervals. Results are shown by year, with the Kuwait crisis being detached and tested separately (we have removed the extreme observation associated with the price change consequent on the onset of the attack on Iraq from this period). For each period we show the skewness and

Table 11.3: Normality Tests on Brent Price Changes.

Periods	Normality			Log-Normality		
	Kurtosis	Skewness	Jarque-Bera	Kurtosis	Skewness	Jarque-Bera
1988	6.439	0.504	136.44	7.505	0.512	226.82
1989	3.907	-0.439	16.95	3.943	-0.449	18.03
1990 (pre crisis)	4.906	0.272	24.38	4.420	0.326	15.17
Kuwait crisis	4.497	-0.345	17.77	4.661	-0.230	19.43
1991 (post crisis)	4.305	0.022	14.41	4.398	0.025	16.57
1992 (until end June)	4.688	-0.295	16.79	4.776	-0.374	19.51

kurtosis of the series. In a normal distribution these will be respectively zero and three, and we also show the value of the Jarque-Bera test for normality which tests the joint hypothesis that they take on these critical values.

The values of the Jarque-Bera test are such that in all periods Brent price changes show a highly significant departure from both normality and log-normality. The source of this failure is in each case excess kurtosis rather than excess skewness. Brent price changes are shown to be highly leptokurtic, i.e. when compared to a normal distribution there are significantly more observations in the tails of the distribution than would be expected. Leptokurtosis has also been found in many other financial and commodity time series.[26] Opinions remain divided as to whether this is because they conform to some other single stable distribution, or represent a mixture of two or possibly more distributions. However, this departure has important implications – in particular the Black-Scholes formula explained in the third section of this chapter for the pricing of options, relies on the log-normality of price changes. The above shows that this assumption cannot be maintained in the case of Brent prices.

Notes
1. See R. Mabro (ed.) (1988), *The 1986 Oil Price Crisis*, Oxford Institute for Energy Studies, and R. Mabro (1987), *Netback Pricing and the Oil Price Collapse of 1986*, Oxford Institute for Energy Studies.
2. The OPEC basket represents the average price of seven crude oils. Six of these are from OPEC countries (Arabian Light, Bonny Light, Dubai, Minas, Saharan Blend and Tia Juana Light) and one non-OPEC (Mexican Isthmus). The value of the basket generally lies between $1.10 and $1.50 per barrel below that of dated Brent.
3. Calculations made from data drawn from Petroleum Argus *Oil Prices Worldwide*. The price series represents Pennsylvania crude prices for the period from 1860 to 1899, US average crude price for 1900 to 1944, and Arabian Light basis Middle East since 1945.

4. For a survey see R. Britto (1985), 'Futures Trading and the Level and Volatility of Spot Prices', Columbia Business School.
5. F. Black and M. Scholes (1973), 'The Pricing of Options and Corporate Liabilities', *Journal of Political Economy* 81.
6. In fact there is no formula for the value of an American call premium, only statistical methods. See R. Geske and K. Shastri (1985), 'Valuation by Approximation: A Comparison of Alternative Option Valuation Techniques', *Journal of Financial and Quantitative Analysis*, 20.
7. See M. B. Garman and M. Klass (1980), 'On the Estimation of Security Price Volatilities from Historical Data', *Journal of Business*, 53.
8. P.A. Samuelson (1965), 'Proof that Properly Anticipated Prices Fluctuate Randomly', *Industrial Management Review* 6. See also P.A. Samuelson (1976), 'Is Real-World Price a Tale Told by the Idiot of Chance?', reprinted in A.E. Peck (ed.) (1977), *Selected Writings on Future Markets*.
9. R.W. Anderson and J.P. Danthine (1980), 'The Time Pattern of Hedging, Volatility of Futures, and the Resolution of Uncertainty', Columbia Business School.
10. See J. Gabillon (1991), *The Term Structure of Oil Futures Prices*, Oxford Institute for Energy Studies.
11. Ibid.
12. A. Serletis, 'Maturity Effects in Energy Futures', *Energy Economics*, April 1992.
13. The market for WTI and the NYMEX light sweet crude oil contract are documented in Chapter 12.
14. Predictability of volatility from its own past values has also been found in stock market prices. See R. Merton (1980), 'On Estimating the Expected Return on the Market : An Exploratory Investigation', *Journal of Financial Economics*, 8.
15. As noted in the previous section, it is highly unlikely to be a factor in the spread between expiring IPE Brent contracts and the Brent forward month they converge onto.
16. Minimum operating levels comprise oil in tank bottoms, pipeline fill, refinery fill and so on. This is normally a substantial amount, for instance in the USA it amounts to some 300 mb of crude oil. (See National Petroleum Council (1989), *Petroleum Storage and Transportation*, vol. 5). While this represents over three weeks' consumption, total stock levels normally exceed it by less than four days' consumption.
17. J.M. Keynes (1930) *A Treatise on Money*, vol. 2.
18. J.R. Hicks (1946) *Value and Capital*.
19. K. Dusak (1973), 'Futures Trading and Investor Returns: An Investigation of Commodity Market Risk Premiums', *Journal of Political Economy*, vol. 81, no.6.
20. For an oil company perspective see A. Binder (1988), 'A Major's View of the World's Oil Market', Shell International.
21. For example see C.S. Rockwell (1967) 'Normal Backwardation, Forecasting, and the Returns to Commodity Futures Traders', reprinted in A.E. Peck (ed.) (1977), *Selected Writings on Futures Markets* vol. 2.
22. E.F. Fama (1970), 'Efficient Capital Markets: A Review of Theory and Empirical Work', *Journal of Finance*, 25.

23. For a sceptical view of chartism, see B. G. Malkiel (1990), *A Random Walk Down Wall Street*, 5th edition, Norton. For a proponent's view see M. J. Pring (1991), *Technical Analysis Explained*, 3rd Edition, McGraw Hill.
24. For an analysis of such occurrences (e.g. the South Sea Bubble, the Dutch tulip mania and so on) see R. J. Schiller (1988), 'Fashions, Fads and Bubbles in Financial Markets', reprinted in R. J. Schiller (1989), *Market Volatility*, Massachusetts Institute of Technology Press.
25. The term derives from a debate over the best method of locating a drunk who had been left in the middle of a field at night, the answer being in the middle of the field since the path of the drunk's walk would be random and expected to sum to zero total movement. See B.G. Malkiel, 'Efficient Market Hypothesis', in J. Eatwell, M. Milgate and P. Newman (eds) (1987), *The New Palgrave : A Dictionary of Economics*, MacMillan Press.
26. See A. Kamara (1982), 'Issues in Futures Markets: A Survey', *Journal of Futures Markets*, 2.

Part IV

World Oil Markets

CHAPTER 12

THE BRENT FUTURES CONTRACT AND ITS RELATIONSHIP TO THE FORWARD MARKET

1. Introduction

In this chapter we consider the IPE Brent contract and its relationship with forward Brent trade. In section 2 we chart the evolution of trade in the IPE contract and its characteristics. Section 3 addresses the issue of what constitutes a futures market, and whether the 15-day Brent is forward or futures. The final section considers the interrelationship between forward and futures, and why an informal and a formal market for the same commodity can co-exist.

2. The IPE Brent Contract

The institutional features and structure of the IPE Brent contract were explained in Chapter 4, with a description of the successful third attempt to launch it on 23 June 1988. Given the earlier problems the scale of this success is quite remarkable. The volume of trade in the contract increased remorselessly over the course of the first two years after the launch. Figure 12.1 shows the total daily volume traded for all delivery months on the IPE, expressed as a weekly average. Consistent growth saw average volume exceed 10 thousand contracts per day in the spring of 1990, equivalent to over 10 mb/d of Brent.

However the greatest impetus to the contract was given by the Kuwait crisis. The average volume of trade more than doubled in just two months. The increase in liquidity arose from the general increase in the desire to risk manage due to added volatility, combined with the advantages of the IPE over NYMEX during the crisis. The IPE begins to trade at 9.30 a.m. London time (i.e. over five hours before NYMEX). Because of time differences, events in the Middle East occurred mainly after the futures markets had closed, so the IPE could react to overnight news well before NYMEX. As a result a lot of trade that would otherwise have gone to NYMEX migrated to the IPE.

Volume peaked in the run-up to and immediate aftermath of the attack on Iraq, since when the daily average has remained in the range

194 *Oil Markets and Prices*

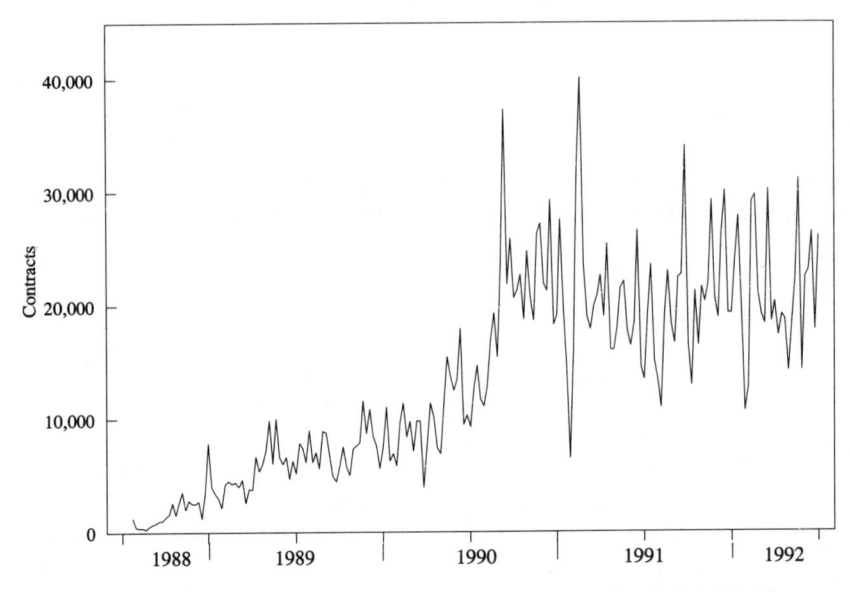

Figure 12.1: Daily Average Number of IPE Brent Contracts Traded. 1988–92.

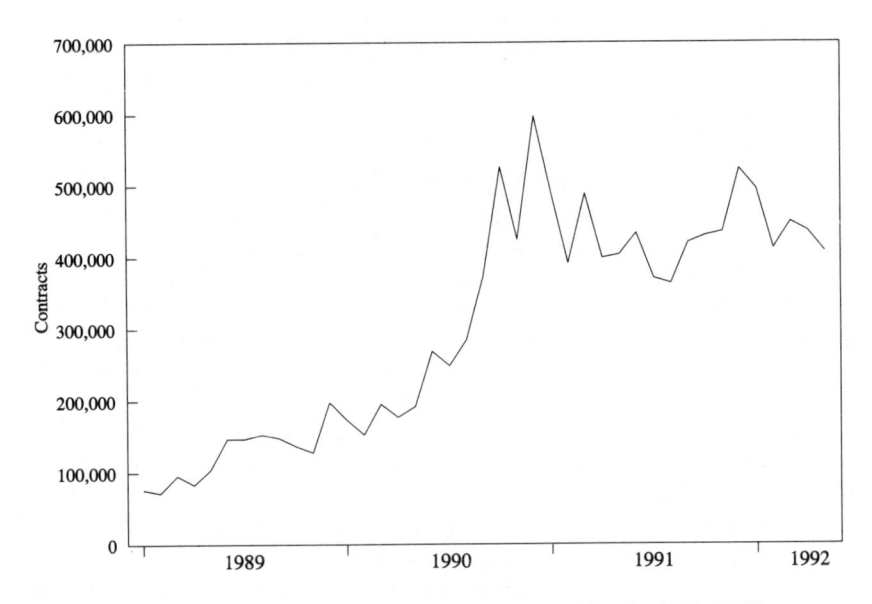

Figure 12.2: Number of Contracts Traded per Delivery Month. 1989–1992.

of 15 thousand to 25 thousand contracts a day. Our estimates of forward market volume from Chapter 7 imply an average of about 35 mb per trading day. It appears then that IPE Brent now trades volumes that are between 50 per cent and 70 per cent of the size of those traded on the forward market.

After the period of sustained growth accelerated by the Kuwait crisis, total volume has shown no significant trends. Volume for the IPE as a whole has continued to grow, but it has been achieved largely by growth in Brent options, together with attempts to launch new oil product contracts, rather than by further expansion in the Brent futures contract. The levelling off of volume in the Brent contract suggests that it is now close to being a completely mature contract. The total value of trades made for the IPE Brent contract in 1991 equates to about $100 billion.

The path of volume is also shown by Figure 12.2, which gives the total volume of trade for each IPE Brent contract month from January 1989 to May 1992, i.e. the time-scale represents delivery rather than calendar months. The Kuwait crisis led to a dramatic increase in the total trade in the last four contracts of 1990 compared to previous delivery months. The peak occurred for the December 1990 contract which was traded 600 thousand times, equivalent to a volume of 600 mb. After this contracts have tended to trade between 400 mb and 500 mb over the course of their life, with no significant trend in total volume for contract months from January 1991 onwards.

Figure 12.3 shows the maximum level of end of day open interest achieved by contract month. Open interest is the number of outstanding positions among participants in the market. As each buy must be matched with a sell (i.e. each long matches a short), open interest must then equal the number of open buy positions, and the number of open sell positions. Generally a market with a large amount of open interest is one where hedging is taking place, i.e. there is stock of long or short positions that are not closed out every day. Figure 12.3 then shows the maximum extent of these open positions over the course of trading of each contract month. Like the path of volume in the IPE contract, the maximum level of open interest increased steadily until the Kuwait crisis, which then accelerated the growth. The highest open interest recorded was for the March 1991 contract, when at one point open interest reached 65 mb. Growth has not been maintained since, and indeed the maximum level of open interest for the May 1992 contract was below that of the July 1990 contract, before Iraq invaded Kuwait.

The path of open interest over the life of a contract is shown by trading days to expiry in Figure 12.4, which averages contracts with 1991 delivery dates. There is some open interest more than four months

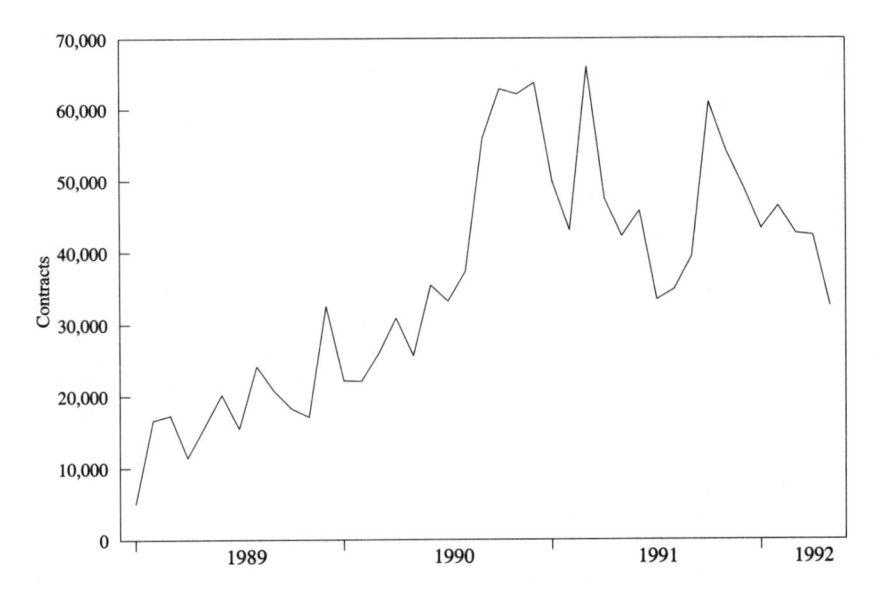

Figure 12.3: Maximum Open Interest per Contract Month. 1989–92. Number of Contracts.

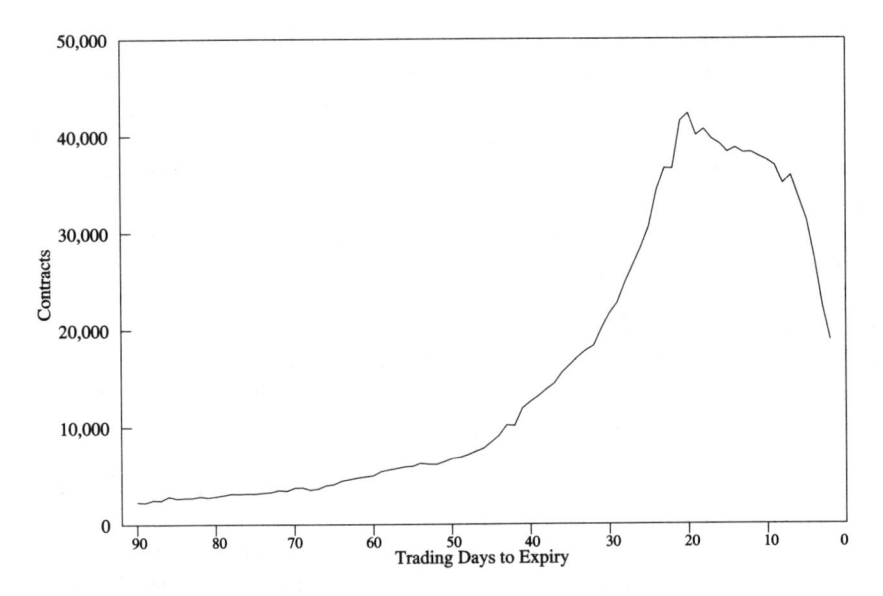

Figure 12.4: Average Open Interest by Trading Days to Expiry. 1991. Number of Contracts.

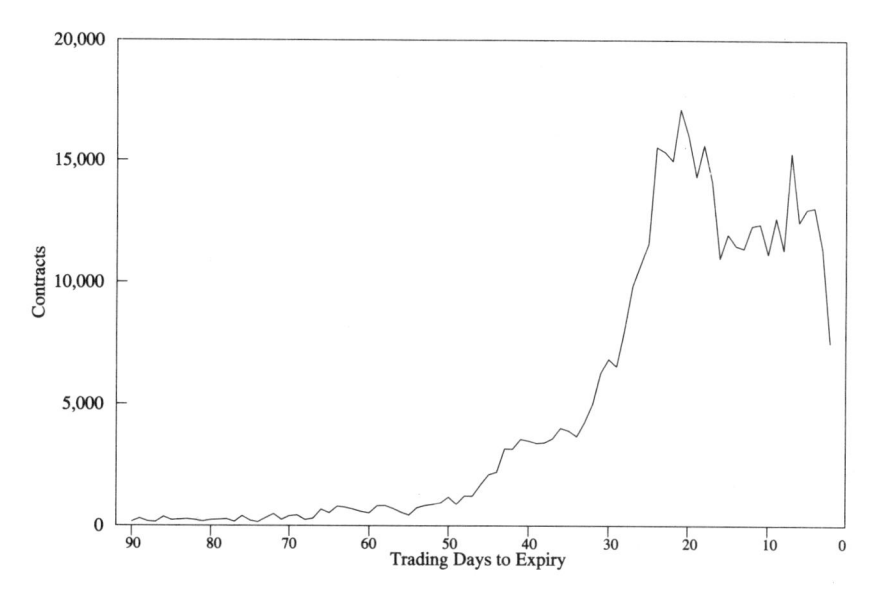

Figure 12.5: Average Number of Contracts Traded by Days to Expiry. 1991.

Figure 12.6: Average Forwardness of IPE Brent Contracts by Month. 1989–92. Number of Days.

away from expiry, but it builds up over the course of the period when the contract is the second forward month traded on the IPE. The maximum is reached just after the contract becomes the first forward month, and in 1991 equated to an average of just over 40 thousand contracts or 40 mb. About one-half of these open positions are closed out over the last month's trading through offsetting buys or sells or through EFPs, so that in 1991 an average of about 20 thousand contracts went to maturity for cash settlement. The average total volume per 1991 contract was about 430 thousand, and hence 4.6 per cent of all trades made were taken to expiry.

A similar pattern to the path of open interest is shown by volume in Figure 12.5, again representing the average of contracts with delivery in 1991. There is very little volume more than three months away from expiry. While the bulk of volume occurs when the month is the first forward month, the peak occurs at the beginning of that period, and volume falls off sharply in the last few days before expiry.

We have constructed a measure of the forwardness of IPE Brent trades for each delivery month as the average number of days to expiry for all trades made for each month. This is shown in Figure 12.6. Forwardness increased, albeit erratically, over the course of 1989. The Kuwait crisis made trade go slightly deeper in time, but since then it has mainly kept within the range of nineteen to twenty-one trading days from expiry. This equates to just under one calendar month. Remembering that the IPE does not trade the first forward 15-day market delivery month, IPE trades are then carried out on average about two months before the start of nominations in the forward market, and therefore three months before the average cargo in a given delivery month loads (i.e. the middle of the delivery month). In Chapter 7 we found that the equivalent figure for the 15-day market ranged in 1991 between fifty-five and seventy calendar days. Trade in IPE Brent is then on average made further forward than in the 15-day market.

3. Differences Between Forward and Futures Markets

In Chapter 9 we pointed out that the question as to what constitutes a forward market is of more than academic interest, since the delineation also marks the extent of the reach of US law. The key point is the interpretation of section 4(a) of the US Commodity Exchange Act, which provides exemption for forward markets from the law that US courts can rule over futures markets in which US interests deal. As seen earlier, the Commodity Exchange Act itself does not attempt any delineation between forward and futures markets, except the observation that in a forward market delivery is deferred for reasons of 'convenience or necessity'. Below we list the major distinguishing features between the two market forms,[1] and provide an opinion as to whether the 15-day Brent market constitutes a futures market.

The first distinguishing characteristic is that futures markets are based in a centralized exchange, trade under the rules of that exchange, and use a clearing house. While it is possible to have a forward market that trades in the same physical location, it is the role of the clearing house that causes the greatest distinction. A forward contract is a bilateral contract with no other parties concerned. However, while a futures contract is traded between agents on the exchange floor, it essentially represents two contracts. The buyer has one contract with the clearing house, and the seller another. Once the original deal is made, there is no linkage between the agents that made them.

This distinction leads to the point that there is a structural difference in the type of default risk in the two markets. In a futures market the only risk of default comes from a collapse of the clearing house. Even the financial collapse of the futures exchange itself does not threaten default as long as the clearing house is a separate entity. In the case of the IPE the clearing house (the International Commodities Clearing House), is owned by the major UK banks and has operations in several futures markets. The risk of default on an IPE contract by the clearing house is then for all practical purposes virtually non-existent, save in the case of a complete collapse of the entire UK banking and financial system. However, as a forward contract is bilateral, the risk of default is potentially more real. Actual defaults are rare, but have happened, and certainly the threat of default influences the choice of trading partner.[2] A company in obvious financial difficulties tends to have difficulty in making further 15-day market trades. By contrast, the status of the counterpart to a potential futures trade need have no effect on the willingness of futures market participants to deal with them.

Financial flows also constitute a major difference. In a futures market payment of a margin (i.e. deposit) must be made for each trade, and the trade is marked to market each day. Hence the book losses of each trade have to be covered on each trading day. By contrast payment in a forward market is made after expiry, with no marking to market and no deposits required.

Futures markets trade standardized contracts, with standardized delivery or settlement procedures. The only distinguishing features of a trade are the delivery month and the price. Trade in a forward market does not imply any such standardization; the specific details of any individual trade can vary beyond delivery months and price. There is no necessity for the delivery and nomination procedures or even the volume traded to be the same for all trades in the same forward market. While most trades in the 15-day Brent market do use the Shell General Terms and Conditions as part of the agreement, there is no necessity to do so.

There is also an issue of transparency in trades and therefore in prices. In a futures market, be it one where trades are arranged solely through open outcry on the floor, or one where more automated methods are possible, each trade is observable by all participants. The only exception to this is trades involving EFPs, which, while they must be reported, are not immediately observable, especially as they may happen outside exchange opening hours. Other than these trades, the level of prices is constantly observable. In a forward market there is no such transparency in trades. Without any centralized clearing house there is no one to report trades to. While many trades made are revealed to price assessment agencies, no company is under any obligation to reveal the details of any trade to any other company or to any assessment agency. The level of prices is then not constantly observable.

Futures markets have institutional procedures on membership and hence on who has the right to operate in a trading pit. Transactions are offered to the general public, who can trade through one of the member firms. By contrast there is no membership procedure in a forward market. Trade is open to anyone who can find someone else in the market to trade with. Hence the size of the forward market trading community is determined by the intersection of the set of firms that wish to participate and the set of firms with which at least one firm is prepared to trade with.

Futures contracts exhibit automatic offset. That is to say that when individual agents have made an equal number of buys and sells for a given delivery month, their net position is balanced and they retain no interest in that contract. In a forward market there is no automatic offset. For instance, a company with an equal number of buys and sells could still find itself taking delivery of a cargo if it is 5 o'clocked. The equality of the number of their buys and sells does not automatically remove their deals from the chains, and their balanced position still requires managing, in respect of the receiving and passing on of nominations.

All the characteristics of a futures exchange listed above are manifested in the IPE Brent contract and trade in that contract.[3] The 15-day market displays none of them. It has no centralized exchange, uses no clearing house, makes no deposits on trade, does not mark to market, has no necessary standardization of contracts nor formal membership procedures, no automatic offsetting and trades are not observable to all participants. This leaves the question as to whether, in the terms of the US Commodity Exchange Act, delivery is deferred for reasons of convenience or necessity. The key issue here is the proportion of trades that result in a physical delivery.

It will be seen in Chapter 13 that in 1991 only 5 mb were delivered through the standard delivery terms of the NYMEX light sweet crude oil contract out of a total volume of 20.5 billion barrels, i.e. 0.02 per cent. However, this is somewhat misleading since the vast majority of deliveries are accomplished by EFPs, and total deliveries in 1991 amounted to 669 mb. Hence the deliveries represented 3.3 per cent of all trades. In the previous section we saw that 4.6 per cent of trades for IPE Brent were taken to maturity and cash settlement.

In Chapter 7 we estimated that 15-day market volume was of the order of about 35 mb per trading day, and in Chapter 3 we showed that loadings from Sullom Voe in 1991 amounted to 730 thousand barrels per calendar day. This equates to 1.06 mb per trading day. Thus the volume loaded is 3 per cent of 15-day market trade, lower than the equivalent proportion on NYMEX, and also the proportion of cash settled contracts on the IPE. In fact, the proportion of trades resulting in the loading of cargoes at Sullom Voe will be lower, since some loadings are internal company transfers that have not gone through the forward market, or sometimes cargoes that have been sold dated but have not arisen out of a 15-day market transaction (i.e. the equity producer has sold the oil on a dated basis and not through the 15-day market). In Chapter 8 we found that over one-half of all cargoes loaded from Sullom Voe had been traded on a dated basis prior to loading. In all, the proportion of 15-day market trades that results in the buyer physically putting crude oil on a tanker they own or have chartered, is probably less than 1 per cent.

The above conclusion that there is actually a greater proportion of trades that end in physical delivery on the NYMEX futures market than on the 15-day Brent market, is correct on the basis of matching physical end cargoes to trades. However on a legal basis the proportion of deliveries can be taken to be much higher. When a Brent cargo is loaded, physical transference under the Shell General Terms and Conditions takes place at the permanent hose connection being utilized by the tanker. If the original seller of the cargo was, say, Shell and the company at the end of the chain was, say, Phibro, then physical ownership of the cargo belongs to Shell immediately before the permanent hose connection, and to Phibro immediately afterwards (unless of course Phibro has sold the cargo on in the market for dated Brent). However, except when the chain consisted only of a sale from Shell to Phibro, there is no direct link between Shell's original sale and

Phibro's purchase. What in fact happens is that at the permanent hose connection ownership passes right through the chain from Shell to Phibro. The cargo is technically physically delivered to Phibro by the company they had bought it from, not by Shell. Hence at the hose connection ownership of the oil is held for an infinitesimally small time by each company in the chain.

Using this legal definition of physical delivery, the correct measure for the proportion of deals that end in physical delivery is then the proportion of total deals that are not eventually booked out, i.e. the proportion of deals that eventually occur in a chain. The size of any one chain can vary from single figures to over a hundred, depending on market conditions. It therefore follows that the proportion of deals resulting in physical delivery for any given delivery month under this approach also varies very widely. The proportion implied by the evidence given by the defendants in the Transnor case,[4] as reported by Sas,[5] is 40 to 50 per cent. This is probably the correct mid-point estimate, but given the magnitude of the variation in average chain length per month, it can vary by at least 25 per cent either side of this range.

Hence using one approach to derive the proportion of deals resulting in delivery in the 15-day market we produce a number which is less than 1 per cent, and using the other we get a range of about 15 to 75 per cent. It should be noted that this range is determined entirely by the feature of no automatic offset, and further that it is impossible to attribute the intention of delivery for all these trades. In particular, deals do get left in chains which either or both parties had wished to book out, but were unable to do. There is no more intention of delivery for these trades than in a pair of automatically offset futures transactions. It should also be noted that refusing to book out, for instance to keep the capacity to play the tolerance game, is only signalling the desire to maintain the option of taking physical possession of a cargo, not necessarily the intention.

The concept of forward trade being deferred for convenience or necessity in fact matches the reasons for the element of forwardness in spot crude oil transactions (as discussed in Chapter 14). The 15-day market does have an important supply function, but it is also possible to both hedge and speculate on the market. The market does enable transference of risk without physical transference of cargoes. The failure of the 15-day market to match any of the characteristics of a futures market listed above implies that it is not a pure futures market. It shows all the characteristics of a forward market bar one, the supply function does not dominate.

The 15-day market is then not a futures market, but, in the

terminology of Sas,[6] a hybrid or developed forward market. It appears inappropriate to consider it as a futures market, although it does, in the form of the IPE Brent contract, have a non-dominating futures market grafted onto it. We now turn to the reasons for this co-existence.

4. The Relationship Between Forward and Futures Brent

The economic theory of finance normally assumes that a forward market is simply an embryonic form of a futures market, whose natural evolution is to become standardized. The implication is that the development of futures markets will supplant forward markets as an industry moves through a stage of just spot trade to one of spot and forward, before maturing to spot and futures. It will be seen in Chapter 13 that the forward market for WTI is in essence simply the market for NYMEX EFPs, and as such is no longer a separate entity. Yet in the Brent market, forward and futures coexist with companies trading in both, with neither market being an appendage to the other.

The conventional theory of a futures market considers the situation where that market has an underlying spot market. When contracts expire prices should have converged onto spot prices if the market is functioning correctly. It should be noted that the IPE Brent contract does not conform to this idealized construct. In particular it does not have an underlying spot market, but rather an underlying forward contract which itself has an underlying spot market. At expiry it replicates, not the spot commodity, but the second month Brent forward contract at the point where it becomes the first month forward. In fact it replicates the comparable forward delivery month over all its life, and it should be convergent on the comparable forward month at all times that it is trading.

The prices will not always be exactly the same for several reasons. First, there may be a convenience yield attached to holding a physical cargo, in which case some convenience yield will attach to holding a paper claim on a physical cargo, if the convenience yield is expected to persist until that claim can be made physical. In a weak market with dated Brent trading below forward Brent this implicit convenience yield can be negative. Theoretically a difference can be caused by the separate nature of default risk in the two markets, and by the transactions costs of trading the arbitrage between the two markets by effecting an EFP. However, for all practical purposes there should in normal market conditions be little difference between the prices of comparable IPE and forward market delivery months.

As prices in the forward market are neither constantly nor exactly observable, a direct test of this proposition is impossible. However prices for EFPs are observable, and these imply that the IPE Brent price only very rarely moves much more than 15 cents away from the forward market price. The only major exception was during the first few months of the exceptional circumstances of the Kuwait crisis, when EFPs as high as a 50 cent premium for the forward market were observed. However, generally there is very close convergence of IPE prices onto the forward market.

In fact as the IPE contract is cash settled, any demise of the forward Brent market would also lead to its demise. Without a physical delivery basis it cannot take over the functions of the forward market, and while physical delivery is possible through the utilization of EFPs, this is achieved by utilization of the forward market delivery mechanism. With the two markets having reached an equilibrium of co-existence, the continued existence of both must imply that they fulfil different functions.

It could be argued that the basing of futures contracts by the IPE on the forward market, initially meant to convince traders that the final price on delivery would be based on adequate verifiable data, is now no longer necessary. We find in Chapters 14 and 15 that the most important price in international oil trade is dated and not forward Brent, and in particular the five-day average of Brent price assessments. There appears to be no reason now why the base of the futures contract should not be the five-day price average. This would be more useful to the oil industry, and also partially decouple the IPE from the forward market.

There are no publicly available data that could be used to give a breakdown of shares in total trade in IPE Brent which parallel those derived in Chapter 7. Even if data were available it could only break down by trade by broker, not by the companies on whose behalf trade was being carried out. However, from interview evidence we believe that the largest users of the IPE contract are by and large the same as those in the forward market. Some important forward market participants prefer to trade Brent options rather than Brent futures, but overall there are very few companies active in forward Brent who do not also trade IPE Brent.

It is of course rational for companies to trade in several markets as a way of diversifying risk. However this does not explain participation in both Brent markets, since price risk is not independent across them. As noted above, prices on the two markets are almost perfectly correlated. While risk might be diversified by trading both, say, Brent and sugar, it is not diversified by trading IPE Brent and forward Brent. Instead we can identify several factors that explain participation in both markets.

The IPE offers greater flexibility in trading a cargo size of one thousand rather than 500 thousand barrels. For instance, assume a refiner has a term contract for Saudi Arabian oil for import into Europe. Following standard Saudi terms cargoes are priced on a dated Brent related formula taking the ten-day average of Platt's assessed dated Brent prices around the fortieth day after loading. Suppose the refiner wishes to lock in the level of prices at time of loading for a 1 mb cargo. This hedge is best accomplished by buying 1,000 IPE contracts on the day of loading, and then selling 100 contracts per day on each of the days when prices are used in the average. The hedge is not in itself perfect, it leaves the risk of movements between dated Brent and IPE Brent as well as the Platt's risk (as explained in Chapter 10). However it will provide a better hedge than, say, buying two forward cargoes at time of loading and selling one on the first and the last days of the pricing period. The same flexibility can be utilized in all other deals that involve pricing over more than one day's assessments. This also applies to trigger priced deals, which are explained in Chapter 14, and to most imports into Europe and some into the USA, as is described in Chapter 15.

However, trade on the IPE is less suited to taking a large position. For example a trader that takes a market view can very quickly go, say, 5 mb long or short on the forward market. Following the same strategy on the IPE, apart from incurring the costs of commissions and tying up capital in margins, would be likely to move the market to the trader's detriment as it involves large, and by the nature of IPE trading, observable transactions. If the trader has developed a market view on a time-spread and wishes to take a large position on it, then the point becomes even more relevant.

Instead of the flexibility of IPE Brent, forward Brent offers lower trading costs. It also provides the supply function lacking in IPE Brent, and is the only relevant market for those wishing to utilize the links with the physical market.

We have already noted that trades in the forward market are not, if ever, immediately observable to the market. There is less than full transmission of the trades made into prices, and this only occurs at discrete intervals. By contrast, transmission of information from IPE trading is almost immediate, and forward market traders tend to always work with a screen display of IPE prices close to view. As reported in Chapter 11, the extension of the IPE's trading hours in January 1990 meant that on the average day most price changes occur while the IPE is open. We found that since the end of the Kuwait crisis the average absolute price change overnight has been 9 cents per barrel, compared with the average 19 cents per barrel movement between IPE open and close. It follows then that the function of short-term price discovery must lie in the futures market during the time of day when it is open.

Notes
1. A large literature exists on this subject. See N. Kaldor (1939), 'Speculation and Economic Stability', *Review of Economic Studies*; 7; L. G. Telser (1981), 'Why There Are Organised Futures Markets', *Journal of Law and Economics* 24; J. C. Cox., J. E. Ingersoll and S. A. Ross (1981), 'The Relation between Forward Prices and Futures Prices', *Journal of Financial Economics* 9.
2. For an empirical study of default risk in the 15-day market see R.J. Weiner (1991), 'Default Risk and the Difference Between Forward and Futures Markets: An Empirical Study', Columbia Business School.
3. As a technical point, under UK law the IPE Brent contract is not a futures contract but a contract for differences as it is cash settled. The distinction has no practical implications.
4. See Chapter 9.
5. B. Sas (1989), 'Legal Aspects of Risk Management of Forward Oil Trading: The "Forward" Oil Markets and their Contracts', *Journal of Energy and Natural Resources Law*, vol. 7, no. 1.
6. Ibid.

CHAPTER 13

THE MARKETS FOR DUBAI, WTI AND EUROPEAN PETROLEUM PRODUCTS

1. Introduction

In this chapter we examine the structure and features of three other major oil markets, and the relationship of Brent to those markets. In section 2 we consider the informal forward market for Dubai and through the use of the Petroleum Argus database construct a parallel analysis to that carried out for the forward Brent market in Chapter 7. We also find a close linkage between Dubai prices and price behaviour in the Brent market. Section 3 considers the market for US light sweet crude oil, as traded on NYMEX. Section 4 considers product trading in North West Europe, which is normally grouped together as constituting the Rotterdam market. Section 5 provides a summary. We also consider relationships between Brent prices and oil product prices. Other spot and forward markets for crude oil are examined in Chapter 14.

2. The Dubai Forward Market

Dubai is a medium (31 degrees API) and high sulphur (2 per cent) crude oil with, until recently, a relatively stable production base of around 400 thousand b/d.[1] Unlike Saudi Arabia, Iran, Iraq and Kuwait, the states of the United Arab Emirates allow equity production by oil companies, and Dubai Fateh crude oil has six equity producers. While the number of producers is considerably less than for Brent, the concentration of ownership among those producers is broadly similar. The percentage shares of each company are shown in Table 13.1.

These shares are the nominal entitlements out of full production. The companies actually receive less than that under the terms of their agreement with the Ruler of Dubai. The Ruler receives a proportion of total production which normally amounts to about four cargoes a month. Of these one is normally sold in the forward market directly, and the others sold under term contracts to companies who may then choose to sell them on in the forward market.

Table 13.1: Equity Shares of Dubai Production by Company. 1993. Per Cent.

Company	% Share
Conoco	30
CFP (Total)	25
Repsol	25
Rheinol/Texaco	10
Sun	5
Wintershall	5

In addition to this share of physical production, the Ruler announces retroactively a price at which the rest of the output for a given month is deemed to have been sold to the companies listed in Table 13.1. These prices are not released publicly, and we have no information concerning their derivation, other than that there appears to be no direct relationship between the retroactive price and the deals actually done in the Dubai market by the equity participants.

The operator of the Fateh terminal is Conoco. The standard parcel size is 500 thousand barrels and hence there are around twenty cargoes of Dubai per month, the bulk of which go into the chains of the forward market. Equity producers tend to take around five or six cargoes a month into their own systems. Normally between ten and fifteen cargoes go into the chains per month. Compare this to Brent where in a normal month there are over fifty cargoes and perhaps forty to forty-five enter the chains.

A typical contract for Dubai, like that for Brent, consists of two parts. Part one, sometimes referred to as the 'special terms', consists of the specifics of the sale as entered into by the two parties. This can be a printed form, telex, letter, fax or any other written document. Part two consists of the general terms of sale, usually taken to be those in the Conoco 'Dubai Crude Oil General Terms and Conditions for f.o.b. Oil Sales' (the GTCs). The current version of the GTCs as of 1992 was published in November 1988 with a modification made to one paragraph in May 1989.

The standard Dubai contract differs from that used for Brent in several ways. The Conoco GTCs leave the question of parcel size and operational tolerance to the parties themselves to specify in part one of the contract. However the norm is, like Brent, for an operational tolerance of 5 per cent at the buyer's discretion. The GTCs are governed by the laws of New York with an explicit statement that the UN Convention for the International Sale of Goods of 1980 does not apply. Arbitration is at the seller's option. Hence while Brent is governed by English law, with the reach of US law being a moot point (as discussed in Chapter 9), Dubai trade definitely falls under the aegis of US law.

The most fundamental difference between the operation of the Dubai market and that of the Brent market concerns the nomination procedures. Dubai has no equivalent of Brent's 15-day nomination system. In the Brent market the three-day loading range is the seller's choice, with the only constraint on the seller being the need to give fifteen days notice to the buyer of this range. Hence the last Brent cargo for loading in March would only become dated on 13 March.

In the Dubai market the choice of loading date is, at least in the first instance, at the *buyer's* discretion. The buyer must nominate a three-day loading range at the latest by the first day of the month prior to the delivery month, i.e. 1 February for a March cargo. The seller then has until the 18th of the month to decide whether they will accept or reject that nomination. Should the cargo have been bought after the first day of the month prior to delivery then the buyer has three days to notify the seller of their preferred range. If this nomination is received by the seller after the 13th of the month prior to delivery then they have five days to accept or reject it.

In practice the buyer's nomination is accepted in the majority of cases. However should the seller reject it, they must submit a three-day loading range back to the buyer together with the rejection. The buyer may then propose another three-day range, but should this also be rejected then it is the seller's nomination that remains in force. Thus while the buyer has the first call, the choice of loading range does effectively lie with the seller.[2]

After the 18th of the month the terminal operator, i.e. Conoco, is in a position to finalize the loading schedule for the following month and this normally appears around the 19th of the month. Hence all March Dubai cargoes become effectively dated around 19 February, some three and a half weeks before the last Brent cargo becomes dated. Further, buyers in effect can have a very strong, but not totally certain, idea of their loading dates for March at the start of February, given that the vast majority of buyer nominations of loading ranges are accepted.

This procedure means that the eventual lifter out of the chains tends to emerge much earlier than in the Brent market. As Conoco begins to accept nominations nearly all those in the market who do not intend to take delivery or maintain any option on taking delivery book out their positions. Hence book-outs in the Dubai market for any given delivery month tend to occur long before those in the Brent market, and the chains of transactions that remain tend to be shorter. When transactions are left in a chain, the financial settlement is made thirty days after the bill of lading.

Trade in the forward market tends virtually to cease by the time the lifting schedule appears, except for the physical transfer of cargoes from the lifter to the eventual end-user. One striking feature of the Dubai market is that there is very little direct involvement in the forward market by the majority of end-users. Some Dubai goes through a tendering procedure to Asian national oil companies, in particular to India (IOC), Thailand (PTT), and the Philippines (PNOC). Of these by far the most important is IOC, the Indian Oil Corporation. IOC prefers to procure supplies of crude oil through a system of tenders, on average for about five cargoes but through 1991 seven or eight cargoes was the norm, with the tenders normally being awarded before the Dubai lifting schedule is finalized. In competing for the tenders companies submit a list of prices and the grades of crude oil offered. A large proportion of these tenders is normally filled by Dubai.

Dubai has fewer add-on markets than Brent. While futures markets for Dubai have been set up in London by the IPE, and in Singapore by the Singapore Monetary Exchange, (Simex), both contracts have failed as did discussions between the exchanges on a link-up of their Dubai contracts. In 1992 the New York Commodity Exchange (Comex), received US regulatory approval for a Dubai contract that would link up with both the IPE and Simex contracts. As of 1993 there was no indication of any launch date for this contract. The only important Dubai market other than the forward market is the trade in partial Dubai, i.e. paper cargoes of 50 thousand barrels, run by market makers such as Morgan Stanley, J Aron, Phibro and BP. The latter two often have physical Dubai through contracts with the Ruler.

The nature and character of the Dubai market and of its participants has changed drastically since its beginnings. The market began around 1984 as spot trading for Arabian Light wound down and then virtually ceased. At first, deals were conducted between a few trading companies producing less than one reported deal per trading day in 1984. The market grew dramatically in 1985, mainly due to the broking firm Amerex Petroleum. Amerex actively sought to get the Japanese trading houses, the sogo shosha, to participate in the Dubai market. Amerex proved successful, and 1985 saw the rapid entry of the sogo shosha in the market. As we detail further below, at points during 1986 their total share of Dubai trade exceeded 50 per cent.

The next wave of entries into the market was the Wall Street refiners who stepped up their involvement in mid-1987. The rapid growth led to Dubai being dubbed as 'the Brent of the East' although as we will see the modern market has very little to do with the East. The zenith of the market came in 1988 by which time its nature had changed markedly.

When the market started, OPEC still retained a fixed price system; however by 1988 Iran, Iraq and Saudi Arabia had been through the period of netbacks, and now linked sales to the Far East directly on Dubai market quotations. Retroactive prices announced by other Gulf states also relied on Dubai quotations. From its genesis the market evolved into a method of pricing about 6 mb/d of crude oil on a base of about fifteen cargoes a month.

The other major development in 1988 was the change in the standard Brent cargo from 600 thousand to 500 thousand barrels. While some trade in the Brent-Dubai differential had existed before, it now became a far more practical proposition and the importance of this particular price spread increased.

The evolution of the Dubai market since 1986 is shown in Table 13.2, with an analysis of the data on reported deals contained in the Petroleum Argus database. This table shows some of the features of the evolution of the Brent market detailed in Chapter 7, but greatly exaggerated. Considering first the total liquidity of the Dubai forward market, from the views of traders supported by the data on reported deals, we believe that the total size of the Dubai market was about one-quarter of the size of the Brent market during Dubai's heyday in 1988, and by 1991 it was about one-sixth. Once Brent futures and other add-on Brent markets are considered, the volume in the various Dubai markets probably amounts to about 10 per cent of that in markets for Brent.

The total liquidity of the Dubai market shows a downwards trend since 1988, with the Gulf crisis of 1990 having had a particularly adverse effect from which the market has still not totally recovered. However, far more striking has been the change in the composition of the liquidity of the market, with spread trades increasing from about 15 per cent of the total in 1986 to over 90 per cent in 1991. The Gulf crisis virtually killed trade in outright prices in the Dubai market (which had been in decline since 1988). In 1991 as a whole sixty-three outright deals were reported, just over one per week. When a market becomes so thin, reporting rates are likely to tail off markedly, but as far as price formation in the Dubai market is concerned it is fair to say that outright deals are now of little importance.

Dubai prices are now derived by price assessment agencies from market talk of, and trading in the Brent-Dubai differential, which became common from the second quarter of 1988 with the change in the standard Brent cargo to the same size as Dubai (effective for contracts for delivery in August 1988 onwards). After peaking at the end of 1988, this trade declined slightly, but there are still about one and a half reported Brent-Dubai deals per trading day. The level of

Table 13.2: Composition of Dubai Deals. Outright and Spreads. 1986-91. Number of Deals.

		Total Deals	Outright Deals	Spread Deals	Dubai Spreads 1 Month	Dubai Spreads 2+ Months	Total Dubai Spreads	Inter-Crude Spreads Brent	Inter-Crude Spreads WTI	Spreads As % of Total
1986	1	62	60	2	2	0	2	0	0	3.2
	2	190	167	23	8	0	8	15	0	12.1
	3	362	327	35	20	0	20	15	0	9.7
	4	217	172	45	26	0	26	19	0	20.7
1987	1	277	204	73	30	0	30	38	5	26.4
	2	199	159	40	38	0	38	1	1	20.1
	3	272	216	56	30	4	34	19	3	20.6
	4	264	200	64	52	0	52	7	5	24.2
1988	1	449	281	168	118	2	120	38	10	37.4
	2	439	228	211	132	0	132	75	4	48.1
	3	489	199	290	150	6	156	125	9	59.3
	4	434	124	310	148	0	148	156	6	71.4
1989	1	437	89	348	204	0	204	138	6	79.6
	2	384	93	291	198	14	212	72	7	75.8
	3	446	104	342	252	6	258	80	4	76.7
	4	407	86	321	214	4	218	97	6	78.9
1990	1	402	98	304	194	6	200	100	4	75.6
	2	398	112	286	198	4	202	82	2	71.9
	3	334	62	272	184	2	186	83	3	81.4
	4	170	11	159	98	0	98	61	0	93.5
1991	1	249	12	237	150	6	156	79	2	95.2
	2	277	20	257	154	4	158	98	1	92.8
	3	354	11	343	256	2	258	84	1	96.9
	4	308	22	286	202	0	202	84	0	92.8

Source: Own calculations from Petroleum Argus database.

Dubai prices is now assessed totally on the basis of these trades and market talk of the differential, as was explained in Chapter 10. Dubai is also very occasionally traded against WTI, and in 1986 and 1987 deals were sometimes done against Oman. However, it is the Brent-Dubai trade that provides the Dubai market with much of its liquidity, as well as being the only way to gauge the level of Dubai prices. By 1991 Brent-Dubai trades accounted for one-third of reported Dubai liquidity in terms of contracts traded, and one-half in terms of deals done. Dubai has become close to being little more than another Brent add-on market. As well as outright trades, Dubai-Dubai and Dubai-Brent spread deals, Dubai-Brent box trades are sometimes reported. Box trades were explained in Chapter 3, and for the purposes of Table 13.2 they have been counted as two Brent-Dubai differential trades.

The structure of the participants in the Dubai market has also changed markedly. We have classified participants into six categories. First, there are the equity producers of Dubai and their associated companies, among which CFP and Conoco are by far the most active, accounting for 60 and 26 per cent of the trades involving this group for the period from 1986 to 1991 as a whole. The gap between the involvement of CFP and Conoco has grown over time, with CFP making fifteen times as many trades as Conoco in 1991. Secondly, there are other oil companies with no interests in Dubai but with equity or production interests in the UAE or Oman. This group includes BP, Crescent, Elf, Exxon, Amerada Hess, Neste and Shell. These companies have equity production whose prices are in some way Dubai related. Several also have refining interests in the Far East.

The third category are the Wall Street refiners, dominated by Phibro, J Aron and Morgan Stanley. Fourthly, we identified the sogo shosha and other Japanese firms. The most important of these are Kanematsu, Mitsui, Marubeni, C Itoh and Nissho Iwai. The category of traders is led by Marc Rich, Arcadia, Cargill and TWO. Finally, we have identified companies with refining interests in Asia or Oceania outside Japan, but with no equity production in the Middle East. There are other companies in the Dubai market who do not fit into any of the above categories, but since they represented less than 1 per cent of the total volume of trade since 1986, they have been omitted.

The shares of these six groups in the total volume of trade for Dubai on a monthly basis are shown in Figure 13.1. Following their entry in 1985 the sogo shosha and other Japanese firms came to dominate Dubai trade, accounting for over half the total volume in mid-1986. The scaling down of their activity after this point was continuous, and by 1991 Japanese firms were only minor players, with less than 10 per cent of the market. By contrast the Wall Street firms scaled up their involvement in 1987 and have maintained a high share, representing about one-third of all volume in 1991, about the same share they had in the Brent market. Other Gulf producer companies, in particular BP and Amerada Hess, increased their relative participation from the start of 1989, and now have a higher share of the market than the equity producers of Dubai. It is striking that Asian refiners outside Japan have very little involvement in the market. They do not use the Dubai forward market as a source of supply, nor do they appear to use it for

214   *Oil Markets and Prices*

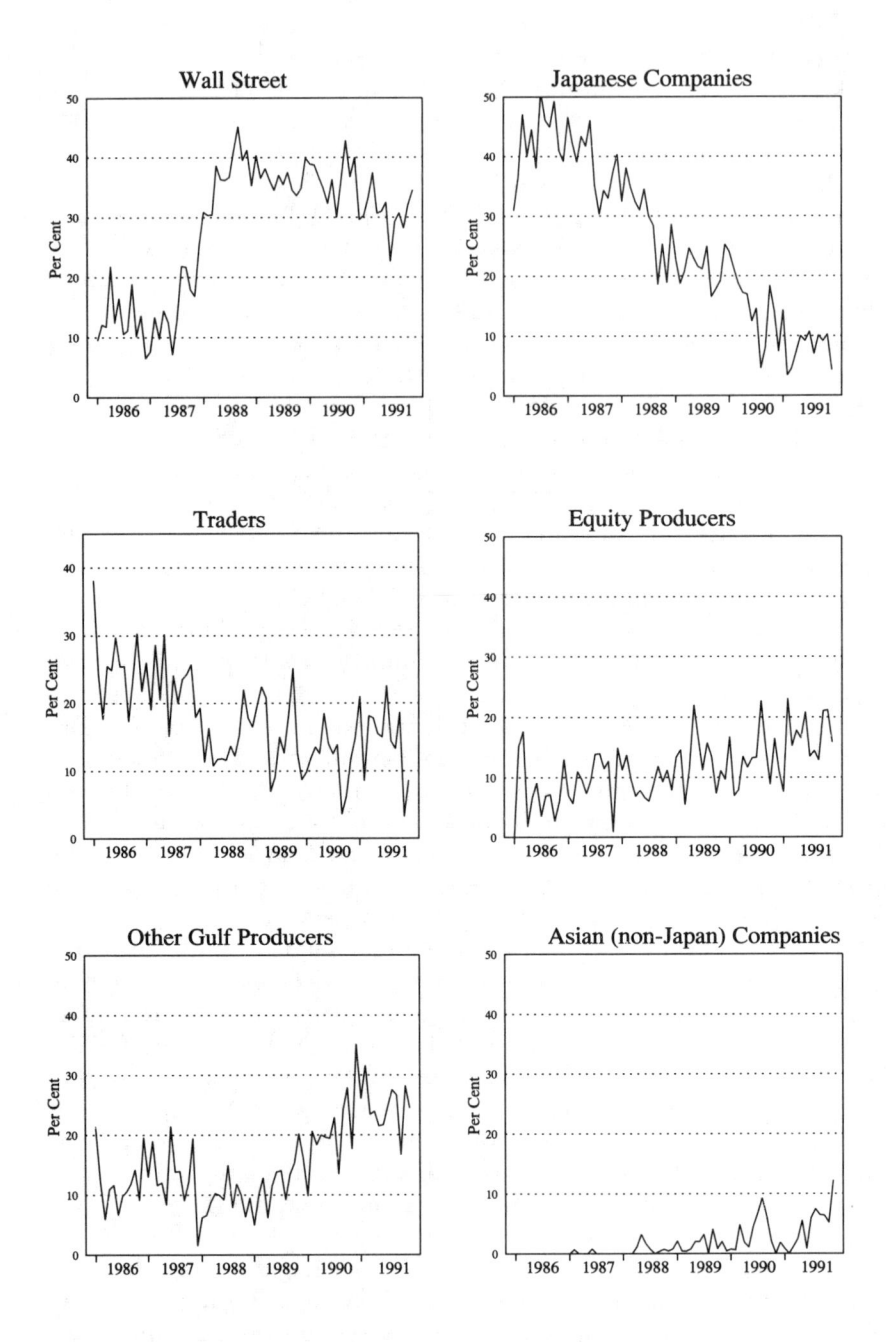

Figure 13.1: Market Shares of Various Categories of Participants in the Dubai Market by Month. 1986–91.

risk management when buying on Dubai price related terms.

The Dubai market is then currently dominated by western oil companies, banks and traders, with very limited Japanese involvement and virtually no involvement by Asian owned refining or state oil companies. There is very little that is Asian about the composition of Dubai players, and, as we detail in our empirical results below, this results in a market which is far more sensitive to western than eastern trading conditions.

Table 13.3 lists the twenty largest traders in the Dubai market with their shares from 1986 to 1991. The listings for 1990 and 1991 bear a striking resemblance to the equivalent table for Brent trades detailed in Chapter 7. Indeed, of the ten largest traders of Brent in 1991 all but Statoil rank in the top eleven traders of Dubai. Like Brent, the market has come to be dominated by Phibro and J Aron. Comparing with Figure 13.1, it is clear that most of the increase in the share of Wall Street firms between 1987 and 1988 is due solely to the scaling up of the involvement of J Aron.

In Chapter 7 we saw that on a monthly basis the 15-day Brent market had between forty and fifty participant companies in 1991, down from a peak in 1987 of between seventy and eighty. We further saw that activity had become more concentrated across companies, with the inverse Herfindahl index for trade having fallen to about 15 in 1991 from a peak of over 30 in 1987. The comparable movements in the nature of the Dubai market since 1986 are shown in Figures 13.2 and 13.3.

The Dubai market is seen to have not only fewer participant companies than 15-day Brent (about twenty less per month on average in 1991), but also to have a more concentrated pattern of trade, with an inverse Herfindahl index that typically lies in the range of 10 to 15. In the average month in 1991 there were five companies active in the market dealing only in intra-Dubai spreads, and not in the Brent-Dubai spreads that determine the level of Dubai prices.

We have already noted that the 1990–91 Kuwait crisis had an adverse effect on the liquidity of the Dubai market. Figure 13.3 confirms that there was an exodus of companies from the market over this period, with the number of participants falling below normal over a seven-month period. At the low point in December 1990, there were only fifteen active companies, with ten of these dealing in Brent-Dubai spreads and therefore having input in the setting of absolute Dubai prices. Indeed at its lowest point the inverse Herfindahl index for these trades fell to just six, compared to its normal level of about ten.

Dubai is then a market used for the pricing of oil heading East from the Arabian Gulf, whose participants are not only limited in number,

216   *Oil Markets and Prices*

Table 13.3: Main Participants in the Dubai Market. Rank and Market Shares. 1986–91. Per Cent.

Rank	1986		1987		1988		1989		1990		1991	
1	Marubeni	10.2	Phibro	8.7	J Aron	16.8	J Aron	15.9	Phibro	16.8	CFP
2	C Itoh	9.2	Kaines	7.8	Phibro	13.3	Phibro	13.9	J Aron	12.4	J Aron	11.3
3	Phibro	9.0	C Itoh	7.2	Kanematsu	9.1	CFP	6.2	CFP	7.9	Phibro	10.3
4	Kaines	7.3	Kanematsu	5.5	Mitsui	6.6	Kanematsu	5.8	Kanematsu	6.2	BP	9.7
5	Kanematsu	5.7	Mitsui	4.7	CFP	4.3	Morgan Stanley	4.1	Morgan Stanley	5.8	Morgan Stanley	7.4
6	Marc Rich	4.8	CFP	4.1	Mitsubishi	3.4	Arcadia	4.0	BP	5.1	Kanematsu	4.9
7	Nissho Iwai	4.3	Nissho Iwai	4.0	Nissho Iwai	3.1	BP	3.9	Arcadia	4.3	Cargill	4.7
8	Mitsui	4.1	BP	3.7	Drexel	2.7	Cargill	3.8	Mobil	4.1	Mobil	4.2
9	TWO	3.9	J Aron	3.6	Conoco	2.6	Mitsui	3.7	Neste	3.7	Shell Internat.	4.1
10	BP	3.9	Mitsubishi	3.6	Shell Int	2.5	Marubeni	3.6	Mitsui	3.3	Marc Rich	3.7
11	Mitsubishi	3.3	Marubeni	3.5	BP	2.5	Conoco	3.5	Marc Rich	3.0	Amerada Hess	3.0
12	Sumitomo	2.9	Marc Rich	3.2	Marubeni	2.4	Marc Rich	3.2	Shell Internat.	2.9	IOC	2.8
13	Sigmoil	2.5	Tradax	3.1	Kaines	2.3	Mitsubishi	3.0	Amerada Hess	2.4	Arcadia	2.4
14	Avant	2.4	TWO	2.9	Elf	2.2	Elf	2.8	Nissho Iwai	2.2	Neste	2.3
15	Marimpex	2.3	Conoco	2.5	Morgan Stanley	2.2	C Itoh	2.5	Caltex	2.1	Bear Stearns	2.1
16	Shell Internat.	2.2	Gotco	2.2	Cargill	2.0	Mobil	2.3	Conoco	2.1	Conoco	1.4
17	Vitol	2.1	Elf	1.9	C Itoh	1.9	Nissho Iwai	2.0	Cargill	2.0	Gotco	1.2
18	Elf	1.8	Exxon	1.8	Marc Rich	1.6	Drexel	1.9	Elf	1.4	Repsol	1.2
19	Gotco	1.6	Vitol	1.5	Elders	1.4	Caltex	1.6	Marubeni	1.1	Caltex	1.1
20	Sun	1.5	Coastal		Scan	1.4	Neste	1.4	Mitsubishi	1.1	Nova	1.1

Source: Own calculations from Petroleum Argus database.

Dubai, WTI and European Products 217

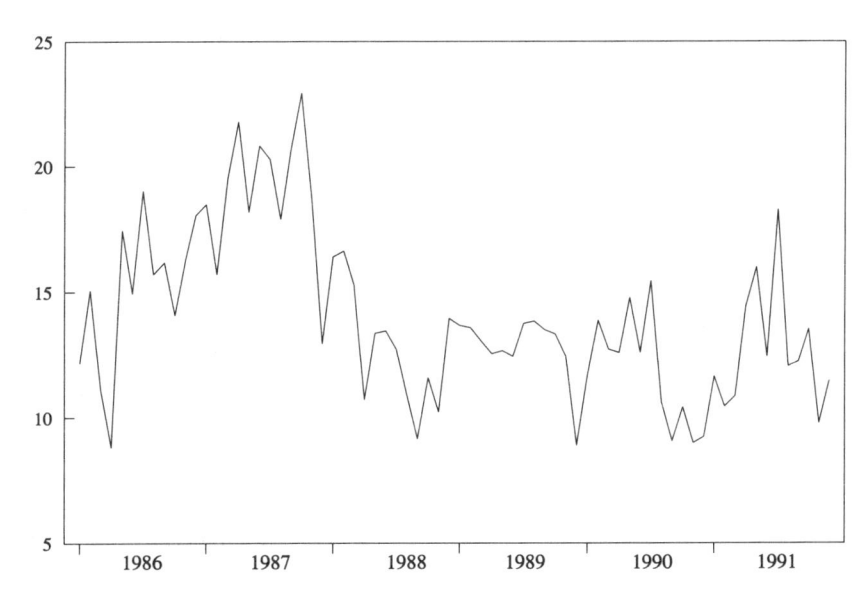

Figure 13.2: Concentration in the Dubai Market by Month. 1988–91. Inverse Herfindahl Index.

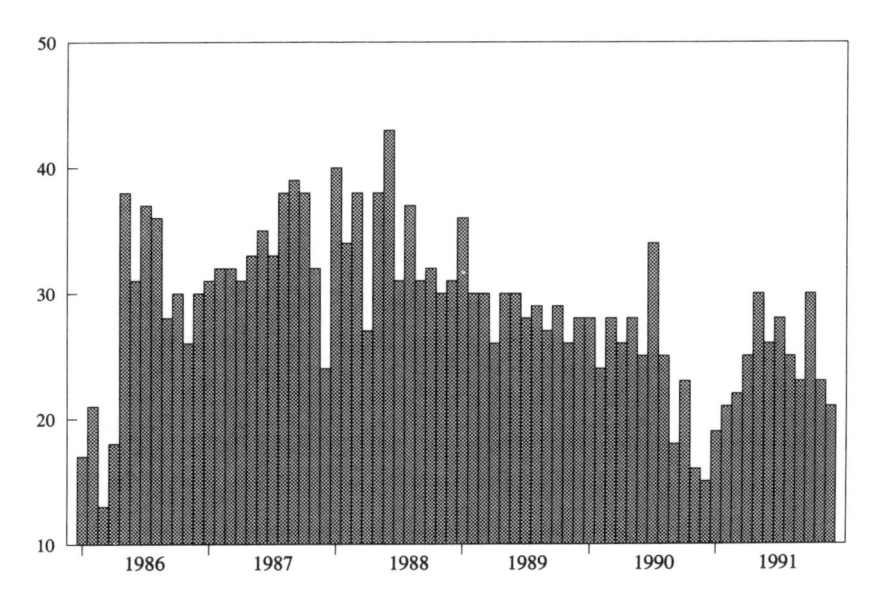

Figure 13.3: Number of Participants in the Dubai Market by Month. 1986–91.

but also dominated by western companies. This then leads to the question of whether Dubai prices reflect trading conditions in the East or the West. We have examined changes in the price of Dubai, in relationship to four main sets of factors.

The first set are changes in the gross product worths (GPWs) achievable through refining Dubai in typical refineries in the three main refining areas, i.e. Singapore, the US Gulf Coast and NW Europe. We have also used changes in Brent GPWs in conjunction with those of Dubai. As Dubai prices are assessed through trades in the Brent-Dubai differential it is, at least a priori, possible that changes in the value of Brent yields could affect the level of Dubai prices.

Secondly, we have considered changes in the time structure of prices in the markets for Brent and WTI. As Dubai is distant from refining areas its value is likely to be affected by the time structure of prices. For example, Dubai takes about thirty days to reach Europe. Hence Dubai prices are likely to be depressed by backwardations in European prices, and pulled up by contangos. Thirdly, we used changes in freight rates for Dubai to both western and eastern locations.

The final set of factors we considered relate to product market volatilities. While a refiner can, should they wish to do so, lock in through forward trade any level of Dubai prices or of the Brent-Dubai differential that occurs, they cannot do the same for the gross product worth. Without a complete set of liquid futures or forward markets for each product in each refining area, as is the current situation, risk management for refinery output is considerably harder than for refinery input. Thus it is possible that greater volatility in product markets might, *ceteris paribus*, tend to reduce Dubai prices given that the greater transport time for Dubai leaves refiners exposed to risk for longer than with other crudes, from the point of time when their purchase is made. We proxied this by calculating the imputed cost of a swap for the value of refinery output, on a daily basis in each refining area.

In analysing the determinants of Dubai prices we have used the following methodology.[3] We first regressed Dubai prices, y, on the vector of explanatory variables, x, i.e.,

$$y_t = \alpha + \beta x_t + \varepsilon_t$$

The error terms from this regression were non-stationary, i.e., did not have a constant variance. Statistical inference on the basis of such an equation would then be misleading. However, the data is stationary in first differences, and hence the model was reparameterized as follows:

Starting from the general equation

$$y_t = \alpha y_{t-1} + \beta_1 x_t + \beta_2 x_{t-1} + \varepsilon_t$$

We have,

$$\Delta y_t = (\alpha - 1) y_{t-1} + \beta_1 \Delta x_t + (\beta_1 + \beta_2) x_{t-1} + \varepsilon_t$$

And rearranging,

$$\Delta y_t = \beta_1 \Delta x_t + (\alpha - 1) [y_{t-1} - (\beta_1 + \beta_2) x_{t-1} / (1 - \alpha)]$$

or,

$$\Delta y_t = \beta_1 \Delta x_t + \beta_3 \text{ECM} + \varepsilon_t$$

Where ECM (Error Correction Mechanism) represents the deviation from a long-term equilibrium, and is simply the error term from the first static regression run in levels. Thus, in the results that follow, the coefficients on our explanatory variables are impact effects, while the ECM picks up the long-term relationship, and the coefficient on the ECM determines how fast is the adjustment to the long-term equilibrium.

Our dependent variable is changes in the price of second month forward Dubai, with an estimation period running from the start of 1988 to the end of 1991. We removed the period of the Gulf crisis from the estimation period. This left a final sample of 867 observations, and the results are shown in Table 13.4. Among all the changes in GPWs used, both contemporaneous and lagged, we found five to be significant. Among these the GPW of Dubai evaluated at the US Gulf Coast and NW Europe are dominant, both being significantly greater in magnitude than the GPW of Dubai evaluated at Singapore. We also found significance in the GPW at the US Gulf lagged by one day. The GPW of Brent in NW Europe enters the equation with a significant negative coefficient.

Taken together the coefficients imply that price changes in Dubai are primarily driven by developments in Europe and the US Gulf Coast. The feedback on Dubai prices from the Singapore market is of a very limited magnitude. The coefficient on change in the GPW at Singapore suggests that, holding GPWs in other areas constant, a rise in the GPW of $1 per barrel would only increase Dubai prices by 8 cents per barrel.

That Dubai prices should be determined at the US Gulf and in Europe rather than in the Far East would follow if these were indeed the marginal markets for Dubai. US import statistics show that in 1991, 65 thousand b/d of crude oil from the United Arab Emirates was imported into US refineries, with all but one cargo of this flow going

Table 13.4: Determinants of Dubai Price Changes. Dependent Variable: Change in Dubai Price.

Variable	Coefficient	T-Statistic
Constant	0.0048	0.752
Changes in Product Worths:		
Dubai (NWE)	0.5338	4.860**
Brent (NWE)	-0.3379	-3.165**
Dubai (USGC)	0.4300	19.140**
Dubai (USGC) 1 lag	-0.1187	-5.074**
Dubai (Singapore)	0.0859	1.792*
One Month Backwardations in Brent:	-1.2798	-11.473**
Error Correction Term:	-0.0316	-3.002**

Other Statistics: R-Squared 0.551, Log-Likelihood 215.096, F-Statistic 129.550

Note: * Significant at 10 per cent level
 ** Significant at 1 per cent level

Table 13.5: UAE Exports to Europe and Japan. 1988–91. Thousand Barrels per Day.

Importing Country	1988	1989	1990	1991
France	0.0	0.0	0.0	25.6
Germany	6.4	21.1	15.1	10.7
Italy	57.2	79.7	73.3	43.4
Netherlands	7.5	12.0	31.9	18.1
Spain	25.1	16.5	27.8	29.9
United Kingdom	2.6	5.5	7.1	11.6
EC	103.3	168.3	188.0	148.8
Japan	652.2	740.1	826.6	1067.3

Source: OECD, *Quarterly Oil Statistics*

to the Amerada Hess refinery at St. Croix in the Virgin Islands. However, all of this oil came from Abu Dhabi. Absolutely no Dubai at all reached the US Gulf Coast, or in fact any other part of the USA, during the course of 1991. The USA does not therefore constitute the marginal market for Dubai.

Unlike US import statistics, European figures do not allow for any decomposition of imports from the UAE by individual emirates. Total UAE exports to Europe are shown in Table 13.5, together with exports to Japan. In addition to the flow of crude oil to Japan shown, a further 0.5 mb/d goes from the UAE to other Asian countries. On the basis of this table it is hard to conclude that Europe represents the marginal market for UAE crude oil in general. If it did, it should take up most of the changes in production levels; yet since 1988 flows to Europe have increased by just 45 thousand b/d compared to the 700 thousand b/d increase in exports to the Far East as a whole. While Dubai does occasionally go into Europe, and very occasionally into NW Europe rather than the Mediterranean, it is difficult to sustain any conclusion that it is NW Europe and not the Far East that in a typical month represents the marginal market for Dubai – especially as much of the volume of Dubai going to Europe will be internal transfers by the equity partners.

However, when the Mediterranean sour crude market is tight, for instance due to the erratic arrival of Russian Urals or Iranian grades, large amounts of Dubai can be pulled westward, primarily through equity transfers. For instance, sour crude market tightness in the spring of 1992 led to about sixteen out of a programme of twenty cargoes in April going west. Most of this was internal transfers to European refineries, with small amounts going to South Africa and South America. Therefore, it seems reasonable to accept that under certain market conditions, Europe does represent a marginal market for Dubai. Europe may in fact increasingly become the marginal market as Far Eastern demand turns further towards light sweet grades, and if a situation arises where declining export availabilities of Russian Urals impinge on the Mediterranean market.

Other than changes in GPWs, Table 13.4 also showed strong significance for the price time structure in the Brent market as a determinant of Dubai prices. The coefficient of the one-month price differential (-1.2798) implies that thirty-eight days of the Brent price time structure is taken into Dubai prices, which is consistent with sailing times from Dubai to NW Europe. We found no separate influence from the time structure of WTI prices.

Changes in freight rates and in product market volatility proved to be insignificant influences on daily changes in Dubai prices. However, their longer-run influence works through the significance of the error correction term shown in Table 13.4. As noted above, this term represents the residual of a static regression of all variables in levels on the level of the Dubai price, with this residual being lagged by one period. It therefore proxies the degree of departure of the Dubai price from its long-run relationship, and the speed of adjustment is reflected in the coefficient on the term. Thus Table 13.4 implies that 3.16 per cent of any departure from the long-run relationship is corrected in any one trading day. This is a very slow adjustment, implying that on a day-on-day basis Dubai prices are primarily driven by the dynamic factors shown in Table 13.4.

We have then established that Dubai prices respond to trading conditions in Europe and the USA far more than they do to the Far Eastern markets. Dubai behaves as if it were being arbitraged in the USA and Europe, which are not normally the marginal markets for Dubai. For the purpose of market related pricing, Dubai does not then serve as an adequate marker against which to price term sales to the Far East. In fact, it would be better to use it for westward rather than eastward liftings of sour crude from the Arabian Gulf as it responds well to changes in the USA and Europe. As a meaningful Far Eastern marker Dubai fails every test. As we have seen, it is a thin market of western companies with little end-user participation, and it is then perhaps not surprising that participants play the market as if they were arbitraging Dubai with Brent in Europe and the USA.

The Brent-Dubai relationship should then in normal times be thought of as a measure of the differences between long and short haul, and sweet and sour crude oil in the West, rather than as an indication of the relative strengths of oil markets in the West and the Far East. The path of this differential is shown in Figure 13.4, which represents the weekly average difference between the price of the first forward month traded in the Dubai market and the comparable month in the Brent market (usually first month forward Brent, but in the early part of a month before Brent contracts expire, the second month forward).

Figure 13.4 shows that the differential has tended to increase over time. From an average level of between $1 and $2 per barrel in 1987, it currently tends to trade in the $2 to $3 range. The trend in the differential reflects the general change in the relationship between sweet and sour crudes, working through the GPWs. Only a small part of the trend is due to trends in freight rates. Figure 13.5 shows freight rates per barrel since 1987 for Dubai moving to NW Europe (assuming a VLCC is loaded), and for Brent to NW Europe (assuming a standard 0.5 mb cargo size). The trend in the differential between the rates is statistically significant but weak, amounting to about a 20 cent per barrel shift since 1987. As noted above, in our empirical results there was no impact effect on Dubai prices of changes in freight rates, and the relationship can then only work through the long-run pattern embodied in the error correction mechanism term.

The Brent-Dubai differential has often been volatile, but, as we will

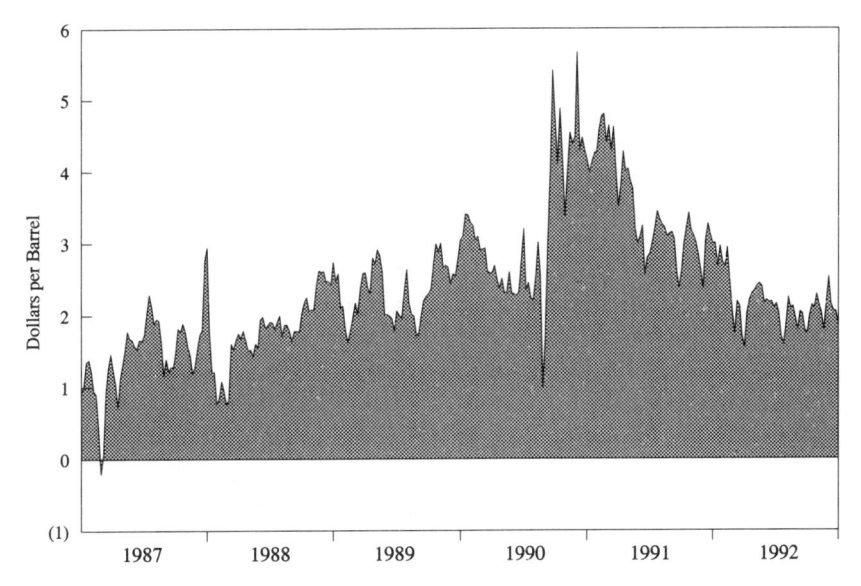

Figure 13.4: Weekly Average Price Differentials between Brent and Dubai (Comparable Delivery Months). 1987–92. Dollars per Barrel.

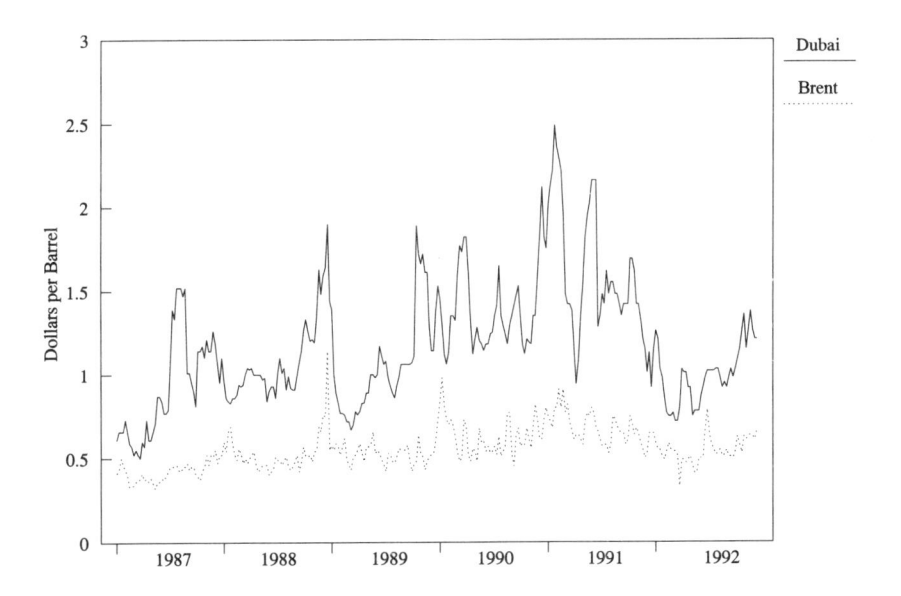

Figure 13.5: Weekly Freight Rates to NW Europe from Dubai and Sullom Voe (Brent). 1987–92. Dollars per Barrel.

see below, tends to move over a much smaller range than the Brent-WTI differential. We noted that, as can be seen in Figure 13.4, the Iraqi invasion of Kuwait in August 1990 lead to a temporary increase in the participation of Asian refiners in the Dubai market. This general scramble to secure supplies is perhaps the only occasion when differential demand patterns in the Far East impinged on the Dubai market. Figure 13.4 shows that it was associated with a relative strengthening of Dubai such that its discount to Brent was almost completely removed, and in fact Dubai did move to an unusual premium to WTI at this time. From that point Dubai weakened drastically against Brent, so that over a few weeks Brent moved to $5.50 premium over Dubai.

If Dubai prices are to be seen as a measure of sweet and sour crude relationships, then the price of Dubai will be heavily affected by expectations about, and the result of, OPEC decisions. This is because changes in OPEC output tend to be heavily biased towards lower value heavy and sour crude oils. After a decision to cut output these grades take most of the cuts, and as a result the average quality of OPEC production improves. This also leads to tightness in the market for sour crude and a relative strengthening of the prices of these grades. Likewise, incremental production from OPEC always tends to be heavier and sourer than existing output, which is inclined to depress sour crudes relatively. This effect is hard to model through the regression analysis used above, first because it is expectationally driven, and secondly, because OPEC output tends to be only observable on a monthly basis. However, observation suggests that before OPEC meetings that are expected to tighten the market, Dubai prices tend to strengthen against Brent, and likewise when production cuts are actually implemented and observed to have been so. However, tight market situations are normally associated with increases in backwardations, and, as we have seen above, the backwardation tends to drive down the price of Dubai and therefore the net effect is a priori indeterminate.

We have noted above that futures markets based on Dubai have not been a success. Our own view is that, in itself, the daily price of Dubai is not a very interesting or useful number to trade. The futures markets have set up trade in the wrong Dubai price. What *is* a useful number is the average of Dubai prices over a month. As we will see in Chapters 14 and 15, this average is of vital importance in both spot trade in Middle Eastern grades, and in term sales to the Far East. A contract, and options on it, for the Dubai average might prove to be a totally different proposition.

3. NYMEX Light Sweet Crude and the Market for WTI

The New York Mercantile Exchange is currently the fourth largest futures market in the world in terms of the volume of contracts traded (after the Chicago Board of Trade, the Chicago Mercantile Exchange, and the London International Financial Futures Exchange), and its light sweet crude oil contract is by far the most actively traded commodity futures contract in the world.

The launch dates of the nine currently active NYMEX futures contracts and the five active options on futures contracts are shown in Table 13.6. NYMEX first entered into energy futures in 1978 with its heating oil contract. However, it was the launch of the light sweet crude contract in March 1983 that provided the impetus for the growth of the exchange. In 1991 the light sweet futures contract and options on the contract had a combined volume of about 27.5 million, 60 per cent of the total volume of the exchange. With each contract being for one thousand barrels, this means that 27.5 billion barrels were traded on NYMEX in 1992. By way of comparison, total world production of crude oil in 1992 was about 22 billion barrels. The record volume of trade for any one day on the light sweet contract (excluding options), equates to 199 mb of crude oil, three times daily world production.

NYMEX is a regulated market. As well as its own internal rules it is overseen by the US Commodities and Futures Trading Commission (CFTC), which must approve all its contracts. It is also subject to the risk of direct interference from the federal government. For example, the 1992 US budget proposals contained a provision for a 15 cent tax

Table 13.6: NYMEX Contracts, 1993.

Commodity	Futures	Options
Platinum	3 Dec 1956	16 Oct 1990
Palladium	22 Jan 1968	-
Heating Oil	14 Nov 1978	26 Jun 1987
Light Sweet Crude Oil	30 Mar 1983	14 Nov 1986
Unleaded Gasoline	3 Dec 1984	13 Mar 1989
Propane	21 Aug 1987	-
Natural Gas	3 Apr 1990	2 Oct 1992
Sour Crude Oil*	28 Feb 1992	-
Unleaded Gasoline (USGC)*	18 Sep 1992	-

* At the beginning of 1993 trading volumes of these two contracts were zero on most days.

Source: NYMEX

on all NYMEX contracts.[4]

The light sweet crude oil contract is often, but in a strict sense mistakenly, described as a contract for West Texas Intermediate. In fact WTI is only one of ten grades (seven domestic and three imported) currently acceptable for delivery under the contract (see Table 13.7). However the price of the contract in any time does, *de facto*, represent the price of WTI.

Until the April 1990 contract, WTI with gravity 40 degrees API and a sulphur content of 0.4 per cent was defined as the par grade, with adjustments to the price of oil delivered under the contract being made for gravities below (but not above) the par characteristics, and for sulphur contents above or below par for any deliveries of imported grades. There are now no gravity or sulphur adjustments made. All oil delivered under the contract must however have a gravity of between 34 and 45 degrees API, and a sulphur content of less than 0.5 per cent.

The basic traded unit is one thousand barrels. Trade is currently conducted for delivery months up to three years away, with twenty-two delivery months being open for trade at any one time. The first eighteen consecutive months are traded, together with four delivery months further out. The exact forwardness of the months these contracts represent at any given time depends on a six-month cycle. Initially the four months were the 21st, 24th, 30th and 36th months forward. After three months a new 24th month contract began trading, and three months after this a new 36th month contract began trading, with this sequence then being perpetually repeated. In all intervening months a new 18th month contract begins trading. Hence the outer contract ranges from thirty-one to thirty-six months distant.

Trade for a given delivery month takes place up to the third business

Table 13.7: NYMEX Deliverable Grades.

Domestic US Crudes	*Imported Crudes*
1. Low Sweet Mix (Scurry Snyder)	1. Bonny Light
2. Mid Continent Sweet	2. Brent
3. New Mexico Sweet	3. Oseberg *
4. North Texas Sweet	(4. Brass Blend)
5. Oklahoma Sweet	(5. Ekofisk)
6. South Texas Sweet	(6. Saharan Blend)
7. West Texas Intermediate	(7. Zarzaitine/El Borma)

Notes: * Added effective from April 1990 contract
( ) Removed effective from April 1990 contract

day before the 25th (or first business day before the 25th if the exchange is not open on that date) of the prior month. On the 25th, pipeline companies begin to schedule the next month's shipping programme. Most participants balance their portfolios in the expiring contract before this time. However should a position be kept until expiry, delivery takes place at Cushing in Oklahoma at any facility that has access by pipeline to the storage facilities at Cushing of either ARCO or Texaco.

Other than the standard terms, there are two other methods of physical delivery. In a standard delivery the buyer and seller are matched by NYMEX. An ADP (Alternate Delivery Procedure) occurs when buyers and sellers matched by the exchange wish to effect the transfer on terms other than those specified in the standard delivery procedures. However, the most flexible method of facilitating delivery is to agree an EFP (Exchange of Futures for Physicals).

An EFP can be agreed between any two participants (there is no matching of buyer and seller by NYMEX as in standard deliveries or ADPs), on any terms they wish to agree. An EFP could transfer any grade of crude oil (not just those shown in Table 13.7), at any location in the world, and at any time of day whether or not the NYMEX trading floor is physically open. While the exchange must be notified of EFPs, no trading floor activity is necessary. While EFPs are normally used to close positions, they can also be used to initiate a position. The price of the transfer is negotiated by the parties as a differential to the price of the light sweet contract.

The annual volume of deliveries and their decomposition made through the NYMEX contract since 1984, together with the total volume of trade, is shown in Table 13.8. This table will underestimate the volume of EFPs since the statistics are only published by NYMEX for the nearest delivery month trading. Table 13.8 shows the rapid increase of the volume of trade up to 1988, and the plateau since 1989. Total volume fell in 1991 for the first time, to below the 1989 level, before rising slightly in 1992. There is a suggestion in these figures that the contract is now mature in the sense that a continuing pattern of further large annual increases in the volume of trade appears unlikely. In 1992 one in every thirty-five trades resulted in a physical delivery, 97 per cent of these being achieved through the use of EFPs.

There is a forward market for WTI also based on deliveries at Cushing, which tends to trade lot sizes of between 50 thousand and 100 thousand barrels. This is essentially the market for NYMEX EFPs. As such, its prices are discussed with reference to the NYMEX screen, and it continues to trade when NYMEX is closed. There is also a market for WTI based on Midland Texas. The market for WTI and price

Table 13.8: Total Volume and Deliveries, NYMEX Sweet Contract 1984–92. Million Barrels.

Year	Volume	Total Deliveries	EFPs	ADPs	Standard Deliveries
1984	1495	67	49	3	16
1985	3581	158	132	2	24
1986	7312	276	256	3	18
1987	12986	434	417	3	14
1988	18518	612	603	2	7
1989	20665	679	664	8	7
1990	23000	719	701	10	9
1991	20467	669	652	12	5
1992	21093	596	577	10	8

Source : NYMEX *Energy in the News*, various issues

relationships in the US market are driven by pipeline logistics. Figure 13.6 shows the major US Gulf crude oil pipelines and their directions of flow.[5] Production of WTI amounts to about 1 mb/d which is gathered and brought into the area of Jal and Midland. From Midland crude can flow to the Gulf Coast refinery areas of Corpus Christi, Houston, Texas City, Beaumont and Port Arthur, the total pipeline capacity to the coast being about 780 thousand b/d. Alternatively it can flow North to Cushing and then on to Chicago. The Basin (382 thousand b/d) and Shell (24 thousand b/d) pipelines go from Midland to Cushing. Once a flow has started on this route it cannot reach the US Gulf. The importance of Midland in the logistics system then is that it is the point where shippers of WTI have the choice of meeting mid-West or US Gulf demand. In other words, the difference between the price of WTI at Midland and at Cushing then reflects both transportation costs, and also the balance of Gulf Coast and mid-West demand. The pipeline tariff between Midland and Cushing is normally between 20 and 30 cents. However, as shown in Figure 13.7, the differential in prices, shown as a weekly average, oscillates widely either side of this range. Particularly striking is the extra volatility of the differential after 1988. Much of this is due to pipeline reversals, which have fundamentally changed both the nature of the WTI market, and in particular its relationship to internationally traded crude oils.

Imported grades of crude oil have always been deliverable under the NYMEX light sweet contract (as shown in Table 13.7). However, before 1988 no imported crude oil could actually reach Cushing. In April 1988 ARCO reversed the flow in their pipeline which runs from

Texas City to Cushing via Jacksboro (as shown in Figure 13.6). This reversal allowed imported crude oil to reach Cushing at the rate of 55 thousand b/d. This has since been increased to nearly 120 thousand b/d, and in the longer term could increase to over 200 thousand b/d. The rate of potential flow from the Gulf Coast to Cushing increased by a further 55 thousand b/d when Texaco reversed their Wichita Falls to Houston pipeline in January 1990. The capacity on this line has since increased to about 70 thousand b/d.

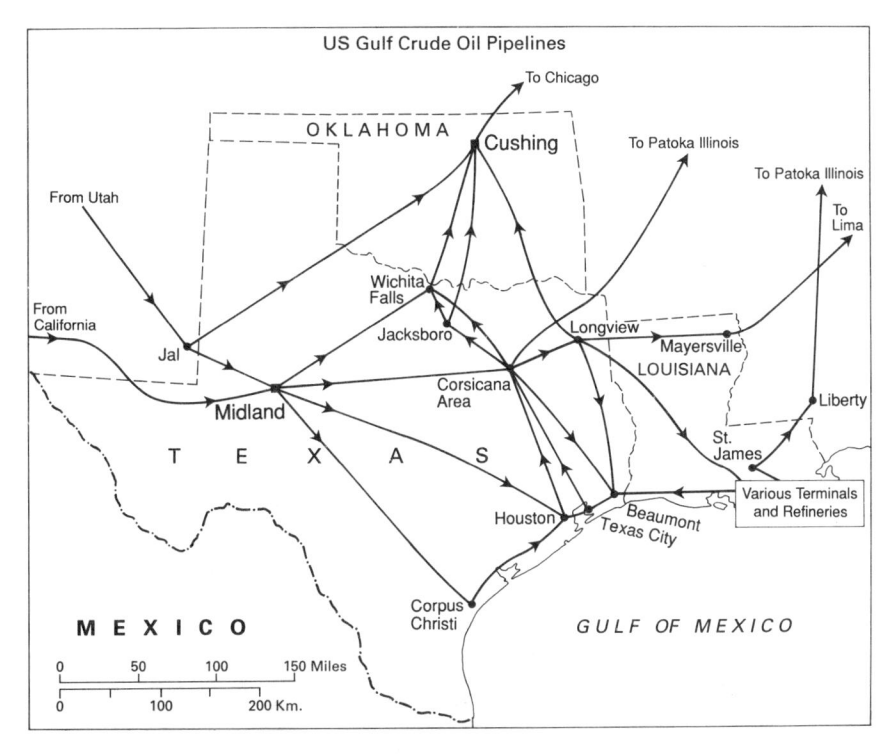

Figure 13.6: Map of US Gulf Crude Oil Pipelines.

While the pipeline reversals allowed imported crude oil to reach Cushing, it also created the current situation where once past Midland, WTI can only flow North. Hence the Cushing-Midland differential became more responsive to differential demand patterns in the mid-West and on the Gulf Coast. These reversals have also had an effect on the relationship between WTI and Brent (see Figure 13.8, showing the weekly average differential adjusted for comparability of delivery months).

230   *Oil Markets and Prices*

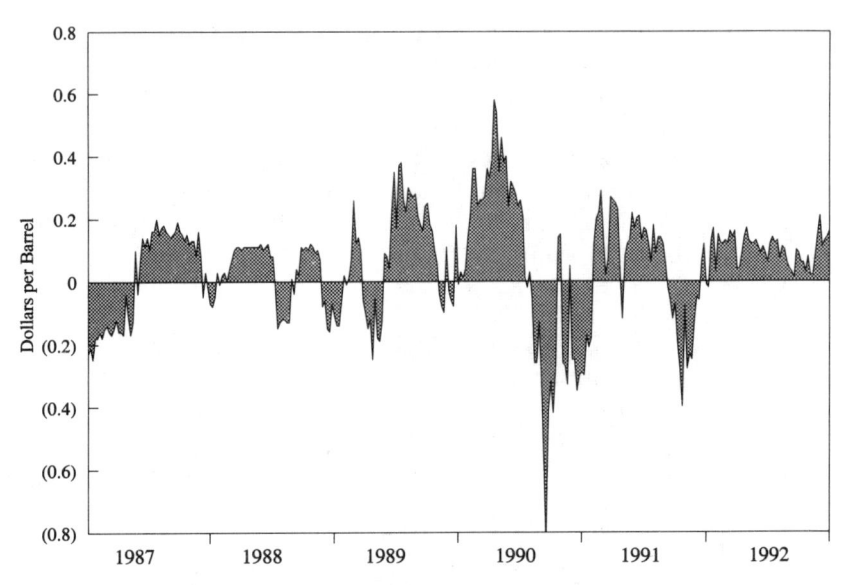

Figure 13.7: Weekly Average Price Differentials between WTI at Cushing and WTI at Midland. 1987–92. Dollars per Barrel.

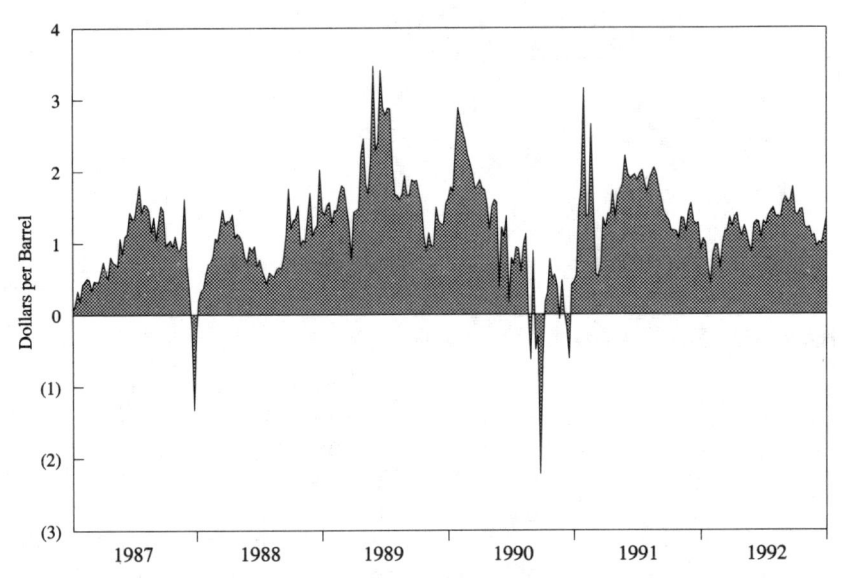

Figure 13.8: Weekly Average Price Differential between WTI at Cushing and Brent (Comparable Delivery Months). 1987–92. Dollars per Barrel.

While the ARCO reversal in April 1988 had allowed Brent and other imports to reach Cushing, the potential flow was not large enough to prevent WTI from totally decoupling itself from the world market. This was manifested in 1989 (note the three large spikes in Figure 13.8). The USA faced a logistical problem in moving imported crude oil through the country. The fall in oil demand in the early 1980s had led to the conversion of two key arterial pipelines (Seaway and Texoma) which moved imports into Oklahoma, to natural gas usage, and left a capacity problem as demand began to pick up and domestic production fell. The result was that Cushing had become isolated.

The Gulf crisis of 1990 showed the other facet to this. While the reversals had allowed imported crude oil to get to Cushing, they had also divorced prices at Cushing from the direct pull of Gulf Coast demand. The result was that Cushing showed a tendency to be primarily influenced by mid-West demand rather than that of the Gulf Coast, where the impact of the cessation of Iraqi exports was most felt (Iraq exported over 1 mb/d to the USA immediately before the invasion of Kuwait). This is shown in the path of the Cushing-Midland differential in Figure 13.7. The crisis also showed the greater flexibility and responsiveness of the Brent market compared to WTI. Scheduling remains a problem in the US market, with pro-rationing still common on major pipelines carrying imported crude oil[6] (in particular Capline), and also at terminals receiving imported crude oil, such as the Louisiana Offshore Oil Port (LOOP).

Brent has inherently greater flexibility than WTI in being both waterborne (and therefore not totally subject to the problems of US pipeline scheduling), and exportable (and thus able to react to demand changes throughout the western hemisphere). The net result of the flexibility in late 1990 was that the price of Brent moved upwards sharply against WTI, reaching a peak premium to WTI of over $3 per barrel (see Figure 13.8).

There is one other important WTI market. Independent producers of US domestic crudes are paid on the basis of posted prices by the companies that operate gathering stations. The price of WTI at Cushing as traded on NYMEX includes gathering costs and pipeline transportation costs. The gap between the posted prices and the NYMEX price has spawned a separate market known as the Postings Plus (or P-Plus) market. This market trades the differential to a specific posting agreed by the traders, normally Koch's (the major US crude oil gatherer).

Posted prices have not been the result of a competitive market. Gatherers normally attempted to tie particular producers to them by the payment of variable bonuses above posted prices to secure supplies, given the continued decline in the output of US sweet crude oil, and thus posted prices have tended to be lower than those that would prevail under competitive conditions.[7] Hence the value of P-Plus reflects gathering costs, transport costs to Cushing, an allowance for the time structure of prices and for the size of the bonuses offered by the gatherers.

4. The Rotterdam Market

The Rotterdam market is the generic term given to trade in oil products in North-West Europe, and takes its name from the large refining and storage complex in the Antwerp-Rotterdam-Amsterdam (ARA) area. Together with trade in the Mediterranean focused on Genoa in Italy and Lavera in France, it constitutes the European spot market for oil products. Like the forward Brent market it has no centralized exchange and trade is carried out by telephone and telex. Table 13.9 shows the products for which price assessments are made by Platt's (as of 1993) on a daily basis.[8]

Three sets of quotations are produced, one for each of the separate elements of the Rotterdam market. There is a barge market for oil products to be moved up the Rhine into Germany, as well as a cargo market for both the import (c.i.f.) and the export (f.o.b.) of oil products.

Table 13.9: Platt's Price Quotations for Petroleum Products, ARA Area. 1993.

Products	Cargoes c.i.f. NWE Basis ARA	Barges f.o.b. Rotterdam	Cargoes f.o.b. NWE
Leaded Gasoline (0.15 G/L)	X	X	X
Premium Unleaded	X	X	X
Regular Unleaded	X	X	X
Physical Naphtha	X	X	
Paper Naphtha	X		
Jet Kerosene	X	X	X
Gasoil 0.2 S	X	X	X
Gasoil 0.3 S	X		
Fuel oil 0.7% S (Straight)			X
Fuel oil 1% S	X	X	X
Fuel oil 3% S	X		X
Fuel oil 3.5% S	X	X	X
E4 Feedstock	X		
MTBE	X		

The cargo sizes traded are typically about 10 thousand tonnes for gasoline and jet kerosene, and 17 thousand to 25 thousand tonnes for other products. Given the diversity of standards across Europe (for instance each major Western European country has different specifications for gasoline), and the diversity in qualities across individual cargoes, assessments relate to basic specifications as defined by each reporting agency. As we saw in crude oil price assessments in Chapter 10, much is left to the skill and judgement of the price reporter.

Rotterdam prices are now accepted as a base to price oil products in trade and in internal company transfers throughout Northern Europe. However the industry has not always accepted the role of the Rotterdam market. Consider the view of one major oil company in 1975.

> In fact, no company involved in the sort of integrated operation – and the associated long term financial commitments – which supplies 90% to 95% of Europe's oil requirements could accept that a market trading only say 3% should set price levels for the rest of the business. This would be a case of the tail wagging the dog with a vengeance.[9]

In addition to spot trade there is also an array of European informal forward markets in gasoil,[10] gasoline, naphtha and heavy fuel oil. Gasoil is also traded in a successful contract on the IPE.[11]

To simplify the analysis we have constructed three price series, relating to the broad refinery cuts of gasoline, distillates and heavy fuel oil. All prices are cargoes NWE c.i.f. basis ARA, with the data converted into dollars per barrel from dollars per tonne through use of the relevant conversion factors for each product. The gasoline series represents the weighted average of leaded and regular unleaded gasoline assessments, the weights being their share in European output. The distillate series is the average of gasoil and jet kerosene weighted by output.

Derivation of a heavy fuel oil series generates three issues. First, the sulphur content of fuel oil for any given crude oil type varies according to the refinery configuration. We therefore generate two series, one for a typical simple refining process, and one for a typical complex refinery. The sulphur content of the fuel oil produced through running Brent is respectively 0.67 per cent and 0.9 per cent for the two processes. We then derive the price of the heavy fuel oil in each case by straight line interpolation of the assessed prices of 1 per cent and 3.5 per cent fuel oil.

Secondly, the fuel oil produced by simple refining is straight run, i.e.

it can still be broken down further into greater yields of lighter products by using it as a feedstock in a complex refining unit. Fuel oil from a complex refinery is cracked, i.e. no more lighter products can be produced save by running it through an even more sophisticated unit. Thus fuel oil from simple refining tends to have a greater value than that from complex refining. We correct for this effect by interpolations from the price of E4 – a Russian feedstock of straight-run fuel oil laced with gasoil. It has a sulphur content of between 2 per cent and 2.5 per cent. The price of E4 is normally quoted as the premium over the means of a set of series for 3.5 per cent straight-run fuel. We have interpolated the premium of E4 over straight-run fuel with the midpoint sulphur content of 2.25 per cent, and adjusted for the gasoil content of E4. This provides an approximation to the premium of straight-run fuel oil over cracked.

The weekly averages of the series for the prices of the derived gasoline, distillate and (complex refining) heavy fuel oil cuts are shown in Figure 13.9 for the period from January 1989 to the end of June 1992. These series, while overall highly correlated, can often move very independently, particularly when any short-term tightness in the market leads to a spike in prices. Note that the 1989 spike on gasoline prices caused by the feedback effects from the tight US market, had little knock-on effects on distillate prices. Likewise the cold snap that hit both the USA and Europe at the end of 1989 and caused spikes in distillate and fuel oil prices, had little effect on gasoline prices. Note also the very brief spike in gasoil prices in August 1991 consequent on the attempted coup in Russia, which had little impact on the other products.

The Gulf crisis had the greatest effect on distillate prices, both in magnitude and in duration. While the gasoline market had reversed nearly all the previous run-up in prices by the end of December 1990 (there was a further brief sharp upwards move before the onset of war), the market for distillates took a further two months to reach the same position. The market for fuel oil, unlike the other products, faces a high degree of possible substitution to other fuels in its main use, i.e. power generation. It therefore soon hit an upper bound beyond which substitution would drive the price down again.

Using the price series for the three cuts we can generate the Gross Product Worths, (GPWs), for simple and for complex refining of Brent, i.e. the combined value of the refined products per barrel of Brent used as refinery feedstock. The refinery yields that we assume are shown in Table 13.10 as weekly averages for the three broad output cuts.

Weighting the price series by these yields produces GPWs gross of refinery costs. We follow the methodology of Platt's in approximating

Dubai, WTI and European Products 235

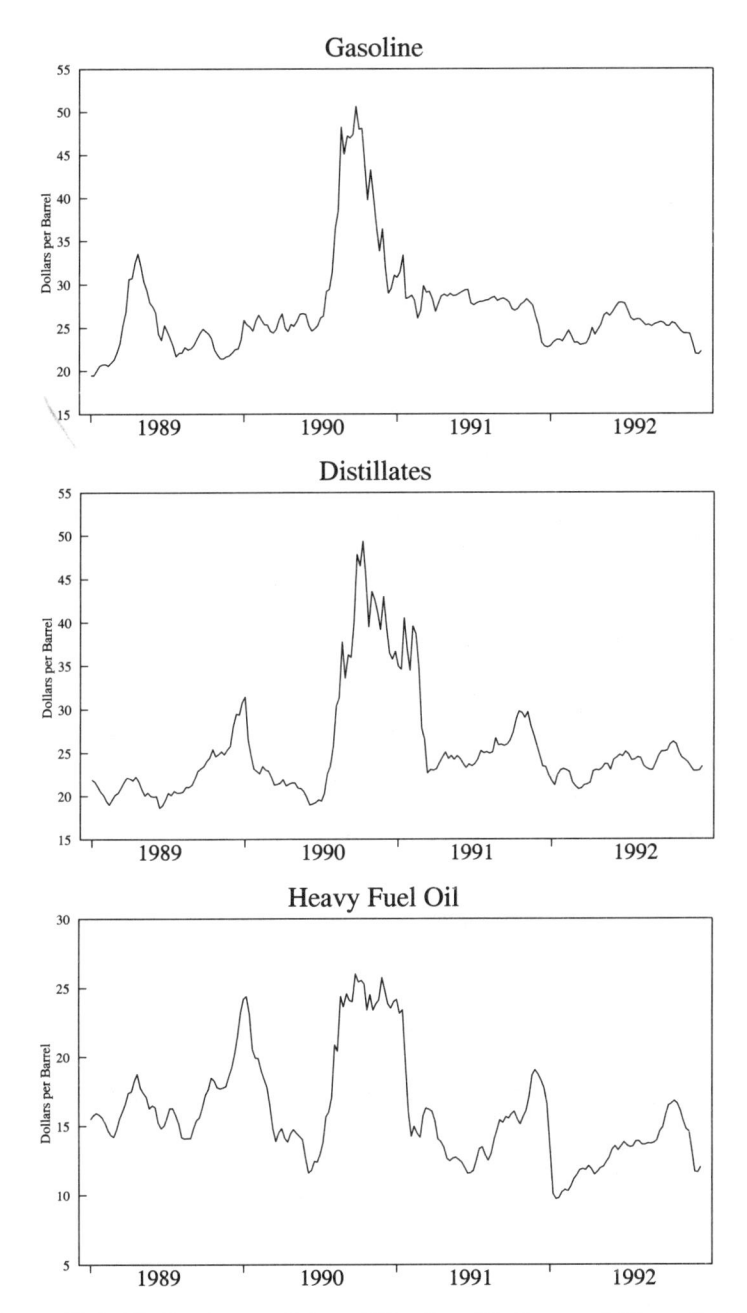

Figure 13.9: Weekly Average Prices of Gasoline, Distillates and Heavy Fuel Oil in the Antwerp-Rotterdam-Amsterdam (ARA) area. 1989–92. Dollars per Barrel.

Table 13.10: Representative Refinery Yields for Brent. Per Cent.

Products	Simple Refining	Complex Refining
Gasoline	0.1745	0.3694
Distillates	0.4521	0.4768
Heavy Fuel Oil	0.3741	0.1538

Source: *Platt's Oil Price Handbook and Oilmanac 68th edition*

costs by assuming a loss of fuel oil in refinery usage and costs such that the above fuel oil yields are reduced by 0.075. Subtracting the price of dated Brent then gives the refinery profit margins for simple and complex refining consequent on running Brent. These are shown in Figure 13.10, together with the difference between them.

Refinery margins have shown considerable volatility, even outside the period of the Kuwait crisis, as has the difference between complex and simple margins, i.e. the gross per barrel return to investment in upgraded capacity. As of 1992 this return lies between $1 and $2 per barrel, having shown a strong downwards trend throughout 1991. The volatility of refinery margins demonstrates how much greater are the problems of risk management for a refiner compared to a solely upstream company. The oil producer's risk arises solely from variations in the absolute price of crude oil, whereas the refiner's arises from variations in price differentials.

Given that the behaviour of the three series shown in Figure 13.9 has often been very different, the question is raised as to whether they separately or jointly impact on Brent prices. The first step is to examine the causality among price changes, and in particular we test for Granger causality between the daily price of Brent and those of oil products. An event Granger causes another if it pre-dates it, and hence in this context we are testing for significant effects on changes in one set of prices, arising from lagged changes in other sets of prices. The results of this exercise are shown in Table 13.11, using twenty lags, with the null hypothesis being that there is no causality, for the period after the end of the Kuwait crisis up to the end of June 1992. The heavy fuel oil series is that produced for complex refining, i.e. without any premium for uncracked material.

These results have very clear implications for the nature of the causality between Brent and oil product prices, at least in the period studied. There is significant causality running from Brent to gasoline

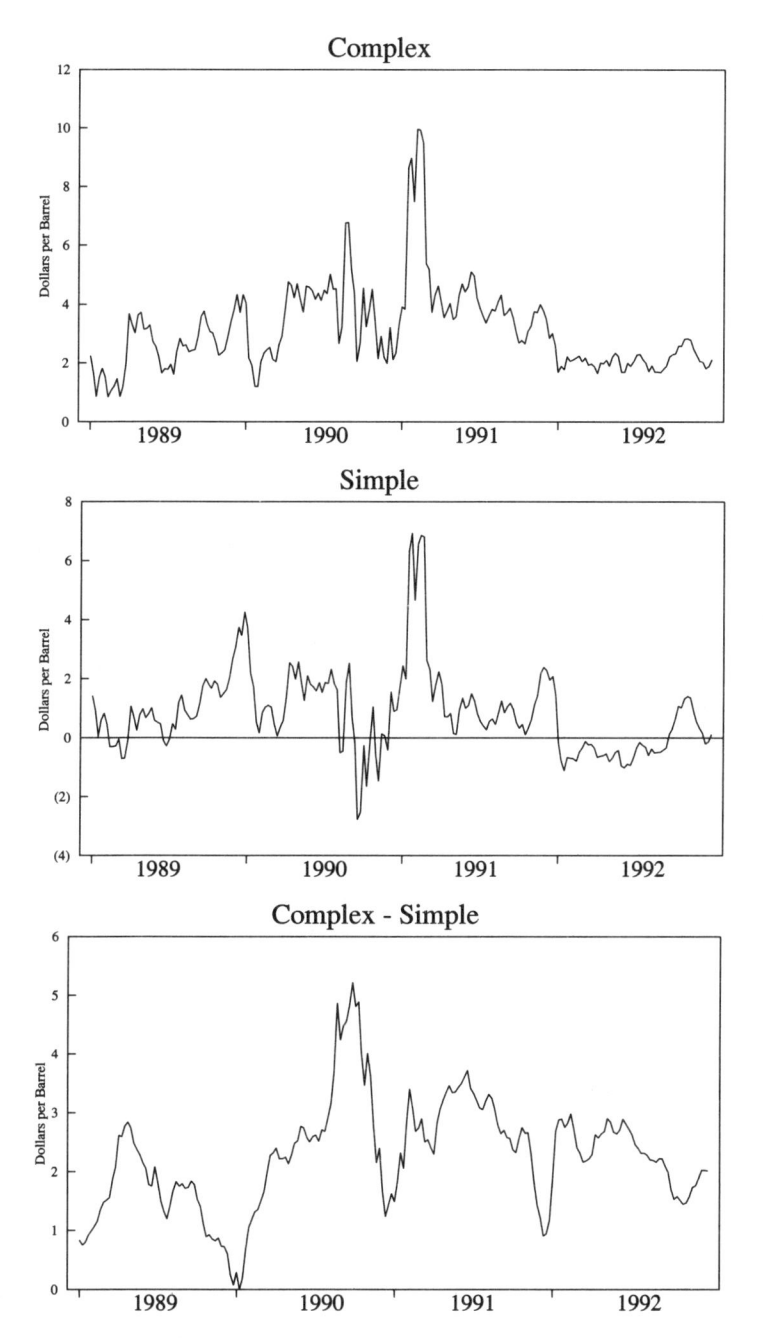

Figure 13.10: Weekly Average Refinery Margins from Brent in the ARA Area. 1989–92. Dollars per Barrel.

Table 13.11: Causality Tests Between Brent and Product Prices.

| Causality from Brent to Product Prices | | Causality to Brent from Product Prices | |
Products	F-Statistic	Products	F-Statistic
Gasoline	1.713*	Gasoline	1.125
Distillates	3.411**	Distillates	1.259
Heavy Fuel Oil	1.323	Heavy Fuel Oil	1.119
GPW (Simple)	4.142**	GPW (Simple)	1.153
GPW (Complex)	3.464**	GPW (Complex)	1.308

Note: * significant at 5 per cent
** significant at 1 per cent

and distillate prices, as well as to both simple and complex GPWs. Only fuel oil price changes are not significantly affected by previous Brent price changes. By contrast, there are no significant causalities running from product prices or GPWs to Brent prices.

The above does not imply that there is no causality between product prices and Brent, but it does imply that any such causality must happen in a period of less than one day, whereas previous days' Brent price changes do have explanatory power for product price changes. To illustrate this we consider the relationship over the same period as above between daily ARA gasoil prices and Brent prices, both expressed in dollars per barrel.

Statistically both series are non-stationary, and hence the analysis cannot be carried out in levels of prices. We therefore use the following two-step procedure, using the same methodology as used in the analysis of Dubai prices. First the static regression of the level of gasoil prices on a constant and Brent prices (dated Brent is used in this example). The equation can be thought of as the long-run relationship between the prices, and hence the residuals of the regression are the deviation of short-run equilibrium from the long-run path. In the second stage the daily change in gasoil is regressed on a constant and the change in the Brent prices and lags of those changes, as well as the lagged residual generated in the first stage. Hence the coefficients on price changes are the impact effect of day-to-day variations, while the coefficient on the lagged first stage residual represents the proportion of any departure from the long-run relationship that is removed each trading day. The results of this procedure are shown in Table 13.12.

A strong contemporaneous correlation between gasoil and Brent price changes is shown in Table 13.2. However, lagged changes in the price of Brent also have explanatory power, particularly the first lag.

The hypothesis that the sum of the coefficients on Brent price changes is equal to one cannot be rejected. Thus, while a change in Brent prices does map through to an equal change in gasoil prices, the transmission of the change does not all take place on the same day. It follows that gasoil prices are not generated in an efficient market, since a given day's price change is in part predictable by previous days' Brent price changes.

Table 13.12: Regression of Gasoil Price Changes. Statistics.

Variable	Coefficient	T-Statistic
Constant	0.0011	0.07
Changes in Brent prices:		
Current	0.5973	10.60**
1st Lag	0.4149	6.98**
2nd Lag	-0.0821	1.43
3rd Lag	-0.1125	1.97*
Correction Term	-0.0784	3.94*

Other Statistics: R-Squared 0.269, Log Likelihood -896.5, F-Statistic 24,587
Note: * significant at 5 per cent
      ** significant at 1 per cent

The significance of the correction term, i.e. the lagged residual from the static equation, shows that the two sets of prices do converge onto a long-run relationship, with 7.9 per cent of any short-run divergences from that relationship being removed on each trading day.

From daily price series it is impossible to determine the causality between Brent and oil products for price changes occurring on the same day. It is however possible to examine the characteristics of the correlations. We have followed the same two-step procedure as in the above exercise over the same time period, as Brent prices and all product prices proved to be non-stationary. The static equation in this case is a regression of dated Brent prices on the prices for the three refinery cuts, using the price of cracked material for the heavy fuel oil series. The dynamic equation considers the relationships between price changes together with the adjustment term derived from the static equation. The results of the dynamic equation are shown in Table 13.13.

No lagged oil product price changes proved to be significant, as would be expected given the result of the causality tests. The strongest

Table 13.13: Regression of Dated Brent Price Changes. Statistics.

Variable	Coefficient	T-Statistic
Constant	0.0052	0.36
Changes in Product prices:		
Gasoline	0.1400	1.90*
Distillates	0.3880	8.70**
Heavy Fuel Oil	0.0800	1.25
Correction Term	-0.0940	3.59**

Other Statistics: R-Squared 0.278, Log-Likelihood -16.050, F-Statistic 29.955
Note: * significant at 10 per cent
 ** significant at 1 per cent

correlation is between Brent price changes and distillate price changes, with a lesser but significant correlation between Brent and gasoline. By contrast, once other product price changes are included, there is no significant correlation between heavy fuel oil and Brent price changes. Together with the lack of Granger causality between the two series we found above, this implies that, at least over the period considered, observation of the market for heavy fuel oil contained no useful additional information for Brent traders. There is also a significant adjustment effect, implying that 9.4 per cent of any departure from the long-run relationship is made up on each trading day.

5. Summary

In this chapter we have considered the two other main forward or future markets beyond Brent, i.e. Dubai and West Texas Intermediate. Dubai, often seen as a marker for the Far East market, was instead shown to be a marker for sour crude oil in western markets. The Brent-Dubai differential is a good indicator of the relative strength in western markets of short haul sweet crude oil compared to long haul sour crude oil. It is not a good indicator of relative market conditions in the western hemisphere as compared to the Far East. We have then suggested that Dubai represents a poor marker crude for the Far East. We also found that Dubai trading is becoming increasingly illiquid, particularly for single cargo fixed price deals. Indeed the price of Dubai can only be defined from the basis of deals done in the Brent-Dubai differential.

WTI, or more exactly the light sweet crude oil contract on the New York Mercantile Exchange, was shown to be the crude oil market with the greatest liquidity in the world, indeed the volume of trade exceeds that of world production. However, this does not mean that the price of WTI is a good indication of world oil prices. WTI is the dominant crude oil for price setting in the US domestic market. This market is based on US pipeline deliveries, whereas most world trade is in waterborne cargoes. We have suggested that not only can WTI prices at Cushing Oklahoma become decoupled from world prices, they can even (because of pipeline logistics) become decoupled from prices at the US Gulf, the major import market into the USA. In sum, the NYMEX contract essentially represents the US domestic crude oil market, and is inappropriate either for price setting or for hedging of the waterborne cargoes that are the basis of most world trade in crude oil.

This chapter has also considered the Rotterdam market, the basis for European oil product trading. We found strong causality running from Brent prices to gasoline and distillate prices as well as to refinery gross product worths, with no significant causality running the other way, at least on daily price series. This was further demonstrated by the significance of past Brent price changes in explaining gasoil price changes. Our conclusion is then that, other than same day effects, Brent prices do lead oil product prices.

Notes
1. By early 1993 output had fallen to about 350 thousand b/d.
2. The seller is not constrained in rejecting nominations by the buyer. There is a view that under the Conoco GTCs the seller cannot 'unreasonably' reject a nomination. (For example B. Sas (1989), 'Legal Aspects of Risk Management and Forward Oil Trading. The Forward Oil Markets and their Contracts', *Journal of Energy and Natural Resources Law* vol. 7, no. 1). In fact the GTCs only state that the nomination of a *vessel* not a loading range can not be 'unreasonably rejected'.
3. This methodology follows that of Hendry. See D. Hendry (1990), *PC-GIVE Manual*, Oxford Institute of Economics and Statistics.
4. A similar proposal was rejected by the US Congress in 1991.
5. A full inventory of US pipelines is given in National Petroleum Council, *Petroleum Storage and Transportation*, vol. V, 'Petroleum Liquids Transportation', NPC 1989. All pipeline capacities quoted in the text are drawn from this unless otherwise stated.
6. Pro-rationing has been virtually perpetual on the Interprovincial Pipeline (IPL) which carries Canadian production out of Alberta. As shippers expect to be pro-rationed they tend to overnominate, and at times this has led to the total of nominations on the IPL far exceeding the level of total Albertan production.
7. In March 1992 Phillips 66 announced an intention to stop bonus payments and raised its posted price, and were closely followed by other gatherers, but not Koch.

Phillips reverted to the old system in August 1992 (see *Oil Daily Energy Compass*, 21 August 1992).
8. Daily hardcopy assessments are also made by Petroleum Argus and London Oil Reports.
9. 'The Rotterdam Market', Shell Briefing Service. For current oil company views of the Rotterdam market see UK Monopolies and Mergers Commission (1990), *The Supply of Petrol*.
10. The various markets for gasoil in Europe are considered in D. Long (1991), *European Gas Oil Markets : Price Relationships, Hedging and Efficiency*, Oxford Institute for Energy Studies.
11. The IPE has also attempted contracts in unleaded gasoline, naphtha and heavy fuel oil. Only the first of these was trading as of 1993.

CHAPTER 14

WORLD OIL SPOT TRADE

1. Introduction

In previous chapters we have considered the markets for Brent, Dubai and WTI. In total these three crudes represent about 3 per cent of the volume of world production, and less than 1 mb/d of a total international trade in crude oil of over 30 mb/d. While the bulk of the remaining 97 per cent of world trade moves under term contracts from producing countries (which is considered in the next chapter), there is significant spot trade in several regions of the world.

This chapter looks at the structure and changes over time of spot trade as reflected in the records contained in the Petroleum Argus database. The analysis is conducted on a regional basis, and we look in turn at markets in the North Sea, West Africa, the Mediterranean, the Middle East Gulf, the Far East and the USA. The final section provides a brief summary.

Our focus in this chapter is on price formation in international spot markets. The particular issue is whether Brent prices are merely representative of other markets, or whether they have a direct impact on price formation. We have already seen in Chapter 8 that spot trade in Brent itself, i.e. dated Brent, is primarily carried out as a differential to forward Brent prices, with outright trade in absolute prices having all but vanished since 1986. There is a question then as to whether similar patterns are found in other markets, and if so how many different marker crudes there are in the world oil market.

While our regionalization is on the basis of producing areas there is also some useful information that can be derived from the import statistics of consumer countries. The appendix to this chapter details the results of an analysis of the import statistics produced by the US Department of Energy and disseminated by the American Petroleum Institute which reports US imports on a shipment-by-shipment basis. These tables will be referred to at several points in the text. No equivalent publicly available data at the same level of disaggregation exist for the UK or any other European country.

The distinction between spot and forward trade in the oil industry is not always a clear one. In other commodities spot trade normally represents sales and purchases of fixed amounts with a fairly rapid transfer of the physical commodity between the parties. However, the nature of crude oil trading is very much driven by infrastructural factors. With loading schedules at terminals and pipeline schedules normally settled well in advance, together with the logistics of chartering tankers, there is very little spot trade in the normal sense.

The sale of a cargo already afloat is normally interpreted as a distressed sale and will tend to have a discount attached. Refiners prefer to have their crude oil slate arranged several weeks in advance, to reduce uncertainty and to help keep inventory holdings close to minimum operating levels. Hence nearly all trade defined as spot in oil does carry an element of forwardness, in some areas of the world often more than two months. In terms of the discussion of futures and forward trade in Chapter 12, this forwardness is a deferral of delivery for reasons of convenience or necessity.

One possible definition of a spot trade in the oil industry is the trade of a specific cargo for loading within a specific narrowly defined range. However this still leaves a grey area, for instance a large-scale producer of a particular grade might be fairly certain that they will have a cargo for loading in, say, the first ten days of a given month, and sell this hypothetical cargo well in advance of the publication of the loading schedule with a ten-day loading range.

Observationally, the difference between spot and forward markets in oil is that there is other activity in a forward market than simple physical transfer of oil in single transactions. In particular, there is trade in claims to cargoes, with the number of transactions usually being a sizeable multiple of the number of cargoes available, and the market can be used for hedging purposes.

2. The North Sea

As well as the various markets for Brent blend, there is also an active trade in other North Sea grades of crude oil, both those from the UK and the Norwegian sectors. In most cases these are purely wet markets, spot trade usually conducted within a month of the loading date of the oil, or occasionally the resale on a delivered basis of cargoes that have already been loaded.

The bulk of UK production is taken by pipeline to one of four onshore loading terminals. Terminal loadings accounted for 1.33 mb/d out of a total UK offshore production of 1.79 mb/d in 1991. Apart from the 0.77 mb/d of Brent blend put into the Sullom Voe terminal, 0.36 mb/d came from the Forties system into Cruden Bay, and 0.18 mb/d from the Flotta system. Output from the Beatrice field is taken by pipeline to Nigg Bay, but in 1991 this amounted to just 0.02 mb/d. The pipeline systems then produce three main tradable grades of crude oil, Brent, Forties and Flotta, plus the minor grade Beatrice. Offshore loadings by tanker from individual or groups of fields produce another half dozen or so grades, of which the most important are Fulmar (0.149 mb/d in 1991), and Beryl (0.105 mb/d). Very minor amounts also come from Argyl, Cyrus, Kittiwake and Maureen (respectively 0.005, 0.006, 0.03 and 0.04 mb/d). The UK also has a share of the offshore loaded Norwegian grade Statfjord, and this share amounted to 0.1 mb/d in 1991. In total then Brent blend comprised 44 per cent of UK output in 1991, Forties 21 per cent and Flotta 10 per cent.

In the Norwegian sector output reached 1.88 mb/d in 1991, exceeding UK output for the first time given the shutdowns during the year in the Brent, Ninian and Forties pipelines. This production is composed of four main marketable grades determined by pipeline and offshore loading systems. In 1991 these four grades each had a larger production base than all grades in the UK North Sea other than Brent. The Oseberg system produced about 0.425 mb/d loaded at the terminal in Sture, and the Ekofisk system produced 0.51 mb/d loaded at Teeside in the UK. The other two main grades are both loaded offshore, Statfjord (Norwegian share 0.6 mb/d in 1991) and Gullfaks (0.37 mb/d). The Norwegian share of the Murchison field is loaded at Sullom Voe as part of Brent blend.

The spot trade for North Sea oil is made up almost entirely of UK and Norwegian grades.[1] Table 14.1 shows the main traded grades ranked by total trade reported to Petroleum Argus since 1986, together with representative gravities and sulphur contents of the crude oils. Trade in Ninian blend ceased with the co-mingling with Brent in 1990. Before this Ninian had been the most actively traded grade in North Sea wet trade.

The composition of reported spot trade in UK and Norwegian grades over time is shown in Figure 14.1, demonstrating the volume of trade by quarter since 1986. Among UK grades by the end of 1991 wet trade represented about fifteen cargoes per week, with the bulk of the activity occurring in the market for dated Brent, as has been the case since the co-mingling of Ninian with Brent.

While UK wet trade volume has remained fairly static, Figure 14.1 shows the sharp increase in the volume of trade in Norwegian grades following a sustained increase in Norwegian output. Total trade in Norwegian grades exceeded that in UK grades in 1991. From being a very thin market reporting about three traded cargoes a week in 1986, it now trades just over fifteen reported cargoes a week. The development

Table 14.1: Major North Sea Spot Traded Crudes.

Crude	Origin	Gravity	Sulphur %
Brent	United Kingdom	37.1	0.43
Forties	United Kingdom	40.3	0.34
Ekofisk	Norway	43.4	0.14
Statfjord	Norway	38.4	0.27
Oseberg *	Norway	33.7	0.31
Flotta	United Kingdom	35.7	1.14
Fulmar	United Kingdom	39.3	0.26
Gullfaks *	Norway	28.6	0.44
Maureen	United Kingdom	35.8	0.55

Note: * Brought on stream in 1986

Sources: Various.

of the Oseberg system and the Gullfaks field has led to a thriving market in these grades, which has been accompanied by a continued growth in the market for Ekofisk and Statfjord. The growth in the Norwegian market has been such that by 1991 the volumes of trade in Ekofisk, Statfjord and Oseberg had all surpassed spot trade in Forties.

The evidence is that the other North Sea spot markets are currently not independent centres of price formation or price discovery. They are almost totally reliant on the various Brent markets to fulfil these functions, and their prices are actively driven by Brent prices. There has been a significant change in the method of price formation (that is outright or differential price) in the North Sea since 1986, with a complete shift towards differential pricing, particularly pricing against dated Brent. This is illustrated in Table 14.2, which shows by year the percentage of reported deals for spot North Sea oil other than Brent with an outright price agreed, and those where the price was agreed as a differential against another price.

Table 14.2 shows that by 1991 outright trade in the North Sea market had virtually ceased, representing just 0.7 per cent of reported trade compared with 87.3 per cent in 1986. The dominant form of trading is to agree a price as a differential to a Brent price. By 1990 the Brent price chosen was almost always dated Brent, but before this time trades against the 15-day market price were not uncommon, particularly before the introduction of a daily quotation for dated Brent by Platt's in July 1987. There are occasional trades made against the IPE Brent futures price, but in 1991 these represented less than 1 per cent of the total.

World Spot Trade 247

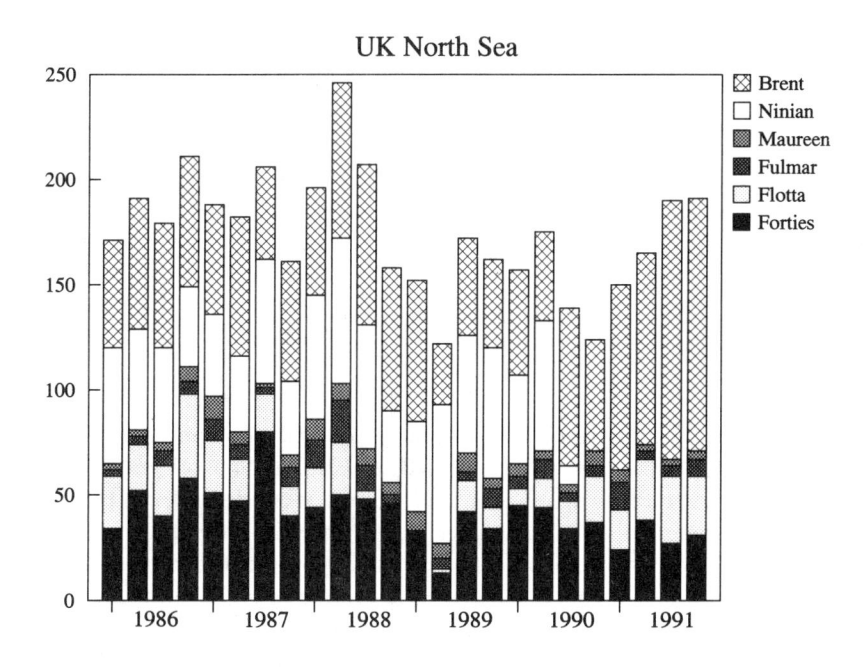

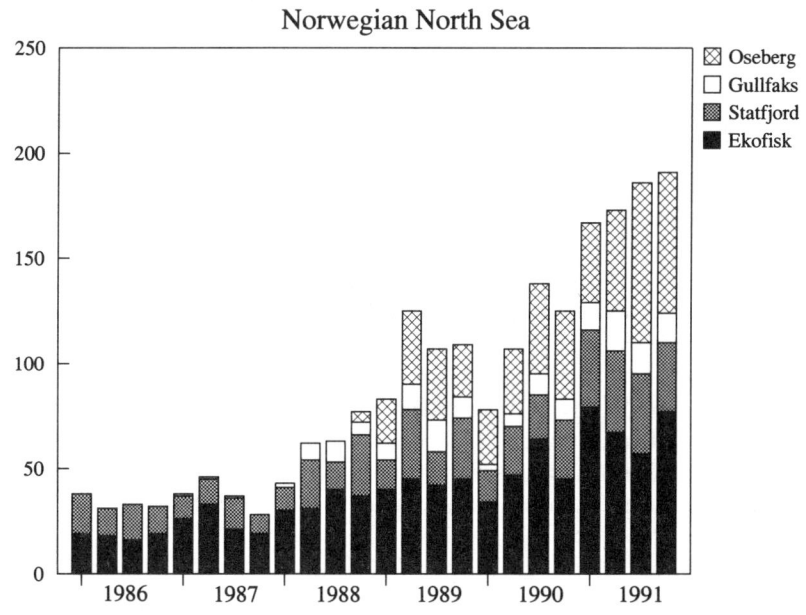

Figure 14.1: Quarterly Composition of North Sea Spot Trade by Crude. 1986–91. Number of Deals.

Table 14.2: Pricing Basis of North Sea Crude Spot Deals. 1986–91. Percentage of Total Deals.

	1986	1987	1988	1989	1990	1991
Outright Price	87.3	76.5	20.7	3.5	2.9	0.7
Differentials Price to:						
Brent	6.0	20.1	74.7	91.7	92.8	96.2
WTI	0.6	1.2	4.0	1.4	1.6	1.4

Source: Own calculations from Petroleum Argus database.

Only a very small proportion of North Sea trade is done against the price of WTI. In fact very little non-Brent North Sea oil goes to the USA. Appendix Table 14.2 shows US imports of crude oil from the UK and from Norway in 1991. Allowing for transport time, the port and harbour records at Sullom Voe reveal that 99 thousand b/d of Brent would have arrived in the USA in 1991. Hence only 18 thousand b/d of other UK grades was exported to the USA, or 1.8 per cent of the non-Brent total. The volume of Norwegian exports to the USA equates to 3.9 per cent of Norwegian output. From inspection of the gravity and sulphur content records of these exports, they appear to have been primarily Ekofisk and Gullfaks. Brent is then a slight oddity among North Sea grades in that while in 1991 about 13 per cent of Brent production went to the USA, the equivalent figure is only 3 per cent for other North Sea grades. Much of this disparity is due to the superiority of the loading facilities and harbour in Sullom Voe compared to those for other North Sea grades, particularly in enabling the loading of cargoes of 1 mb and more with their superior freight economics. Except for Brent, the USA then constitutes a relatively unimportant market for North Sea crude oils.

Forms of pricing other than those presented in Table 14.2 have been reported to Petroleum Argus, with occasional trades being made against the assessed prices of other North Sea grades or against unknown formulae which are almost certainly Brent related. However, dated Brent remains the dominant marker used in establishing the price of deals in the North Sea.

The shift in behaviour in North Sea trade towards formula pricing using a differential against assessed Brent prices is shown in more detail in Figure 14.2, which displays on a monthly basis the proportion of North Sea deals made on an outright basis, and the proportion linked to Brent. The move towards Brent related pricing began in July 1987

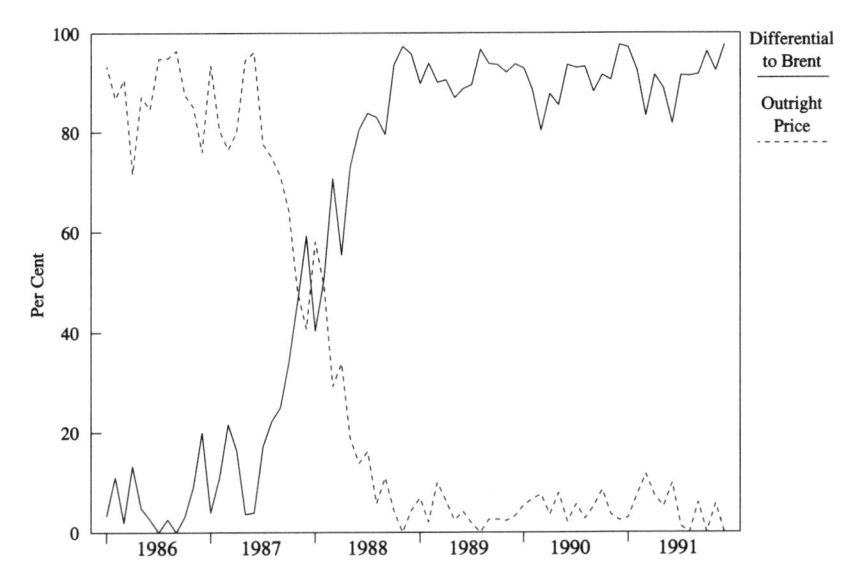

Figure 14.2: Pricing Basis of North Sea Spot Deals (other than Brent) by Month. 1986–91. Percentage of Total Deals.

(when Platt's introduced a daily quotation for dated Brent) and then gathered pace. By the end of 1988 outright trade had been all but eliminated. This innovation in the method of North Sea pricing then took eighteen months to diffuse and to become dominant. Formula prices involving the use of triggers (as explained in Chapter 8), are also common in North Sea trade.

If spot trades were all carried out on or after the day of loading of a cargo, then formula pricing using that day's prices would have few implications, it would merely provide a way of allowing the deal to follow the market, should the price move between the time of day the deal was made and the time-stamp on the relevant price assessment. However, sellers do not like the leverage given to buyers which such pure spot trade involves – it would appear to be a distressed sale – and refiners prefer to have their crude slate arranged some time in advance. Thus wet North Sea trades are normally done a few weeks in advance of the loading date of the cargo. Trade tends to have a forwardness on average of about two weeks.

The major implication of differential pricing has been the concentration on the Brent market as a centre of price formation. The other North Sea markets lose any role as independent centres of price discovery. Differential pricing also increases the complexity of the task faced by price assessment agencies. A deal for Forties done at, say, a 10 cent premium to dated Brent prices carries different information if the relevant dated Brent price is before, averaged around, after, or on, the loading date. This becomes a particular problem in times of a steep time profile in prices, given that the element of forwardness in a North Sea deal means that relative prices as discussed in deals are not invariant to changes in the time profile.

There are some potential asymmetries between the preferences of buyers and sellers which could create the opportunity for intermediation. North Sea trade is conducted on a f.o.b. basis, although there are end-users who wish to buy on a c.i.f. basis.[2] There may also be cases where producer and end-user cannot agree on a form of pricing; the producer may want the locking in of current prices given by an outright trade, while the refiner wants the insurance against market moves offered by formula pricing. While as noted above US consumption of non-Brent North Sea grades is slight, what there is may come from buyers wishing to buy on a WTI related basis while the sellers wish to sell on a Brent related basis. There is then some scope for intermediary trade in the North Sea. However, with the major companies more prepared to handle their own risks, the degree of intermediation by Wall Street firms and trading companies is in fact relatively slight and also declining, as is shown in Tables 14.3 and 14.4. The share of North Sea wet trade other than that in Brent held by participant companies is shown in Table 14.3 for UK grades and Table 14.4 for Norwegian grades. Transactions by subsidiaries have been aggregated with their parent companies in these tables.

As Table 14.3 shows, trade in non-Brent UK grades is dominated on the selling side by BP, reflecting BP's dominance of production. In 1991 BP produced about 270 thousand b/d in the UK North Sea (outside of the fields that contribute to Brent blend), some 27 per cent of the total. Other major producers of grades other than Brent were Shell and Exxon (around 80 thousand b/d each), Texaco and Amerada Hess (60 thousand b/d), Mobil (45 thousand b/d), Marathon (40 thousand b/d), and Enterprise (35 thousand b/d). Just as the selling side of the market is now dominated by equity producers, the major buyers are European refiners. The role of intermediary firms has declined substantially from the major share of the market that was taken by J Aron and in particular Phibro from 1986 to 1989, making the UK North Sea spot trade predominantly an oil company market without the high level of Wall Street and oil trading company involvement we have observed in the Brent market. Both sides of the market have become more concentrated over time. In 1986 the four main sellers had a combined market share of 41.1 per cent, and by 1991 this had reached 52.2 per cent. Likewise the 38.4 per cent share for the four major buyers in 1986 had risen to 53.8 per cent in 1991.

In Norway Statoil is the largest seller, given its large share of production. In 1991 Statoil had production in the four Norwegian grades amounting to about 900 thousand b/d. Other major producers were BP (120 thousand b/d), Conoco (110 thousand b/d), Norsk Hydro and Mobil (100 thousand b/d) and Phillips (90 thousand b/d). Shell and Exxon had entitlements to about 60 thousand b/d each (in fact Shell has more production in Denmark than it has in Norway). As Table 14.4 shows the trade in Norwegian oil is, like the UK North Sea, dominated by oil companies with a limited and declining role for intermediaries. Among the oil companies there are differences in their trading profiles. For instance despite their respective production entitlements, Shell is a far more active trader of Norwegian oil on both sides of the market than BP.

Price differentials in the North Sea tend not to be prone to sudden sharp movements. The reliance on formula pricing based on dated Brent reduces the direct role for other markets in the process of price discovery, and hence they rarely move sharply away from Brent even for short periods. However, it is by no means easy for the market, particularly when informationally constrained, to find the correct level for price differentials.

Figure 14.3 shows the weekly average differential between Forties and dated Brent from the beginning of 1989 to the end of 1992. The series is shown as a 20-trading day moving average. Until the last two months of 1990 the differential was normally a 10 cent premium for Brent, with slight movements either side of this figure. Starting in the last two months of 1990, Forties increased in value relative to Brent. The differential continued to move in favour of Forties throughout 1991, reaching a 25 cent premium by the end of the year, before falling back towards Forties in 1992.

The major reason for the change in the behaviour of Forties relative to dated Brent has been changes in the quality of the two crude blends. The API gravities for Brent and Forties shown in Table 14.1 are not those normally found in reference works, which tend to put Forties at around 37 degrees and Brent at around 38 degrees. The gravities shown come from crude oil assays carried out in fairly typical months in 1991 and 1992, and show a significant improvement in the quality of Forties relative to Brent. It took an inordinately long time for the market to begin to reflect this in price differentials. As shown in Figure 2.3, the low point for Brent quality was reached in mid-1990, when the average quality was around 35 degrees API, and the quality of some cargoes even worse. We know of two refiners who received cargoes of

Table 14.3: Main Buyers and Sellers in UK Crude Oil Spot Trade. Rank and Shares. 1986–91. Per Cent.

(a) Main Sellers in UK Crude Oil Spot Trade (excluding Brent)

Rank	1986		1987		1988		1989		1990		1991	
1	BP	16.7	BP	12.9	BP	20.1	BP	21.7	BP	20.9	BP	21.2
2	Phibro	9.5	OPA	9.5	Phibro	8.0	Phibro	8.9	Shell	8.0	Texaco	11.3
3	OPA	9.1	Phibro	9.1	Shell	6.4	Elf	7.2	Elf	7.0	Amerada Hess	10.2
4	Shell	5.8	J Aron	5.8	Marathon	5.6	Shell	6.0	Texaco	5.6	Marathon	9.5
5	Occidental	5.2	Occidental	5.2	J Aron	5.0	Marathon	4.7	Marathon	5.6	Shell	6.6
6	Texaco	4.8	Shell	4.8	OPA	4.2	J Aron	4.5	Chevron	4.9	Phillips	4.4
7	Marathon	4.0	Exxon	4.0	ICI	4.0	TWO	4.3	Occidental	4.4	Phibro	3.6
8	Chevron	3.4	Tradax	3.4	Cargill	3.6	Texaco	3.4	CFP	4.4	Cargill	2.9
9	Citizens Energy	2.6	Marathon	2.6	Elf	3.4	Chevron	3.4	Cargill	4.1	Enterprise	2.9
10	Exxon	2.6	Texaco	2.6	Texaco	3.4	CFP	3.0	Enterprise	3.6	Elf	2.9

(b) Main buyers in UK Crude Oil Spot Trade (excluding Brent)

Rank	1986		1987		1988		1989		1990		1991	
1	Phibro	12.9	BP	12.9	Phibro	8.5	Shell	11.9	Shell	19.5	Shell	20.7
2	BP	8.8	CFP	8.8	BP	8.5	BP	11.3	Exxon	10.5	Exxon	16.5
3	Shell	8.8	Elf	8.8	CFP	7.0	Texaco	9.2	CFP	7.4	BP	8.3
4	CFP	7.9	Shell	7.9	Exxon	6.8	Phibro	8.6	BP	6.8	URBK	8.3
5	Elf	5.2	Exxon	5.2	Shell	6.8	J Aron	8.2	Phibro	5.5	CFP	7.9
6	Marathon	5.0	Phibro	5.0	Elf	5.4	CFP	4.9	Texaco	4.5	Chevron	6.8
7	Exxon	3.4	Chevron	3.4	Texaco	3.9	Irish NPC	4.3	Morgan Stanley	3.9	Repsol	4.0
8	J Aron	2.9	J Aron	2.9	J Aron	3.9	TWO	3.5	Irish NPC	3.7	Neste	3.8
9	Texaco	2.9	Texaco	2.9	Ultramar	3.9	Exxon	3.1	Koch	3.4	Petronor	3.4
10	Norsk Hydro	2.7	Sun	2.7	Mobil	3.7	Elf	2.3	URBK	3.2	Phibro	3.4

Source: Own calculations from Petroleum Argus database.

Table 14.4: Main Buyers and Sellers in Norwegian Crude Oil Spot Trade. Rank and Shares. 1986–91. Per Cent.

(a) Main Sellers in Norwegian Crude Oil Spot Trade

Rank	1986		1987		1988		1989		1990		1991	
1	Conoco	13.2	Statoil	13.7	Statoil	29.8	Statoil	32.1	Statoil	23.8	Statoil	26.1
2	Elf	11.6	Elf	9.6	BP	8.7	Phibro	7.6	Shell	7.6	Shell	8.0
3	Phibro	9.1	Conoco	8.9	Phibro	7.0	Shell	5.5	Phillips	5.3	BP	5.2
4	BP	9.9	Exxon	8.2	Phillips	5.4	TWO	3.8	Norsk Hydro	4.8	Vitol	5.0
5	Statoil	7.4	BP	9.6	Shell	5.4	Elf	3.6	Vitol	4.8	Norsk Hydro	4.9
6	Shell	5.8	Phibro	6.8	Conoco	4.1	Dreyfus	3.3	Phibro	4.6	Chevron	4.3
7	Britoil	5.0	Tradax	4.1	Exxon	3.7	Norsk Hydro	3.3	Amoco	3.9	Conoco	4.1
8	Norsk Hydro	5.0	J Aron	3.4	Elf	3.3	Phillips	3.3	BP	3.7	Cargill	3.2
9	Amoco	4.1	TWO	3.4	Texas Eastern	3.3	Amoco	3.1	Conoco	3.7	Phibro	3.1
10	Chevron	4.1	Shell	2.7	Amoco	2.9	Conoco	3.1	Elf	3.4	Coastal	2.9

(b) Main Buyers in Norwegian Crude Oil Spot Trade

Rank	1986		1987		1988		1989		1990		1991	
1	Shell	16.3	Shell	16.2	Shell	21.7	Shell	20.6	Shell	23.0	Shell	22.7
2	CFP	10.6	CFP	12.5	CFP	13.6	Exxon	12.7	Exxon	12.0	Exxon	6.3
3	BP	8.1	ICI	8.1	Exxon	8.6	CFP	12.5	Phibro	5.6	Texaco	5.8
4	Chevron	8.1	Sun	7.4	ICI	6.6	BP	6.0	CFP	5.4	CFP	5.5
5	Texaco	4.9	Petrofina	6.6	Phibro	6.6	Phibro	6.5	BP	4.3	Chevron	3.6
6	ICI	4.1	Exxon	5.1	BP	5.6	Mobil	4.1	J Aron	4.1	BP	3.3
7	Phibro	4.1	Mobil	5.1	Sun	4.5	TWO	3.5	Texaco	3.3	Phibro	3.2
8	Amoco	4.1	Amoco	4.4	Mobil	4.0	Texaco	2.7	Conoco	2.8	Cargill	3.0
9	Bear Stearns	3.3	Chevron	4.4	Conoco	3.5	Petrotrade	3.0	Chevron	2.6	Bear Stearns	2.9
10	Conoco	3.3	BP	4.4	Petrofina	3.0	J Aron	2.4	Neste	2.6	Kuwait	2.9

Source: Own calculations from Petroleum Argus database.

Brent over this period with gravities between 33 and 34 degrees API. However the market did not begin to reflect this until the end of 1990. The differential continued to move in favour of Forties over the course of 1991, during which time there was an improvement and stabilization of the quality of Brent relative to Forties. Based on average final quarter of 1991 product prices, we estimate the premium of the gross product worth of Forties compared to that of Brent to be about 40 cents a barrel, a level the price differential never achieved.

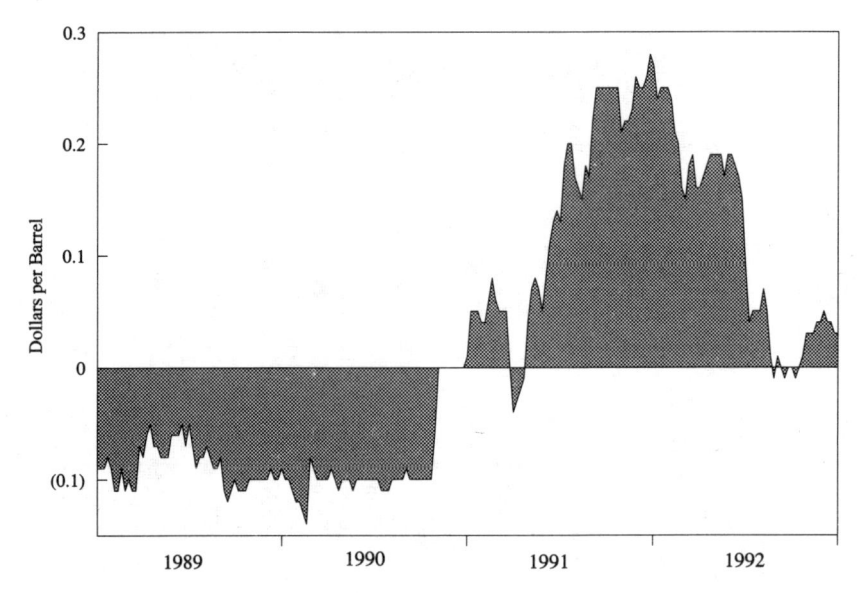

Figure 14.3: Weekly Average Differential between Forties and Brent. 1988–92. Dollars per Barrel.

Other factors beyond gross product worths should impinge on the dated Brent to Forties differential. The terminal for Forties is closer to the major European refinery areas, but is also a more difficult and less flexible one in which to operate for many users, given the usage arrangements they currently work under. In addition, the loading schedule for Forties is known further in advance than that for Brent in that a refiner will normally know the exact loading date for a purchase of Forties further ahead than for a purchase of dated Brent.

Most price assessment agencies try to standardize their North Sea quotations to reflect cargoes loading from between five and fifteen or ten and twenty days from the date of quotation. As a large number of

Forties trades are for cargoes loading more than twenty days in advance, while very few dated Brent sales occur before the 15-day chains are made wet, this method makes assessment of the true differential a matter for skilled judgement, particularly in a heavily backwardated market.

The only major factor that might tend to move the steady state price differential in Brent's favour is the flexibility given by the underlying forward and futures markets. However the short-term basis risk between the two grades for periods up to a month has never been large. Further there is in fact also a forward market in Forties, albeit small, mainly confined to equity producers, and whose activity and prices are not currently reported into the public domain. It is unlikely that extra flexibility in trading Brent would be sufficient to outweigh the factors in favour of Forties noted above, and also to result in a steady state value of the differential too far from that implied by gross product worths.

In sum it does appear that the market has undervalued Forties relative to dated Brent, and has shown itself to be very slow to react to changes in crude oil quality. In the second and third quarters of 1990 Forties appears to have been undervalued relative to Brent by over 50 cents per barrel on average, and even by 1992 the undervaluation is still of the order of 10 to 20 cents per barrel.

The market for North Sea grades is not a marginal market on the supply side. The North Sea never acts as a swing producer or in consort with swing producers; output is kept at the sustainable maximum, regardless of price, for all price levels likely to be encountered. For field output to be driven down at all by price, it would probably have to fall below $5 per barrel before the most marginal field became shut in. The largest producing fields such as Brent, Ninian and Forties have very low marginal operating costs and prices would have to be even lower before they became shut in and any major fall in North Sea output was observed. Over all realistic price levels North Sea output is virtually inelastic with respect to price, other than any endogeneity in the timing of field and pipeline maintenance programmes.

The only major effect that price has on North Sea output is very long term, in that persistently low levels would reduce research and development on technology as well as the level of exploration effort and field developments, if low prices also led to low price expectations, and if there was not sufficient compensation made through changes in the fiscal regime. But in the short run the level of output will not respond. There is in fact a ratchet effect at work – high prices and high price expectations led to the development of the North Sea, but low prices will not take North Sea production off stream (as once developed a field's marginal costs are low), but merely reduce the level of future development.

Just as North Sea output does not constitute a marginal source of supply, neither do North Sea spot sales. Spot sales are production minus internal transfers by integrated companies minus stock changes minus any term sales. While the level of internal transfers is certainly affected by patterns in price changes for tax optimization reasons, there is no unique mapping on them from any given level of price.

Hence the price of oil in the North Sea is attempting to clear a market where North Sea oil is not the marginal source of supply. Consequently, the market then needs information on the production of and the demand for the marginal barrel. As movements of non-North Sea oil are subject to long decision and transport lags, and often not immediately if ever observable, a large role is left to market perceptions and expectations.

3. West Africa

An active spot trade exists for West African crude oil, with a particularly active cross Atlantic trade. Total production in the area was 3.1 mb/d in 1991, with the largest producers being Nigeria (1.9 mb/d), Angola (0.5 mb/d), Gabon (0.3 mb/d), Congo (0.16 mb/d) and Cameroon (0.15 mb/d). Around 2 mb/d are available for export, and as Appendix Table 14.3 shows, about 1.15 mb/d of this went to the USA in 1991, with Sun, Shell, Chevron and BP accounting for 0.6 mb/d. The bulk of the remainder of exports goes into Europe, with minor amounts moving into Far Eastern markets.

While the majority of exports move under term contracts, a substantial volume is spot traded, including a significant amount traded at the US Gulf Coast. However, despite the strong pull of the US market on West African supplies, we find that like the North Sea, West African trade primarily uses Brent as a marker.

The major spot traded grades are shown in Table 14.5, ranked by their share of total spot trade since 1986. West African grades are typically sweet, with medium to light gravity. The volume and the composition over time of the West African spot market is illustrated in Figure 14.4, which shows Nigerian and other West African crudes separately. This shows that the market is made up primarily of Nigerian grades, despite an increase since 1986 in the trading of the Angolan grades Takula, Palanca and Molongo. Among the Nigerian grades the primary sources of liquidity in the market are the trades for Forcados and Bonny Light. By 1991, total reported deals in the West African

Table 14.5: West African Traded Crudes

Crude	Origin	Gravity	Sulphur %
Forcados	Nigeria	31	0.2
Bonny Light	Nigeria	37	0.1
Takula *	Angola	33	0.2
Bonny Medium	Nigeria	26	0.1
Brass River	Nigeria	42	0.1
Kole	Cameroon	34	0.3
Palanca	Angola	n.a.	n.a.
Qua Iboe	Nigeria	37	0.1
Djeno	Congo	28	0.2
Molongo *	Angola	n.a.	n.a.
Rabi	Gabon	34	0.1
Escravos	Nigeria	36	0.1
Mandji	Gabon	30	1.2
Lokele	Gabon	n.a.	n.a.
Soyo Blend	Angola	34	0.2
Anten	Nigeria	35	n.a.
Pennington	Nigeria	36	0.1

Note: * Now part of Cabinda Blend
Sources: Various.

market had risen from about four a week in 1986 to fifteen per week in 1991, compared to the thirty per week recorded in the North Sea.

Equity producers provide the liquidity for the West African spot trade. In Nigeria the state company Nigerian National Petroleum Corporation holds a 60 per cent share of all fields leaving 40 per cent to equity partners. Thus, in 1991 equity companies received an entitlement to nearly 800 thousand b/d. Among the equity partners Shell is dominant, with a 30 per cent share of the Bonny fields and Forcados giving it around 300 thousand b/d of production, more than Shell's production in any other country in the world. The other major equity producers are Chevron, Mobil and Elf. Elsewhere in West Africa, equity production mainly accrues in Gabon to Elf and Shell, in Cameroon to Elf and CFP, in the Congo to Elf, in Zaire to Chevron and Fina, and in Angola to Chevron, Fina, Texaco and Elf.

Given their large equity shares, Elf and Shell dominate the selling side of the West African spot market, as can be seen in Table 14.6. There is also a substantial trade through intermediaries, in particular Phibro. While Phibro does run West African crude through its own refineries (see Appendix Table 14.3), Table 14.6 shows it to be very active on both the selling and the buying side of the market. The major

258 *Oil Markets and Prices*

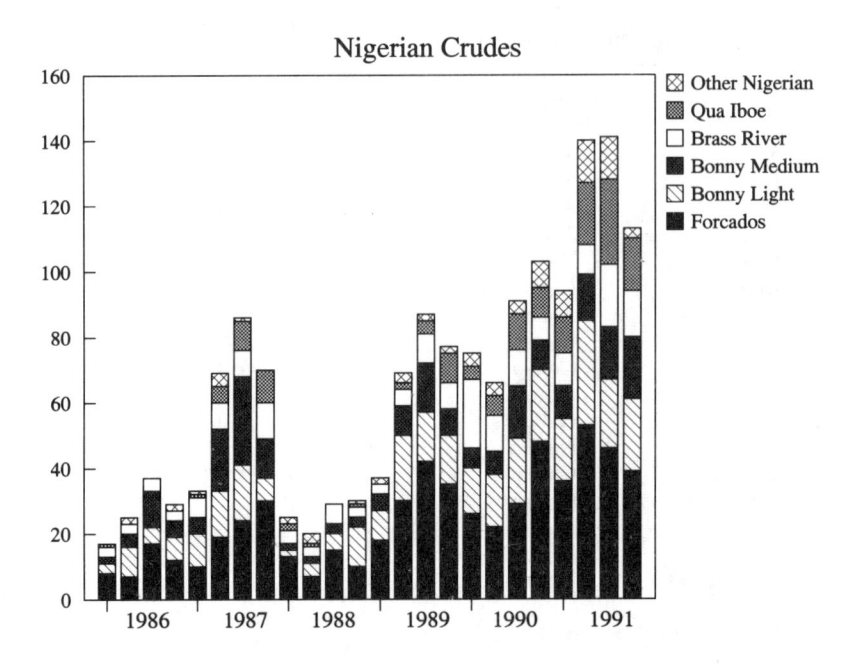

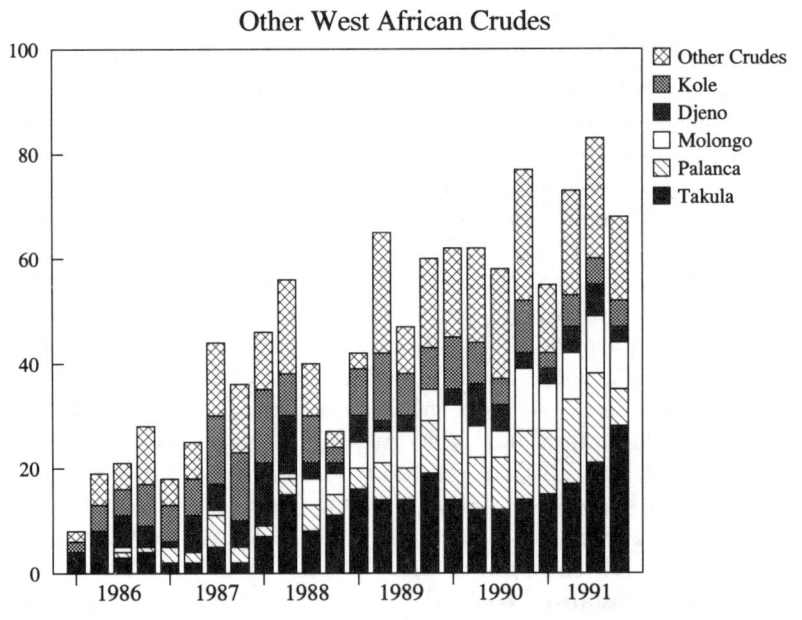

Figure 14.4: Quarterly Composition of West African Spot Trade by Crude. 1986–91. Number of Deals.

buyers are BP, CFP and, despite its marketable surplus of Nigerian crude oil, Shell.

The pricing method of spot deals in the West African market is very similar to that which we found in the North Sea. Table 14.7 shows the proportion of outright trades, and the proportion priced against other crude oils. By 1991 outright trade had vanished, with any residual outright trade having gone totally under cover and being no longer reported. Dated Brent has become the dominant marker for West African trade. While the majority of exports from West Africa goes to the USA, trade against WTI is slight and much of this arises from trade in the US Gulf Coast. It is not uncommon for an intermediary to match up a spot sale f.o.b. West Africa priced against dated Brent with a trade with a US refiner who wishes to buy c.i.f. the US Gulf Coast on WTI related terms. Hence West African spot trade generates one source of liquidity in the WTI-Brent arbitrage market, and West African term contracts (priced off dated Brent), provide another.

Occasionally trades are made against another West African crude oil, usually Forcados or BBQ. The BBQ price is in fact the price of a basket of three Nigerian Crudes, (Brass River, Bonny Light and Qua Iboe). However, given that the underlying price of BBQ and Forcados are derived from dated Brent, trades made against their price are essentially also Brent related. They do not represent an alternative marker or centre of price discovery beyond Brent.

One indigenous price marker that has been suggested for at least some West African grades is Angolan Cabinda. This is a blend first produced in 1992, of which the dominant stream used to be traded separately as Takula. This was a relatively heavy grade (33 degrees API) but sweet, and as such was fairly typical of most export grades from Angola, Zaire, Congo, Gabon and Cameroon. As Figure 14.4 shows, by the end of 1991 the volume of trade in Takula was only surpassed by Forcados among West African grades. Cargoes are normally traded in volumes of around 900 thousand barrels which on a production base of 190 thousand b/d in 1991 implies an availability of only one wet cargo per week.

While, as we will see in the section on the American market, once established a forward market can survive on such a small base, it is not sufficient for the development of a marker crude oil nor an underlying forward market. Co-mingling of Takula with Molongo (80 thousand b/d) in 1992 together with other field developments, has produced a crude blend which is of a very similar quality to Takula. Production of Cabinda will be between 280 and 320 thousand b/d by the end of 1992, or about ten cargoes a month.

260 Oil Markets and Prices

Table 14.6: Main Buyers and Sellers in West African Crude Oil Spot Trade. Rank and Shares. 1986–91. Per Cent.

(a) Main Sellers in West African Crude Oil Spot Trade

Rank	1986		1987		1988		1989		1990		1991	
1	Elf	14.2	Phibro	16.0	Shell	17.6	Shell	19.7	Shell	15.9	Elf
2	Phibro	11.8	Elf	15.0	Elf	15.7	Elf	15.9	Elf	14.4	Shell	11.7
3	Shell	10.1	Shell	7.3	Chevron	8.4	Agip	8.5	Agip	9.5	Phibro	8.2
4	Attock	8.3	Kaines	7.1	Phibro	7.7	Phibro	7.6	Phibro	9.3	Chevron	5.5
5	Kaines	7.7	Attock	5.8	Addax	6.1	Addax	7.0	Chevron	6.7	Agip	5.4
6	Sigmoil	7.7	Marc Rich	5.2	SNH	4.2	Chevron	5.7	Sonangol	4.2	Coastal	5.0
7	Chevron	7.1	Scan	3.9	Agip	3.8	Vitol	4.0	Addax	3.7	Marc Rich	4.5
8	Marc Rich	3.6	SNH	3.7	Seagas	3.8	Sonangol	3.6	Attock	3.3	Sonangol	4.3
9	Bomar	3.0	J Aron	3.4	BP	3.1	Coastal	2.5	Texaco	3.2	Morgan Stanley	3.6
10	Agip	2.4	Seagas	3.1	J Aron	2.7	SNH	2.5	Vitol	3.0	Addax	3.5

(b) Main Buyers in West African Crude Oil Spot Trade

Rank	1986		1987		1988		1989		1990		1991	
1	BP	12.2	BP	18.3	BP	14.2	BP	13.1	Shell	12.5	Shell	10.5
2	Phibro	7.9	Shell	7.5	Shell	10.8	Phibro	7.8	BP	12.5	CFP	9.3
3	Shell	6.5	Phibro	7.5	Phibro	9.2	Coastal	6.8	Phibro	9.4	BP	8.3
4	Chevron	5.8	Petrofina	6.5	Exxon	7.1	Shell	6.3	CFP	8.9	Phibro	8.0
5	Hess	5.0	Chevron	5.0	Coastal	4.6	Exxon	6.1	Coastal	6.6	Coastal	6.2
6	Sun	5.0	CFP	4.7	Hess	4.2	Sun	5.8	Exxon	6.4	Sun	5.9
7	TWO	5.0	J Aron	3.4	Petrobras	4.2	Amoco	5.3	Sun	6.2	Exxon	5.8
8	Exxon	3.6	Kaines	3.4	Chevron	2.9	Chevron	5.3	Chevron	4.4	Chevron	4.4
9	Agip	2.9	Elf	2.8	Seagas	2.9	Hess	3.6	Elf	3.5	Repsol	4.2
10	Marathon	2.9	Hess	2.8	CEPSA	2.1	Kerr McGee	3.6	Repsol	2.7	Elf	2.7

Source: Own calcualtions from Petroleum Argus database.

Table 14.7: Pricing Basis of West African Spot Deals. 1986–91. Percentage of Total Deals.

	1986	1987	1988	1989	1990	1991
Outright Price	87.1	56.9	11.4	3.2	1.5	-
Differential Price to:						
Brent	5.9	37.2	76.5	80.2	76.0	80.5
WTI	4.8	4.1	11.4	15.0	8.4	8.1
BBQ	-	-	-	0.6	8.4	5.0
Forcados	-	-	-	0.4	4.2	2.4

Source: Own calculations from Petroleum Argus database.

4. The Mediterranean

Unlike the North Sea and West Africa, the Mediterranean does not have large-scale exportable equity production by the major oil companies, given that what active equity production exists is primarily in the hands of smaller international companies. The spot market consists of production by countries in the area together with volumes sold c.i.f. in the Mediterranean by the Russians and the Iranians. Production in the Mediterranean area was about 4 mb/d in 1991, with the largest producers being Libya (1.5 mb/d), Egypt (0.9 mb/d), Algeria (0.8 mb/d) and Syria (0.5 mb/d).

Table 14.8 details the major spot traded grades produced in the Mediterranean area or sold c.i.f. in the area. Spot trade in indigenous production is made up primarily of light sweet Libyan grades. Libya exported about 1.2 mb/d in 1991. However, trade in Libyan oil is heavily affected by the US sanctions on trade with Libya imposed in 1986, and *de facto* toughened in 1992 with the first imposition of fines against US companies and companies with US subsidiaries violating the sanctions. Libyan crude oil cannot be exported to the USA, and is almost entirely confined to the European market. The US political stance means that most major oil companies, both US and European, tend to shy away from purchases of Libyan oil. Hence the main users of Libyan oil are the European equity partners Agip and Veba, and Tamoil, Libya's own European downstream operation. There are five US equity partners in Libya, but their participation is currently frozen.

It has been suggested that the cut-off of the US market and the reduction in the level of interest in Libyan oil from many European companies results in a downwards bias in the price, the so-called

Table 14.8: Major Mediterranean Trade Crudes.

Crude	Origin	Gravity	Sulphur %
Urals (c.i.f.)	Russia	32	1.0
Iranian Heavy (c.i.f.)	Iran	31	1.6
Iranian Light (c.i.f.)	Iran	34	1.4
Es Sider	Libya	37	0.5
Zarzaitine	Tunisia	42	0.1
Suez Blend	Egypt	33	1.4
Saharan Blend	Algeria	44	0.1
Zueitina	Libya	41	0.2
Syrian Light	Syria	37	n.a.
Sirtica	Libya	41	0.4
Brega	Libya	40	0.2
Sarir	Libya	36	0.2
Ras Budran	Egypt	24	n.a.
Ashtart	Tunisia	29	1.0
Amna	Libya	36	0.2
Belayim Blend	Egypt	26	1.6

Sources: Various.

embargo factor. Our analysis found no statistically significant difference between the refining margins achievable with Libyan Es Sider and other Mediterranean grades in the period from 1987 to 1992. The idea that there is an embargo factor at work on Libyan prices can be rejected. In fact the cut-off of the US market does not disadvantage Libya compared to other countries in the area. As is shown in Appendix Table 14.2, the flow from the area to the USA is very minor, with combined exports from Syria, Algeria, Egypt and ultra heavy Italian crude oil amounting to just 72 thousand b/d in 1991.

The composition of trade from 1986 to 1991 in the Mediterranean is detailed in Figure 14.5, where Libyan grades other than Es Sider and Zueitina have been aggregated. Among indigenous grades there is no dominant source of liquidity in the market. Since 1988 between two and three spot trades have been reported per week in total. While a market in Libyan grades had achieved some significant liquidity during 1986 and 1987, by 1990 this trade was thin, particularly in Es Sider which, on a quarterly basis, has not traded more than once a week since 1987. The spot market in indigenous grades is then thin to non-existent.

As Figure 14.5 shows, the bulk of the liquidity in the Mediterranean market comes from the spot trade of imported sour crude oils from Russia and Iran priced c.i.f. Europe. However this trade is highly variable. Spot sales of Russian Urals had always been of an erratic

World Spot Trade 263

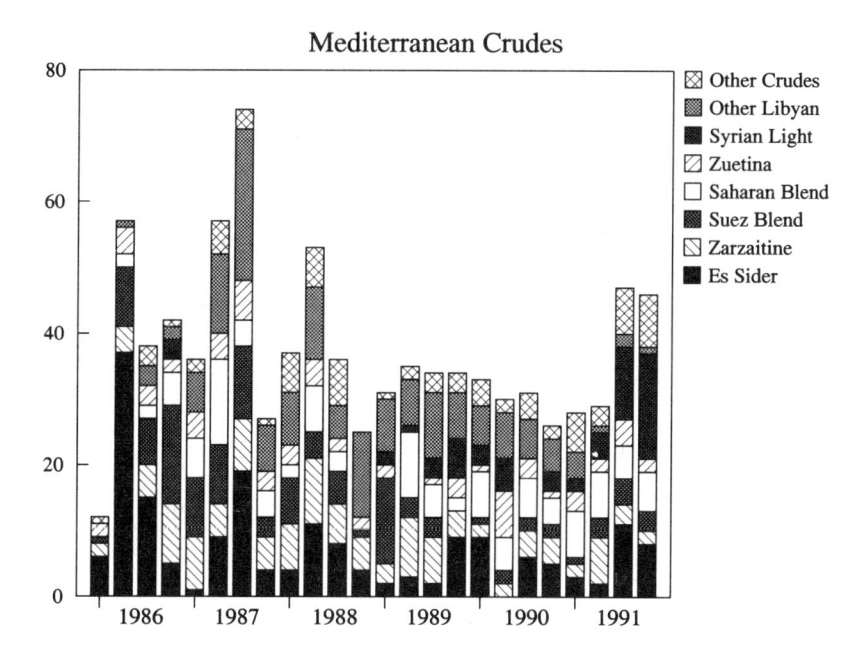

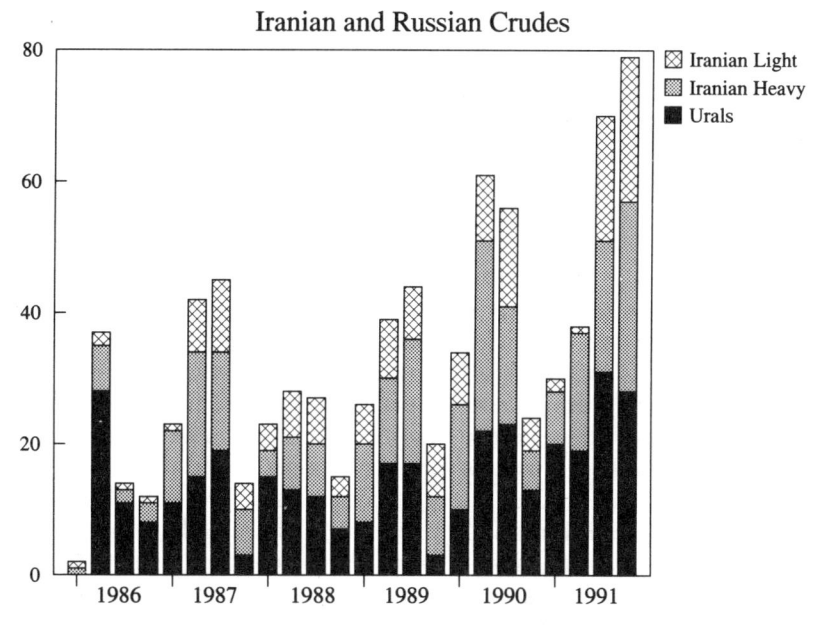

Figure 14.5: Quarterly Composition of Mediterranean Spot Trade by Crude. 1986–91. Number of Deals.

volume, and since total sales themselves became highly variable in 1990 this tendency has been increased. As of 1992 Urals has a habit of arriving in bunched cargoes, often no supplies trade for several weeks, and then there is a glut of cargoes.[3] Likewise the flow of Iranian crude oil onto the spot trade can be variable, being highly dependent on the level of floating Iranian stocks and the level of European demand for sour crude oil.

Spot trade in the Mediterranean tends to be agreed as a differential to dated Brent. Table 14.9 shows the evolution of the pricing basis of spot deals for indigenous grades, and shows exactly the same pattern as the one we observed for North Sea and West African trade.

Table 14.9: Pricing Basis of Mediterranean Spot Deals. 1986–91. Percentage of Total Deals.

	1986	1987	1988	1989	1990	1991
Outright Price	91.3	87.3	13.9	1.5	0.8	-
Differential Price to:						
Brent	1.4	8.4	76.9	87.3	95.8	74.7
Official Prices	0.7	3.0	2.0	2.2	-	1.4
WTI	-	-	-	6.0	0.8	-
Es Sider	-	-	-	-	1.7	19.2

Source: Own calculations from Petroleum Argus database.

By 1991 outright trade had completely ceased, with Brent being the dominant marker. Very little trade is ever done against the price of WTI, but as noted above, very little crude oil from this region ever goes to the USA. In 1991 a significant volume of trade was made as a differential to the quoted price of Es Sider. This mainly followed from Syria's decision to price its terms sales against Es Sider in preference to Brent. However, as the price of Es Sider is discussed relative to dated Brent, and as Figure 14.5 showed, there is not enough trade in Es Sider to make it an independent centre of price discovery – pricing against Es Sider is just an indirect way of pricing against dated Brent. Syria's decision to move back to Brent in term contracts in 1992 should reduce the volume of trade differentially priced against Es Sider.

By 1991 Iranian and Russian oil were also priced against dated Brent in over 96 per cent of cases, with no outright trades having been reported since 1988. Iranian oil, like Libyan, faces legal restrictions in the USA, with an embargo being placed in 1988. Licences for limited amounts were granted in 1991 with payment being made against an escrow account in the Hague, and these limited volumes are shown in Appendix Table 14.4. We have found no significant downward bias in Iranian crude oil prices as a result of the US embargo.

5. The Middle East Gulf

The major market in the Gulf is the Dubai forward market, to which the other Gulf markets are either directly or indirectly linked, and which was examined in Chapter 12. We now consider the spot market for other crude oils from the region. While the Gulf is the major oil-exporting area in the world, comparatively little oil from the region is sold on a spot basis. The volume spot traded other than that traded through the Dubai market, normally lies between 0.5 mb/d and 0.7 mb/d compared to the 12.4 mb/d produced in the Gulf countries in 1991 (excluding Iran). The bulk of Gulf exports is sold on formula priced term contracts. Limited amounts of Saudi Arabian grades are currently sold spot,[4] and then only with the permission of the Saudis.

There has in the past been some trade in Iraqi and Kuwaiti grades. However the major sources of oil for spot trade in the Gulf have been the two countries with the most active equity participation by international oil companies – Oman and the United Arab Emirates (and within the UAE, in particular Abu Dhabi). There is also limited trade in the minor production of Qatari oil (total Qatari production was 0.39 mb/d in

Table 14.10: Major Gulf Spot Traded Crudes.

Crude	Origin	Gravity	Sulphur %
Oman	Oman	36	0.8
Murban	Abu Dhabi	40	0.8
Qatar Marine	Qatar	36	1.5
Lower Zakum	Abu Dhabi	40	1.1
Qatar Land	Qatar	41	1.2
Arabian Medium	Saudi Arabia	31	2.3
Kuwait	Kuwait	31	2.5
Kirkuk	Iraq	36	2.0
Umm Shaif	Abu Dhabi	37	1.4
Arabian Light	Saudi Arabia	34	1.7
Upper Zakum	Abu Dhabi	34	1.8
Arabian Heavy	Saudi Arabia	27	2.8
Marib Light	Yemen	40	0.1

Sources: Various.

266 *Oil Markets and Prices*

1991), and an emerging market in the currently limited volumes of Yemeni grades (production of 0.2 mb/d in 1991).

The major spot traded grades are shown in Table 14.10, ranked by total trade since 1986, together with representative API gravities and sulphur contents. Among these, over 80 per cent of all trade has been in the first six grades listed. Gulf crude oils tend to have a relatively high sulphur content (with the exception of Marib Light), but the main traded grades are all relatively light. As elsewhere in the world, there is little genuine spot trade in cargoes just about to load or already loaded. In reality what is termed spot trade in the Gulf is normally carried out between one and two months in advance of loading. The evolution over time of Gulf trade is shown in Figure 14.6, where the limited trade in Saudi grades has been aggregated.

Price formation for the Gulf spot trade is one of the most complicated in any region of the world. It owes much to the mechanics of the derivation of official selling prices (OSPs) in Oman, Qatar and Abu Dhabi. The OSP for a particular grade represents the price for all transactions with state oil companies, as well as representing the taxation or royalty reference price. In all three countries OSPs are announced retroactively, and apply to all cargoes loaded in the previous month.

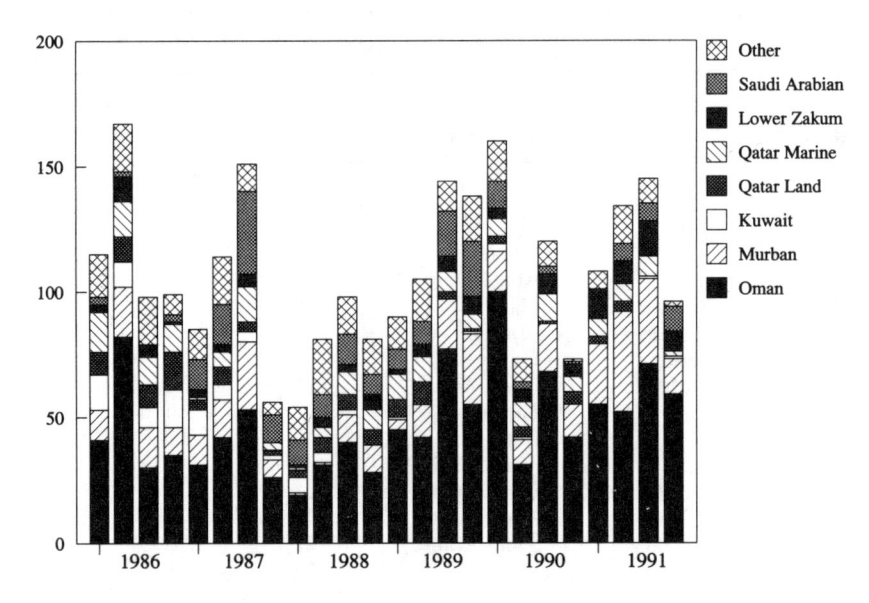

Figure 14.6: Quarterly Composition of Gulf Spot Trade by Crude. 1986–91. Number of Deals.

The Omani retroactive price is known as the MPM price (after the Omani oil ministry) or the PDO price (after the state oil company). The Qatari state oil company, QGPC, announces retroactive prices for both Qatar Marine and Qatar Land. In Abu Dhabi the state oil company, ADNOC, announces prices for each of its four grades (Upper Zakum, Murban, Lower Zakum and Umm Shaif).

The exact method of derivation for MPM, QGPC and ADNOC prices has never been revealed, but it is relatively easy to infer the general principles involved. We explain this with the aid of Table 14.11, which infers the relationship between Dubai forward, MPM, QGPC, and ADNOC prices for the last nine months of 1991. The second column of Table 14.11 shows the average price of the first forward month, i.e. for cargoes loading in the next month, in the Dubai market over the course of each month. The Oman MPM, which is announced as an absolute price, bears a very close relationship with the Dubai average as is seen in the third column which expresses the MPM as a differential from Dubai.

The MPM moves within a range of a 78 cent and a 96 cent premium to the average Dubai price over the course of the nine months. This fluctuation is small enough to be totally consistent with the idea that perhaps the Omanis use a different set of assessed prices for Dubai than those shown, or even an average of quotes from price assessment agencies. Over these nine months the degree of discretion used by Oman in setting OSPs appears to have been minimal, and the Oman MPM seems to have been almost or wholly determined by Dubai average prices. While Oman is considerably sweeter than Dubai (0.8 per cent sulphur content as opposed to 2 per cent), there appears to be

Table 14.11: Dubai Prices and Gulf Official Selling Prices. 1991.

Month	Dubai (D)	Oman (O)	Qatar Land (QL)	Qatar Marine	Upper Zakum (UZ)	Murban (M)	Lower Zakum	Umm Shaif
April	15.36	D+0.84	O+0.60	QL-0.05	D+0.29	UZ+1.50	M-0.10	M-0.30
May	15.94	D+0.96	O+0.60	QL-0.05	D+0.31	UZ+1.70	M-0.10	M-0.30
June	15.41	D+0.87	O+0.60	QL-0.05	D+0.39	UZ+1.80	M-0.10	M-0.30
July	16.27	D+0.78	O+0.60	QL-0.05	D+0.33	UZ+2.20	M-0.10	M-0.30
August	16.63	D+0.82	O+0.60	QL-0.05	D+0.27	UZ+2.00	M-0.10	M-0.30
September	17.86	D+0.86	O+0.85	QL-0.05	D+0.34	UZ+2.10	M-0.10	M-0.30
October	18.90	D+0.80	O+0.85	QL-0.05	D+0.20	UZ+2.00	M-0.10	M-0.30
November	18.34	D+0.86	O+0.80	QL-0.05	D+0.26	UZ+2.00	M-0.10	M-0.30
December	15.22	D+0.90	O+0.85	QL-0.05	D+0.13	UZ+2.00	M-0.10	M-0.30

no relationship between the MPM-Dubai differential and movements in the relative market prices of sweet and sour crudes. Note that the link between Dubai prices and the MPM is rather counter-intuitive – the MPM announced in, say, May for cargoes that loaded in April, is related to the average price over April of Dubai cargoes due to load in May.

As the fourth and fifth columns of Table 14.11 show, QGPC prices are determined from the MPM with some, albeit limited, discretion used. In fact, QGPC prices are not announced in absolute terms but as a differential to the MPM. Over the period considered the OSP for Qatar Land was set at a constant 5 cent premium to that for Qatar Marine. Among Abu Dhabi grades the ADNOC price for Upper Zakum, which is of very similar quality to Dubai, bears a close relationship to the Dubai average. The OSPs for the three higher quality Abu Dhabi grades were kept with a fixed differential between them, but considerable discretion was used, particularly from April to July, in the differential between them and Upper Zakum (and therefore Dubai).

In sum, on the basis of Table 14.11, it can be seen there is a very close relationship between average Dubai prices and Gulf OSPs, with some flexibility in the OSP differential between Abu Dhabi's premium grades and that for Lower Zakum occasionally being exercised by ADNOC.

The retroactive OSP system has come to mean that most spot trade is now conducted as a differential to OSPs. For example Table 14.12 shows the evolution of price formation in the market for Oman. After the abandonment of fixed reference price OSPs in 1986, there was a brief flowering of outright and Dubai, Brent or Oman market price related trading before the current system of OSPs was introduced in late 1987. Since then virtually all spot trades have been conducted on

Table 14.12: Pricing Basis of Omani Crude Deals. 1986–91. Percentage of Total Deals.

	1986	1987	1988	1989	1990	1991
Outright Price	37.2	80.7	5.9	0.5	0.4	-
Differential Price to:						
MPM	44.6	-	78.0	97.3	94.2	99.1
Dubai or Oman	16.5	11.3	12.7	0.5	2.1	-
Brent	1.1	1.3	-	0.9	0.4	0.4

Source: Own calculations from Petroleum Argus database.

the basis of differentials to the relevant MPM price, which is of course unknown when the deal is struck. Trades are then being discussed as differentials to the expected average price of Dubai in the next month plus, as shown in Table 14.11, a relatively stable, but still unknown at the time of sale, premium.

Similar patterns hold in the other Gulf spot markets. Table 14.13 shows the price basis (outright or differentials to other crudes) of Abu Dhabi spot sales. By 1991, nearly all trade was conducted on the basis of differentials to the (unknown at time of trading) ADNOC retroactive price, with little outright or directly market related trade taking place. Table 14.14 shows the evolution of pricing for Qatari spot trade. As with Omani and Abu Dhabi spot sales, trade is currently conducted as a differential to official prices, with no outright trade observed since 1987. Hence, as shown in Table 14.11, trade is being conducted relative to expected average Dubai prices over the next calendar

Table 14.13: Pricing Basis of Abu Dhabi Crude Deals. 1986–91. Percentage of Total Deals.

	1986	1987	1988	1989	1990	1991
Outright Price	48.3	54.9	3.5	-	-	-
Differential Price to:						
ADNOC	17.8	45.1	45.6	98.0	91.8	98.2
MPM	28.0	-	24.6	-	-	-
Dubai or Oman	4.1	-	3.5	-	5.1	-
Brent	0.8	-	7.0	2.0	1.0	1.2

Source: Own calculations from Petroleum Argus database.

Table 14.14: Pricing Basis of Qatari Crude Deals. 1986–91. Percentage of Total Deals.

	1986	1987	1988	1989	1990	1991
Outright Price	50.5	36.6	-	-	-	-
Differential Price to:						
QGPC	-	61.0	79.1	94.4	100.0	100.0
MPM	33.7	-	7.0	3.7	-	-
Dubai or Oman	12.7	2.4	2.3	-	-	-
Brent	-	-	7.0	-	-	-

Source: Own calculations from Petroleum Argus database.

month, plus the expected level of two unknown premia, the premium of the MPM over average Dubai prices, and the premium of QGPC prices over the MPM.

In sum, the prices paid in the Gulf spot markets are related to the three sets of OSPs represented by MPM, QGPC and ADNOC prices. These in turn are related to average Dubai prices over each calendar month, and hence the Dubai market does not have the same immediate daily transmission to other spot prices inherent in the relationship between dated Brent and spot trade in the North Sea, West Africa and the Mediterranean.

While there is some limited flexibility in the retroactive prices, the determination of Dubai prices by western rather than eastern trading conditions we have found above, means that OSPs in the Gulf are also primarily driven by western factors. Thus the characteristics of Dubai prices feed through to a much greater volume of crude oil. They affect all term sales priced off Dubai (i.e. Saudi, Iranian, Kuwaiti, and, when they are able to export, Iraqi sales to the Far East), all term sales based on OSPs (i.e. Abu Dhabi, Oman and Qatar), and all Gulf spot trade. This totals about 5 mb/d.

We saw in Chapter 13 that Dubai prices are strongly affected by the GPW of Brent and in particular the degree of backwardation in the Brent market. Hence the markets for Brent help to set the price of all this 5 mb/d, in conjunction with the effect of product market prices in Europe and in the US Gulf. Further, the price of some Latin American exports to the Far East are either directly or indirectly affected by the Dubai market, and, as we shall see in the next section, much of Far Eastern spot and term sales are also related to Dubai prices. The total volume of international crude oil trade affected by the determination of prices in the Dubai market is then in the order of over 6 mb/d.

6. The Far East

As well as being a large importer of crude oil from the Middle East, the Far East and Asia also trade grades of crude oil indigenous to the region. Spot trade is primarily concentrated on Indonesian and Malaysian grades, with some trade in Australian, Chinese and Vietnamese grades. The major spot traded crude oils are shown in Table 14.15, ranked by their shares in total spot trade since 1986. This table also shows that Far Eastern crude oil tends to be light and sweet. Duri is a notable exception, being the rare case of a crude oil that is both heavy and sweet. The bulk of trade occurs in the multiplicity of Indonesian grades.

Table 14.15: Major Far Eastern Spot Traded Crudes.

Crude	Origin	Gravity	Sulphur %
Tapis	Malaysia	44	0.1
Minas	Indonesia	34	0.1
Labuan	Malaysia	33	0.1
Duri	Indonesia	20	0.2
Cinta	Indonesia	28	0.1
Arun Condensate	Indonesia	54	0.1
Attaka	Indonesia	44	0.1
Gippsland	Australia	48	0.1
Kakap	Indonesia	45	0.1
Lalang	Indonesia	39	0.1
Jabiru	Australia	42	0.1
Widuri	Indonesia	33	0.1
Miri	Indonesia	36	0.1
Walio	Indonesia	34	0.1
Bima	Indonesia	20	0.3
Ardjuna	Indonesia	37	0.1
Bekapai	Indonesia	41	0.1

Sources: Various.

Figure 14.7 details the composition of trade, split between Indonesian and other grades, with Australian crude oils being aggregated. The volume of reported trade is volatile, ranging from only two deals a week in the second quarter of 1990, to over ten a week in the second quarter of 1991.

Far Eastern crude oil pricing is the most opaque in the world. Deals tend to be priced as a differential to either the assessments of the Asian Petroleum Price Index (APPI) or the Indonesian Crude Price (ICP). The APPI prices are produced on a weekly basis by a panel of companies including a balance of traders, producers and refiners. The spot assessments are generated by averaging the assessments of the companies on the panel, having rejected statistical outliers. APPI prices suffer from several severe drawbacks. Their weekly nature is a disadvantage in itself, particularly in fast moving markets. However, more importantly there are strong reasons to believe that they do not, even on average, reflect genuine spot prices.

A balanced panel of companies in the market might be expected to produce unbiased prices given the interest of one component of the panel in high prices and the interest of another for low prices. However there are two problems with the set-up of the APPI panel. The minor problem is that the individual assessments of panel members do not

272   *Oil Markets and Prices*

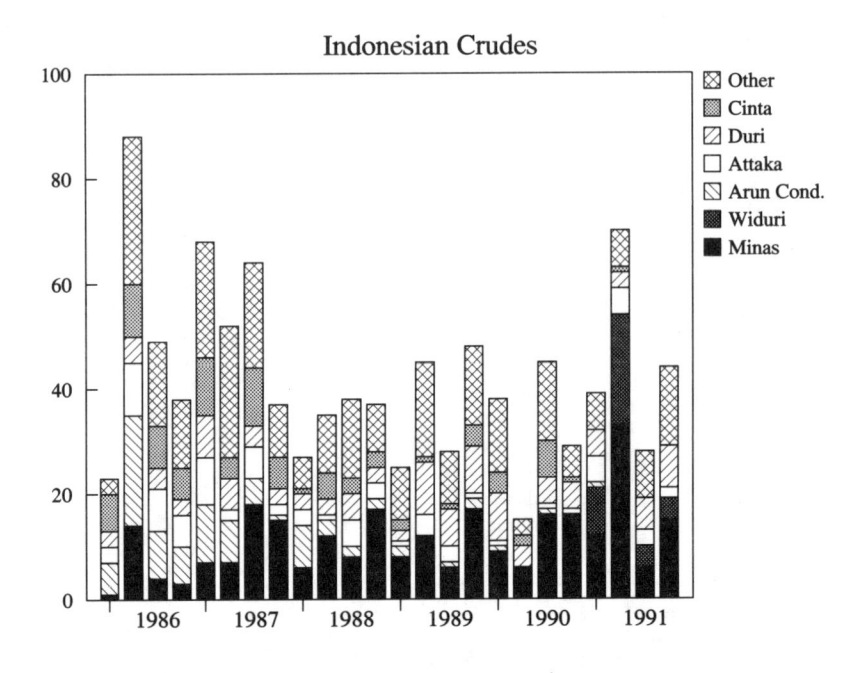

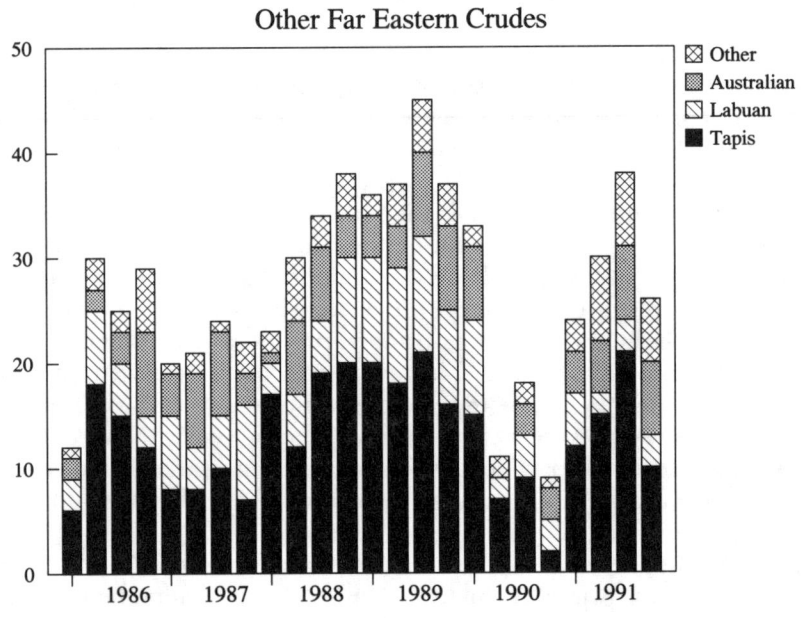

Figure 14.7: Quarterly Composition of Far Eastern Spot Trade by Crude. 1986–91. Number of Deals.

reflect their relative weights in the volume of trade when they are averaged. A large producer for a given grade receives the same weight as a trader who rarely if ever trades that grade. In fact, the correct weighting needed to achieve an estimate of the spot price should be the share in *marginal* trade, not total (including intra-marginal) trades. This provides a severe problem for pricing panels, as these marginal weights are unobservable. Given that the spot price is a marginal concept, average assessments are of limited usefulness.

The second problem is more serious in its implications for the veracity of APPI prices. The motives of buyers and sellers in the Far Eastern market are *not* symmetric and offsetting. There is a systematic bias in the panel's motivations which tends to produce prices that are consistently below genuine spot levels. Refiners obviously have an incentive to try to bid prices down. However, the producers of Indonesian crude oil have no offsetting incentive to bid prices up due to the structure of the Indonesian taxation system. Indonesian production is taxed against the ICP (which is derived from APPI prices), at a rate of 56 per cent, and not against the actual sales receipts of the companies involved. It is therefore in the interests of producing companies to drive APPI prices down and, in effect, create a two-tier Far Eastern market. At one level there is the hypothetical market that is reflected in APPI prices, and at the other the real market where the oil is actually sold. The objective of the companies producing in Indonesia is to create as much of a premium as possible in favour of the latter market without creating so large a distortion as to lead to any radical reform of the Indonesian taxation system. From our own observation and from evidence from interviews, we believe that APPI prices normally lie between 50 cents and $1 per barrel below true spot prices.

The ICP is a complicated arrangement derived in the following manner. To derive the official price of a given grade for a given month, say Handil in June, the average of assessments between 16 May and 15 June is calculated for a basket of five crude oils. This basket comprises Oman, Dubai, Gippsland, Minas and Tapis. The average assessment of this basket is also calculated over a 52-week period and is deducted from the 52-week average assessment for the individual crude, in this case Handil. This 52-week average differential of Handil from the price of the basket is then added to the monthly average assessment of the five crude basket to derive the ICP for Handil.

This procedure is both clumsy and inappropriate. A yearly average differential added to the basket price ignores all seasonality or any short-run factors or demand shifts affecting an individual grade. The ICP can therefore be far away from actual average spot prices, and, as noted above, will not even be correct on average due to its reliance on

APPI prices. Another bias is added by the composition of the basket. Dubai and Oman prices are, as we saw in the last section, discounted by the time structure of Brent prices. Hence a tax reference price for short to medium haul crude is being established with respect to long haul crudes that are primarily determined by factors outside the Far East. Further, as the level of the basket is set on a monthly basis, whereas the value of the individual crude oil only enters on a yearly basis, short-run factors in Europe and the USA that affect Dubai and therefore Oman prices are given a greater weight than short-term factors affecting an individual crude.

The above procedure is currently used for all Indonesian export grades. The heavy grade, Widuri, was linked to Cinta prices, but the method was changed to the above in late 1991. A major problem with the ICP as a taxation reference price is its treatment of heavy and light grades. This is mainly due to the yearly differential component of the ICP which means that the ICP will always lag behind any trend in prices. There has been a continued shift in demand in the Far East towards light grades. End-user demand for oil products has become heavily biased towards middle distillates, and with refining constraints being hit, there has been a continued trend in the differential between light and heavy grades in favour of the light grades. This creates two problems for the producers of Indonesian heavy grades. With the trend in the light/heavy differential, spot values for the heavy grades can be consistently below the relevant ICPs even with the downwards bias in ICP prices. Equity producers in Indonesia are not allowed to sell equity entitlement at prices below the ICP, and hence producers of the heavy grades will occasionally find themselves having to shut in production. Producers of lighter grades by contrast receive a double benefit. They have little risk of being shut in, and their effective taxation rate (i.e. taxation paid as a proportion of actual sales receipts) will be lower than for the heavy grade producers.

While efforts to create a Dubai futures contract in Singapore have failed, there is a forward paper market in the Far East based on Tapis. However it bears no resemblance to the structure of the Brent and Dubai forward markets, and is really better described as a price swap market. The paper Tapis market is made up of a series of bilateral deals, normally highly personalized, equivalent to 'over the counter' swap arrangements. There is less than total standardization, but generally lots of 100 thousand barrels are traded. These deals are cash settled and no physical oil changes hands through the market. The settlement price is usually the average APPI assessment for Tapis for the delivery month being traded. The major participants in paper Tapis appear to be BP, Morgan Stanley, Phibro, J Aron, Shell, Merrill Lynch,

Banque Paribas and Crédit Suisse.

Paper Tapis does not then provide an alternative to ICP or APPI pricing. It merely provides a hedging mechanism for those trading physical oil on an APPI related basis, and hence its role as a marker is limited. Like the APPI, the paper Tapis market will not provide a true measure of the spot value of Tapis. Indeed as paper Tapis is normally traded one or two months ahead, the paper market will produce even lower numbers for Tapis than the APPI in a backwardated market. There is also currently little scope for a satisfactory physically settled forward market in Tapis to arise without the active co-operation of Petronas, which currently moves 300 thousand b/d of Tapis through term contracts.

There also appears to be little scope as yet for a meaningful and sustainable market in an Indonesian export grade. The development of such a market would require two conditions to be met. First it would need the active co-operation of the state, and a change in Indonesian taxation policy. However even if the Indonesian government moved to a fiscal regime more akin to the UK, a second condition would still have to be met, i.e. a viable physical base. The problem with this is that the future of Indonesia as an exporting country is by no means certain.

In 1991 Indonesia produced about 1.4 mb/d and consumed 0.65 mb/d, leaving 0.75 mb/d available for exports – that is to say, it is already a minor exporter in world terms. However, Indonesia's spare production capacity is concentrated in its heavier grades, which are becoming hard to market, and are certainly no longer those required by marginal demand. Furthermore, the low level of upgrading in domestic refineries makes it difficult to run more heavy material in order to release light grades for export. The overall production profile is set to dip. By the year 2000, Indonesia should be producing between 0.8 and 1.1 mb/d, depending on investment levels over the course of the 1990s, with domestic demand towards the bottom of this range. The level of exports will therefore be very limited, and net exports could even be negative.

A final complication is the multiplicity of export grades produced, and with the grades with the highest current production being those that also have the greatest proportional fall-offs in their production profiles over the course of the 1990s, the tradable export base for a given grade is likely to be very limited.

The current method for producing the ICP was introduced by Indonesia in April 1989. Table 14.16 shows that most trade in the Indonesian grades is now discussed as a differential to the ICP. Before April 1989 trade was primarily done in terms of outright prices. Indonesia maintained a virtually fixed OSP throughout the period when other countries were experimenting with netbacks, but was prepared to negotiate discounts to the (at least on paper) fixed OSP. By 1991 there was proportionately more trade in outright prices than we have found in other regions, but the volume of such trades is still fairly insignificant.

Table 14.16: Pricing Basis of Indonesian Spot Deals. 1986–91. Percentage of Total Deals.

	1986	1987	1988	1989	1990	1991
Outright Price	99.5	46.6	85.4	11.0	3.2	6.7
Differential Price to:						
ICP/OSP	-	51.6	11.0	76.0	87.9	86.0
Tapis	-	-	1.5	8.9	4.0	1.7
Attaka	-	0.5	-	0.7	2.4	1.1

Source: Own calculations from Petroleum Argus database.

Nevertheless, as can be seen in Table 14.17, trade in outright prices is still dominant in the market for Malaysian grades (primarily Tapis and Labuan), despite a growth in recent years in the number of trades priced as a differential to APPI assessments. While the market for Malaysian crude is the only one we have found where absolute prices are not mainly determined by one of the various forms of differential formula pricing, as Figure 14.7 showed the spot market is still fairly thin, with less than two deals per week being reported for Malaysian grades in 1991.

Table 14.17: Pricing Basis of Malaysian Spot Deals. 1986–91. Percentage of Total Deals

	1986	1987	1988	1989	1990	1991
Outright Price	97.2	96.7	99.0	88.9	69.0	62.7
Differential Price to:						
Official Prices	1.4	3.3	1.0	6.4	6.9	6.0
APPI	-	-	-	3.2	12.1	18.1
Tapis	-	-	-	0.8	3.4	2.4
WTI	-	-	-	-	5.2	6.0

Source: Own calculations from Petroleum Argus database.

In summary we believe that there are serious defects in the Far Eastern crude oil market, and also in the method of compilation of the ICPs for the Indonesian grades, particularly its use of panel price assessments. This is compounded by the use of Dubai and Oman in the basket used to derive the ICPs. The Far East is in need of a liquid market in an appropriate marker crude oil, and the results of Chapter 13 rule out the use of Dubai in this context.

7. The USA

The USA is by far the largest market for crude oil in the world. In 1991 it produced 7.46 mb/d of crude oil, a level only surpassed by Russia (9.3 mb/d) and Saudi Arabia (8.2 mb/d). As is detailed in the appendix to this chapter, this left a shortfall of domestic production under domestic crude oil demand of just over 6 mb/d which was covered by imports. Of this total more than a quarter came from Saudi Arabia alone, and 80 per cent came from Saudi Arabia, Mexico, Canada, Venezuela and Nigeria combined, with the residual amount being drawn from no less than thirty-one other countries.

The major US market is that for the NYMEX light sweet crude contract and WTI which was considered in Chapter 13. We briefly document the rest of the US market in three sections. We look in turn first at the forward market for Alaskan North Slope (ANS), secondly the market for other US domestic grades, and finally we consider the NYMEX sour crude oil contract.

While the USA imports over 1.75 mb/d of crude oil from Latin America (as shown in Appendix Table 14.6), there is only limited spot trade in these grades, primarily due to restrictions placed by the major exporters. The only grades spot traded in any significant volumes are Colombian Cano Limon and Ecuadorian Oriente, trade normally being conducted as a differential to WTI or ANS. US domestic crudes cannot generally be exported, except in the form of refined products, due to US legal restrictions, and thus are not internationally tradable. The only exceptions to this are the export licences granted for the export of Californian production in late 1991, small quantities of Alaskan Cook Inlet crude, and a volume of Alaskan North Slope allowed into Canada under the provisions of free trade agreements between Canada and the USA.

a) The ANS Forward Market

Alaskan North Slope is a medium heavy (27.9 degrees API) sour crude oil (its sulphur content is 1.05 per cent), with a current production level of about 1.8 mb/d. ANS therefore represents more than one-quarter of total US crude oil output. It is mainly produced in the Prudhoe Bay field, and then transported 800 miles through the Trans-Alaska Pipeline System[5] to Valdez, where it is loaded onto tankers. From Valdez about 70 per cent of ANS usually goes to the US West Coast, with the rest continuing south to Panama where it is unloaded, and after crossing the country by pipeline, is loaded onto smaller tankers to go to the US Gulf Coast.

Cargoes bound for the Gulf Coast are the base of forward ANS trade. The delivery chain into the forward market is therefore rather tortuous, involving two pipeline journeys and two tankers. From the West Coast, some ANS goes into Midland Texas along the All-American pipeline (see Figure 13.6). It is not sold spot to any significant extent and would not in any case add to the liquidity of the ANS forward market which is a cargo rather than a pipeline market. ANS is not internationally tradable, which has often led to the threat of legal action against the federal government by the State of Alaska, which believes that the restriction has led to an undervaluation of ANS.

The production of ANS is in the hands of seven companies, dominated by BP (50 per cent), ARCO (20 per cent) and Exxon (20 per cent). Minor shares are held by Amerada Hess, Mobil, Phillips and Union. Exxon and ARCO tend to use most of their entitlements in their own refineries, and hence virtually all ANS traded comes from BP's share. Typical ANS forward trades have some very striking differences compared to typical 15-day Brent trades. The ANS market is conducted on a c.i.f. delivered basis rather than the f.o.b. terms of Brent. It trades a smaller standard parcel size (400 thousand barrels). As a consequence of being a c.i.f. market the loading tolerance is at the seller's rather than the buyer's discretion. This tolerance is also far greater than in the Brent market, 15 per cent as opposed to 5 per cent. Thus in a standard delivery from the ANS forward market any cargo size between 340 and 460 thousand barrels is acceptable.

The Brent forward market is called the 15-day Brent market due to its nomination procedures. By the same token ANS could be called the 10-day ANS market, as this is the minimum notification time of a three-day delivery range that the seller must give the buyer. The buyer nominates the desired port of entry for the cargo at least fifteen days before the start of the delivery month. There are no partial or futures markets based on ANS (although ANS is a deliverable crude oil in the NYMEX sour crude contract launched in 1992). Attempts in the late 1980s by Morgan Stanley and TWO to launch a paper partial ANS market both failed. A market for ANS exists on the US West Coast, and

BP has also sold cargoes on a f.o.b. Valdez Alaska basis.

ANS is normally traded as a differential to WTI. By 1992 trade had become confined in the prompt month, just as with US pipeline crudes other than WTI. It was mainly being carried out between the holders of physical barrels and end-users, with the number of trades being a very low multiple of the number of available cargoes (which by 1992 was down to two or three per week). The forward market for ANS has then almost completely ceased to exist, its reported prices are almost exclusively hypothetical, since they are simply the judgement of price assessment agencies based on market talk of where the market would be trading were there to be any trade. The volume of physical ANS reaching the US Gulf has been in steep decline, as has the proportion of this being traded on the forward market. While, as we will see in the next chapter, a large volume of oil is linked to ANS prices, to call this market related pricing is stretching the concept rather a long way.

b) Other US Domestic Grades

Other US domestic grades tend to be traded in the prompt month for scheduling delivery in the next month. On the West Coast, which mainly consumes a diet of ANS, Canadian and Asian crude oil, there is some trade in Californian output. This is primarily very heavy, the major traded grades being Kern River, THUMS and Line 63 (a blend of Kern River and NGLs). However, the bulk of spot trade occurs for Gulf Coast produced crude oils, in particular West Texas Sour (WTS), which like WTI is gathered into the Midland area, or Light Louisiana Sweet (LLS). The basing point for LLS is St. James Louisiana, from which it can either go to southern refineries, or into Illinois through the Capline via Liberty (see Figure 13.6).

The cash markets for WTS and LLS tend to trade a flow rather than a stock of oil, usually about 2.5 thousand b/d over the next month. Trade is carried out almost exclusively in terms of formula prices against the price of WTI, with each grade normally trading about 300 times per month.

In recent years there have been profound changes in the nature of US spot trade. In total they have led to a continuing decline in the liquidity of the market and hence in its transparency. There are three main factors at work in this. The first has been the evolution of new trading techniques. Other than the increase in swap deals, there has also been a growth in the trading of non-WTI US pipeline crudes through either 'strips' or options. A strip is a medium term deal, usually of between three and nine months duration, between producers and refiners. The deal is priced against the average of NYMEX prices for a consecutive series of months (i.e. the average of a 'strip' of prices). By entering into a strip deal both parties are restricting their interest in the spot market.

Alternatively both producers and refiners can trade in options for non-WTI crudes. These are tailor-made options provided by market makers who offer the right, but not the obligation, to trade a specified grade at a set differential to WTI prices. They therefore offer the opportunity to manage the basis risk between WTI and other US crudes. For the payment of a premium (normally between 5 cents and 25 cents per barrel depending on market conditions), producers and refiners can limit the risk attached to unfavourable movements in the differential without having to give up the benefit of any favourable movements.

A second factor reducing liquidity in the cash market has been the tendency of refiners to trade in larger flow sizes, often 10 thousand b/d or more. Without reducing the volume spot traded, this has reduced the number of deals done. However in the market for WTS, deals of as little as 1 thousand b/d are still very common.

c) NYMEX Sour Crude

We have already noted that the forward market for ANS does not represent a credible way of pricing sour crude oil. Yet there is a need for a transparent way of pricing sour crude oil relative to sweet, particularly due to the increasing level of sour imports into the USA. The NYMEX sour crude oil contract was designed to fill this gap, especially given the *de facto* demise of the ANS market.

Launching a new crude oil futures contract can be a hazardous process. Prior to the launch of the NYMEX sour crude contract, there had been a total of nine crude oil contracts launched, out of which only two (NYMEX light sweet and IPE Brent) had survived (and only one of these allowed for physical delivery of oil). The first failure was a contract launched by the New York Cotton Exchange. The Chicago Board of Trade (CBOT) had failed with a contract for Light Louisiana Sweet launched at the same time as the NYMEX light sweet contract, the IPE had two unsuccessful Brent contracts and one Dubai contract, Brent futures in Rotterdam had failed as had Dubai futures in Singapore.[6] The list of failed oil product contracts is even longer. However, the contracts that failed did so mainly due to specific design faults. In relation to these the NYMEX sour crude contract has no glaring shortcomings, and its failure to take off may say more about the general problems of launching a new contract than about the contract itself.

The sour crude contract has many common features with the light sweet contract, but with a few notable differences. As with light sweet futures, the basic trading unit is one thousand barrels, with the last trading day for any given month's delivery being the third business day before the 25th of the prior month, with the first eighteen consecutive months being traded. There are seven deliverable grades. Six of these are waterborne, ANS, Dubai, Flotta (UK), Iranian Light, Oman and Oriente (Ecuador), and one is a domestic pipeline crude, West Texas Sour/New Mexico Sour. Deliverable quality is of a minimum API gravity of 26 degrees, and a sulphur content between 0.5 per cent and 2.2 per cent. The typical par qualities of the deliverable grades range from API gravities of 27.9 (ANS and Oriente) to 35.7 (Flotta), and sulphur contents of 0.9 per cent (Oriente) to 2 per cent (Dubai).

Instead of a single point of delivery as in the light sweet contract, delivery can take place in one of three ways. Transfer can occur at one of three marine terminals on the Texas coast (ARCO in Texas City, Oiltanking in Houston and Sun in Nederland), by pipeline at specific connections to Rancho and Texaco systems, or out of storage in one of four facilities (Amerada Hess, Oiltanking and Texaco, all in Houston, and Sun in Nederland). Comparable ADP and EFP procedures exist as in the light sweet contract.

The contract began well, trading 1853 contracts on its first day on 28 February 1992. This compares with the 1884 contracts traded on the first day of the light sweet contract. It could, however, be argued that the comparison is not a fair one, since in 1983 the oil industry had less experience with futures and was wary of crude oil futures in particular. Further, the light sweet contract had a direct competitor in the CBOT LLS contract, and did not have the additional source of potential liquidity that trading the sweet-sour spread represents. All the same, the first day's volume was still encouraging. On the second day volume fell to 611 contracts, on 16 March volume was just one contract, and the first day of no trade at all was 30 March. After that date, in the rest of 1992, the contract traded sporadically and on most days there was no trade at all.

8. Summary

Throughout the various spot markets for crude oil in the world that we have considered, one overwhelming trend has emerged. Oil trade has become a trade of differentials, with markers having taken an increasing role in the process of price formation. Apart from some trade in Far Eastern grades, outright trade, while dominant in 1986, has all but vanished. Price levels are set by markers, and spot markets set the differentials from those markers for any given grade. We have found four main markers in spot trade. By far the most important is dated Brent, the dominant marker for trade in the North Sea, the Mediterranean and West Africa, while WTI is the marker for trades of US domestic crude oils.

In other areas trade is focused on differentials from retroactive (and thus unknown at the time of trade), official prices. They are functions of monthly averages rather than daily assessments. In the Middle East spot trade is carried out against official prices which are themselves close functions of average Dubai prices over a month. In the Far East the main marker is the ICP, a complicated and unsatisfactory concept involving both monthly and yearly price averages.

Outside of the USA, the Brent market is seen to be the major dynamic in setting price levels. While dated Brent is the most important marker crude, we saw in Chapter 8 that there is virtually no outright trade in dated Brent, with 99.8 per cent of trades in 1991 being conducted as a differential, normally to forward Brent. Hence forward Brent sets the level of prices, the dated Brent market sets the differential of spot from forward oil, and the differential of other North Sea, West African and Mediterranean grades from dated Brent is set by trade in those grades.

The forward Brent price also sets the level elsewhere in the world. We saw in Chapter 13 there was little outright trade in the Dubai forward market, with Dubai prices being set by trades and market talk of the Brent-Dubai differential. Average monthly assessed Dubai prices feed into the retroactive official prices set by Abu Dhabi, Oman and Qatar, and spot trade is conducted as differentials to these. The Dubai average, together with its strong influence over Oman prices, then feeds through into the compilation of the ICP. In short, there is very little spot trade outside of the USA and US bound cargoes, that does not directly or indirectly depend on the prices set in the Brent forward market in the derivation of the general level of prices. With Brent being the only internationally tradable crude that generates a significant amount of outright trade on a daily basis, it has become the ultimate centre of price formation for international spot trade.

Notes
1. Occasional trades are reported for Danish oil (Danish production was 0.146 mb/d in 1991). There has been no reported trade in the minor production of Dutch oil (which amounted to 0.044 mb/d in 1991).
2. Particularly as c.i.f. deals transfer the environmental risk of spillage during transit to the seller.

3. Variations in quality have led traders to split Urals into four grades. Urals Heavy (28 degrees API), standard Urals (32 degrees API), Siberian Light (35 degrees API), and Siberian Extra Light (36.5 degrees API).
4. BP (130 thousand b/d) and Shell (270 thousand b/d) have availabilities of Saudi oil to sell as part of a defence contract between Saudi Arabia and the UK (the al-Yamamah deal).
5. A good description of the development of the Alaskan oil infrastructure is given in P.A. Coates (1991) *The Trans-Alaska Pipeline Controversy*, Associated University Presses.
6. A cash settled Dubai contract was proposed in 1991 by the Commodity Exchange (COMEX) and has received CFTC approval. Other contracts currently on the drawing board include a Brent contract in Singapore, and a futures contract to be traded in Budapest.

Appendix to Chapter 14

Table A14.1: US Crude Oil Imports by Country of Origin and Users by Company. 1991. Thousand Barrels per Day.

1. Origin

Country	Volume	Country	Volume
Saudi Arabia	1723.7	Zaire	27.0
Mexico	772.6	Malaysia	23.5
Canada	736.8	Australia	21.5
Venezuela	712.9	Yemen	19.5
Nigeria	703.5	Egypt	17.3
Angola	267.7	Cameroon	17.0
Colombia	145.4	Kuwait	5.6
United Kingdom	117.1	Syria	4.4
Indonesia	102.0	Argentina	4.2
Gabon	97.3	Benin	3.8
China	87.4	Oman	3.6
Norway	74.0	Thailand	3.2
Trinidad	72.4	Italy	2.9
UAE	65.0	Guatemala	2.9
Congo	56.9	Brunei	2.9
Ecuador	53.4	Peru	1.8
Algeria	45.3	Bahamas	1.5
Iran	39.0	Bolivia	0.5

2. Users of Imported Crude

Company	Volume	Company	Volume
Chevron	604.7	Caribbean Pet. Corp.	26.6
PDVSA	449.6	Valero	21.6
Sun	395.3	Cenex	17.0
Exxon	377.6	Hunt	16.6
Mobil	355.8	Unocal	12.4
Shell	314.8	Texaco	12.3
BP	253.3	Trifinery	10.2
Marathon	219.7	Unknown	9.2
Koch	192.2	Total	8.2
Coastal	188.9	Cibro	7.7
Ashland	185.8	Ergon	6.9
Phibro	185.1	Laketon	5.4
Hess	171.5	US Oil	5.0
Lyondell	167.7	Montana Refining	4.9
Conoco	150.0	Golden West	4.6
Phillips 66	116.6	Indian Refining	4.5
Fina	113.3	Tosco	3.6
Clark	100.1	LL&E	2.1
Kerr-McGee	61.0	Sound Refining	1.8
United Refining	55.1	Sinclair	1.3
Murphy	50.5	Crystal	0.5
Crown Central	49.6	Frontier	0.1
Hawaiian Ind.	45.6		

Source: Own calculations from *Imported Crude Oil and Petroleum Products*, American Petroleum Institute, various issues.

Table A14.2: US Imports of North Sea and Mediterranean Crude Oil By Company. 1991. Thousand Barrels per Day.

Imports from the United Kingdom		Imports from Norway	
Company	Volume	Company	Volume
Kerr-McGee	19.9	Phillips 66	23.0
Crown Central	17.3	Fina	12.6
Fina	14.7	BP	11.6
Sun	12.3	Amoco	9.9
Chevron	11.0	Crown	5.5
Hess	10.7	Mobil	4.1
Clark	6.1	Exxon	2.8
Ashland	4.1	Sun	1.6
Phillips 66	4.0	Clark	1.6
PDVSA	2.8	Marathon	1.4
Marathon	2.5	Total	74.0
Lyondell	2.2		
Amoco	1.4	Imports from Algeria	
Murphy	1.4	Company	Volume
Unknown	1.4	Shell	38.0
Koch	1.3	LL&E	2.1
Mobil	1.3	Koch	1.4
Total	117.1	Crown	1.3
		Kerr-McGee	1.0
Imports from Egypt		Sun	1.0
Company	Volume	Phibro	0.5
Star Enterprise	17.3	Total	45.3
Total	17.3		
		Imports from Italy	
Imports from Syria		Company	Volume
Company	Volume	Chevron	2.8
Phibro	2.7	Kerr-McGee	0.2
Clark	0.8	Total	2.9
Total	4.4		

Source: Own calculations from *Imported Crude Oil and Petroleum Products*, American Petroleum Institute, various issues.

Table A14.3: US Imports of West African Crude Oil By Company. 1991. Thousand Barrels per Day.

Imports from Nigeria		Imports from Angola	
Company	Volume	Company	Volume
Sun	196.7	Chevron	69.1
BP	175.8	Exxon	33.0
Shell	116.3	Phibro	31.7
Chevron	91.3	BP	31.5
Amoco	55.3	Coastal	21.6
Hess	18.0	Kerr-McGee	18.2
Phillips 66	17.0	Crown	17.5
Phibro	6.9	Hess	10.7
Coastal	6.8	Phillips 66	9.4
Koch	5.8	Lyondell	6.1
Crown	5.6	Shell	5.4
Marathon	3.2	Fina	3.8
Unknown	2.5	Mobil	2.9
Kerr-McGee	1.2	Amoco	2.8
Lyondell	0.9	Sun	2.7
Star Enterprise	0.4	Murphy	1.3
Total	703.5	Total	267.7

Imports from Gabon		Imports from Zaire	
Company	Volume	Company	Volume
Coastal	38.0	Chevron	19.2
Phibro	31.7	BP	3.4
Hess	12.0	Mobil	1.5
Exxon	9.7	Exxon	1.1
Sun	2.3	Phillips 66	0.9
Mobil	2.0	Phibro	0.8
Chevron	0.8	Total	27.0
BP	0.8		
Total	97.3		

Imports from Cameroon	
Company	Volume
Amoco	10.4
Exxon	5.7
Coastal	0.9
Total	17.0

Imports from Congo	
Company	Volume
Hess	29.3
Phillips 66	21.7
Phibro	4.9
Chevron	1.0
Total	56.9

Imports from Benin	
Company	Volume
Mobil	3.8
Total	3.8

Source: Own calculations from *Imported Crude Oil and Petroleum Products,* American Petroleum Institute, various issues.

Table A14.4: US Imports of Middle Eastern Crude Oil By Company. 1991. Thousand Barrels per Day.

Imports from Saudi Arabia		*Imports from UAE*	
Company	Volume	Company	Volume
Star Enterprise	519.5	Hess	63.5
Exxon	237.2	Fina	1.5
Chevron	214.1	Total	65.0
Ashland	152.8		
Marathon	140.9	*Imports from Iran*	
Amoco	116.9	Company	Volume
Lyondell	61.8	Coastal	24.2
Mobil	59.7	Hess	6.6
Shell	57.7	Fina	2.7
Fina	44.2	Chevron	2.7
Sun	43.8	Marathon	1.4
Phillips 66	40.5	Lyondell	1.4
Phibro	15.2	Total	39.0
Hess	11.6		
Hunt	3.0	*Imports from Yemen*	
Koch	2.8	Country	Volume
Texaco	1.4	Shell	5.5
Clark	0.8	Koch	4.0
Total	1723.7	Clark	2.9
		Fina	2.7
Imports from Kuwait		Coastal	2.7
Company	Volume	BP	1.8
Amoco	2.6	Total	19.5
Fina	1.4		
Total	5.6	*Imports from Oman*	
		Company	Volume
		Fina	1.8
		Chevron	1.8
		Total	3.6

Source: Own calculations from *Imported Crude Oil and Petroleum Products*, American Petroleum Institue, various issues.

Table A14.5: US Imports of Canadian and Far Eastern Crude Oil By Company. 1991. Thousand Barrels per Day.

Imports from Canada

Company	Volume
Koch	157.6
Amoco	119.5
Mobil	102.7
United	55.1
Clark	52.8
Sun	51.6
Conoco	42.3
Ashland	28.9
PDVSA	20.4
Exxon	19.1
Cenex	17.0
BP	16.2
Marathon	13.8
Murphy	10.6
Total	8.2
Laketon	5.4
Montana	4.9
US Oil	3.0
Shell	2.0
Hess	1.7
Sinclair	1.3
Tosco	1.0
Unknown	0.7
Crystal	0.5
Indian	0.5
Frontier	0.1
Total	736.8

Imports from China

Company	Volume
Phibro	33.8
Valero	21.6
Coastal	18.8
Exxon	7.2
Chevron	3.9
Hawaiian Ind.	2.4
Total	87.4

Imports from Brunei

Company	Volume
Shell	1.8
Total	1.8

Imports from Indonesia

Company	Volume
Chevron	46.5
Hawaiian Ind.	19.0
Coastal	10.0
Unocal	7.9
PDVSA	4.7
Phibro	4.7
Unknown	3.2
BP	2.0
Shell	1.5
Exxon	1.5
Koch	1.1
Total	102.0

Imports from Australia

Company	Volume
Hawaiian Ind.	11.9
Shell	3.4
Exxon	2.0
Phibro	1.2
BP	1.1
US Oil	0.7
Unocal	0.7
Coastal	0.6
Total	21.5

Imports from Malaysia

Company	Volume
Hawaiian Ind.	10.4
Coastal	4.0
Phibro	3.2
Shell	2.0
Unocal	1.9
Amoco	1.4
Golden West	0.7
Total	23.5

Imports from Thailand

Company	Volume
BP	1.8
Unocal	1.3
Total	3.1

Source: Own calculations from *Imported Crude Oil and Petroleum Products*, American Petroleum Institute, various issues.

Table A14.6: US Imports of Latin American Crude Oil By Company. 1991. Thousand Barrels per Day.

Imports from Mexico

Company	Volume
Chevron	130.7
Mobil	101.6
Lyondell	79.7
Shell	74.7
Amoco	63.7
Marathon	56.5
PDVSA	47.0
Coastal	33.9
Clark	33.9
Exxon	32.8
Sun	31.3
Conoco	31.3
Fina	21.1
Murphy	16.6
Koch	9.6
Hunt	5.7
BP	1.0
Hess	0.8
Tosco	0.7
Total	772.6

Imports from Colombia

Company	Volume
Phibro	33.8
Mobil	21.6
Sun	21.0
Murphy	20.6
Kerr-McGee	6.8
BP	6.3
Exxon	5.5
Fina	2.8
Crown	1.6
Shell	1.4
Lyondell	1.3
Indian	1.2
Conoco	0.9
Total	145.4

Imports from Peru

Company	Volume
Mobil	1.5
Total	1.5

Imports from Argentina

Company	Volume
Cibro	1.1
Koch	1.1
Exxon	1.1
Phibro	0.8
Hess	0.8
Total	4.2

Imports from Guatemala

Company	Volume
Amoco	1.8
Exxon	0.6
Mobil	0.6
Total	2.9

Imports from Venezuela

Company	Volume
PDVSA	370.3
Conoco	73.5
Mobil	36.5
Star Enterprise	36.3
Sun	31.0
Caribbean Pet.C	24.8
Coastal	21.3
Exxon	18.4
Amoco	17.8
Texaco	10.9
Chevron	10.0
Trifinery	9.9
Phibro	9.2
Lyondell	8.2
Koch	7.0
Hunt	6.9
Ergon	6.9
Cibro	6.6
Sound	1.8
Unknown	1.4
Shell	1.0
Clark	0.8
US Oil	0.4
Total	712.9

Source: Own calculations from *Imported Crude Oil and Petroleum Products*, American Petroleum Institute, various issues.

Table A14.6: US Imports of Latin American Crude Oil By Company. 1991. Thousand Barrels per Day. (continued)

Imports from Ecuador		Imports from Trinidad	
Company	Volume	Company	Volume
Mobil	14.7	Amoco	70.4
Coastal	6.1	Phibro	1.2
Lyondell	6.0	Clark	0.6
PDVSA	4.4	Trifinery	0.3
Shell	4.3	Total	72.4
Fina	3.9		
Golden West	3.9	Imports from the Bahamas	
Phibro	3.0	Company	Volume
Tosco	1.9	Hunt	1.0
Hawaiian Ind.	1.9	Total	1.0
Caribbean Pet. C.	1.8		
US Oil	0.9	Imports from Bolivia	
Unocal	0.5	Company	Volume
Total	53.4	Koch	0.5
		Total	0.5

Notes to Tables A14.1 to A14.6.
Note 1: Total US Imports in 1991, 6.03 mb/d.
Note 2: The refinery interests of PDVSA in the USA (both wholly and partly owned) are aggregated and are listed under PDVSA.

Source: Own calculations from *Imported Crude Oil and Petroleum Products*, American Petroleum Institute, various issues.

CHAPTER 15

THE EXPORT OF CRUDES AT MARKET-RELATED FORMULA PRICES

1. Historical Context

Formula pricing is a method for defining the sale price of an export crude by relating it to the spot or forward price of another crude taken as a reference. This method, now applied by most oil-exporting countries, was adopted as early as March 1986 by Mexico. By 1988 it had become a common and widely accepted pricing method.

The adoption of formula pricing ushered in a new chapter in the history of oil price determination. The 1986 crisis was the watershed that separated this episode from a radically different one during which the international prices of crude oil were strongly influenced, if not almost fully determined, by a reference price set by OPEC at meetings of its conferences of oil ministers. Oil-exporting countries then fixed official selling prices for their own crude varieties related through some estimate of relative values (taking into account API gravity, sulphur content and location) to the OPEC reference price, that of Arabian Light 34° API, the marker crude. The period during which world oil prices were subject to OPEC's administration began in late 1973 and ended in 1985; this episode lasted therefore twelve years. It was preceded by a much longer period of price administration by seven or eight major oil companies, a period which sometimes evokes nostalgia for a lost golden age of price stability.

The 1986 crisis brought to an end the episode of OPEC's price administration and ushered in the era of market-related price formulae. The old system collapsed because the burden of holding the oil price line, as administered by OPEC, had become intolerably heavy on Saudi Arabia which saw its production dwindling from a peak of some 11 mb/d in 1980 down to 3.0–3.5 mb/d in 1985. In fact total OPEC production fell during the first half of the 1980s from a peak of some 31 mb/d to a low of 16 mb/d. This was due to three major factors: (a) the coming on stream of an additional 1 mb/d, on average, every year between 1978 and 1985 of additional non-OPEC oil production, mainly from the former Soviet Union, the North Sea, Alaska, Mexico, West Africa and Oman, (b) a world economic recession causing a decline in the demand for energy and therefore oil; (c) interfuel substitution against oil and energy conservation measures which affected oil demand more significantly than other fuels. The oil price shocks of 1973-4 and 1979-80 were blamed, almost exclusively, for all these developments. The true story is naturally more complex. It has been shown by Adam Seymour in a recent study,[1] for example, that more than half of the increase in non-OPEC oil output of the period 1975-85 would have obtained regardless of the price increases because irreversible investment decisions had already been made before the shocks. Furthermore, the economic recession which reduced energy demand was due to many factors besides the oil price rises; and the energy efficiency and inter-fuel substitution drive owed some of its momentum to security rather than economic considerations. In short, the problems faced by OPEC in the mid 1980s cannot be attributed in their entirety to the rises in oil prices. A number of other factors – geological, political, fiscal, economic and strategic – played a role. More importantly, it was the *manner* in which prices were administered (the suddenness of the 1973-4 rises and the failure to lower prices in 1981 after the Iranian crisis) rather than the *principle* of price administration, which can be conceived and implemented in many different ways, that caused some of the problems.

Many within OPEC, and most authorities outside the organization, concluded from the experience of the early 1980s that the principle of price administration is inherently flawed. The notion that a full recognition of the nature and functions of a market can be reconciled with flexible forms of price policy (as the analogy of foreign-exchange markets and policy suggests) has not yet crystallized.

1986 was a watershed because it witnessed the wholesale rejection of the old oil pricing system. Interestingly, a system different from both OPEC price administration and its successor, market-related pricing formulae, was tried for a short time. This was netback pricing introduced by Saudi Arabia and quickly adopted by most other oil-exporting countries in a competitive race for market shares.[2] The short experiment was traumatic as it led to a price collapse.

Market-related price formulae thus emerged as the only possible alternative to the disgraced system of price administration and the disastrous netback pricing experiment. It was pioneered by Mexico in March 1986 as an alternative to netback pricing which Pemex intensely disliked. It spread later during that year and in 1987, and soon became almost universal (the exception being recourse to retroactive pricing by some countries).

2. The Method: its Objectives and Application

The adoption of formula pricing is meant to achieve three objectives:

(a) To relieve exporting countries from the burden of discovering the 'economic' price of oil. 'The market performs this task best when left on its own' is the widely accepted wisdom;
(b) To ensure, through the formula, that the exporter realizes prices which reflect movements in the general oil price level in the world petroleum market;
(c) To ensure competitiveness between the export crude which a country wants to sell and the set of close substitutes which other countries also sell in the same market, or even more narrowly, to the same refiner.

The method chosen to achieve these objectives appears very simple at first sight. It is a method of differential pricing often expressed by the formula:

$$P_X = P_R \pm D \tag{1}$$

where X is the export crude (say, Arabian Medium); R is the crude chosen as a market reference in a particular area; and D is the value of the price differential between X and R as estimated from time to time by the exporting country. It is known as the adjustment factor and is sometimes broken up into two or three elements. This however should not detract attention from the fact that the critical part of (1) is the difference, however expressed, between P_X and P_R.

It is useful to discuss the relationships between this simple method and the objectives of market-related pricing as stated above. The comparison of means with aims can provide insights into the economic significance of this system and at the same time explain several features of formula pricing as applied in practice by oil-exporting countries today.

(a) The Economic Price

Formula pricing raises the question of whether the spot, forward or other type of market in which the reference crude R is traded is the locus where supply and demand balance at the margin and yield the economic price of oil for the region. A positive answer to this question is tantamount to making very strong assumptions about the structure and performance of markets. The purist will always be inclined to say that they can never be satisfied. To stick to this position is clearly futile since imperfections are inherent features of all markets and indeed any institution. The opposite position which argues that, things being what they are, there is no other course than to accept that the markets for the chosen reference crudes constitute the true market. This realism has its merits if it does not degenerate into complacency and, by a peculiar inversion, into a dogmatism as dangerous as that of the purist. The more positive approach is to recognize that while one may have to accept the recourse to the reference crude markets *faute de mieux* there are essential tasks to be continually performed to identify imperfections, to attempt to remove some of them, to improve the structure and mode of operations of markets, and to create, if necessary, more representative and economically meaningful ones.

The current practice is to take Brent as the reference crude for sales to Europe; ANS, sometimes in combination with LLS, WTS or Brent for sales to North America; Dubai, Oman or an average of the two for the Far East. It is possible to argue that Brent has a central role in this system. Its significance for crude oil pricing extends beyond Europe because of its influence on the determination of Dubai prices and its use by some exporting countries as a partial or full reference crude for sales to the USA.

Brent is the only reference crude in this list that is traded in a market which displays many of the essential economic characteristics required for eligibility. It is an active, multi-layered market, centrally placed in the heart of a large oil-consuming region, and is well linked through active arbitrage to WTI in the USA and Dubai in the Gulf. Its imperfections and peculiar features raise interesting economic issues but do not affect its rank at the top of the merit order of reference crudes.

The use of ANS as reference for sales to the USA seems to owe much to this crude being waterborne. Pipeline crudes are not generally favoured because logistical bottlenecks often cause accidental squeezes. It is difficult to make a case in favour of ANS on other important grounds: market size, location, price transparency and so on. Dubai is discussed in some detail elsewhere in this study.

(b)   Price Equivalence with the Reference Crude and Competition with Substitute Crudes

The exporter's dual purposes are: to track as closely as possible the general movement of oil prices, and, at the same time, to set the price of his crude X in line with the prices set by close competitors for crudes with similar characteristics. There would be no problem reconciling these two objectives if (i) refiners were able to switch easily from one crude variety to another irrespective of how far apart they lie on the (multi-dimension) quality spectrum, and (ii) if, partly as a result of this substitutability, the relative prices of any pair of crudes reflected at all times the correct economic valuation of their characteristics, that is differences in GPWs, processing, transport and other costs.

In practice the set of export crudes traded in the world is segmented and competition is to a large extent limited to sub-sets which include crudes of fairly similar gravity and sulphur characteristics. Thus, Arabian Heavy is not in the same sub-set as Brent; Arabian Light competes more closely with Iranian Light, Dubai, some Iraqi and Egyptian crudes and Urals than with North and West African or with North Sea crudes.

Furthermore, the relative prices of crudes in different sub-sets do not usually move in very close harmony in the short period. In other words the equilibrium condition that relative prices are such as to make a refiner indifferent as between buying this or that crude is an ideal towards which the market may tend but which is naturally never realized. In a market context, distortions give rise to arbitrage. But in setting in advance the value of D, the differential or adjustment factor, the exporting country cannot easily reconcile strict adherence with the principle of equivalence between the price of its export crude X and that of R, and the main competitive objective which is to price X in relation to that of [Y], the sub-set of close substitutes.

Put differently, formula (1) implies that an oil-exporting country needs to be only concerned with the differential between R and X, while in reality it has to watch very closely how its competitors are pricing their crude Y in relation to R. As the decisions of different countries are made separately, the dates at which everyone announces the chosen value of D for the formula acquires significance. A country that announces its formula first is at a competitive disadvantage. If undercut by its competitors it may respond in the next round by adjusting its new price downward, or by delaying the announcement, or both.

In short, the setting of a value for D would rarely reflect at first the economic differential between the prices of X and R but may involve a complex process of lagged adjustment.

(c) Further Implications of the Competitive Equivalence Principle

The notion of equivalence through differential pricing of X and R, or X and Y (as the case may be), for the marginal buyer raises the complex issue of the relevant location where this equivalence should be sought.

A very strict application of this principle would multiply the number of relevant locations and therefore the number of formulae for every export crude. It would involve discriminatory pricing on a large scale, which is both undesirable and impractical. The current practice is to distinguish three (and sometimes four) broad regions: North America or more broadly the Western Hemisphere, Europe (sometimes North West Europe and the Mediterranean separately) and the Far East. Because the set of markets across the world is incomplete and the transport infrastructure not always fully adequate, arbitrage is not absolutely perfect. This provides some opportunities for a modicum of price discrimination between the regions supported by destination restrictions on some sales contracts and naturally gives rise to some buyers' complaints. On the other hand, the recognition by oil-exporting countries that the circumstances of individual buyers in a given region are sometimes different induce some of them, when the balance of bargaining power is in the buyers' favour, to modify slightly the terms of the relevant formulae depending on the customer. This seems to be the marketing practice followed by Iran, and before the Gulf War by Iraq. Those who benefit from these minor concessions naturally do not complain.

Thirdly, the 'equivalence to the buyer' principle means that the point of comparison must be close to destination rather than to the point of origin. This is tantamount to c.i.f. pricing. Yet many oil-exporting countries wish to retain the notion that their export crudes are sold f.o.b. and their pricing formulae states that the point of sale is at a certain port or terminal f.o.b. In practice the way around this apparent contradiction is found by (a) stipulating a time lag between the loading and the pricing dates and by including freight rates elements in the computations that set D, the differential parameter, in the price formula (as generically expressed by equation (1)). The time lags can be as long as fifty days, as in the Saudi formulae for sales to the USA. In important cases, however, like Saudi Arabia's sales to the Far East or Mexico to the Western hemisphere there is no time lag. This means the risks of price changes during the haul period are carried by the buyer.

The key parameter of the price formula, D in equation (1), is in certain cases set some time in the month preceding the month in which the formula is applied; and in some cases only quarterly. The first step in the process that leads to the choice of a value for D is to estimate it in a way that reflects as accurately as possible the difference in GPWs obtained from refining the two crudes (X and R), the difference in freight costs involved in moving these two crudes from their respective origins to the point of comparison (e.g. Brent from Sullom Voe to Rotterdam and Arabian Light from Ras Tanura to Rotterdam) and differences in refining costs (RC). The equivalence implies,

$$D = P_R - P_X$$
$$= (GPW_R - GPW_X) + (freight_X - freight_R) + (RC_x - RC_R) \qquad (2)$$

The setting of D at a value that reflects fairly exactly (2) at the time and point of delivery involves certain practical problems. The first arises because of the time discrepancy between the date at which D is usually set and announced (two or more weeks before the beginning of the applicable month) and the date at which the crude reaches its destination. Although the time lag in pricing covers for possible changes in the level of the reference price during the haul, the pre-setting of D means that the differential in the formula is always bound to be out of date. The time discrepancy between the date at which D is set and the date of arrival of a cargo can be very long in the extreme case when D is set at the beginning of the month preceding the applicable month on the basis of data of say the previous two or three weeks, the cargo lifted at the end of the applicable month for a destination involving a six week haul. In this case the time discrepancy can be as long as fifteen or sixteen weeks.

The second is a classical measurement problem. Since a price formula usually applies to a whole region the setting of D involves the choice of a typical point of destination for computing the freight element and that of a marginal refinery, or of a particular refining model for calculating GPWs. This means that the value set for D will never be identical to the relative valuation put by individual refiners in the region on the two crudes. The circumstances of various refiners naturally differ.

The second step is to compare the resulting value with the behaviour of competitors and make accordingly an adjustment based on marketing experience and judgement. It is also likely that the setting of D will often involve some attempt to look at conditions expected to prevail two or three months ahead; and in many instances oil-exporting countries sound the views of their main customers before finally setting D.

Problems arising from the pre-setting of D are probably ironed out to some extent by the pattern of sequential adjustments as mentioned earlier. Thus if D is set in January for liftings in February at a level that yields too high a price P_X relative to P_R at the time of arrival in March, there will be buyers' pressure to adjust the value of D set in March for April liftings. It is possible, of course, that this adjustment yields a price P_X for April that turns out to be too low in the circumstances prevailing in May or June at the time of delivery. This will induce the seller to adjust upward in the subsequent month.

For these and other reasons the pattern of changes in the values of D for any given formula may sometimes seem erratic when compared *ex post* with the actual movements of GPWs and freight differentials; but this does not prove that attempts to set D as close as possible to its expected market value are not continually made through a mixture of forecasting, analysis of recent data, consultations and adjustments for past discrepancies.

Biases introduced by the measurement problem (the choice of reference location and of the marginal refining yield) against crude X for particular refiners are perhaps removed, albeit partially or occasionally, through individual bargaining. It may be however, that in a buyers' market, the most common state of affairs, the exporting country will set D at a level that makes its crude X competitive with the reference crude for the refiner that values X least (relatively to R). In practice this means that crude X will be undervalued relatively to R for all buyers except one when uniform pricing is applied.

In short, market-related formula pricing inevitably involves compromises between (a) the sellers' main objectives which are to offer their crudes at prices that are both comparable (after all adjustments for quality, transport costs and so on are made) with that of a reference crude taken to represent the market and in line with competitors' prices; (b) their desire to price as uniformly as possible (within every broad region) and to retain the appearance of an f.o.b. base.

3. Saudi Arabia's Pricing Formulae

As it is impossible to analyse in detail all the pricing formulae of exporting countries, we limit the discussion in this section to Saudi Arabia. We chose this country for this illustration partly because it is the largest oil exporter and partly because of a greater availability of data. The description of other important formulae can be found however in an Appendix to this chapter.

The introduction of formula pricing by Saudi Arabia did not follow immediately the end of the 1986 crisis. In early 1987 Saudi Arabia returned for a while to official pricing and this was associated with a rather strict adhesion to quotas. This position, however, could not be held for very long considering that many oil-exporting countries were adopting the much more flexible system of formula pricing thus threatening Saudi Arabia's market share. Sometime during the first half of 1987 Saudi Arabia began to show flexibility in setting contract terms and in pricing. The explicit adoption of price formulae dates probably from October 1987 although this was initially done secretly and press reports about their introduction strenuously denied.

Published data on Saudi Arabia's price formulae provide information starting in October 1987 for Arabian Light sales to Aramco partners for US destinations; in December 1987 for other crude varieties also to Aramco partners for the USA; and as late as April 1988 for sales to Aramco partners for Europe and the Far East.

All the Saudi price formulae are of the general form

$$P_X = P_R \pm D$$

There is only one reference crude in all formulae for European and US destinations, Brent and ANS respectively; and now the average of Oman and Dubai is used in formulae for Far Eastern destinations. The latter case amounts to having Dubai alone as the reference crude because the Dubai/Oman differential as assessed by Platt's tends to remain constant for very long periods of time. The relevant Brent price in the formulae has been changed from dated to first month forward in January 1989 and back to dated in May 1991. It seems that in the past some customers were allowed to opt for either a dated or forward Brent pricing formula, but that Saudi Arabia now wishes pricing with reference to dated Brent to become universal.

The basic formulae are for sales to Aramco partners. In these the point of sale is stated as f.o.b. but the formulae involve long time lags for sales to Europe (forty days) and the USA (fifty days). There is no time lag in formulae for the Far East as mentioned earlier on. The market quotes of the reference price are however averaged over ten days around the pricing date for Europe and the USA, and over the calendar month that includes the loading date for the Far East.

The D term in the Saudi pricing formulae for Europe and the USA consists in fact of two parts, the first termed the adjustment factor and the second the freight adjustment factor. The former is supposed to reflect differences in GPWs between the relevant export and the reference crude, differences in refining costs and, *grosso modo*, the difference between the freight rate involved in moving the reference crude say, in the case of Brent, from Sullom Voe to Rotterdam, and a basic freight rate for the haul of the export crude from Ras Tanura to the oil-consuming region. The latter was set in the past at WS40, and since December 1990 at a fixed level of $7.36 per long ton for the USA and $7.39 per long ton for Europe. The second element, the freight adjustment factor, adds to or subtracts from the price the difference between the freight rate and the base rate depending on whether the actual rate is below or above the base.

300 Oil Markets and Prices

The formulae applied to non-Aramco sales are less well documented. The important point is that since mid-1989 these formulae involve a c.i.f. point of sale which means that the pricing date is the actual delivery date. The general principle of Saudi oil pricing in this context is that the prices yielded by formulae for non-Aramco buyers should track the results of Aramco formulae despite differences in the way these algorithms are specified. Although some flexibility may be involved to suit the circumstances of individual customers, it is generally said that small differences in formulation are not allowed to yield, other than in an insignificant manner, non-uniform pricing. Table 15.1 summarizes Saudi Arabia's main oil pricing formulae.

Table 15.1: Saudi Arabian Oil Pricing Formulae. 1988–91.

Crude/Destination	Period	Formula
1. All crudes/Aramco Europe	April 88 – December 88	Dated Brent − adj. factor − freight disc.
	January 89 – April 91	Forward Brent − adj. factor − freight disc.
	May 91 –	Dated Brent − adj. factor − freight disc.

Notes: Point of sale, f.o.b. Ras Tanura. Date of pricing is now forty days after the date of loading. Market price quotas are averaged over ten days around the pricing date. For freight discount, see text. The adjustment factor was negative for all crudes (Arab Light, Medium, Heavy and Berri) every month in 1988–91.

| 2. All crudes/Aramco USA | October 87 | ANS − adj.factor − freight disc. |

Note: Point of sale f.o.b. Ras Tanura. Date of pricing is now fifty days after the date of loading. Market price quotes are averaged over ten days around the pricing date. For freight discount, see text. The adjustment factor was negative for all crudes throughout Oct 87 – 91 except for Berri 39° API which was at a discount until September 1990 and at a premium since.

| 3. All crudes/Aramco Far East | April 88 – May 88 | Dubai ± adj.factor |
| | June 88 – | 0.5 (Dubai + Oman) ± adj.factor |

Notes: Point of sale f.o.b. Ras Tanura. Date of pricing is now the loading date. Market price quotas are averaged over thirty days. There is no freight discount. The adjustment factor was positive (except in December 1988, minus five cents) for Arabian Light, always negative for Arabian Medium and Heavy, and always positive for Berri 39° API.

Source: Own calculations from *MEES*, *PIW*, and other sources.

An interesting analytical question relates to the setting of the adjustment factor. Does the setting of the adjustment factor every month by the relevant Saudi authorities take other elements into consideration than the data on GPWs, freight and refining costs available to the authorities at the time when the value of the adjustment factor is being fixed? Let us recall that the pricing formula applicable to loadings in a given month (say, May) is announced at the beginning of the preceding month (in this case, April) and must therefore be calculated on the basis of data from the month before (March and perhaps the first two or three days of April). We can test the hypothesis that the actual adjustment factor for month M is set exclusively through recourse to the relevant data (GPW, etc . . .) of the second month prior to M. The hypothesis would be proven true if there is a close match between the actual adjustment factors and their values as computed by us using data lagged *back* by two months. Small random discrepancies which one always expects would not upset the hypothesis. But if the discrepancies turn out to be either large or systematic, we would have to reject the simple hypothesis that the adjustment factor is set mechanistically by churning out equation (2) with data from month M−2 for the pricing formula for month M; and this would raise new questions for analysis.

We have applied this test for the period April 1988 to December 1991 (forty-five observations) comparing the adjustment factor in pricing formulae for sales of Arabian Light to Aramco partners for European destinations in each month M of our period with our calculations using data for months M−2 of

[$GPW_x - GPW_R$] + [freight rate Sullom Voe/Rotterdam − WS40 (or $7.39 per long ton)] − [difference in refining costs assumed to be $0.15 per barrel higher for Arabian Light than Brent]

We have assumed that the marginal refining capacity in NW Europe is simple refining and the GPWs calculated accordingly. We have attempted two sets of computations, one using GPW data for the last two weeks of month M−2, the other using GPW data for the whole of month M−2. The resulting discrepancies between the actual adjustment factor and our computed value are presented in Table 15.2.

The results in Table 15.2 show that the adjustment factor set the price of Arabian Light below Brent by a wider margin for month M than implied by the data for month M−2 (the data available to the pricing authorities when the adjustment factor was decided upon) in thirty out of the forty-five months comprised in our period. On nine occasions the differential was narrower than expected from the data,

Table 15.2: Comparison of the Adjustment Factor in Saudi Arabia's Pricing Formula (Aramco/Europe) in Month M with GPW, Freight and Refining Costs Difference in Month M−2. Dollars per Barrel. 1988–91.

Month of Application		Adjustment Factor for Month M	GPW and Freight Rate Difference in Month M-2	Discrepancy
1988:	April	−1.50	−1.85	+0.35
	May	−1.50	−1.67	+0.17
	June	−1.50	−1.34	−0.16
	July	−1.80	−1.71	−0.09
	August	−1.80	−1.80	0.00
	September	−1.80	−1.81	+0.01
	October	−1.80	−1.75	−0.05
	November	−1.80	−1.67	−0.13
	December	−1.80	−1.74	−0.06
1989:	January	−2.00	−2.12	+0.12
	February	−1.90	−1.63	−0.27
	March	−1.90	−1.92	+0.02
	April	−2.00	−1.92	−0.08
	May	−1.95	−1.66	−0.29
	June	−1.95	−1.99	+0.04
	July	−2.05	−2.21	+0.16
	August	−1.90	−1.63	−0.27
	September	−1.80	−1.58	−0.22
	October	−1.80	−1.35	−0.45
	November	−1.80	−1.49	−0.31
	December	−1.80	−1.63	−0.17
1990:	January	−1.90	−1.39	−0.51
	February	−1.90	−1.58	−0.32
	March	−1.90	−2.98	+1.08
	April	−2.00	−2.56	+0.56
	May	−2.40	−1.78	−0.62
	June	−2.40	−1.86	−0.54
	July	−2.75	−2.08	−0.67
	August	−2.75	−2.30	−0.45
	September	−2.00	−2.37	+0.37
	October	−1.20	−2.63	+1.43
	November	−1.70	−3.77	+2.07
	December	−2.70	−2.88	+0.18
1991:	January	−2.70	−2.43	−0.27
	February	−2.00	−1.67	−0.23
	March	−2.00	−1.43	−0.57
	April	−2.00	−1.89	−0.41
	May	−2.50	−2.41	−0.39
	June	−2.50	−2.46	−0.34
	July	−2.30	−1.91	−0.69
	August	−2.30	−1.79	−0.81
	September	−2.30	−1.95	−0.65
	October	−2.20	−2.02	−0.48
	November	−2.20	−2.52	+0.32
	December	−2.20	−2.17	−0.03

Sources: Adjustment factor: *MEES*. Other columns: our calculations.

and in one month only there was no discrepancy at all.

Examining closely the months M in which the adjustment factor was set at a lower level[3] than indicated by the GPW and cost data of months M–2 we find that:

(a) In three cases – September 1988, March and June 1989 – the discrepancy is of the order of US cents 1–4 and therefore negligible.
(b) In four other cases – May 1988, January and July 1989, and December 1990 – the discrepancies were between US cents 12 and 18, and therefore not very significant.
(c) In March 1990 the adjustment factor was set at a significantly lower level than indicated by the GPW and cost data of January 1990. There was a gasoil price spike at the turn of 1990 (December 1989/January 1990) which raised the GPW of Brent relative to Arabian Light which the Saudi authorities seem to have rightly treated as a temporary distortion. This suggests that judgement about the state of the market in the months ahead is made when the adjustment factor is set. Spikes shown in current data are ignored.
(d) During the Gulf crisis of 1990, the discrepancy was very high in two months – October and November 1990. Again this suggests that a judgement was made that the widening GPW differential between Brent and Arabian Light that obtained just before and in the first two months of the crisis would not persist.

Looking again at the period as a whole we observe a discontinuity. Between April 1988 and December 1989 the discrepancies were not very large. In 1990 the discrepancies were very significant and generally reflected adjustment factors set at a much lower level than indicated by the GPW and cost data available to the pricing authority at the time of setting. The picture changes in 1991 when from January to October the discrepancy reflected bigger adjustment factors than indicated by the GPW and cost data.

This analysis is about *ex ante* decisions. It reveals that the setting of adjustment factors for pricing formulae is not exclusively based on the information about the market in the recent past except when the state of the market is judged to be stable. When there is turmoil, there is an attempt, albeit not often successful, to look ahead. It also reveals changes in the Saudi intentions as regards the pricing of oil during the years 1988–91. In 1988–9 there was no apparent intention to discount the price of Arabian Light relative to Brent. In 1990 there was a view that Arabian Light would be worth more in the months ahead than contemporary information suggested, hence a tendency to set adjustment factors at a relatively low level. In 1991 the Saudi intentions seem to have changed in the opposite direction and the adjustment factors were set higher than the levels implied by the contemporary data. These are signs of competitive intentions. Things may have changed again towards the end of 1991 and in 1992. By then Saudi Arabia had achieved a production volume objective, to attain and sustain an oil output of 8.0–8.5 mb/d. At this stage a revenue-maximizer naturally begins to switch from a volume to a price objective and consequently to blunt the edge of competitive policies.

We made another comparison – the price of Arabian Light with that of Iranian Light for Far Eastern sales – as they emerge from the relevant formulae. These two crudes are close competitors. Although each country sets the adjustment factor in its own formula separately the need to remain competitive means that each one then watches closely the pricing behaviour of the other.

The results of the comparison in Table 15.3 show that most of the time the price of Arabian Light turns out to be slightly higher than Iranian Light. But from November 1989 until the Gulf crisis (August 1990–January 1991) the gap closed significantly and the differential was usually very small in the range of US cents 1.0–5.0 per barrel. The Gulf crisis was a disturbance which made price relativities move in all directions, not only in this particular instance. After the crisis, the prices of the two crudes become almost identical every month with a differential of US cents 2.0–3.0/barrel only.

These analyses of prices generated by Saudi formulae tend to confirm a description of the procedures followed by the Saudi Arabian Oil Company for setting the adjustment factor every month which we obtained from reliable sources. The procedure involves the following steps: (a) An estimation of the 'correct' differential obtained by comparing GPWs and freight rates using a refining model. The data used are the most recently available at the time of the estimation; (b) The value thus obtained is then modified on the basis of judgements that take into account information about the behaviour of competitors, a critical assessment of the views expressed by major customers in informal consultation, and a forecast of the market situation in the two or three months ahead.

The second step of this procedure explains the achievement of a close relationship between the prices of Arabian Light and Iranian Light observed in recent periods, excluding the Gulf crisis. It is also consistent with the twin observations of, first, a lack of correspondence between the adjustment factor and the underlying parameters (GPWs and so on) to which it is supposed to relate, and, secondly, lagged corrections which seem to bring, over a period of time, the average discount between Arabian Light and the equivalent Brent price close to its intended value.

In other words, oil-exporting countries, as exemplified in this illustration by Saudi Arabia, attempt to fulfil a competitive marketing objective with a combination of means: an analysis of theoretical price

Table 15.3: Comparison of Arabian Light and Iranian Light Prices as Per Formulae. Far East. Dollars/Barrel. 1989–91.

		Arabian Light	*Iranian Light*	*Difference*
1989:	January	14.62	14.42	0.20
	February	14.80	14.60	0.20
	March	16.37	16.04	0.33
	April	17.42	17.41	0.01
	May	16.21	16.07	0.14
	June	15.91	15.76	0.15
	July	15.92	15.78	0.14
	August	15.55	15.41	0.14
	September	16.17	16.03	0.14
	October	16.69	16.54	0.15
	November	16.56	16.52	0.04
	December	17.58	17.54	0.04
1990:	January	17.90	17.86	0.04
	February	16.43	16.20	0.23
	March	17.31	17.86	0.04
	April	14.76	14.74	0.02
	May	15.02	14.99	0.03
	June	13.70	13.69	0.01
	July	15.51	15.48	0.03
	August	24.87	24.44	0.43
	September	31.06	31.36	(0.30)
	October	32.49	32.51	(0.02)
	November	29.54	29.53	0.01
	December	24.48	24.11	0.37
1991:	January	20.38	20.15	0.23
	February	15.43	15.36	0.07
	March	15.94	15.87	0.07
	April	16.59	16.61	(0.02)
	May	16.45	16.43	0.02
	June	16.03	16.00	0.03
	July	16.88	16.85	0.03
	August	17.25	17.23	0.02
	September	18.49	18.46	0.03
	October	19.68	19.66	0.02
	November	19.11	19.09	0.02
	December	16.00	15.97	0.03

Source: *MEES*.

relativities, a continual reference to the behaviour of exporters of crude varieties that are close substitutes, an attention to the desiderata of their customers, and unavoidably trials and errors that lead to long, and at first sight unavoidable, sequences of adjustments. The customers put up with errors that may affect them from time to time because they can seek subsequent corrections. The term contract, by its very nature, provides the two parties with the security that time is available for adjustments and corrections. A further consideration is that moving in and out of term supply contracts involves costs. This means that a company with an established relationship with an important exporting country will be reluctant to give it up when the exit costs exceeds costs occasionally incurred through imperfect pricing.

4. The Place of Brent in Oil Pricing Formulae

Apart from Saudi Arabia which, as seen in Table 15.1, uses Brent as the reference price for sales to Europe, all of the following oil-exporting countries include Brent in pricing formulae:

1. Algeria, for Saharan Blend (44° API) and Zarzaitine (42° API)
2. Libya's price formulae for all crudes were based on 50 per cent Brent and 50 per cent products netbacks until the second quarter of 1989. Thereafter the full price reference was Brent.
3. Iran for all crudes to Europe.
4. Iraq until the UN embargo for all crudes to Europe
5. Russia prices Urals on dated Brent for term contracts.
6. Egypt now uses Brent with a 60 per cent weight as a base for setting the price of Suez Blend.
7. Syria initially used Brent, then switched to Es Sider whose price is in any case related to Brent.
8. Nigeria, for all crudes, both to Europe and the USA. This practice is probably followed by all West African exporters.
9. Mexico includes Brent in its pricing formulae for sales to Europe. It includes it also, albeit with a small weight, in some formulae for the USA.
10. The Yemen now uses Brent as a reference for the sales of Marib Light (40.4° API) to both Europe and the USA.

In 1991, world crude oil trade was estimated at just over 30 mb/d. OECD Europe total imports in 1991 (including intra-regional international trade) amounted to 10.9 mb/d, and Eastern European imports (not including the states of the CIS), amounted to 1.2 mb/d.

Total European imports, all Brent linked or Brent derived, were 12.1 mb/d. On the basis of the appendix to Chapter 14, 1.4 mb/d of US imports were solely linked to Brent (there is also 0.7 mb/d of Mexican exports that are linked to Brent and other crudes). We then have a total of 13.5 mb/d linked to Brent or some 45 per cent of world trade. When one considers Brent linked trade within Africa, and between the states of the CIS, we believe what happens in the Brent market directly affects the pricing of over 50 per cent of world trade in crude oil, or more than 15 mb/d.

We have shown elsewhere in this study that the determination of the Dubai price which serves as reference for exports to Asia (26.5 per cent of world trade) is the result of arbitrage on the Atlantic Basin where Brent is the lynchpin. Ignoring Brent influences on the price of ANS, the third world crude marker, one can safely say that, in a rather close sense, the prices of some 75 per cent of internationally traded crude oil are predicated on Brent.

5. Formula Pricing and other Pricing Systems

The old OPEC system of administered oil prices had some merits and major defects. One merit is that a reference price was posted for everyone to see. But its more important advantage for all producers – be it OPEC, non-OPEC countries or companies with upstream equity – is that it sought to provide an insurance against an oil price fall towards the very low levels set by the cost floor in the short or medium term. But it can only provide this insurance if the exporting countries that administer the price are able to absorb adverse swings in demand. In this respect OPEC proved to be very successful between 1974 and 1978, that is for a relatively short period of five years. It struggled to prevent a sharp fall in oil prices after 1980 and this uneasy period lasted another five years, that is between 1981 and 1985. The major problem with the price administration system is not, as the conventional wisdom wants us believe, the determination of price differentials with the marker crude. As we have seen in this chapter, formula pricing as now practised is inherently a system of differential pricing. And we have seen that despite many internal difficulties and inconsistencies it is made to work through trial and errors, compromises and the use of commercial common sense.

The fundamental problem of the old OPEC pricing system is that the volume of residual demand for OPEC oil is a wild variable whose movements are not entirely due to prices but to a combination of other factors (economic, geological, political). The ability to hold stable prices comes episodically under severe strain because of large variations on the call for OPEC oil. If this demand exceeds the volume of capacity available to OPEC (as happened in 1979 and in August/September 1990 for example), prices immediately rise and OPEC loses control over their levels.

Whenever demand falls short of capacity by a very significant amount (as happened between 1982 and 1989), the burden put on the residual supplier in terms of revenue and market share losses becomes intolerable. This could cause a loss of control as happened in 1986.

The alternative system, netback pricing, used extensively in 1986 is entirely geared to securing a positive refinery margin to the buyer of crude oil. Contrary to a commonly held opinion it is not netback pricing as such that causes prices to collapse, but its use in combination with a marketing policy aiming at volume maximization without any supply restraint. The main defect of netback pricing, apart from insulating one set of agents (the refiners) from the vagaries of the market, is that the absolute crude oil price emerges only *ex post* as a residual. This hinders the fulfilment of its normal economic role as the signal that helps determining *ex ante* supply and demand decisions.

The current system of market related formula pricing enables exporters to set their prices close to those of competitors in the place where crude oil is refined. In this sense it has commercial merits for both buyers and sellers. Refiners are not as fully and exclusively protected under this system as under netback pricing but are less exposed to risks of significant price discrimination. Exporting countries can more easily protect their market shares under this system than under the old OPEC price administration arrangements. Its main disadvantage however is that it does not afford by itself any protection against a significant oil price fall. The producers have no direct influence on the oil price level in this system. They can only seek this influence through production policies whose effects on prices always prove uncertain, sometimes perverse and almost always widely different (because of inevitable under or over-shooting) from the intended result.

Notes
1. A. Seymour (1990), *The Oil Price and non-OPEC Supplies*, Oxford Institute for Energy Studies.
2. See R. Mabro (1987), *Netback Pricing and the Oil Price Collapse of 1986*, Oxford Institute for Energy Studies.
3. A smaller adjustment factor than suggested by the GPW and cost data means implicit *ex ante* over-pricing of Arabian Light relative to Brent.

APPENDIX TO CHAPTER 15

A Review of Oil Pricing Formulae

A. Mexico

This appendix considers market-related pricing formulae only. The official selling price and the retroactive pricing systems of Abu Dhabi, Oman, Indonesia and Qatar were considered in Chapter 14.

In so far as we can establish, Mexico was the first major oil-exporting country to adopt a price formula system. This was introduced in March 1986 and represented Mexico's alternative to netback pricing, the method applied by several oil-exporting countries at that time, which Pemex, for good reasons, strongly disliked. Mexico's reluctance to abandon the official pricing system at the beginning of 1986 when almost everybody else was competing for market share through the netback system cost it a significant loss of export volumes. It tried to retrieve the situation with formula pricing; in the circumstances of 1986 this alternative idea may not at first have yielded better export prices than the netback system (because crude oil prices fell for a while faster than product prices which determined the netbacks). Later there may have been some convergence of results, nevertheless Mexico can claim that it pioneered a new system whatever its merits and drawbacks.

The Mexican formulae are more complex than those offered by other countries as they use more than one reference crude (in the case of Western Hemisphere sales) and involve in some instances a link with fuel oil prices. The use of several reference crudes is an insurance against the effects on occasions of erratic performance in particular markets. The reference crudes used during the period 1987–91 were a varying combination of WTI, WTS, LLS, ANS and dated Brent. WTI, however, was abandoned in August 1989 because of a realization that WTI spot price movements are sometimes strongly influenced by local factors and thus become decoupled from the general movements of world oil prices.

Pipeline crudes are prone to accidental squeezes arising from logistical difficulties. The view that pipeline crudes are unsuitable for use as reference is widespread (hence the inclusion of ANS in the pricing formulae for Western Hemisphere sales of other countries). Mexico tries to mitigate the problem by retaining a mixture of pipeline crudes (WTS and LLS), a US non-pipeline crude (ANS), and an international marker (Brent). The closeness of Isthmus properties to

Table A15.1: Mexico's Pricing Formulae, 1987-92

1. Isthmus 34° API Western Hemisphere Sales

Period	Formula
Jan 87–Jul 91	0.33 (WTI + WTS + ANS) – 0.15 (fuel oil 1%S – fuel oil 3%S) ± adj.factor
Aug 89–Apr 90	0.50 (WTS + ANS) ± adj.factor
May 90–	0.30 (WTS + LLS) + 0.20 (ANS + dated Brent) ± adj.factor

Notes: The formula of sale is f.o.b. The reference prices are Platt's spot quotes averaged five days around the date of loading (there is no lag to allow for difference between the dates of loading and delivery).

2. Isthmus 34° API European Sales

Period	Formula
Jan 87–Mar 88	0.85 (dated Brent) + 0.5 (fuel oil 3.5%S) – 0.21 (fuel oil 1%S – fuel oil 3.5%S) ± adj.factor
Apr 88–	0.887 (dated Brent) + 0.113 (fuel oil 3.5%S) – 0.16 (fuel oil 1%S – fuel oil 3.5%S) ± adj.factor

Notes: The point of sale is f.o.b. The reference prices are Platt's spot quotes averaged five days around the 15th day after loading.

3. Maya 22° API Western Hemisphere Sales

Period	Formula
Jan 87–Jul 89	0.21 (WTI+WTS+ANS) + 0.37 (fuel oil 3%S) – 0.28 (fuel oil 1%S – fuel oil 3%S) ± adj.factor
Aug 89–Apr 90	0.33 (WTS + ANS) + 0.335 (fuel oil 3%S) ± adj.factor
May 90–	0.246 (WTS) + 0.147 (ANS) + 0.099 (LLS + dated Brent) + 0.394 (fuel oil 3%S) ± adj.factor

Notes: Same as for Isthmus 34° API Western Hemisphere sales.

4. Maya 22° API European Sales

Period	Formula
Jan 87–Mar 88	0.47 (dated Brent) + 0.13 (fuel oil 3.5%S) – 0.17 (fuel oil 1%S – fuel oil 3.5%S) ± adj.factors
Apr 88–	0.527 (dated Brent) + 0.467 (fuel oil 3.5%S) – 0.25 (fuel oil 1%S – fuel oil 3.5%S) ± adj.factor

Notes: Same as for Isthmus 34° API European Sales
Source: Data supplied by PEMEX.

WTS makes it difficult to discard WTS as a reference crude; and the importance of the US Gulf Coast to Mexican sales makes the recourse as reference to Texan and Louisiana crudes, whatever the qualms, almost unavoidable.

It is in this context that the introduction of Brent as reference for sales of such a different crude as Maya in the Western Hemisphere can be explained. The inclusion of Brent, however, increases the volatility of the formula and places a burden on the adjustment factor.

The formulae are constructed in a way that seeks to equalize the refinery yield of the relevant Mexican crude with the composite yield of the set of reference crudes (given the weights attributed to them) included in the formula. The fuel oil element in the pricing formula is there to bring the two sets of yields to full equivalence and to correct for sulphur contents. These tasks are performed imperfectly by the fuel oil element and the resulting discrepancies are mitigated by changes in the adjustment factor. The freight rate element is also dealt with by the adjustment factor. Whether changes in this factor are used, in addition, as a competitive instrument cannot be established from the data.

Table A15.1 presents the formulae offered for Isthmus and Maya sales to the Western Hemisphere and Europe during the period 1987–92. The European formulae take dated Brent as the only reference crude. They involve a 15-day time lag which approximates the duration of the haul across the Atlantic. The Western Hemisphere formulae do not involve a time lag. There is also a pricing formula for Olmeca 39° API for Western Hemisphere sales introduced in August 1988 soon after the discovery of this crude. Since May 1990 it defines the Olmeca price as a simple average of the prices of WTS, LLS and dated Brent with a small adjustment factor. Mexican sales to the Far East did not use pricing formulae until October 1992. Retroactive pricing (at the end of the month) was used instead. There is little doubt that Dubai/Oman prices influenced the setting of these retroactive prices.

B. Algeria

Algeria since September 1989 has been using for its official selling price a formula of the standard type. It is dated Brent plus or minus an adjustment factor. The formula applies to Saharan Blend (44° API) and Zarzaitine (42° API). The adjustment factor is set every month and seems to be set at the same value for both crudes.

C. Iran

Iran has experienced difficulties in the marketing of its crude oil largely because of disruptions caused by the revolution and the long war with Iraq. Logistical bottlenecks put f.o.b. sales at a disadvantage, and the practice now is to sell c.i.f. Some Iranian pricing formulae reflect this fact with prices set on a c.i.f. basis at the date of delivery.

In so far as we can ascertain, the formulae for c.i.f. sales of Iranian Light (34° API) and Iranian Heavy (31° API) for Europe are dated Brent minus an adjustment factor. The pricing date is that of delivery, and prices are averaged over five days. The f.o.b. formulae also take dated Brent as a reference minus the adjustment factor. The pricing date is the 25th after loading and the market quotes are averaged over five days.

The formulae for sales to the Far East are on a f.o.b. basis. The reference crude for Iranian Light (34° API) is Oman and for Iranian Heavy (31° API) is Dubai. Market quotes for the reference crude are averaged over the month of loading. This is the common practice of Gulf countries for sales to the Far East.

D. Iraq

The price formulae for f.o.b. sales of Kirkuk (37° API) and Basrah (35° API from Ceyhan) to Europe, before the Gulf crisis of 1990-1, were dated Brent minus an adjustment factor. Interestingly the pricing date was set at only five days after loading, with market quotes averaged over ten days.

Formulae for the Far East took the Oman/Dubai average as reference plus or minus an adjustment factor. The usual monthly price averaging applied.

Formulae for the USA had ANS and sometimes in the past the average of WTI, WTS and ANS as reference price, minus an adjustment and sometimes an additional freight discounting factor. The unusual feature is a short lag between loading and pricing date which was initially between ten and fifteen days and further reduced to five days in 1990.

Although Iraqi pricing formulae were officially expressed as f.o.b. and naturally in a unique form, the Iraqi marketing approach was known to be flexible with prices often agreed cargo by cargo and buyers' preference for c.i.f. sales accommodated in many instances.

E. Libya

In the first half of 1989 Libya adopted formulae involving 50 per cent dated Brent plus or minus an adjustment factor with different values for the individual export crudes (Zueitina, Brega, Sirtica, Es Sider, Sarir and Amna), and 50 per cent products netback consisting of the following:

premium gasoline (20 per cent), jet kerosene (11 per cent), gasoil (25 per cent), low sulphur fuel oil (36 per cent), naphtha (4 per cent) less a fee for processing and freight

In the second half of 1989, it adopted the simpler formula of dated Brent plus or minus an adjustment factor. The point of sale is f.o.b. The pricing date was initially the date of loading but lags of ten to fifteen days seem to have been introduced in 1991. Market quotes are averaged over five days.

F. Egypt

Egypt used to price its crudes through official posting on a half-monthly basis. After the start of the Gulf war in August 1990 it changed to retroactive daily posting. This caused offtakers to complain about uncertainty. The system was changed in response to these complaints with effect as from 1 October 1991. The new system is formula pricing for Suez Blend (33° API). The formula consists of (60 per cent Brent minus an adjustment factor) + (20 per cent Iranian Heavy minus an adjustment factor) + (20 per cent Spot Suez Blend). The adjustment factors are set twice a month. Market quotes are averaged over five days.

Other Egyptian crudes are each linked to Suez Blend by an adjustment factor also set twice a month.

The structure of the Egyptian formula is therefore close to the Mexican in that it attempts to set as reference a synthetic crude with similar refining properties to Suez Blend.

G. Nigeria

The Nigerian formulae for sales to the USA and Europe are all of the general form: dated Brent plus or minus an adjustment factor. The formulae are f.o.b. It seems that since December 1990 pricing for all destinations is based on the average of five market quotes from the 14th to the 19th day after loading.

Press reports suggest that pricing is not uniform as among buyers, and that the option of netback pricing is sometimes given. We have not been able to verify these reports.

H. Syria

The Syrian pricing formula for Syrian Light (37° API) is of the standard type, reference crude plus or minus an adjustment factor. The reference crude was initially Brent then changed in November 1990 to Es Sider. The basis is f.o.b. Banyas with market quotes averaged over five days. The pricing date is five days after loading (sales to Europe).

I. Yemen

For sales to Europe of Alif, renamed in 1988 Marib Light, the pricing formula until the end of 1988 used as reference the average price of Brent and Dubai. This was changed to dated Brent as from January 1989. For sales to the USA the reference was also the average price of Brent and Dubai until the end of 1988. This was then replaced by WTI, a very rare choice of a reference crude, between January and September 1989. From then on, WTI was abandoned and there is only one reference crude for sales to all destinations, which is dated Brent. The pricing formula is f.o.b. Ras 'Isa, with pricing date on day of loading and market quotes averaged over five days – two days before through two days after the loading date.

J. Kuwait

Kuwait's pricing formula for sales to the Far East is of the standard type. The reference price is the average of Oman and Dubai plus or minus an adjustment factor. Kuwait however has a clause in its contracts providing for price revisions (quarterly) that take into account the prices generated by Saudi formulae for Arabian Medium.

K. Vietnam

Vietnam sells most of its production to Japan through term contracts. It links the prices of its major export grade (Bach Ho, 33° API) to the APPI quotation for Indonesian Minas. APPI quotations and their defects were discussed in Chapter 14.

CHAPTER 16

CONCLUSIONS

1. Introduction

The prices of crude oil in international trade, or more precisely the prices which serve as markers for physical crude oil transactions across national borders, and within free-market economies, emerge from a small constellation of spot, forward and futures markets that deal with Brent in the North Sea, WTI in the USA, and Dubai in the Gulf. This study has shown that a set of Brent markets (the dated, the 15-day forward and the IPE futures market) plays a central and leading role in the formation of crude oil prices in large parts of the world. The focus of our study on the Brent market is entirely due to its centrality in pricing, and to its privileged place in the web of inter-relationships that links it closely with Dubai, WTI and other marker crudes.

The proposition that Brent is at the heart of *crude oil price formation* does not provide us, however, with a complete understanding of this most important subject. A full picture involves a study of the structure of the world petroleum market and of its constituent parts, an analysis of the influence that OPEC and other institutional or political factors may have on prices, and of the modes of operations of the particular markets in which marker prices emerge.

An assessment of these various issues would help in clarifying the debate between those who argue that world oil prices are determined by the interplay of economic forces in a market typical of any primary commodity; and those who emphasize the significance of non-economic factors (which include the policies of OPEC and of oil-consuming countries) in the formation of energy prices.

2. The Structure of the World Petroleum Market

We have seen that the world petroleum market broadly consists of two parts.

The first is the large physical market for crude oil exports from most OPEC countries and many producers in the developing world, such as Mexico, Syria, the Yemen and so on. This market involves an interface between these oil-exporting countries or their national oil companies on the selling side, and oil companies or commodity traders from the rest of the world on the buying side. The numbers of buyers and sellers are fairly large. They continually engage in arm's length transactions undertaken within the framework of commercial contracts.

As discussed in Chapter 15, oil is generally priced in these contracts through formulae which take as their main parameter the price of a marker crude: either Brent, or Oman/Dubai, or ANS. Pricing methods other than formulae, such as retroactive and differential pricing, are sometimes used; but these methods rely also on the prices of the same set of marker crudes.

This 'producing-countries market' covers the bulk of physical crude oil movements in international trade. Although precise estimates are difficult to make, it may be assumed rather conservatively that the volume involved is of the order of 25 mb/d, representing 80 per cent of the total amount of world crude oil exports in 1991 or 1992 (31 mb/d). Despite its size and significance very little is ever said or written about this very large segment of the world petroleum market. The reason is that the most interesting questions about the behaviour of participants, the bargaining tactics of oil companies and commodity traders who lift oil in this market, and the commercial strategies of the sellers, governments or national oil companies, cannot be researched because information is shrouded in commercial secrecy.

The second constituent part of the world petroleum market has a much smaller physical base. It is comprised of the set of spot, forward and futures markets for the marker crudes mentioned before, and other spot markets for certain OPEC and non-OPEC crudes. These 'marker crudes markets' *make* prices which the 'producing-countries market' *takes* as reference in pricing formulae.

At first sight there seems to be a complete dichotomy between these two parts of the world petroleum market. The smaller segment that deals with marker crudes displays all the attributes of a market as a place where economic agents can buy and sell oil using a wide, and continually evolving, range of trading instruments. These were described in Chapter 4. They can be used not only to lift physical oil but for hedging and speculation. The prices generated in this segment of the world market have a term structure and thus provide information about both the current and the expected supply/demand balance in future months.

The larger segment, where the bulk of physical oil in international trade changes hands, is also a market precisely because there is buying and selling between willing parties. But the role of the 'producing-countries market' in price formation is more difficult to define. On the face of it this market appears to be completely passive since it takes marker prices as they emerge and uses them almost automatically in pricing formulae.

In fact there are interactions between the 'marker crudes' and the 'producing-countries markets'.

First, although the producing countries take the marker crude prices as given they exercise discretion in setting the adjustment coefficients in pricing formulae. These coefficients, which define the differential between the marker price and that of the export crude concerned, are set at regular intervals on the basis of a judgement about relevant market conditions, that is the state of competition and the balance of bargaining power between the producing country and its customers. The prices at which the producing countries sell their crudes are not therefore rigidly determined by marker crudes. A producing country may underprice its crude relatively to the market in order to increase sales, or overprice it when it wishes to reduce exports or when it judges that general supply conditions are tight and that buyers can therefore be made to pay more.

The ways in which adjustment coefficients are set provide information to the 'marker crudes market' about producing countries' perceptions and commercial strategies. This information is bound to influence the formation of marker prices.

The second and most important influence exercised by producing countries on the 'marker crudes markets' arises from the strong perception that some OPEC member countries, more particularly Saudi Arabia, are vested with significant potential power over oil supplies.

This power is not only a function of size, of the fact that the main OPEC member countries produce large volumes of oil and are endowed with considerable petroleum reserves. Saudi Arabia's power over supplies also arises from unusual technical flexibility in oil production and from financial strength.

On the technical side, the rate of oil output can be varied, up and down, over a wide range in Saudi Arabia as was abundantly demonstrated in the 1980s (when output fell from 11.0 mb/d to less than 3 mb/d over a period of five years) and during the Iraq–Kuwait crisis of 1990 (when output was increased by 3 mb/d over three months). These rates can therefore be changed very rapidly, and, in many instances, without great additions to production costs. This is due, first, to the existence of a cushion of surplus capacity in Saudi Arabia even at times when production levels are thought to be high; and, secondly, to favourable technical characteristics of the oilfields which enable production rates to be varied without serious loss of pressure or damages to the reservoirs.

On the financial side, Saudi Arabia has a greater ability to cope with reduced oil revenues than most other OPEC countries (except the UAE and Kuwait). Although its financial position has been much weakened in recent years the perception that it is a wealthy country dies hard. Hence the belief that Saudi Arabia's power over oil supplies is not constrained by insuperable financial problems.

Furthermore Saudi Arabia has been seen since the early 1970s as a leader in the world of oil with responsibilities that are not limited to OPEC and its fellowships. The OECD countries, developing nations, the oil and other energy industries and international financial institutions hold Saudi Arabia ultimately responsible whenever the price of oil moves sharply and in a destabilizing manner. They expect it to act whenever there is a price crisis, that is a sudden and significant rise or the threat of a price collapse.

The complication, however, is that Saudi Arabia resents being burdened with such heavy responsibilities and being cast in the role of the residual supplier. The official policy, emphatically and repeatedly stated on many occasions since the mid 1980s by the King himself and his ministers, is that Saudi Arabia will never again play this role *on its own*. It will always require full co-operation from other OPEC member countries and seek that of some non-OPEC producers. There is no reason to doubt that these statements accurately reflect Saudi intentions. As this is the case, and considering that since 1986 OPEC member countries have rarely manifested a genuine commitment to a collective production policy, one may question the relevance of Saudi Arabia's potential power over supplies. Some may wish to argue that although this potential power exists, the unwillingness to use it, combined with the continuing failure of other producers to co-operate, rob it of much of its significance.

It would be wrong to go that far. The correct view about the role of Saudi Arabia (and by implication OPEC) in influencing the 'marker crudes market' involves different aspects that may appear contradictory but must be held together. The first is that the potential power over supplies is real and significant because of size, financial and technical flexibility. The second is that Saudi Arabia has been unwilling to use this power in the past seven years. The third is that the power over supplies cannot be ignored because Saudi Arabia may at any time decide to reverse its current policy stance in pursuit of some economic or political objective, or in retaliation against inimical energy policies of consuming countries. The fourth is that Saudi Arabia may be called upon again by the USA or other important countries to play again the role of residual supplier in certain circumstances.

All this means that the 'marker crudes market' will generally tend to ignore the possibility of effective OPEC or Saudi intervention on supplies when oil prices fluctuate within sight of the level which OPEC takes for its preferred target (this is generally believed to be $18/barrel for the OPEC basket of light crudes despite the frequent but unconvincing reference to a target of $21/barrel made since July 1990). And it will take into account the possibility of policy intervention over supplies when oil prices begin to move some distance away from the OPEC target.

The influence of the 'producing-countries market' on the formation of marker crude prices is therefore twofold. First, this market contributes to the short-term price volatility of marker prices when it signals increases in competition over export volumes or, on the contrary, a tightening of supplies. These signals take different forms: from changes in the adjustment coefficients of price formulae and changes in the volume of producing countries' stocks (particularly those held close to the main oil-importing regions) to official statements from OPEC ministers about their production policies. These signals are watched carefully by market participants. Hence, the importance of news about OPEC, and more particularly about Saudi Arabia. Needless to add, some degree of short-term price volatility provides an incentive to trade, and is therefore welcome to market participants.

Secondly, the producing countries, either on their own, or as a result of political pressures from a wider coalition of interests are capable of occasional, but effective, intervention on the oil supply front. They are perceived as the guarantor of oil prices in *the last resort*. They are expected to act when prices move outside a band whose limits are more a matter of judgement than precise definition. And it is this belief which may lead market participants to reverse the direction of a movement that takes prices outside this band. The mechanism is simple. A price fall is reversed when an increasing number of participants start buying when they think that the decline has gone too far and may cause an OPEC intervention. Conversely a price rise is reversed by an increased propensity to sell from participants who think that the price increase will trigger some action.

The world petroleum market thus consists of two parts which interact in specific ways. The large 'producing-countries market' which takes the prices that emerge in the 'marker crudes market' has some influence on their formation. The first linkage (the price taking) between the two sets is strong, the second (the producing countries' influence) is generally weak, always dependent on perceptions and only manifesting itself in special circumstances.

It is precisely for these reasons that the Brent market which leads in the formation of marker crude prices is of particular significance. So much depends on Brent in the world petroleum market that it is necessary to ask searching questions about its mode of operations, the economic behaviour of its participants, its relationships with other crude oil markets and its future, which may become threatened by a narrowing of the physical base.

3. Brent

The Brent market emerged during the 1980s in response to fundamental changes in the structure of the world petroleum industry following vertical de-integration in the OPEC region and a very significant growth in non-OPEC production and exports. De-integration naturally required the development of external markets for large volumes of oil which previously moved within (or between) a small group of major oil companies. The emergence of sizeable and growing amounts of non-OPEC oil for exports called for the development of hedging mechanisms because most non-OPEC countries did not participate in the OPEC system of administered prices.

A number of special features and circumstances favoured the emergence of a market suitable for price discovery, hedging and speculation in the North Sea. The physical base (production and exports volume) was adequate, the location near the large consuming region of NW Europe favourable to trade both because of the presence of buyers and the short haul between crude oil export terminals and refining centres. Production in the North Sea was in the hands of private oil companies better equipped than national oil corporations and governments to use effectively the wide range of trading instruments imported from financial and other commodity markets. Finally, the UK oil tax regime created additional incentives for developing a market for North Sea crudes. Oil companies producing in the North Sea needed an external market where oil prices are discovered and established for fiscal purposes. They also needed it for undertaking tax optimization exercises. These involve arm's length transactions by vertically integrated companies whenever the price of oil in open market sales happens to be lower than the fiscally assessed price for internal transactions between the producing and refining subsidiaries of the oil corporation. It also involves complex uses of trading instruments for shifting profits from the upstream sector, where they are subject to high taxation rates, to the trading department of the company where they are more lightly imposed. Tax optimization was partly responsible for the birth of the 15-day Brent market, and continued to provide a motivation to trade until the end of the period covered in this study (1992) despite several reforms of the UK oil fiscal regime.

This incentive to trade which the fiscal regime involved for UKCS producers liable to PRT has nothing to do with the economic functions of markets: exchange, hedging and speculation. Tax optimization influences trading patterns and therefore price formation. But it is impossible to say whether the influence on prices is of a random nature or involves systematic biases. All those, other than North Sea producers, who have an interest in the outcome of the Brent market have reasons to feel uneasy about an important marker price subject to influences that are not well understood.

The 15-day Brent market has other unusual features: (a) One of these is the five o'clock closing time in the nomination procedure which could continue to give rise to litigation by aggrieved parties in the future. We have not been able to find a plausible alternative to the five o'clock rule which may well remain an inevitable feature of the market; (b) Another unusual characteristic of 15-day Brent lies in the discretion enjoyed by producers in determining the loading window in the delivery month. This feature can easily be explained by infrastructural reasons: the need to spread evenly the slots for tankers' liftings over the month. It has nevertheless important implications as it causes dealings on 15-day Brent for a particular month to take place at times when other deals for that month are being nominated. For this reason there is no punctual convergence between 15-day Brent and dated Brent prices. The absence of convergence provides opportunities for further dealings and arbitrage; (c) The discretion enjoyed by producers over the nomination schedule puts buyers at a disadvantage. When they buy a cargo for a forward month they do not know the day of the relevant month on which their contract will mature. We believe that the generous concession given to buyers in the form of a 5 per cent lifting tolerance is meant as a compensation for the disadvantage suffered by the nomination procedure. This study has shown that the lifting tolerance is widely used by buyers to their benefit.

These odd features are not completely neutral in their effects on short-term price movements, but we have not found evidence that the impact is significant.

More worrying perhaps for economists who have reasons to prefer very competitive markets to those which are dominated by a small number of agents, is that the degree of market concentration has tended to increase in 15-day Brent in the years 1990–1. The number of significant participants in this market has always been small but their share of total transactions has recently increased. The main participants consist of four or five Wall Street institutions and commodity traders, and seven or eight oil companies, most of the latter with producing interests in the North Sea. In 1991-2 there was no significant participant from outside these two groups. Even the sogo shosha's involvement which was large in the mid-1980s declined rapidly towards the end of that decade and became negligible in the early 1990s.

We have found that 15-day Brent is a robust market, despite its many odd features and its informal nature. Some may say, however, that informality is its real strength. This market has not yet suffered from a shortage of liquidity. It has been able to deal successfully with occasional squeezes and odd cases of default which ended up in court. It survived the traumas of 1986, and proved resilient to the changes in fiscal procedures introduced by the OTO in 1987. Although the benefits from tax optimization trading strategies became smaller, they remained positive and thus continued to provide UKCS producers with an incentive to participate. More impressively, the producers found a solution to the problem which the market faced when the production of Brent blend declined in the late 1980s. Co-mingling of Brent and Ninian streams restored the physical base of the market.

Price formation in the Brent market involves the relationships between its constituent parts – 15-day, dated and IPE. The IPE provides price data immediately available on the screens. This information influences pricing in the 15-day Brent market because it is immediately available to all participants. But the prices of 15-day Brent themselves are not as immediately and perfectly transparent to the outside world as futures prices. Market participants are inclined to argue that this does not matter because prices are transparent to them. This is not entirely true however. Participants in the forward Brent market are continually engaged in conversation with fellow participants, brokers and price reporting agencies for the purpose of price discovery.

The futures contracts are settled on the IPE price index which is the average price of 15-day Brent on their expiry day every month. There is thus a loop which links forward and futures trading, and it is difficult to single out one of them as an autonomous centre of price formation.

Dated Brent which is widely used in price formulae is a market involving a limited number of transactions. Until 1990 the average number of deals a month was of the order of 15-20 but there was a noticeable increase in 1991 when the average was about thirty-five deals and appears to have increased during the year. Dated Brent is not traded for an outright price (we only observed one such instance in 1991) but as a differential to forward. This feature brings the focus back on the 15-day market which seems to play the central role in the formation of the Brent price used as a marker by many producing countries.

The relationships between Brent and other marker crudes are both complex and interesting. We have seen that while Brent is the marker for the pricing of crude oil exports to Europe and of some sales to the USA, Dubai (sometimes together with Oman) is the marker for the Far East, and ANS for a large proportion of crude oil exports to the USA. The important finding about Dubai in this study is that its price is arbitraged in the Atlantic Basin, not in the Far East where Dubai is used as a marker crude. This implies a very strong link between Brent and Dubai; stronger indeed than may be inferred from the well documented fact that Dubai is generally traded as a differential on Brent.

ANS is a crude whose market, active as it may be in certain places and certain seasons, lacks sufficient visibility. Its price is assessed on the basis of market 'talk' to a greater extent than is the case for other crudes. The price assessment also refers to WTI, the typical US domestic crude. For this reason there is at some remove a link with Brent. Because of cross-hedging and arbitrage the Brent and WTI price movements tend to correlate, albeit less perfectly than one may expect. The imperfections are largely due to pipeline logistics which drive the WTI market and crude oil price relationships in the USA, and to the ban on the exports of US crudes which makes WTI a purely domestic commodity. These imperfections, however, should not distract us from the main observation: that WTI prices generally move in some harmony with Brent.

All that builds a picture of the world petroleum market in which crude oil *relative* prices find their equilibrium in the Atlantic basin thanks to efficient arbitrage. Price movements become more erratic, and their relationships more distorted, the further one moves away from the Atlantic basin. The analogy of a cantilever which is fixed at one end and subject to deflection at the free end aptly illustrates the point.

A number of conclusions about Brent may now be drawn. Brent owes its role and significance in the formation of world crude oil prices to a mixture of historical circumstances and favourable structural factors which were mentioned before: location, the fairly large production volume particularly after co-mingling with Ninian, diversified ownership of production, in the Brent and Ninian systems, and the excellent infrastructure at Sullom Voe for lifting the blend. Brent, partly because it is a UKCS blend of crude, benefits from the support of major oil companies which have a strong interest in its continuing existence and smooth performance for the purposes of price discovery, hedging and fiscal optimization.

In fact Brent emerged to its privileged position partly because of a lack of meaningful alternatives. It compares well with the WTI market which deals with a domestic crude subject to squeezes because of pipeline bottlenecks and to many other local influences. It compares very well indeed with Dubai which has a very narrow (and recently declining) physical base and suffers from suspicions about standards of behaviour; and with ANS which is neither very transparent nor sufficiently liquid. And there are no other autonomous centres of oil price formation outside the markets for these marker crudes. OPEC has ceased to administer prices (even if it attempts from time to time to influence the direction of their movements) since 1986 and has not evolved a market within its own region that could generate a reference price.

But does Brent have a future? For evident reasons, Brent will eventually give way to another crude or blend because of a shrinkage of the physical base. The volume of the co-mingled streams may not be large enough to support efficient trading by the end of this century. We agreed in Chapter 9 that Forties may be the most likely successor to Brent.

The existence of a large physical base is not however a sufficient condition for continuing trading. The survival of the 15-day Brent market also depends on the willingness of two main groups of participants – oil companies and Wall Street refiners – to continue to trade within its framework. We believe that this willingness will remain, partly for fiscal reasons, and more significantly for hedging purposes. The fiscal motive will only disappear if PRT were to be abolished (the 1993 Finance Bill lowered the PRT rate on old fields and exempted new ones but did not do away with this tax), or when the market valuation principle is to be replaced by another method of evaluation. The latter is unlikely.

The 15-day Brent market is not significant *by itself* for hedging purposes but plays an important role in this respect because of its relationship with the IPE futures market. The IPE, which offers greater, more flexible, and ever expanding opportunities for hedging and speculation, is critically predicated on the forward market. The IPE futures contract which does not involve physical deliveries would not be workable without a physical forward market. Any party interested in the survival of the IPE contract as a hedging and speculation instrument is by the same token committed to the survival of 15-day Brent.

4. Oil Prices and Markets

We have argued in a previous section of this chapter that the world price of oil is determined in the 'marker crude markets' which are themselves subject to some influence from the larger 'producing-countries market' that takes their price. The smaller set of markets leads in this relationship because the intervention of producing countries – be it OPEC, or a sub-set of member states, or Saudi Arabia – is occasional and often weak.

The question is whether Brent and other 'marker crude markets' can set world oil prices in an economically meaningful and efficient way? This issue begs at least three further questions.

(a) What is the nature and quality of the information available to the 'marker crude markets', and how much 'noise' affects price formation?
(b) Are the 'marker crude markets' at the economic margin of the world petroleum system?
(c) Can 'marker crude markets' which are mainly concerned with price relatives, as we have seen in this study, determine the economic price level of oil?

This set of questions may not yield definitive answers but give rise to certain considerations.

(a) *Information and Noise.* Brent, and other marker crude, markets are regional in character. Although they receive much information from outside they are naturally affected by local news and shocks. To give one example, the shut-down of a North Sea platform for maintenance works, or as a result of an accident, often has a disproportionate effect on prices. Marker prices tend to move sharply in response to a regional demand/supply imbalance which may well be insignificant in relation to the real state of the global balance.

The absence of major oil-producing countries and other important parties from these 'marker crude markets' that set oil prices for the world means that trading does not reflect significant information available to all the key economic agents. Prices move in response to the dealings of minor agents which interpret, second hand, always partially, and often incorrectly information about supply, demand, stocks and, most importantly, the policies of producing countries.

There are other imperfections. Tax optimization strategies may move short-term prices in directions which are totally unrelated to fundamental expectations about supply and demand. Cross-hedging by Wall Street speculators brings exogenous forces from other primary commodity or foreign exchange markets to bear on oil prices irrespective of prevailing conditions in the petroleum world. The disturbing feature, here, is the concentration of transaction volumes in 15-day Brent (which also applies, albeit to a lesser degree, to both spot and futures Brent) in the hands of a few Wall Street refiners with widespread speculative interests in areas other than oil.

(b) *The Economic Margin.* Brent, and all other markers, are not incremental crudes on the supply side of the world petroleum market. The supply margin is where the large Gulf producers are, not in the North Sea, the USA or in such a minor producing state as Dubai. It is disturbing for an economist to observe a commodity whose price is set by an intra-marginal source of supplies. The argument sometimes advanced in defence of Brent that its price equilibrates in the short term the market of a major consuming region, and that this role cannot be performed by the Gulf incremental crudes without long delays (because of the long haul) is not very convincing. These delays can be bridged either physically through stock changes, or financially through forward and futures trading. The question of why intra-marginal crudes have become price setters for world oil is for producing countries to answer.

(c) *Price Relatives.* The markets that make the oil price are largely concerned with price relatives. This is clearly reflected in the composition of transactions as between spread and outright deals. The fundamental reason for this dominant interest in spreads and differentials as opposed to absolute price levels lies in the composition of economic agents involved in oil trading.

Only two groups are primarily interested in absolute prices: producing countries and final consumers. Neither is very active on the price-setting markets. Some important participants are essentially concerned with differentials: refiners with the margins between crude and product prices and, of course, crude differentials; and Wall Street and other speculators with all types of price spreads.

The participants in 'marker crude markets' are not in a position to set the level around which oil prices can safely fluctuate in the short term. Economics does not provide them with very useful information in this context. It only says that the competitive cost floor for the price of crude oil is in the range of $3–7/barrel and that the monopolistic ceiling is probably of the order of $30–45/barrel, as a guess estimate. But everybody in the market, and outside it, knows that neither the floor, nor the ceiling are politically acceptable. If oil prices were to fall to the level of the cost floor, energy industries around the world would either be decimated or require huge subsidies. Many OECD governments would not cherish this prospect, not only for budgetary but for strategic reasons of energy security. The fall in oil revenues would also destabilize many oil-producing countries in the third world, and this represents a political risk which the USA, Europe and Japan may not be willing to accept.

Conversely if oil prices were to rise close to the monopolistic ceiling, the world economy would be threatened with severe recession and the oil-producing countries would fear the consequences of long-term losses in their share of world energy markets.

The 'marker crude markets' are therefore left to their own perceptions to decide about the width of the band within which oil prices can safely fluctuate. The political factor in oil pricing is not OPEC, Saudi Arabia, OECD or the USA, but a market perception of what these various powers would like to happen. Whether the perception is sharp or muddled is often impossible to say. Pity the market, in any case, because it continually observes political agents who are sometimes themselves unclear about their own objectives and policies.

We can only conclude that the world oil price made by markets is not an economic market price. However, this is not an undesirable state of affairs. The economic price obtained under competitive conditions may prove extremely disruptive, inflicting higher costs on the world economy than the benefit derived from theoretically correct allocative efficiency.

This study, thus, concludes with a paradox. We have argued that there is much to be desired in the current mechanisms of crude oil price formation. There are too many oddities, defects and flaws for comfort. At the same time, we are inclined to argue that any attempt to improve this second-best state of affairs may worsen the situation if attempted without great care and deep understanding.

We are not advocating, however, a complacent acceptance of the status quo. On the contrary, our belief is that the governments of both producing and consuming countries, the oil industry and other economic agents with direct or indirect interests in oil often tend to be complacent. The place of oil in world trade and in the international economy requires more serious consideration than it is receiving from those who believe, or are being induced to believe, that everything must be in good order because it is dealt with efficiently by invisible hands in The Market.

INDEX

Abse, Dannie 107
Abu Dhabi 158, 220, 265–70, 282, 309
Abu Dhabi National Oil Company (ADNOC) 267–70
Adelman, M.A. 4
Aerochem 145
Agip 261
Agreement for the Sale of Brent Blend Crude Oil on 15-Day Terms 40, 41, 78, 121, 124, 141, 200–1
Alaskan North Slope crude oil, *see* ANS
Algeria 38, 158, 170, 261–2, 306, 311
Alif crude oil 314
Alwyn North field 11, 15, 19
Amerada Hess 21, 25, 213, 220, 250, 278, 281
Amerex Petroleum 210
American Petroleum Institute (API) 162, 176, 243
Amna crude oil 313
Amoco 21
Andersen, R.W. 175
Anglo-Suisse 101
Angola 256–7, 259
Annex B permission 11, 12, 21, 36, 147
ANS crude oil 3, 5, 39, 81, 121, 155, 159–61, 277–81, 294, 299, 307, 309, 312, 316, 323–4
ANS forward market 277–80
 partial ANS 278
 tolerance 121, 278
Antwerp, Rotterdam, Amsterdam area (ARA) 46, 155, 232–3, 236, 238
AP Dow Jones 158
Asian Petroleum Price Index (APPI) 165, 271, 273–6, 314
Arabian Heavy crude oil 295
Arabian Light crude oil 74, 210, 291, 295–6, 299, 301, 303–4
Arabian Medium crude oil 314
Aramco partners 299–301
Aran Energy 22
Arcadia 213
Argyl field 245
Atlantic basin 22, 33–4, 38, 76, 256, 307, 311, 323
Atlantic Richfield Company (ARCO) 22, 227–8, 231, 278, 281
Attock 103
Australia 270–1
Austria 26, 116
Avant 141

Bach Ho crude oil 314
Backwardation 44, 45, 48, 91, 134, 179–83, 185, 218, 224, 270
Baghdad 169
Banque Paribas 275
Banyas 314
Basis risk 87–8, 108, 110, 118, 255, 280
Basrah crude oil 312
BBQ crude oil basket 259
Bear Stearns 104

Beatrice crude oil 245
Beaumont, Texas 228
Beryl crude oil 245
Binks, Adrian 6
Bloomberg 156
Bonny Light crude oil 158, 256, 259
BP 21–2, 25, 29, 33–4, 78, 104, 119, 141–3, 148–9, 210, 213, 250–1, 256, 259, 274, 278, 279
Brass River crude oil 259
Brazil 26
Brega crude oil 312
Brent blend 11–13, 26, 38, 41, 47, 76–8, 104, 147–50, 155
 cargo sizes 34–5
 co-mingling with Ninian 13, 15, 20, 26, 104, 147, 244, 322–3
 consumption (UK) 33
 consumption (US) 34
 exports 31
 gravity 19–21
 lifting 28, 29
 lifting tolerance 29, 111, 119, 121, 124, 126–30, 161, 321
 producers of 25, 26, 42, 43, 137, 138
 quality 19–21, 251, 254
Brent field 11, 13, 15, 18–21, 26, 35–7, 255
Brent forward market 40–3, 47–9, 56, 57, 101, 109, 113, 116, 128–30, 132, 143, 169, 180–3, 185–7, 199–205, 208–9, 211, 215, 231–2, 245–6, 282, 299, 315, 320–2, 324
 bookouts 40–2, 48, 50, 127, 141, 202
 chains 42, 84, 113–14, 116, 120–2, 124, 126–30, 134, 137, 139–41, 145, 183, 185, 200–2, 208–9, 255
 clearing process 42–3
 concentration 95, 100–1, 103–5, 146, 321, 325
 discipline 79, 138, 146
 efficiency 185–7
 five o'clocking 41–3, 78, 113, 118, 127, 129, 140–1, 145, 183, 200, 321
 forwardness 89–92, 198
 future of 147–50, 324
 and IPE Brent futures 46, 203–6
 and IPE EFPs 50, 52
 loading procedures 29
 loading ranges 41
 nominations 40–3, 78, 114, 145, 209, 321
 origin 73–9
 parcel size 28
 partial Brent 28–9, 47, 57
 participants 94–5, 100–1, 103–5, 107, 322
 reform proposals 80, 130, 141
 squeezes 130–5, 137–8
 tolerance game 121, 124, 126–30, 202
 volume 84, 85, 87–9, 93, 201
Brent pipeline system '2, 11, 13, 15–16, 18–19, 21–2, 25–6, 35, 111, 137, 147, 244
Brent platforms

Index   329

Alpha 13, 18
Bravo 13, 18
Charlie 13, 16
Delta 16
Brent price 82, 110, 118–19, 130, 132, 134, 137, 156, 161–2, 164, 165, 171–2, 174–5, 183, 187, 204–5, 207, 221, 236, 238–41, 243, 246, 248, 250, 274, 282, 299, 304, 321–2
  price assessment 161–2, 165
  price history 167, 169, 170
  time structure 179–83, 185
  volatility 171–3
Brent refinery yields 234, 236
Brent Spar 13, 15, 18
Brent spot, see Dated Brent
British Gas 25
British National Oil Corporation (BNOC) 62, 67, 76–8
Britoil 22, 25
Brokers 111–12
Burmah 25

C Itoh 213
Cabinda crude oil 259
California 157–9, 161, 277, 279
Cameroon 256–7, 259
Canada 26, 31, 116, 277
Cano Limon crude oil 159, 277
Cargill 104, 116, 119, 130, 145, 147, 213
Ceyhan 312
Chartism 185
Chevron 21, 34, 54, 256–7
Chicago, Illinois 225, 228, 280
Chicago Board of Trade 225, 280–81
Chicago Mercantile Exchange 225
Chicago Research and Trading (CRT) 54
China 270
Cinta crude oil 274
Claymore field 21
Colombia 277
Commodities and Futures Trading Commission (CFTC) 54, 142–5, 225
Compagnie Française des Pétroles (CFP) (or Total) 21, 105, 213, 257, 259
Concentration of Brent production 26, 75
Congo 256–7, 259
Conner, Judge D. 143–5
Conoco 21–2, 78, 140–4, 208–9, 213, 251
Contango 44–5, 48, 91, 134, 179–83, 185, 218
Contract for differences (CFD) 56, 183
Convenience yield 181, 203
Cook Inlet crude oil 277
Cormorant Alpha 13, 16, 18, 20, 26, 115, 169
Corporation tax 36, 37, 60–1, 64
Corpus Christi, Texas 228
Cosmo 103
Crédit Suisse 275
Crescent 213
Cruden Bay 244
Cushing, Oklahoma 46, 131, 227–9, 231–2, 241
Cyrus field 245
Czechoslovakia 116

D'Amato, Senator 144
Danthine, J.P. 175

Data sources 6, 83
Date swap 113, 119
Dated Brent 43, 48, 113–16, 118–20, 126, 130, 132, 140, 160–1, 183, 185, 201, 203–5, 235, 246, 250–1, 254–5, 259, 264, 282, 309, 312–3, 315, 322
  definition 40, 113
  forwardness 114, 118
  price, see Price of dated Brent
  price assessment 165
  price determination 116, 118–19
  specifications 160
  swap 56
  volume 115
  wet chains 115–16, 119
De-integration 73–5, 320
Default 139–40, 142, 145–6
Denmark 251
Department of Trade and Industry (DTI) 143–4
Derivatives 109–10, 156
Deveron field 11, 13, 21
Diesel 37
Distillates 233–4, 238, 240–1
Don field 11, 13, 15, 19
Drake, Edwin 171
Dubai forward market 3, 44–5, 81, 155, 101, 150, 207–13, 215, 218–20, 240, 265, 267–9, 282, 299, 315, 323–4, 326
  bookout 209
  chains 209
  concentration 215
  general terms and conditions (GTCs) 208–9
  and Gulf official selling prices 267–8
  nominations 209
  partial Dubai 210
  participants 210, 213, 215
  prices 218–19, 221–2, 224, 238, 240, 269, 274, 282, 294
  price assessment 165, 211–2
  tolerance 121, 208
  volume 211–2, 215
Dubai, futures markets for 210, 274, 280
Dunbar field 11, 21
Dunlin Alpha 13
Dunlin field 11, 13, 15, 22, 25
Duri crude oil 270
Dusak, K. 182

E4 234
Ecuador 277, 281
Efficient markets hypothesis 185–7, 239–40
Egypt 159, 261–2, 295, 306, 313
Eider field 11, 15, 21
Ekofisk crude oil 245–6, 248
Elf 213, 257
Energy demand 292
Energy efficiency 292
Enterprise Oil 25, 250
Erskine field 148
Es Sider 262, 264, 306, 312, 314
Europ-Oil Prices 157
Europe 3, 33, 52, 73–4, 105, 110, 118, 149–50, 157–8, 162, 164, 173, 183, 205, 207, 218–19, 221–2, 232–4, 241, 243, 250, 254, 256, 261–62, 264, 270, 274, 294, 296, 299, 301, 306–7, 311–14, 320, 323, 327

330   Oil Markets and Prices

Exchange of futures for physical (EFP)   46, 50–2, 56, 164, 198, 200–1, 203–4, 227, 281
Exchange of futures for swap (EFS)   56
Exxon   22, 26, 28, 33, 104, 116, 129, 130, 140–4, 213, 250–1, 278

Far East   57, 74, 164–5, 211, 213, 219, 221–2, 224, 240, 243, 256, 270–1, 273–4, 277, 281–2, 294, 296, 299, 304, 311–12, 314, 323
Far North Liquids and Associated Gas System (FLAGS)   19
Fina   257
Finland   26
First National   111
Flotta crude oil   148, 245, 281
Forcados crude oil   256–7, 259
Forties
   blend   33, 76, 78, 148–50, 245
   field   21, 36–7, 255
   forward market   255
   pipeline system   148–9, 244
   quality   251, 254
   spot trade   246, 250
France   26, 116, 232
Frigg pipeline system   19
Fulmar field   148, 245
Futures markets, *see* IPE and NYMEX

Gabon   256–7, 259
Gannet field   148
Gas   19
Gas Levy   36
Gasoil   233, 238–41
Gasoline   37, 169, 233–4, 240–1
Gatoil   139–41, 145–6
Genoa   232
Germany   26, 31, 116, 158, 232
Gippsland crude oil   273
Goal   25
Grangemouth Refinery   33
Greaves, Walter   107
Gross product worth (GPW)   218–19, 221–2, 234, 238, 254, 270, 295–9, 301, 303–4
Gullfaks crude oil   245–6, 248

Haltenbanken Area   149
Handil crude oil   273
Heather field   11, 19, 21
Heating oil   169
Heavy fuel oil   233–4, 236, 238, 240
Hedging   48, 74, 79–80, 87–91, 107–8, 110–11, 128, 162–3, 182–3, 195, 198, 205, 275, 316, 320, 323–5
   categories of   108
Herfindahl Index   26, 100–1, 215
Hicks, J.   182
Hill Petroleum   101
Houston, Texas   48, 157–8, 162, 228–9, 281
Hudson field   11
Hunt   130
Hutton field   11, 19, 22, 25

Idemitsu   103
Imperial Chemical Industries (ICI)   25, 130
Independent Chemical Information Services   157–8

Indian Oil Corporation (IOC)   210
Indonesia   164, 270–1, 273–5, 277, 309, 314
Indonesian Crude Price (ICP)   164, 271, 273–5, 282
Insider trading   50
International Commodities Clearing House (ICCH)   49
International Petroleum Exchange of London, *see* IPE
Inventory   134, 137, 162, 181, 244, 319
IPE   6, 46–9, 118, 162, 164, 169, 204–5
   and Dubai futures   210
   clearing house   49, 199
   membership   49
IPE Brent futures   46–50, 52–3, 56–7, 87, 93, 110–11, 145–6, 162–3, 165, 193, 195, 198–201, 203–5, 246, 248, 315, 322, 324
   and forward Brent   203–6
   Brent index   48–9, 52
   default risk   199, 203
   forwardness   198
   margins   47
   open interest   195, 198
   volatility   174–9
   volume   193, 195, 198
IPE Brent options   52–5, 176–7, 195, 198, 204
IPE gasoil contract   233
Iran   1, 77, 111, 159, 207, 211, 221, 262, 264–5, 270, 292, 296, 306, 311–12
Iranian Heavy crude oil   312–13
Iranian Light crude oil   281, 295, 304, 312
Iraq   37, 111, 169–70, 207, 211, 231, 265, 296, 306, 312
Iraq Petroleum Company   157
Ireland   26, 116
Isthmus crude oil   309, 311
Italy   232, 262

J Aron   57, 104, 115–16, 119, 124, 210, 213, 215, 250, 274
Jacksboro, Texas   229
Jal, New Mexico   228
Japan   26, 73, 87, 103, 105, 116, 210, 213, 215, 221, 314, 327
Jet kerosene   233

Kanematsu   105, 213
Kern River crude oil   279
Keynes, J.M.   182
Kirkuk crude oil   312
Kittiwake field   245
Kloeckner   141–2, 146
Knight Ridder   156
Koch   143, 231
Kuwait   26, 37, 169–70, 207, 265, 318
Kuwait crisis (1990–1)   57, 83, 85, 90–1, 95, 134, 158, 167, 169, 172, 174–8, 182–3, 186, 193, 195, 198, 204–5, 211, 215, 219, 224, 231, 234, 236, 303–4, 312, 317

Labuan crude oil   276
Latin America   101, 221, 277, 270
Lavera   232
Libya   38, 170, 261–2, 264, 306, 312
Line 63 crude oil   279
Litigation   139–47
Light Louisiana Sweet (LLS) crude oil   279–81, 294,

309, 311
Loading programme
  Brent 29, 42, 113–14, 138–9, 148
  Forties 254
London 6, 7, 39, 41, 46–9, 52, 78, 141, 143, 145, 156–8, 162, 177, 193, 210, 225
London and Scottish Marine Oil (LASMO) 21, 25
London International Financial Futures Exchange 47, 225
London Oil Reports (LOR) 48–9, 156–8, 162
Long Beach, California 159
Louisiana Offshore Oil Port (LOOP) 231
Lower Zakum crude oil 267–8
Lyell field 11, 15

Magnus field 11, 15, 19, 21, 25
Maintenance 15, 16, 21, 325
Malaysia 270, 276
Marathon 250
Marc Rich 140, 213
Marcus Hook refineries 34
Marib Light crude oil 266, 306, 314
Marimpex 142
Marker 3, 8, 74, 81–2, 119, 155–6, 165–6, 222, 240, 243, 248, 256, 259, 264, 275, 277, 281–2, 291, 307, 309, 315–27
Market 1, 2, 4, 5, 73, 74, 292–4, 327
Marubeni 213
Maureen field 245
Maya crude oil 311
McGraw-Hill 157
Medine field 148
Mediterranean 3, 33, 156, 158, 164, 221, 232, 243, 261–2, 264, 270, 282, 296
Merrill Lynch 54, 274
Mexico 34, 76, 277, 281, 291–2, 296, 306–7, 309, 311, 313, 315
Middle East 38, 78, 164, 178, 193, 213, 224, 243, 265, 270, 282
Midland, Texas 227–9, 231, 278–9
Milford Haven refinery 33
Minas crude oil 273, 314
Ministry of Petroleum and Mines (Oman) see MPM
Mitsubishi 140
Mitsui 141, 213
Mobil 250–1, 257, 278
Molongo crude oil 256, 259
Monan field 148
Morgan Stanley 54, 57, 80, 119, 130, 210, 213, 274, 278
MPM 160, 267–70
Mungo field 148
Murban crude oil 267
Murchison field 11–12, 19, 22, 25, 244

Naphtha 233
Nasmyth, Jan 157
National oil companies 35, 73, 76, 105, 111, 143, 156, 210, 215, 257, 266, 315–16, 320
Nationalization 73
Nederland, Texas 281
Neste 105, 130, 213
Netback pricing 79–80, 155, 211, 276, 292, 308–9, 313
Netherlands 116

New Mexico Sour crude oil 281
New York Cotton Exchange 280
Nichimen 140
Nigeria 34, 38, 159, 162, 256–7, 259, 277, 306, 313
Nigerian National Petroleum Company (NNPC) 257
Nigg Bay 245
Ninian
  blend 12–13, 20, 76, 78, 104, 149, 150, 244
  blend gravity 20
  field 11, 13, 22, 35–7, 255
  pipeline system 2, 11–13, 15, 18–19, 21–2, 25–6, 35, 111, 137, 147, 244
Nissho Iwai 142, 144–5, 147, 213
Norsk Hydro 251
North Cormorant field 11, 13, 19, 21
North Sea 3, 6, 12, 15, 21, 25, 31, 35–7, 50, 56, 59, 63–4, 75–8, 80–1, 85, 87–8, 101, 103, 105, 107, 111, 118–19, 121, 131, 135, 137, 147, 149, 150, 185, 243–6, 248–51, 254–7, 259, 261, 264, 270, 282, 291, 295, 315, 320–2, 325–6
North West Hutton field 11, 15, 21, 25
Norway 12, 25–6, 38, 76–7, 87–8, 110, 149, 156, 244–6, 248, 250–1
  oil fiscal regime 76–7, 88
  Petroleum Price Board 77
New York Mercantile Exchange, see NYMEX
NYMEX 6, 47, 54, 131, 162, 169, 175–7, 193, 203, 225–7, 229, 231
  ADP 227, 281
  contracts 225
  EFP 227, 281
  light sweet crude oil contract 46, 75, 201, 225–7, 229, 231, 241, 281
  options 225
  sour crude contract 277, 280–1
  volume 225, 227, 241

Official selling price (OSP) 266–8, 270, 275–6, 282, 291
Oil and Pipelines Agency (OPA) 140
Oil companies 21–2, 73, 82, 107–8, 110–11, 146, 155, 171, 207, 250–1, 261, 265, 273, 316, 320, 322
Oil demand 79, 170, 231, 274, 277, 292, 308
Oil-exporting countries 3, 5, 18, 25, 33, 37, 42, 55–6, 61, 73–4, 81, 103, 108, 111, 113, 114, 128–30, 137, 146, 155, 158, 161, 165, 172, 201, 213, 236, 243–4, 250, 255, 273, 275, 291–8, 305–9, 316–7, 319, 322, 325–7
Oil output valuation principle 61–4, 67–9, 76–7
Oil price 1, 2, 5, 74, 79, 81, 93, 126–7, 131, 135, 137, 139, 155–66, 204–6, 208, 235, 238–41, 245, 255–6, 293, 315, 319, 324–7
  normality 186–7
  volatility 89, 91, 160, 170–9, 186, 218, 319
Oil price crisis (1973) 292
Oil price crisis (1979) 292
Oil price crisis (1986) 79–81, 139, 142, 167, 291–2, 298
Oil production 13, 15, 18, 20, 22, 26, 38, 74, 77, 170, 225, 243–4, 256–7, 259, 265–6, 275, 291, 317
Oil Taxation Office (OTO) 61–6, 68–9, 80–1, 83, 322
Oilfields 18, 21, 36, 37

Oilfields (continued)
   discovery 11
   production start 11
Oiltanking 281
Olmeca crude oil 311
Oman 160, 212–13, 265–8, 270, 273–4, 277, 281–2, 291, 294, 299, 309, 311–12, 314, 316, 323
OMV 22
OPEC 1, 2, 8, 37–8, 63, 73–4, 76, 79–81, 155–6, 167, 169, 178, 211, 224, 291–2, 307–8, 315–20, 324–5, 327
Operators 21
Options 279–80
Options pricing 53, 173, 187
Organisation for Economic Co-operation and Development (OECD) 33, 170, 306, 318, 326–7
Oriente crude oil 277, 281
Oryx 22, 25
Oseberg crude oil 245–6
Osprey field 11, 13, 15, 19
Outright trades 85, 87–9, 92–3, 160, 165, 211, 249–50, 259, 264, 268–9, 275–6, 281, 322
Over the counter (OTC) options 54, 55, 111
Ownership 21–2, 25, 26
Oxford Institute for Energy Studies 6

Palanca crude oil 256
Panama 278
Panel pricing 160, 165, 271, 273, 277
Papua New Guinea 103
Patrick Victor Mazzarolli Oil Associates (PVM) 111
Pelican field 19
Pemex 292, 309
Petrobras 25
Petrofina 25
Petrogulf 103
Petroleum Argus 6, 8, 44, 48–9, 80, 83–5, 87, 93, 104, 115, 126, 156–8, 162, 207, 211, 243, 245, 248
Petroleum Authority of Thailand (PTT) 210
Petroleum Development Oman (PDO) 267
Petroleum product prices 233–4, 236, 238–40, 254
Petroleum Revenue Tax (PRT) 25, 35–7, 60–6, 68–9, 80–1, 321, 324
   nomination procedures 64–8, 81
Petronas 275
Phibro 101, 104, 115–6, 119, 158, 201–2, 210, 213, 215, 250, 257, 274
Philadelphia refineries 34
Philippine National Oil Company (PNOC) 210
Phillips 251, 278
Platt's 6, 48, 52, 56, 156–8, 160, 162–4, 205, 232, 234, 246, 249, 299
Platt's risk 52, 163, 164, 205
Poland 116
Port Arthur, Texas 228
Price differentials 34, 44–5, 56, 60–1, 65, 68, 88–9, 91, 118–19, 132–3, 135, 156, 160–1, 164–5, 183, 211–13, 218, 221–2, 224, 227–9, 231, 236, 240, 243, 246, 248–1, 254–5, 264, 267–9, 271, 273–7, 279–82, 293, 295–9, 301, 303–4, 307, 316–17, 322–3, 326
   Brent-Dubai 44–5, 109, 165, 211–13, 215, 218, 222, 240, 282
   Brent-WTI 88, 109, 224, 229, 231, 259

   dated Brent-Forties 251, 254–5
   WTI-Dubai 212, 224
Price discovery 75, 79, 171, 206, 246, 249, 251, 259, 264, 320, 322, 323
Price discrimination 296, 308
Price formula 3, 5, 118, 119, 155, 162, 205, 248–251, 265, 276, 279, 291–301, 303–309, 311–314, 316, 317, 322
Price of dated Brent 1, 3, 5, 44, 48, 52–5, 61, 66–7, 74, 76, 81, 88–9, 93, 108, 119, 124, 126, 131–2, 141–2, 156, 160, 163–5, 167, 169, 173, 175, 177, 179–83, 218–9, 222, 224, 226–8, 231, 233, 234, 236, 238–41, 248, 256, 259, 264, 267, 269, 270, 273, 279, 291, 293–5, 301, 303–4, 306–7, 314, 316, 318, 320, 322, 324, 326
Price Reporting 89, 112, 119, 155–66, 200, 211–12, 233, 245, 249–50, 254–5, 271, 273, 322
Price spreads 5, 165
Pricing strip 279–80
Producer nations, see Oil-exporting countries
Prudhoe Bay, Alaska 278

Qatar 265–70, 282, 309
Qatar General Petroleum Corporation (QGPC) 267–8, 270
Qatar Land crude oil 267–8
Qatar Marine crude oil 267–8
Qua Iboe crude oil 259

Ras 'Isa 314
Ras Tanura 296, 299
Refiners 33–4, 111, 113–14, 116, 118, 162–3, 218, 224, 233–4, 236, 250, 254, 273–5, 280, 295, 301, 308
Refinery margins 235, 262
Repsol 25
Reserves 11–12, 18, 37
Retrospective price 155, 208, 211, 266–70, 282, 292, 309, 311, 313, 316
Reuters 48–9, 156, 158
Rheinoel 140
Ring-fence 60–1
Rotterdam oil futures 47, 280
Rotterdam products market 232–4, 236, 238–41
Royalty 35, 37, 60
Ruler of Dubai 207–8, 210
Russia 76, 101, 149, 158, 170, 174, 221, 234, 262, 264, 277, 306

Saharan Blend crude oil 306, 311
Salomon Brothers 101
Samuelson, Paul 174–5
Sarir crude oil 312
Sas, Blanche 202–3
Saudi Arabia 1, 34, 79, 81, 139, 158, 169, 172, 205, 207, 211, 265–6, 270, 277, 291–2, 296, 298–301, 303–6, 314, 317–19, 325, 327
Saudi Arabian Oil Company 304
Secretan affair 130
Serletis, A. 175
Seymour, Adam 292
Shell 15, 21–2, 26, 28–9, 33, 40–1, 78, 103–4, 116, 119, 121, 124, 140–4, 200–2, 213, 228, 250–1, 256–7, 259, 274
Shellhaven refinery 33

Shetland Islands 11, 29, 31, 122
Shutdown 16, 18, 26, 115, 244, 325
Sidi Kerir crude oil 159
SIMEX 210
Singapore 155, 157, 210, 218–19, 274, 280
Sirtica crude oil 312
Sociéte Générale 54
Sogo shosha 87, 101, 103, 105, 107, 158, 210, 213, 322
Sour crude market 221, 224, 240
South Africa 221
South Cormorant field 11, 13, 15, 19, 21
Soviet Union 291
Spain 26
Spectron 111
Speculation 88, 90, 108, 110–11, 119, 182, 316, 324–6
  and volatility 171
Speculative bubbles 185
Spot market 6, 8, 50, 52, 62, 74–5, 77, 101, 108, 110, 112–3, 118, 155–6, 160–2, 164, 166, 175, 181, 203, 210, 224, 232–3, 243–6, 249–50, 256–7, 259, 261–2, 264–6, 268–71, 276–7, 279–82, 316
Spot price 78, 203, 270–1, 273, 309
Spread trading 43–5, 48, 85, 87–9, 91–3, 213, 326
  and volatility 89
  box trade 45, 213
  crack spreads 109
  inter-crude 44–5, 87–8
  inter-month 43–4, 85, 87–9
  legged spreads 89
  risk 88
  volume in Brent market 85, 87–9
Squeeze 130–5, 137–8, 169, 176, 180, 185, 322, 324
  accidental 138
  defined 131, 134
  gasoline 169
  heating oil 169
St. Croix refinery 220
St. Fergus terminal 19
St. James, Louisiana 279
Staffa field 11, 15, 19
Stanlow Refinery 33
Statfjord crude oil 19, 76, 245, 246
Statoil 105, 215, 251
Stocks 21, 170, 180–1, 264, 319, 325
Storage 13, 21, 114, 180–2
Strategic Petroleum Reserve 158
Strathspey field 11, 19
Sture 244
Suez Blend crude oil 306, 313
Sullom Voe terminal 11–13, 15, 18, 21, 28–9, 31, 34, 40–3, 47, 76, 78, 113–15, 119–22, 124, 137, 149–50, 160–1, 201, 244–5, 248, 296, 299, 301, 323
Sumitomo 130
Sun Oil 25, 34, 140–1, 256, 281
Swap 55, 56, 109–11, 156, 274
Sweden 116
Switzerland 116
Syria 261–2, 264, 306, 314–5
Syrian Light crude oil 314

Takula crude oil 256, 259
Tamoil 261
Tapis crude oil 159, 165, 273–6

Tax optimization 59, 61, 66, 68–9, 77, 79–81, 256, 320–3, 325
Tax spinning 63–9, 78, 82
Technical trading 185
Teeside 245
Telerate 48–9, 156, 158
Tenneco 25
Term contracts 52, 73–4, 77, 110–11, 205, 207, 222, 224, 243, 256, 259, 264–5, 270, 275, 279, 306, 314
Tern field 11, 15, 19, 21
Texaco 21, 116, 140, 227, 229, 250, 257, 281
Texas City, Texas 228–9, 281
Texas Eastern 25
Thailand 210
Thistle field 11, 13, 15
THUMS crude oil 279
Tiebacks 13
Time-stamp 160, 162, 164, 249
Tokyo 48, 157–8, 162
Transnor 139, 142–6, 202
Tricentrol 22
Trigger pricing 118–19, 205, 249
TWO 135, 213, 278

Ultramar 25
Umm Shaif crude oil 267
Union 278
United Arab Emirates (UAE) 207, 213, 219, 221, 265, 318
United Crude 111
United Kingdom 26, 143–4, 199, 244, 248
  Financial Services Act 1986 40, 49
  oil exports 37–8
  oil fiscal regime 59–69, 76–7, 87–8, 275, 320–1
  oil production 37–8
  oil tax revenues 35–7
  refineries 31, 33
  trade restrictions 33
United Kingdom Continental Shelf (UKCS) 12, 18–19, 63, 76–7, 87, 321–3
United Nations 15, 169, 208, 306
United Nations Convention for the International Sale of Goods 1980 40, 208
Unitization 21–2
  payback 22, 26
Unocal 21
Upper Zakum crude oil 267–8
Urals crude oil 158, 221, 262, 264, 295, 306
US Atlantic Coast 34, 88
US Commodity Exchange Act 142–5, 198–9, 201
US Department of Energy 243
US Gulf 34, 113, 122, 155, 157–61, 218–20, 228–9, 231, 241, 256, 259, 270, 278–9, 311
US pipelines 228–9, 231, 241
  ARCO 228–9, 231
  Basin 228
  Capline 231
  Rancho 281
  Seaway 231
  Shell 228
  Texaco 229, 281
  Texoma 231
  Trans-Alaska (TAPS) 278
US West Coast 278

USA 3, 6, 26, 31, 34, 38, 74, 76, 116, 119, 135, 142–5, 158, 162, 164, 169, 198–9, 201, 205, 209, 220, 222, 225, 231, 234, 241, 243, 248, 250, 256, 259, 261–2, 264, 274, 277, 280–2, 294, 296, 299, 306, 312–15, 318, 323, 326–7
   crude oil imports 248, 256, 259, 261–2, 264, 277

Valdez, Alaska 278–9
Veba 261
Venezuela 34, 158, 277
Vertical integration 59, 61–3, 67, 68, 73, 77
Vietnam 270, 314
Virgil 107
Voest Alpine 142

Wall Street refiners 47, 57, 80–1, 88, 93, 101, 103–5, 107–12, 124, 135, 146, 156, 182, 210, 213, 215, 250, 321, 324–6
Warrant 111
West Africa 3, 34, 38, 110, 156, 164, 243, 256–7, 259, 261, 264, 270, 282, 291, 295, 306
West Texas Intermediate, *see* WTI

West Texas Sour (WTS) crude oil 279–81, 294, 309, 311–12
White Nights project 101
Wichita Falls, Texas 229
Widuri 274
Wood Mackenzie 6, 36, 147
Working, Holbrook 108
WTI 3, 44, 75, 119, 159, 164, 218, 221, 231, 241, 248, 250, 259, 264, 277, 279–80, 282, 294, 309, 315, 323
   forward market 169, 203, 227
   postings plus 160, 231–2
   price 226–7, 231
   production 228
   quality 226

Yemen 266, 306, 314–15

Zaire 257, 259
Zarzaitine crude oil 306, 311
Zeschmar, Wolfgang 141
Zueitina crude oil 262, 312